Discovering Microsoft Works for the IBM® Personal Computer

DAVID SACHS
BABETTE KRONSTADT

Pace Computer Learning Center
Pace University

JOHN WILEY & SONS
New York / Chichester / Brisbane / Toronto / Singapore

This Microsoft program was reproduced by John Wiley & Sons under a
special arrangement with Microsoft Corporation. For this reason,
Wiley is responsible for the product warrenty and for support. If
your diskette is defective, please return it to Wiley, who will
arrange for its replacement. PLEASE DO NOT RETURN IT TO
MICROSOFT. Any product support will be provided, if at all, by
Wiley. PLEASE DO NOT CONTACT MICROSOFT FOR PRODUCT SUPPORT.

Copyright © 1989, by John Wiley & Sons, Inc.

All rights reserved. Published simultaneously in Canada.

Reproduction or translation of any part of this work beyond that
permitted by Sections 107 and 108 of the 1976 United States
Copyright Act without the permission of the copyright owner is
unlawful. Requests for permission of the copyright owner should
be addressed to the Permissions Department, John Wiley & Sons.

Microsoft is a registered trademark of Microsoft Corporation.

IBM is a registered trademark of Internation Business Machines Corporation.

Library of Congress Cataloging in Publication Data:

Sachs, David, 1955-
    Discovering Microsoft Works for the IBM Personal Computer/David
Sachs, Babette Kronstadt.
    p. 288 cm.
    Includes Index
    ISBN: 0-471-61728-8 (5 1/4" Disk)
    ISBN: 0-471-50817-9 (3 1/2" Disk)
    ISBN: 0-471-51767-4 (without software)
    1. ICM Personal Computer—Programming. 2. Microsoft Works (computer program)
    I. Kronstadt, Babette. II. Title.

QA76.8.I2594S22   1989   88-7928
005.265—dc19   CIP

Printed in the United States of America

10 9 8 7 6 5 4

Preface

Welcome to the wonderful world of personal computing! The technology that you are about to encounter is the result of an enormous amount of progress that has occurred during the past ten years. Today's hardware and software offer power that is increasingly extensive and adaptable, for a price that is amazingly inexpensive.

The Purpose/Orientation of This Book

This book will provide you with a comfortable introduction to the world of personal computing in general, and to the world of *Microsoft Works for the PC* in particular. After a quick overview of personal computers and of the *Works* "look," each chapter will introduce you to one of the main types of software applications used with personal computers and to ways of using applications together in an integrated program such as *Works*. Since the amount of class and practice time allotted to *Works* will vary depending on the overall content of the course in which it is being used, a final chapter has been included for those courses that devote more time to *Works*. This chapter will give you an opportunity to extend your knowledge of the three main applications introduced in the preceding chapters.

The emphasis is on learning by doing and on learning skills in context. Therefore, after the introduction, you will learn the relevant skills by following instructions to complete projects. Each new chapter, and each project within the chapters, will reinforce previously learned skills as well as introduce new ones. After the instructional projects, several independent projects will incorporate previously taught skills.

Extended Version

A preliminary version of *Discovering Microsoft Work* was published in mid-1988. The current version contains all of the material in the initial version, and has been extended to include a brief introduction to telecommunications and projects for those of you who need to increase your skills with the word processor, database, and spreadsheet portions of *Works*. These new projects include an introduction to *Works* database reporting and spreadsheet charting capabilities, and to one of the most popular ways in which databases and word processors are used together—the creation of personalized form letters.

What is Microsoft Works?

Works is a software program for IBM and IBM-compatible computers that provides the most popular computer applications—word processing, database management, a spreadsheet with graphics capabilities, and telecommunications—all for a little more than the cost of a ticket to a concert or a compact disk. In the computer industry, *Works* is known as an "integrated software package." This means that while the four separate components, or tools—word processor, database, spreadsheet, and communications—are capable of performing well on their own, they interact with each other more easily than do stand-alone programs that are purchased separately. With *Works,* it's possible to move from one task to another directly, without exiting from one program and starting another. Also, information may be moved easily from one tool to another.

Equally important is the fact that learning to use the individual Works' tools is much easier than learning several unrelated packages. Many of the commands in each tool are similar, the screens are alike, and the methods of communicating with the program are consistent.

By the time you have finished learning *Works*, you will be able to do your writing for school and work in a faster, more effective fashion, by using the **Word Processor** tool.

The **Database Manager** tool is the answer if you have a lot of data in your life, such as the names and addresses of friends, or the names and addresses of possible employers or clients. You will be able to store this information in an orderly fashion, modify it when necessary, and print it, whenever it is needed.

The **Spreadsheet** tool is wonderful if you work with financial information or any numeric data requiring calculations. If you need to compare and contrast the prices for a new car, a spreadsheet is your answer. If you need to calculate the averages and ranges of grades for your students, a spreadsheet will do the trick. And if you need to prepare the budget for a club or organization, a spreadsheet is indispensable. What's more, you may use the spreadsheet's graphics capabilities to create charts so that you can see the trends or relationships among your data. Charting is also a great way to actually see the mathematics equation you're learning, or to create a model illustrating a basic engineering concept.

The **Communications** tool of *Works* allows your computer to communicate with other computers. This tool will be discussed only briefly in this book, however, since most users of the educational version of *Works* do not have access to the hardware necessary for computer communications.

Overview of Things to Come

For the most part, the world of personal computing with *Works* is a friendly and inviting one. It does have its own language, which means that you will have to learn some new vocabulary words. We will keep the jargon to a minimum, but there will be some terms and concepts that will be new and will perhaps seem a little unusual at first. Key terms will be highlighted in bold type to help you become familiar with them.

Our first order of business will be to acquaint you with the elements of **computer hardware**. Without the hardware, of course, you would be unable to run the software, so it is important that you have some basic ideas about the various components and how they work.

After that, we will introduce you to what is known as the *Disk Operating System*, or *DOS*. This program is vital if you are going to use any computer software, now or in the future. We will provide you with the fundamentals of the Disk Operating System, so that you can prepare all of your disks for use, make copies of your files, and keep track of all of the files that you will prepare with your word processor, database manager, or spreadsheet.

Next, we will introduce you to the special world of *Works*. This guide will give you experience with the basics of the Word Processor, Spreadsheet, and Database tools. Equally important, your explorations should provide an overall feeling for what the computer can do for you.

An integrated program such as *Works* is perfect for an introductory journey through the common applications of personal computing. Since the interface is consistent, you will find that learning *Works* is a pleasant, comfortable experience. Creating a spreadsheet requires different skills than writing a letter, but once you've seen the word processing screen, the spreadsheet screen will look familiar. Having "opened" or "saved" or printed a spreadsheet you'll be able to guess how to do the same with a database.

At the end of our first look at *Works*, we'll show you how the separate tools in *Works* can be "integrated." Each of the component parts has been carefully designed to work comfortably with the others. This ability greatly enhances the power and usefulness of each individual tool.

Next, we will take another look at the Word Processor, Spreadsheet, and Database tools and another way in which they can be integrated. In this chapter you will extend previously learned skills, learn new ones, and hopefully develop a greater appreciation for the power of computing.

Finally, we will take a brief look at the Communications tool. Since many of you will not have the hardware to complete activities, instructions will be general. The goal of this chapter is to provide a feeling for the added dimension communications gives the personal computer rather than to ensure a mastery of specific skills.

Acknowledgments

Discovering Microsoft Work was written by two of us, but it truly represents the work of many more individuals and organizations. We have received enormous institutional support from Pace University and the School of Computer Science and Information Systems at Pace. In particular, much personal and professional support for our work has come from the Dean, Dr. Susan Merritt.

From another perspective, this book also is a product of the **Pace Computer Learning Center**, a loose affiliation of approximately 15 professors and staff, who have provided more than 1500 days of instruction to over 10,000 individuals in corporate settings throughout the United States and around the world during the past four years. Many of these people have become good personal and professional friends, and our shared experiences in the development and teaching of these courses was an ideal preparation for writing this book.

Access to the state-of-the-art hardware and software made an enormous difference in the production of this text. In addition, we were assisted with some of the actual writing (and rewriting) by Judy Van Wormer, Elizabeth Lo Sacco, Christine Lowden, and Donna Swift. Donna's energy, enthusiasm, and attention to detail are evident throughout this book, and without her work during the past few months, *Discovering Microsoft Works* would have had a much more difficult time seeing the light of day.

In addition to our colleagues at Pace, we've received many invaluable comments and suggestions from instructors at other schools who were kind enough to review the manuscript. Our thanks go out to:

Judith Ernst, Santa Fe Community College;
Stewart A. Myers, Rancho Santiago College;
Glenn Brown, Oklahoma State University;
Clifford H. Peterson, Concordia College;
Stoughton Bell, University of New Mexico;
Dana L. Johnson, North Dakota State University

Our work with John Wiley & Sons has been made wonderfully smooth by the support provided by our editors, Joe Dougherty and Carolyn Henderson. They gave us assistance when we asked for it, quick answers when we needed them, and lots of responsiveness to our needs and concerns.

DAVID SACHS
BABETTE KRONSTADT

August 1988
White Plains, New York

Contents

1 INTRODUCTION TO COMPUTING WITH MICROSOFT WORKS   1
- Objectives 1
- Introduction to the Computer 1
  - Parts of a Computer—The Hardware 1
  - Care and Handling of Disks 5
- DOS (The Disk Operating System) 6
  - FORMAT 8
  - DISKCOPY 10
  - DIR 11
  - COPY 13
  - DEL 14
- Installing Microsoft Works 15
- The Microsoft Works Interface 16
- Rules for Naming a File 29
- The Five Dialog Box Elements—A Summary 30
- The Educational Version of Microsoft Works for the PC 31
- Exiting from Works 32
- Conventions and Notations Used in This Text 32
- Conclusion 33
- Key Terms 34

2 THE WORD PROCESSOR: AN INTRODUCTION   35
- Objectives 35
- What Is a Word Processor? 35
- Creating a New Word Processor Document 35
- The Word Processor Screen 36
- Word Processor Project 1—Debbie's Letter 37
  - Objectives 37
  - Entering Text 38
  - Moving Around the Screen 40
  - Editing a Document 41
  - Saving a Document as a File 44
  - Printing a Document 46
  - Selecting the Text Printer 47
- Word Processor Project 2—Paul's Letter 49
  - Objectives 49
  - Creating a New Word Processing Document 50
  - Directions For Entering the Text 51
  - Proofreading and Saving a Document 53
  - Another Look at Editing Text 54
  - Saving a Document for a Second Time 61
  - Changing the Layout of a Printed Document 62
- Conclusion 63
- Key Terms 63
- Independent Word Processor Project 1 63
- Independent Word Processor Project 2 65

3 THE SPREADSHEET: AN INTRODUCTION   69
- Objectives 69
- What Is a Spreadsheet? 69

Starting a Spreadsheet File 69
The Spreadsheet Screen 70
Moving around the Spreadsheet Screen 71
Entering Labels and Values 72
Practice Exercise 1 72
Spreadsheet Project 1—Budgeting Expenses 75
   Objectives 75
   Entering Labels 75
   Correcting Errors 78
   Entering Values 79
   Moving Around a Spreadsheet 80
   Entering a Formula 81
   Copying Cells 84
   Formatting Labels and Values 86
   Save and Save As 89
   Printing the Spreadsheet 91
Spreadsheet Project 2—Monitoring Travel Expenses 92
   Objectives 93
   Starting the Spreadsheet File 93
   Entering the Labels and Values 94
   Changing Column Widths 95
   Right Justifying Labels 96
   Entering Values 96
   Using Formulas and Functions 99
   Printing the Spreadsheet 102
Conclusion 102
Key Terms 103
Independent Spreadsheet Project 1 103
Independent Spreadsheet Project 2 104

4 THE DATABASE MANAGER: AN INTRODUCTION   107

Objectives 107
What Is a Database? 107
Starting a Database File 107
Designing a Database 108
Database Project 1—Paul's Piano Students 108
   Objectives 108
   A Tour of the Form Design Screen 109
   Entering Field Names 110
   Entering Data 112
   Saving a Database 114
   Viewing Records in the Database 115
   Changing from *List View* to *Form View* 117
   Changing Field Width in *List View* 119
   Editing Data 120
   Searching for Data 122
   Printing Records 124
Database Project 2—Debbie's Painting Clients 126
   Objectives 126
   Designing the Database 126
   Entering Data 127
   Changing Field Width in *Form View* 130
   Viewing Records in the Database 136
   Changing Field Width in *List View* 136
   Searching for Data 137
   Sorting Records 138
   Printing Records 140
   Hiding Fields in *List View* 140
   Redisplaying Hidden Fields in *List View* 141
Conclusion 144

Key Terms 144
Independent Database Project 1 144
Independent Database Project 2 146

5 INTEGRATING *WORKS*: AN INTRODUCTION 147

Objectives 147
Integrated Project 1—Using Information from a Databas in a Word Processor Document 148
    Objectives 148
    Opening More Than One File at a Time 148
    Using the Window Command to Switch Between Files 150
    Copying From the Database to the Word Processor 150
    Reformatting Copied Information 153
Integrated Project 2—Including Information from a Databas in a Word Processor Document 156
    Objectives 156
    Managing the Files 156
    Copying from the Database to the Word Processor 158
Integrated Project 3—Including Information from a Spreadsheet in a Word Processor Document 161
    Objectives 161
    Managing the Files 161
    Copying From the Spreadsheet to the Word Processor 162
    Reformatting Copied Information 162
    Saving All Open Files 166
Conclusion 166
Key Terms 167
Independent Integrated Project 1 167
Independent Integrated Project 2 168

6 EXTENDING YOUR KNOWLEDGE OF MICROSOFT WORKS 171

Objectives 171
The Word Processor Tool 172
Formatting Text 172
Extended Skills Project 1—Enhancing Paul's Letter 172
    Objectives 172
    Formatting Shortcut Keys 175
    Using the Format Character Option 176
Independent Extended Skills Project 1—Enhancing Paul's Resume 177
Extended Skills Project 2—Changing Tabs, Line Spacing and Margins 178
    Objectives 179
    Tab Settings 179
    Setting Tab Stops 180
    Using the Shift + Enter Keys 181
    Changing Existing Tab Stops 182
    Changing the Line Spacing 183
Independent Extended Skills Project 2—Using Tabs in a Letter 184
    The Spreadsheet Tool 185
    Relative and Absolute Copying 185
Extended Skills Project 3—Relative and Absolute Copying 186
    Objectives 186
    Inserting Columns 186
    Creating Absolute Cell Address References 186
    Hiding Columns 191
    More about Functions 193
Extended Skills Project 4—More Functions 193
    Objectives 193
    Using More of the Spreadsheet 193
    The Min, Max, and Sum Functions and Pointing 194
Independent Extended Skills Project 3—Using Absolute Cell Addressing and Statistical Functions to Summarize Spreadsheet Data 198

Charting 201
Setting Up Works to Display Graphics 201
Extended Skills Project 5—Charting Your Monthly Expenditures 205
- Objectives 205
- Creating a Speed Chart 206
- Naming and Saving a Chart 212
- Printing a Chart 213

Independent Extended Skills Project 4—Charting Changes in Budget Figures 215
The Database Tool 217
Database Queries 217
Extended Skills Project 6—Locating Records in Debbie's Database 218
- Objectives 218
- Adding a Field to the End of a Database 218
- Querying the Database 221
- Queries Using Criteria in More Than One Field 227

Independent Extended Skills Project 5—Practicing Queries 228
Creating Reports From Your Database 228
Extended Skills Project 7—Reporting on Debbie's Painting Clients 229
- Objectives 229
- Creating a Speed Report 229
- Modifying a Speed Report 231
- Naming and Saving a Report 235

Independent Extended Skills Project 6—Creating a Second Report 237
Integrating Works 238
Creating Form Letters 238
Extended Skills Project 8—Paul's Personalized Parent Letters 238
- Objectives 239
- Creating a Word Processor Document Containing Variable Information from a Database 239
- Selecting Database Records to Merge 241
- Printing the Merged Document 241

Independent Extended Skills Project 7—Debbie's Customized Form Letters 242
Conclusion 243
Key Terms 244

7 A BRIEF LOOK AT COMMUNICATIONS 245

Objectives 245
What Is Communications Software? 245
The Hardware—A Modem 246
Communications Example: Communicating with an On-Line Information System 247
- The Communications Screen 247
- Setting Up Works for Communication 248
- Making a Connection 253

Conclusion 254
Key Terms 254

Appendix A SYSTEM REQUIREMENTS 255

Appendix B MICROSOFT WORKS MENU COMMANDS 257

Appendix C MICROSOFT WORKS FUNCTION KEYS 265

Appendix D MICROSOFT WORKS FUNCTIONS 267

Appendix E MODEM SETTINGS 271

Subject Index

Chapter 1
Introduction to Computing with Microsoft Works

In this chapter you will learn:

- Some of the terminology used to describe computer hardware.
- The functions of some of the special keys on the keyboard.
- What **DOS** is, and how to use **DOS** commands to prepare a disk for use, to copy entire disks and parts of disks, and to obtain a listing of the contents of a disk.
- How to get ready to use *Works*.
- How to start *Works*.
- How to create, open, and save *Works* files.
- How to use the *Works* menu and Dialog Boxes.

Introduction to the Computer

Your computer is really a complex system of parts, all of which have an important relationship to each other. If you are new to the world of personal computing, perhaps the simplest way to think about these components is as the **hardware** and **software** that make up this system. The hardware is the physical equipment that comprises your computer system. Software consists of programs or sets of instructions to the computer.

Parts of a Computer—the Hardware The computer hardware you most likely will encounter will be the **system unit,** which contains the **CPU** (central processing unit), the **keyboard,** the **monitor** or **CRT** (cathode ray tube), one or more **disk drives,** and the **printer.** These components allow you to "input" or enter information, process the information, "output" or display the information, and store the information for future use. While your particular configuration may differ slightly, we will describe below the common configurations found on an IBM PC.

The System Unit—The Central Processing Unit

The **System Unit** is the heart of the computer. It contains the **Central Processing Unit** or **CPU,** which controls all of the processing of the data, the main memory,

Introduction to Computing with Microsoft Works

which stores the commands and data being used, and the circuitry needed to control the rest of the hardware.

The Keyboard

The computer keyboard is the main input device of the computer. As Figure 1-1 shows, the computer keyboard in many ways resembles a typewriter keyboard. There are some additional keys that are used to help give the computer instructions. Below is a further description of some of the keys on the keyboard.

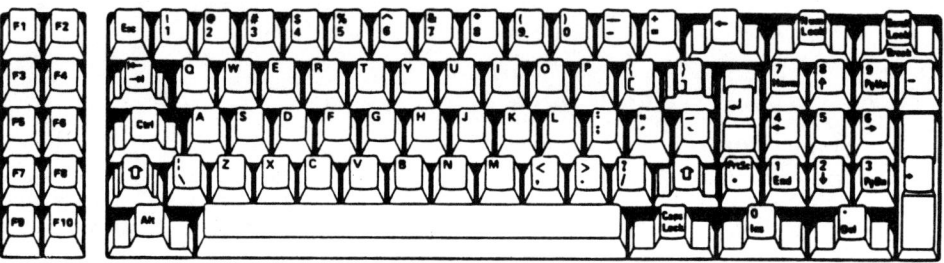

Figure 1-1

The TAB Key and SPACE BAR

The **TAB** and **SPACE BAR** are typical typewriter keys. On some computer keyboards the **TAB** key may be hard to recognize because it is indicated by an arrow pointing left over an arrow pointing right. The specific effect of the **TAB** key is different in each tool (i.e., word processor, database, spreadsheet, communications) of *Works*, but in general it causes the cursor to move a greater distance than one space at a time. The **SPACE BAR** is the big key in the middle of the bottom row of the keyboard, and it is used to create a space.

NOTE: The **cursor** is the blinking line on the computer screen. It indicates where the next character typed will appear, or which item on a menu is being selected.

The SHIFT and CAPS LOCK Keys

These keys also are found on typewriter keyboards. On some computer keyboards the **SHIFT** key is indicated by an outline of an upward arrow; other keyboards also include the word "Shift." To type a single capital letter, press the **SHIFT** key and hold it down while typing the letter.

CAPS LOCK is used to type multiple capital letters. It is a toggle key, which means that each time you press the key it changes its state from off to on or vice versa. When **CAPS LOCK** is on, or activated, all letters you type will be capitalized. **CAPS LOCK** affects only the letters A to Z; you still have to press **SHIFT** in order to type the top characters on any keys that print two characters. The letters *CL* appear on the *Works* screen when **CAPS LOCK** has been activated.

Introduction to the Computer 3

In *Works* the **SHIFT** key also can be used in conjunction with non-letter keys to change the effect of those keys. These key combinations typically are used as shortcuts for tasks that can be accomplished in a variety of ways.

The CTRL and ALT Keys

The **CTRL**, or Control, key and the **ALT**, or Alternate, key are similar to the **SHIFT** key in that they typically are used in conjunction with other keys to change the effect of pressing these other keys. For example, *Works* uses **CTRL** key combinations to move the cursor around the screen. In the word processor, if you press the **END** key by itself, the cursor moves to the end of the line. If you press **CTRL** and **END** together, the cursor moves to the end of the document.

The **ALT** key has a more significant role in *Works*. The **ALT** key is pressed any time you want to access the menus. This is one of the few times when the **ALT** key can be used by itself. It also is used in conjunction with other keys to provide information necessary to carry out commands.

Always depress the **CTRL** or **ALT** key first and keep it depressed while you press the other key.

The BACKSPACE Key

The **BACKSPACE** key, as it is used in *Works*, is a destructive backspace. As it moves the cursor to the left, it erases any characters that are there. The **BACKSPACE** key is usually located on the top row of the main part of the keyboard. On some keyboards it is represented only by an arrow pointing to the left, while on others it has an arrow and the word "Backspace."

The ESC Key

The **ESC** key typically is used to back out of, or escape from, the current situation. Among its uses in *Works* are to leave a menu, cancel a Dialog Box, cancel a command, quit from *Extend*, cancel editing changes, stop printing, or erase material from the Formula Bar. (These concepts will be clearer by the end of this book!) The general rule is that **ESC** can be used to escape from an operation *before* it is completed.

The ENTER Key

In DOS, the **ENTER** key is used to indicate that you have finished typing a command and are ready for DOS to execute it. In *Works*, the **ENTER** key has several different functions. It can be used to make selections from a menu or to tell *Works* that you have finished providing the information it needs to carry out a command. It also has specific uses in each of the tools that will be explained in the following chapters.

The Function Keys

The function keys are located at the top or left-hand side of most keyboards and are labeled with the letter **F** followed by a number. *Works* only uses keys **F1** through **F10**, although some keyboards contain additional function keys. Some software programs use the function keys as the primary way of giving commands. *Works* typically uses the function keys alone, or in conjunction with the **CTRL** or **SHIFT** keys, as shortcuts or alternative methods of issuing commands. Appendix C lists the function keys and their uses.

The Numeric Keypad

The numeric keypad is an extra set of numeric keys arranged in a square on the right-hand side of most keyboards. It functions as an alternative method of entering numerals. However, since the numerals share the keys with arrows or other cursor movement controls, a numeral is produced only if **NUM LOCK** is activated or if the key is depressed in conjunction with the **SHIFT** key.

The ARROW, PGUP (Pageup), PGDN (Pagedown), HOME, and END Keys

These keys are called the cursor movement keys, because they are used to control the movement of the cursor around the screen. The **ARROW** keys move the cursor one space, line, or row in the direction of the arrow. The other keys cause bigger jumps in the cursor movement. The specific effects of these keys in each of the tools will be discussed in the appropriate chapters.

On most IBM or IBM-compatible keyboards, these keys are located on the numeric keypad at the right of the keyboard. Some models also contain an additional set of cursor-control keys in between the alphanumeric keyboard and the numeric keypad.

The NUM LOCK Key

Sometimes you press a cursor control key and either nothing happens or a numeral appears on the screen. That is probably because **NUM LOCK** has been activated. **NUM LOCK**, like **CAPS LOCK**, is a toggle key. *Works* indicates that **NUM LOCK** has been activated by placing the letters *NL* at the bottom of the screen. When **NUM LOCK** is activated and you press a key on the numeric keypad, the number is typed, or, if the cursor is on a menu where the number has no meaning, nothing happens. To correct this problem, press **NUM LOCK** to deactivate it and try the cursor control key again. If your keyboard contains only one set of cursor control keys, it is generally advisable to leave **NUM LOCK** deactivated and type numbers using the top row of the alphanumeric keypad. If you have a second set of cursor-control keys, you may want to keep **NUM LOCK** activated and use the numeric keypad to type numbers.

The Monitor (CRT)

The monitor is one of the principle output devices. It displays information you enter from the keyboard, responses that are generated by the software that you are using, and the results of the commands you use.

The Printer

The printer is the main output device used to obtain a printed copy of your work. In order to use a printer with *Works*, you must give the program some information

Introduction to the Computer

about the printer that you are using and how that printer is connected to your computer. We'll learn how to do this in the next chapter when we print our first document.

The Disk Drive(s)

Disk drives are the type of auxiliary storage units that your computer is most likely to use. The computer can only carry out instructions or manipulate data that is in its main memory. Since this memory is limited and the information in memory is lost when the computer is turned off, disks are used to store both the programs that tell the computer what to do and also the output of the programs. Anything stored on a disk is stored in a file.

There are two types of disk drives: floppy drives and fixed (or hard) drives. Floppy disk drives have openings into which you insert a diskette (which we will refer to as a disk). Disks are currently either 5 1/4 in. or 3 1/2 in. in size, and are transportable. This portability makes floppy disks excellent storage facilities for data. The names **Drive A** and **Drive B** are usually applied to floppy disk drives. **Drive A** is also referred to as **A:** or **a:**, and **Drive B** is referred to as **B:** or **b:**.

Many computers also have at least one fixed disk drive. Fixed disk drives are usually not easily portable, but they hold much more information than floppy disks and are accessed at faster speeds. If a computer has one fixed disk drive, that drive typically is referred to as **Drive C**, or **C:**.

We must use disk drive names whenever we want the computer to read information from a disk or to store information to a disk.

Care and Handling of Disks
You already have a floppy disk containing the *Works* program, and soon you will be creating and saving files of your own. Floppy disks are wonderful data-storage facilities that may be used again and again. They must be handled carefully, however, because when a disk gets damaged there is a good chance that the files on it will be partially or totally destroyed. You will learn how to make backup copies of both individual files and entire disks a little bit later on in this chapter, but for now let's think about ways to avoid damaging disks and losing files as a result.

Floppy disks are sensitive to heat, cold, dust, moisture and magnetic devices, so keep the following guidelines in mind:

- Never store your disks in a location where the temperature will be above 125° Fahrenheit or below 50° Fahrenheit.
- Always store 5 1/4 in. disks in their disk jackets.
- Avoid eating and drinking at your computer work area or disk storage area.
- Never expose your disk to a magnet or leave a disk on top of a computer, television, stereo, or other electrical device, as these generate an electromagnetic field.
- Avoid passing your disks through magnetic sensors such as those in libraries, stores, and airports.
- Never touch any exposed area of a disk.
- Never paperclip a disk to another disk or to papers, as the paperclip may put a crease in the disk.
- Never bend a disk.

Note: People often bend disks inadvertently while trying to insert them into disk drives. *NEVER* try to force a disk into a drive. If the disk does not slip into the drive smoothly, pull it back out and make sure you are holding it correctly. Then gently try to insert it again; you may find that you need to adjust the angle at which you are inserting it.

To insert a 5 1/4 in. disk into a disk drive:

1. Remove the disk from its jacket.
2. Hold the disk so that the label faces up and the small notch in the side is on the left. (This is called the write protect notch; sometimes it is covered with a piece of tape called the write protect tab.)
3. Carefully insert the disk into the disk drive and close the door.

To insert a 3 1/2 in. disk into a disk drive:

1. Hold the disk so that the label faces up and the end with the sliding metal cover enters the drive first.
2. Carefully insert the disk into the drive until it clicks into place.

DOS (The Disk Operating System)

PC-DOS or **MS-DOS** is the **Disk Operating System** typically used with IBM or IBM-compatible personal computers. DOS is the collection of programs that lets you begin to use your personal computer. It serves as the intermediary between your software program and the **Central Processing Unit**. Without first "loading" DOS, you would be unable to proceed to the next step, which is to load the actual software you wish to use. To **load** a program means to copy at least part of it from the disk into the computer's memory. Loading DOS is sometimes referred to as **booting** the disk or booting the system, because DOS "pulls itself up by its own bootstraps" without the help of other programs.

Thus far, in this book, you've been reading general information about *Works* or about computers. For the rest of the book, you'll be trying activities as we discuss them. We're ready to turn the computer on and try some DOS commands. Instructions for starting your computer are given separately for computers with and without hard drives.

If your computer has only floppy disk drives:

1. Put your DOS disk in Drive A and close the door.

Note: If your computer has more than one floppy disk drive, Drive A is usually the left or top drive.

DOS (The Disk Operating System)

2. Turn on the system unit, monitor, and printer.

   Don't worry if nothing much happens for a while. The computer is checking that its components are working.

   Then, the following message will appear:

   Current Date is Tues 1-01-1980
   Enter new date (mm-dd-yy):

3. Type the date in the form: mm-dd-yy

   For example, if the date is September 11, 1988, type: **9-11-88**

4. Press the **ENTER** key.

   Whenever you have completed giving DOS a command or the information it requests, you must press the **ENTER** key to tell DOS that you are done.

   A new message will appear on the screen:

   Current time is 0:00:23:23
   Enter new time:

5. Enter the current time in the form: hh:mm

   DOS uses a 24-hour clock. Therefore, to enter P.M. times, add 12 to the current time. For example, if it is 1:30 P.M., type: **13:30**

6. Press the **ENTER** key.

7. The system prompt, *A>*, should appear on your screen.

If your computer has a hard disk:

1. Make sure that there are no disks in the floppy disk drives.

2. Turn on the system unit, monitor, and printer.

   As with the computers that only have floppy drives, the computer will check that the necessary components are functioning.

3. What appears on your screen next will vary depending on how the hard disk was set up. If you are prompted to enter a date and time, proceed with steps 3-6 above.

4. Your screen should contain the system prompt, *C:\>*, or instructions on how to get to the *C* prompt or how to enter DOS commands.

The Current Drive

The **current drive**, which is sometimes called the **active** or **default drive**, indicates where the computer will look when it needs to find a file or to save a file. When you first turn on the computer, the active drive is the drive that contains the DOS files. The name of the active drive is included in the prompt that appears on the screen. Unless you give the computer other instructions, it will look on the disk in the active drive for any files it needs and will assume that any commands you give it apply to the disk in the active drive.

Now we're ready to start using some DOS commands. While the Disk Operating System is actually quite complex, for our purposes there are just five fundamental commands that you will need to know. These are **FORMAT**, **DISKCOPY**, **DIR** (for directory), **COPY**, and **DEL** (delete). In addition, our goal is only that you know enough about these commands to be able to work effectively with *Works*. Therefore,

Introduction to Computing with Microsoft Works

detailed explanations of the commands and all of their variations will not be provided.

Format The **FORMAT** command is important because it gets your data disks ready for use. It cleans off the disks and puts tracks, sectors, and space for a directory on the disk so that all of your files may be kept in order and may be accessed readily.

Let's format a disk so that we will have some place to store our *Works'* data files once we create them. Be sure to follow the directions carefully. Since the **FORMAT** command cleans off the disk, if you accidently format a disk that contains information you still need, you will lose that information.

Note: Some of the DOS responses to your commands and the exact format of the commands may be different in your system than those described in this book. These discrepancies are caused by the many revisions that have been made to DOS. The commands and prompts given in this book are from DOS version 3.2. Versions of DOS that differ only by the decimal (e.g., DOS 3.0 and DOS 3.1) contain minor variations. A change in the integer portion indicates a greater revision. None of the differences between versions had a major effect on the commands we will learn, and we will note any significant variations.

If you are using a system with only floppy drives:

1. Make sure your DOS disk is still in Drive A.
2. Place a blank disk in Drive B.
3. Type: **format b:**
   You may use any combination of uppercase and lowercase letters when you type a DOS command.

Note: If you omit the B:, DOS will assume that you want to format the disk in the A drive, since that is the current drive.

---

4. Your screen now should say:
   A> Format B:
   Press the **ENTER** key.
5. You will be prompted to enter a new diskette for Drive B. Since you have already done that, press the **ENTER** key.
6. When the formatting is complete, DOS will give you a message telling how much space is available on the disk and if any part of the disk is bad. It will then ask if you want to format another. (Figure 1-2 shows all of the DOS messages from the time you enter the **FORMAT** command until it is completed. The messages you see may be slightly different if you are using a different version of DOS.)

DOS (The Disk Operating System) 9

```
A:\>format b:
Insert new diskette for drive B:
and strike ENTER when ready

Format complete

    362496 bytes total disk space
    362496 bytes available on disk

Format another (Y/N)?
```

Figure 1-2

7. The next response is up to you. Many people like to format an entire box of disks at one time. If you want to format another disk, type **y**. If you do not want to format additional disks, type **n**.

   Press the **ENTER** key. (It is not necessary to press the **ENTER** key if you are using early versions of DOS.)

8. Remove the last formatted disk from the disk drive.

   Put a label saying *Exercise Disk* on one of the disks. We will use this disk later in this chapter and in the following chapters when we want to save our work.

If you are using a system with a hard drive:

1. Put a blank disk in Drive A.

2. Type: **format a:**

   You may use any combination of uppercase and lowercase letters when you type a DOS command.

Note: If you omit the **A:**, DOS will assume that you want to format the C drive, since that is the current drive.

---

3. Your screen now should say:

   C> Format a:

   Press the **ENTER** key.

4. Follow steps 5-8 above to finish the command.

Introduction to Computing with Microsoft Works

DISKCOPY The **DISKCOPY** command is important because it lets you make an *exact duplicate* of any floppy disk. **DISKCOPY** is a very powerful command, but it also can be dangerous. In the process of copying all of the files from one disk (the **source** disk) to another (the **target** disk), **DISKCOPY** also formats, and therefore erases the target disk. For this reason, **DISKCOPY** should be used only when the disk that you are copying to is blank, or contains information that you are sure you will not want to use again.

We will use the **DISKCOPY** command to make a **backup** copy of your *Works* disk. Then you can put the original disk in a safe place and use your backup copy. That way if your *Works* disk is accidently ruined, you can get the original disk, make another copy, and continue working.

Once you start saving your own data on disks, you will probably want to use **DISKCOPY** frequently to make backup copies of your work disks.

Although we think of disks as providing permanent storage, they can be damaged in ways that will cause you to lose information—or you may accidently erase some of the information. Disks can be damaged by exposure to intense sunlight, heat, cold, magnetic fields (such as those generated by TVs, radios, and even your computer), fingerprints, spilled coffee, etc. They also can be damaged by some of the errors that occur while you are using them in the computer. To be safe, use the **DISKCOPY** command to make frequent backups.

The general format of the **DISKCOPY** command is:

DISKCOPY <source> <target>

where **<source>** is the letter, followed by a colon, of the drive containing the disk you want to copy, and **<target>** is the letter, followed by a colon, of the drive containing the disk onto which the copy will be made.

We will use the **DISKCOPY** command to make a backup copy of the *Works* program disk.

If Your Computer Has Only Floppy Disk Drives:

1. Insert the DOS disk in Drive A.
2. Type: **diskcopy a: b:**

    You will see the following prompts to insert the source and target diskettes in the drives you designated in the command.

    Insert source diskette in drive A:

    Insert target diskette in drive B:

    Strike any key when ready

3. Remove DOS from Drive A and replace it with your Microsoft *Works* disk.
4. Put a blank disk in Drive B and press any key. Screen prompts relating to the copy process will appear. When DOS is finished, you will be prompted:

    Copy another (Y/N)?_

5. Since this is the only disk that you want to copy, type: **n**
6. Remove and label the disk. Now put the original away in a safe place, and use the copy of the *Works* disk whenever you are told to use the *Works* disk.

DOS (The Disk Operating System) 11

**If You Are Using a Computer with DOS on the Hard Disk
and One Floppy Drive**

The process is somewhat more complicated in this case because the same disk drive is used for the source and the target. DOS will prompt you to change drives.

1. Make sure you are at the *C>* prompt.
2. Type: **diskcopy a: a:**

    You will see the following prompts:

    Insert source diskette in drive A:

    Strike any key when ready

3. Insert the *Works* disk into Drive A. Press any key.

    When the contents of the disk are copied into the computer's memory, you will be prompted to:

    Insert target diskette in drive A:

    Strike any key when ready

4. Remove the *Works* disk and insert the blank disk in Drive A. Press any key.
5. Depending on the amount of computer memory available, you may have to swap the Source and Target disks a few more times. If this is necessary, you will be prompted. Follow the screen prompts.
6. When the diskcopy is completed, you will be prompted:

    Copy another (Y/N)?_

7. Since this is the only disk that you want to copy, type: **n**
8. Remove and label the backup copy of the *Works* disk.

DIR The **DIR** (Directory) command is valuable because it lets you "see" which files you have stored on a disk. Just like the directory in an apartment building, the directory of a floppy disk will tell you the names of the occupants and a little bit about them. In an apartment building, this would be the last names of the tenants. In a computer, this information includes the name of the file, its extension (if it has one), the date that it was last saved, the time that it was last saved, and the amount of storage space the file requires. (Storage space is measured in **bytes**, where one byte is the space taken up by one character.)

Let's look at a directory of your *Works* diskette.

1. Put the backup copy of your *Works* system disk in Drive A.

Note: Unlike the **FORMAT** and **DISKCOPY** commands, the **DIR**, **COPY**, and **DEL** commands are placed in the computer's memory when DOS is loaded. Therefore, we can issue DOS commands without keeping the DOS disk in the A drive.

Introduction to Computing with Microsoft Works

2. Type: **dir a:**

   A listing of all of the files on Drive A should appear on the screen (Figure 1-3).

```
A:\>Dir A:

Volume in drive A has no label
Directory of    A:\

WORKS      EXE    313622    1-27-88    9:13a
WORKS      INI        50    2-10-88   11:54a
CGA        GSD      4825    9-22-87    6:10p
HERCULES   GSD      5113    9-22-87    6:11p
EGA        GSD      1765    9-22-87    6:10p
MCGA       GSD      2485    9-22-87    6:11p
TANDY      GSD      2739    9-22-87    6:12p
F00225     RFT      7604    9-24-87   10:10a
F001       SFT      7704    9-24-87   10:10a
COMM       SCD      3014    9-22-87    6:13p
EPSONFX    PRD      2832    9-21-87    5:55p
EPSON      GPD       746    9-21-87    5:55p
HIEPSON    GPD       753    9-21-87    5:55p
SAMPLE     WDB       907    3-29-88    2:07p
SAMPLE     WKS      1300    3-29-88    1:59p
SAMPLE     WPS      1309    3-29-88    2:05p
       16 File(s)      367616 bytes free

A:\>
```

Figure 1-3

We are most interested in the *file names* part of the **DIR** listing. File names are of the form:

filename.ext

where the **filename** component may contain from one to eight characters. The **ext**ension is optional, but if it is used, it always is separated from the filename by a period. When the name of the file is displayed in the directory, the period (.) is replaced by a space, and any filename shorter than eight characters is padded with blank spaces.

Most of the files on the *Works* disk are the programs required to make *Works* function. However, we have added three data files that we created using *Works*. Like many applications programs, *Works* adds its own extensions to the names of files you save. In fact, it adds a different extension depending upon which tool you used to create the file. The *Works* extensions are:

Extension	Tool
.WPS	Word Processor
.WKS	Spreadsheet
.WDB	Database
.WCM	Communications

DOS (The Disk Operating System) 13

Note: Some of these extensions are used by other software programs as well.

These extensions help *Works* to recognize which of the files on a disk were created using *Works*. In later chapters we will learn how to display a partial directory using *Works* rather than DOS commands. This listing will contain only files whose extensions begin with a **W**, or only files with one of the specific tool extensions, depending on how you give the command. You also can use these extensions to help you sort out your files. If you look at your directory, you can find the three files that we created using *Works*.

COPY The **COPY** command is used to make copies of one or more files. Just as **DISKCOPY** is used to back up an entire disk, **COPY** is used to back up individual files. Even if you want to copy all of the files from one disk to another, you must use the **COPY** command rather than **DISKCOPY** if the disk you are copying to already contains files you wish to keep. Let's use the **COPY** command to copy two of our *Works* files from the *Works* system disk to our newly formatted Exercise disk.

First we will copy the file **SAMPLE.WKS**, and then we will copy the file **SAMPLE.WPS** from the *Works* disk to your formatted exercise disk. The format of the command to copy a file from one floppy disk to another *without* changing the file name is:

copy a:filename.ext b:

To copy files using a computer with two floppy disk drives:

1. Put the backup copy of the *Works* disk in Drive A:.
2. Put your formatted Exercise disk in Drive B:.
3. Type: **copy a:sample.wks b:**
4. Press the **ENTER** key.

    DOS will return the following message:

    1 File(s) copied

5. To copy the second file, type: **copy a:sample.wps b:**
6. Get a directory of your Exercise disk (Figure 1-4).

To copy files using a computer with only one floppy disk:

1. Put the backup copy of the *Works* disk in Drive A.
2. Type: **copy a:sample.wks b:**
3. Press the **ENTER** key.

    DOS will copy the file **SAMPLE.WKS** from the disk in Drive A to the computer's memory. It then will display the following message:

    Insert diskette for drive B: and strike
    any key when ready

    If you only have one floppy disk drive on your computer, it serves as *both* Drive A and Drive B.

```
A:\>Dir B:

Volume in drive B has no label
Directory of  B:\

SAMPLE    WKS      1300   3-29-88   1:59p
SAMPLE    WPS      1309   3-29-88   2:05p
        2 File(s)      350400 bytes free

A:\>
```

Figure 1-4

4. Therefore, put your formatted Exercise disk in the floppy disk drive.
5. Press any key.

    DOS will return the following message:

    1 File(s) copied

6. To copy the second file, type: **copy a:sample.wps b:**

    This time DOS will prompt you to:

    *Insert diskette for drive A: and strike
    any key when ready*

7. Insert your backup copy of the *Works* disk into Drive A and press any key.

    DOS will prompt you to:

    *Insert diskette for drive B: and strike
    any key when ready*

8. Insert the Exercise disk in Drive B and press any key.
9. Obtain a directory of your exercise disk.

Note: The directory will appear exactly the same whether you copy the files using a computer with two floppy disk drives or a computer with only one floppy disk drive The only difference between your screen and the one shown in Figure 1-4 is that a **C** prompt should appear in place of the **A** prompt.

DEL (Delete) The **DEL** (delete) command is used when you wish to remove a file (or files) from a disk. If you are new to computing, our advice would be to use this command sparingly, since you may accidently erase the wrong file(s) or may decide at a later point in time that you wish that you still had the file(s) that you erased. Disk storage space is very inexpensive compared to the time that it might take to reconstruct the work that went into creating the file(s) in the first place. We will not practice the delete command, but if you want to use it, the format is:

DEL d:filename.ext

where **d:** is the drive containing the file you wish to delete.

Installing Microsoft Works

If Your Computer Has Only Floppy Drives

If you are using *Works* on a computer system that has only floppy drives, the first step is to make a copy of your program (the *Works* system disk) onto a backup disk. If you did not do this when we introduced the **DISKCOPY** command, go back to that section and follow the directions given for making a backup copy of a disk.

The retail version of *Works* has a setup procedure that allows you to tell it what type of monitor and printer you are using. This is not included in the educational version, but the monitor and printer setup can be changed from within *Works*. We will select a printer the first time we use the printer in the chapter on word processing. Instructions for adjusting the monitor will be given later in this chapter.

If Your Computer Has a Hard (Fixed) Drive

If your computer system has a hard or fixed disk, then you might prefer to have the program copied onto it. In the retail version of *Works*, there is a setup procedure that guides you through this task. Using the educational version, you will need to do this yourself by creating a subdirectory for your new program, then changing to that subdirectory, and finally copying all of the files from *Works* into that subdirectory. Follow the directions below to do this:

1. Make sure you are at the *C>* prompt.
2. Type: **md\works**

   Press the **ENTER** key.

   This command *makes* a *directory* (**md**) named **"works"**.
3. Type: **cd\works**

   Press the **ENTER** key.

   This command *changes* to the *directory* (**cd**) named **"works"**.
4. Put your *Works* system disk in Drive A:.
5. Type: **copy a:*.***

   Press the **ENTER** key.

   The * is a DOS wildcard. Any character or characters can be replaced by an asterisk. Therefore, this command will copy every file from the disk in Drive A to the subdirectory **works** on the hard disk.

The setup procedure in the retail version of *Works* also allows you to specify the printer and monitor that you are using. Since the educational version does not have this procedure, we will tell you how to change the monitor and printer setup from within *Works*. Instructions on selecting a printer will be given the first time we use the printer in the chapter on word processing. Instructions for adjusting the monitor will be given later in this chapter.

The Microsoft Works Interface

One advantage of an integrated software package is that the components usually have the same interface. This means that the screens in each tool of the program are similar (if not identical) in many respects. It also means that the actions that you will perform to do certain activities in different tools will be similar or identical. We'll use the Word Processor tool to take our first look at *Works*, but we could just as easily use any of the other tools in *Works*.

Starting Works In order to take a look at *Works*, we must copy at least part of the program into the computer's memory. This is called **loading the program**. The procedure is easy, but operates a little differently depending on whether you have installed *Works* onto your fixed disk, or are using the floppy disk.

Loading Works—From a Floppy Disk System

1. If you have not already started your computer:
   a. Put your DOS diskette in Drive A.
   b. Turn on your computer system.
   c. Enter the correct date and time.
   d. Remove the DOS diskette from Drive A.
2. Once the *A>* prompt appears on the screen, you are ready to load *Works*.
   a. Place your *Works* disk in Drive A.
   b. Type: **Works**
   c. Press the **ENTER** key.

Loading Works—From a Fixed Disk System

1. If you have not already started your computer:
   a. Make sure that there are no disks in the floppy disk drives. Turn on your computer system.
   b. Enter the correct date and time, if necessary.
2. When the *C>* prompt appears on the screen, you are ready to load *Works*.
   a. Type: **cd\works**

      This will change the current directory to the *Works* subdirectory that you created when you installed *Works* on your hard drive.
   b. Type: **works**
   c. Press the **ENTER** key.

At the Beginning When you start *Works*, a copyright screen briefly appears, followed by a screen that allows you to select a tool (Figure 1-5). In order to use Works, you must be working on a file that will be created with one of the four tools—word processor, spreadsheet, database, or communications.

The Microsoft Works Interface 17

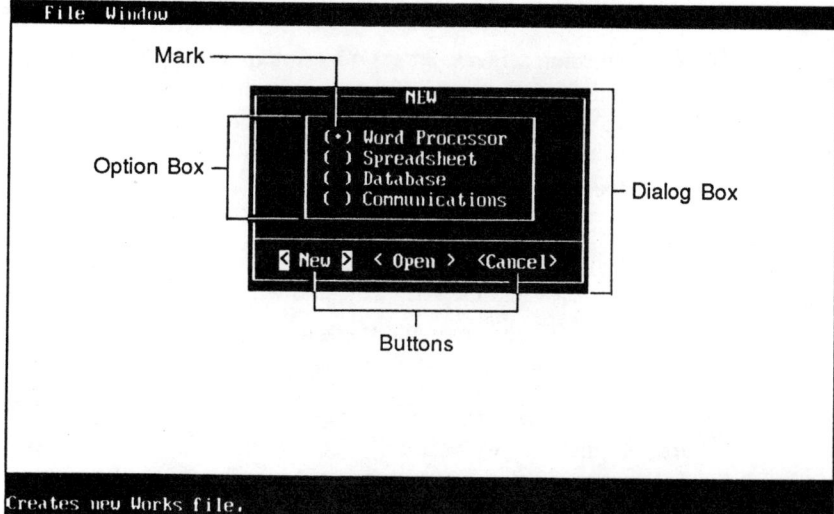

Figure 1-5

Works Dialog Boxes The box in the center of the screen contains all of the information that we need to select a tool. This box is referred to as the NEW Dialog Box. **Dialog Boxes** are used throughout *Works*, as a means of allowing you to specify the information needed to carry out a task. Every Dialog Box contains one or more of five elements: *Text Boxes, Check Boxes, Option Boxes, List Boxes,* and *Buttons*. To use a Dialog Box, select an option from the Text, Check, Option or List Boxes and then select a Button to tell the program to proceed with the command.

The NEW Dialog Box contains only two of the elements: an Option Box and Buttons. The Option Box contains the names of the four *Works* tools: *Word Processor*, *Spreadsheet*, *Database*, and *Communications*. The mark beside *Word Processor* means that the word processor is the currently selected option. Only one option in an Option Box may be selected at a time.

Changing an Option in an Option Box The blinking line under the mark is the **cursor**. The cursor indicates which part of the Dialog Box is active. Since the cursor is in the Option Box, we can use it to move the mark to the other options.

1. Press the **DOWN ARROW** key once.

   The mark moves down with the cursor, selecting the **Spreadsheet** option.

2. Keep pressing the **DOWN ARROW** until **Communications** is selected. Press the **DOWN ARROW** again.

   The cursor moves back up to **Word Processor**, the first choice in the Option Box.

There is another method you can use to change options.

1. Press the **ALT** key.

   One letter in each of the names is **bold**.

Introduction to Computing with Microsoft Works

Note: On some screens, letters may not appear in bold, or the bold letters may become invisible because the default screen setting is inappropriate for your monitor. Once we enter the word processor we will change the screen setting to correct any such problems. Until then, continue following the instructions even though the screen doesn't appear as it should.

---

2. Press the **ALT** key, and while holding it down, type: **d**

   The cursor and mark move to **Database**.

Note: Sometimes we will use the notation **ALT+LETTER** to indicate that you should press the first key and then hold it while pressing a second key. Therefore, if we wanted you to carry out step 2 above, we would say, press **ALT+D**.

---

3. Since we want to select the word processor, press **ALT+W** to move the mark back to **Word Processor**.

Carrying Out a Command

We've chosen the option that we want. Now we need to choose a Button to carry out the command. Every Dialog Box contains Buttons that ask you whether you want to carry out or to cancel the task. Most Dialog Boxes contain only two buttons—one such as **<OK>** or **<Print>** (if we're using the **PRINT** command), which tells *Works* to carry out the command using the current settings in the Dialog Box, and one which says **<Cancel>**. The NEW Dialog Box contains three Buttons [Figure 1-5]. The first two, **<New>** and **<Open>**, allow you to carry out related tasks. **<New>** creates a new file of the type marked in the Option Box. **<Open>** retrieves, or "opens," a file that you have already created and saved on a disk.

Notice that the brackets around **<New>** are highlighted. In every Dialog Box, one Button is enclosed in highlighted brackets. This is referred to as the **default** button because it automatically is highlighted when the Dialog Box appears. The Button in the highlighted bracket will be selected if you press the **ENTER** key. To create a new word processor file:

1. Check that the mark is next to **Word Processor**. If it isn't, use the **UP** or **DOWN ARROW** keys to move it there.
2. Press the **ENTER** key to select the **<New>** Button.

   The word processor screen should appear.

The Works Screen

The screen for each tool is slightly different. However, there are many similarities. Let's use the word processor screen (Figure 1-6) to see what the common elements are.

The **Menu Bar** lists the names of the menus. Most tasks in *Works*, except for entering text or data, involve the use of the menus. Some of the commands listed in the Menu Bar are different in the different tools, or even change within a tool as you are engaged in different tasks. However, many of the menus and much of the

The Microsoft Works Interface 19

Figure 1-6

contents of each menu are the same. More important, once you learn how to select from the menus, the same procedures can be used in each of the tools.

The **Work Area** is used to enter and edit information.

The **Status Line** helps you to keep track of your work. The name of the active file (the file currently displayed on the screen), and the part of the file on which you are currently working are recorded here. Additional information is also displayed, at times, in each tool.

The **Message Line** displays prompts, instructions, or descriptions that primarily are designed to help you to use the menus.

A First Look at Menus

Let's follow the instruction on the Message Line to get a closer look at the *Works* Command Menus.

Right now the cursor is in the Work Area; *Works* is expecting us to enter some text. To give *Works* a command, we must follow three steps:

- Move the cursor to, or *activate*, the Menu Bar.
- *Open* the menu containing the command we want to use.
- *Choose* the command.

To activate the Menu Bar:

1. Press the **ALT** key.

   You should notice three changes on the screen (Figure 1-7):

   - The cursor no longer appears in the Work Area;
   - One letter in each of the menu names is **bold**; and the first menu name, **File**, is in an inverse highlight box. (We will refer to this inverse highlight box as the highlight.)
   - A new instruction appears in the Message Line.

Introduction to Computing with Microsoft Works

Figure 1-7

As the prompt in the Message Line indicates, there are two ways to open a menu—either type the **bold letter**, or use the **RIGHT** and **LEFT ARROW** keys to move the highlight bar to the menu name you want and then press the **ENTER** key. These are similar to the two methods we used to select options in the NEW Dialog Box. Let's try opening the Window menu.

1. Type: **W**

    Notice that the Window menu opens, displaying a list of commands (Figure 1-8). Each of the commands in the Window menu now has a letter in bold, but none of the letters on the top Menu Bar remains **bold**. The Message Line has a description of the first command, because it is highlighted. If you use your **DOWN ARROW** key to highlight a different command, the description in the Message Line will change.

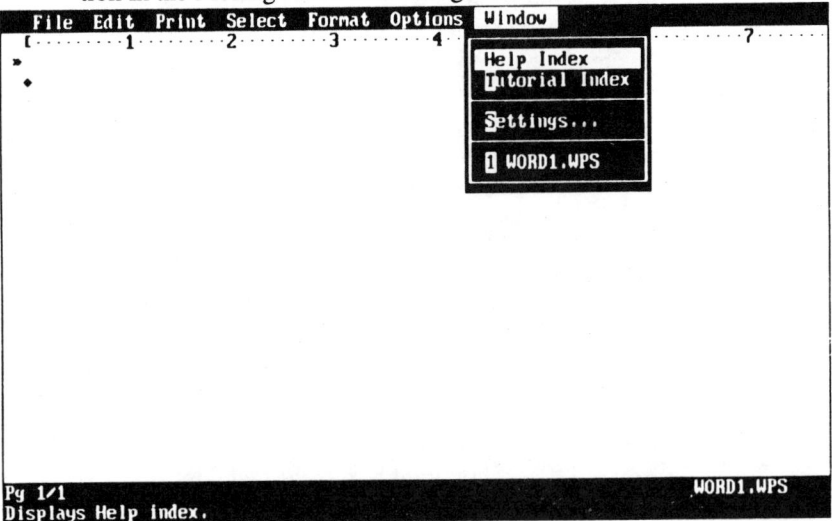

Figure 1-8

The Microsoft Works Interface 21

Note: Only commands beginning with a bold letter may be selected from a menu. At times you will notice one or more commands in a menu that do not begin with a bold letter. This means that those commands are not active and therefore may not be selected from the menu at that time.

Changing the Screen Settings If you have *not* been able to see the bold letters and/or highlight bar on your screen, follow the instructions in this section. Otherwise, go to the next section, Closing a Menu.

If your screen has not shown all of the information it should, it was probably because the *Works* program was set up for a color monitor and you are using a different type of monitor. The following directions should correct this.

1. Use the **DOWN ARROW** key to highlight **Settings...**
2. Press the **ENTER** key.

   The cursor should be under the mark before the **Color 1** setting (Figure 1-9).

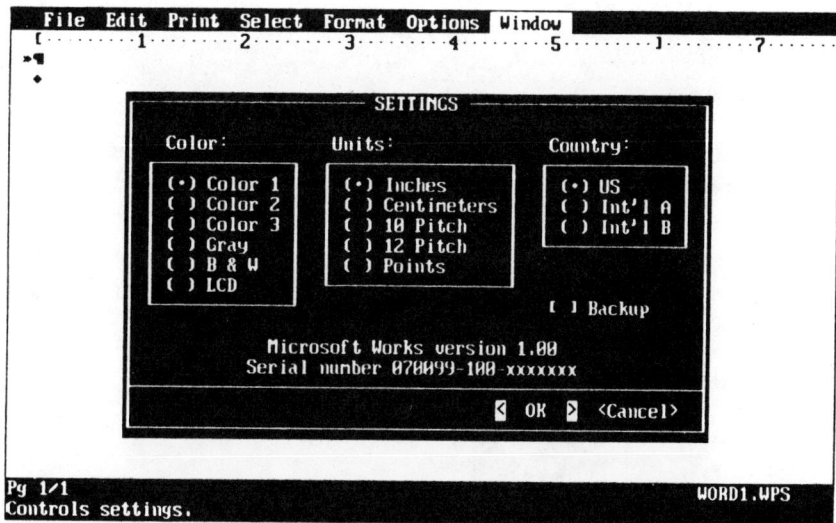

Figure 1-9

3. Use the **DOWN ARROW** key to move the highlight to the type of monitor that you are using. If you have a monochrome monitor, choose **B & W**. Some portable computers use **LCD**. If you're not sure which setting to choose, make a guess. You can always try again.
4. Press the **ENTER** key.
5. Press the **ALT** key to activate the Menu Bar.
6. Type: **W** to Open or "pull down" the **Window** menu.

Introduction to Computing with Microsoft Works

7. If your screen still is not showing the bold letters and highlight bar, repeat steps 1-6, selecting a different monitor setting until it does.

Closing a Menu What happens if you open the wrong menu? Let's see how to close the menu.

1. Press the **ALT** key again.

   This will close the Window menu, but keep the Menu Bar activated.

2. Now press the **ESC** key.

   When the Menu Bar is active, or a menu has been opened, pressing **ESC** returns the cursor to the work area.

Let's select the Window menu again, this time using the ARROW Key Method.

1. First press the **ALT** key to activate the Menu Bar.
2. Then use the **RIGHT** or **LEFT ARROW** key to move the highlight to **Window**.
3. Press **ENTER**.

   Once one menu is opened, the **ARROW** keys can be used to open other menus without pressing **ENTER**.

4. Use the **RIGHT** or **LEFT ARROW** keys to open the File menu (Figure 1-10).

More About the File Menu The File menu and all of its commands are the same in all of the tools. Let's explore some of these commands while learning more about using menus.

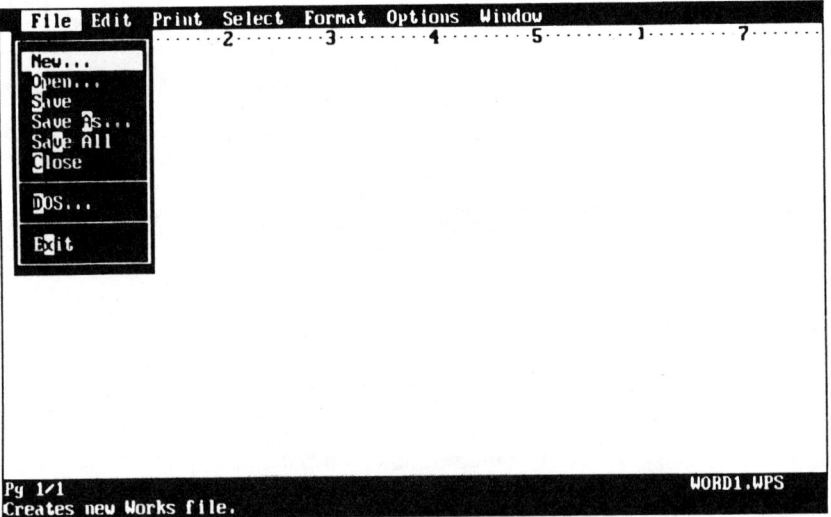

Figure 1-10

The Microsoft Works Interface

Works responds in several different ways when you select a command. Sometimes, it immediately carries out the command. At other times, instructions appear on the Message Line. The command is executed as soon as you carry out the instructions.

Often, *Works* needs more information before it can carry out the command. The commands on the File menu that require more information are **New...**, **Open...**, **Save As...**, and **DOS...**. Notice that each of these command options is followed by an ellipsis (...), which is *Works'* way of telling us that it's going to need more information before it can complete the task. Let's see what happens when we choose one of these commands.

1. The **New...** command on the File menu should be highlighted. If it is not, use the **UP** and **DOWN** arrow keys to move the highlight.
2. Press the **ENTER** key to select the highlighted command, **New...**.

Note: There are two ways to choose a command. In the foregoing example, we suggested that you first use the **ARROW** keys to highlight the command and then press **ENTER**. This is the slower method, but it allows a description of the highlighted command to appear on the Message Line—a good way to learn about *Works*. You also can check that the highlighted command is the one that you actually want to choose.

Alternatively, you may type the bold letter in the command name you want to use. This is faster, but may cause errors because you may not have an opportunity to check that you have selected the desired command before it has been executed.

Do you recognize the box on the screen? Anytime *Works* needs more information about a command, it opens a Dialog Box. When we loaded the *Works* program, it automatically selected the **File/New** command. Therefore, the first screen we saw contained the NEW Dialog Box.

Remember that each Dialog Box is made up of one or more of five basic elements: Text Boxes, Check Boxes, Option Boxes, List Boxes, and Buttons. To use a Dialog Box, you choose from among the options in the various boxes and then choose a Button to carry out the command. There are some differences in the way selections are made in each type of box, so learning to move around the Dialog Boxes may, at first, appear to be a little tricky. Don't worry, we'll give you lots of practice and help throughout the book, and we've summarized the characteristics and procedures associated with each type in a section near the end of this chapter that you can refer back to anytime. By the time you finish this chapter you already will have worked with four of the five elements just by using the NEW and OPEN Dialog Boxes. What's more, once you learn how to work each of the elements, you've learned how to use any Dialog Box that *Works* opens—in the word processor, spreadsheet, or database.

You've already practiced using Option Boxes and Buttons, when you used the NEW Dialog Box. Last time, we used the NEW Dialog Box to create a new word processor file. Let's see what happens if we select the **<Open>** Button instead of the **<New>** Button:

24   **Introduction to Computing with Microsoft Works**

1. Press the **ALT** key and hold it down to see which letter in the **<Open>** Button is bold.
2. While still holding down the **ALT** key, type the letter **O** to open a previously created file.

   The OPEN Dialog Box (Figure 1-11) should appear.

Note: The OPEN Dialog Box also is displayed when the **File/Open** command is selected.

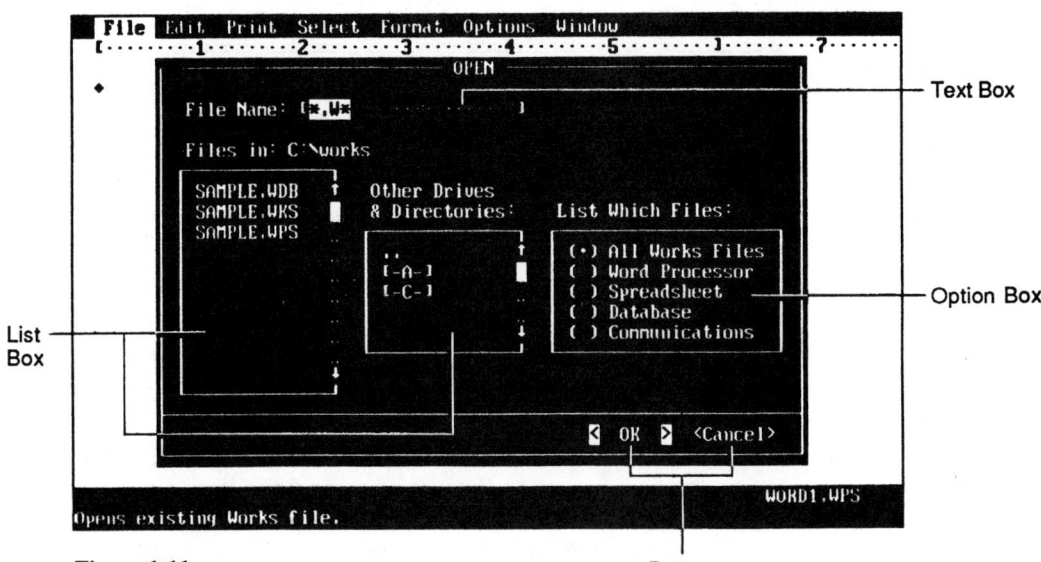

Figure 1-11

The OPEN Dialog Box is used to open a file that has been saved on a disk. In addition, it also acts a little bit like the DOS **DIR** command, by listing the names of the files on a particular disk. It does not provide the rest of the information that the **DIR** command does (e.g., the size of file, and date and time last saved), but it allows you to easily limit the files listed to those with the extensions *Works* uses.

The OPEN Dialog Box contains four Boxes and two Buttons. The File Name is specified using a Text Box. A list of the files in the active disk drive or directory, and a list of the currently available drives and directories, are contained in the two List Boxes on the left and center of the Dialog Box. The List Which Files Option Box allows you to specify which type of files will be listed under the Files in heading. The two Buttons are **<OK>** and **<Cancel>**.

We want to open the file named **SAMPLE.WPS**. We could just type the name of the file that we want in the File Name Text Box. However, we can also let *Works* do that for us, and learn more about using Dialog Boxes in the process. We will change the file name by selecting one of the files listed in the Files In List Box.

Before we can change the selections in a box that does not contain the highlight, we must move to that box.

The Microsoft Works Interface

Moving Between Elements in a Dialog Box

There are two ways of moving from Box to Box — the **TAB** key method and the **ALT** key method. Let's try the **TAB** key method first:

1. Press the **TAB** key once.

    The highlight disappears completely. The cursor should move under the first letter of the first file listed in the Files In List Box.

2. Press **TAB** again.

    The cursor will move to the beginning of the first entry under the Other Drives & Directories List Box.

3. Keep pressing the **TAB** key until the cursor moves back to the File Name Text Box. Notice the pattern of jumps the cursor makes.

Note: Since the **TAB** key, like most computer keys, repeats when it is held down, the cursor may jump rapidly from box to box.

Let's try the **ALT** key method:

1. Press the **ALT** key and keep it down to see which letters are bold.

    In Text and List Boxes, only a letter in the *name of the box* is bold. In Option Boxes, a letter in *each option* is bold.

2. While holding the **ALT** key down, press the letter **O**. Then press **ALT+F**, and then **ALT+N**. The cursor or highlight box moves among the boxes.

3. Now press **ALT+S**.

    When you use the **ALT** key method to move to an Option Box, *Works* simultaneously moves to the box and moves the mark to the option whose key letter you typed.

4. Press **ALT+A** or just press the letter **A** to select **All Works Files** again.

    Once the cursor is in a box, you may move it to a *different option in that box*, or options in some, but not all, other boxes by typing the bold letter *without* the **ALT** key. However, it is always permissible to use the **ALT+letter** combination. Many people find it easier to always use the key combination than to remember when the **ALT** key is needed and when it is not!

5. Use either the **TAB** key or the **ALT** key method to move the cursor to the Files In List Box.

Changing the Drive

When we discussed the disk drive and DOS commands at the beginning of this chapter, we noted that each drive has a name that is used to tell the computer where to find or save files. The first time we try to open or save a file after loading *Works*, it assumes that we are going to look for the file on the drive and directory that contains the *Works* system files. By looking at either Figure 1-11 or Figure 1-12 you can see that *Works* was loaded from the **Works** subdirectory on Drive C. Therefore, the heading for the first List Box is Files in: C:\works. If you loaded *Works* from a disk in Drive A, the heading would be Files in: A:\.

Introduction to Computing with Microsoft Works

Your copy of the educational version of *Works* came with a few data files on it. Typically, however, you will want to save your data to a different disk or drive than the one containing the *Works* program. If you did the exercises in the **COPY** section of this book, you copied two data files to an Exercise disk, which should be in a different disk drive than your *Works* disk. Therefore, we want to use the Other Drives & Directories List Box to change the drive to the drive containing our data, or exercise files.

Selecting Options from a List Box

To change the drive from which files will be opened:

1. Press the **ALT+O** keys, or use the **TAB** key to move the cursor to the Other Drives & Directories Box.

   When you switch to a List Box, the cursor appears under the top item in the list, but none of the options are selected. To select an option in a list box, use the **UP** and **DOWN ARROW** keys to highlight the desired item on the list.

2. Press the **DOWN ARROW** key once.

   The first entry in the list is now selected (Figure 1-12).

Note: Since the active directory in Figure 1-12 is a subdirectory, the first entry is a double period (..). Selecting the double period will take you up one directory in the directory tree. We will not be using this option since we will select a floppy disk drive.

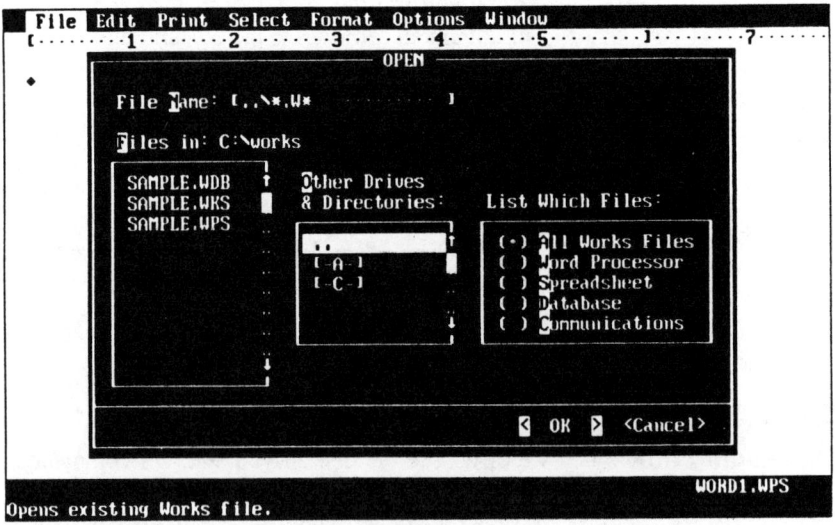

Figure 1-12

The drive name has been inserted at the beginning of the File Name Text Box.

The Microsoft Works Interface

3. If the first drive is *not* the drive that contains your Exercise disk, keep pressing the **DOWN ARROW** until the correct drive is highlighted. (If you are using a system with two floppy drives, the exercise disk should be in Drive B. If *Works* is on the hard drive, the exercise disk is probably in Drive A.)

   As each drive is highlighted, its name appears in the File Name Text Box.

4. Press the **ENTER** key.

   The light on the selected disk drive should be lit while *Works* produces a directory of the *Works* files (and any other files with extensions beginning with a **W**) on the newly selected drive.

   Figure 1-13 shows the OPEN Dialog Box after we changed the Directory to Drive A. The heading for the file listing is now Files in: A:\, and only the two files that we copied onto the exercise disk are listed.

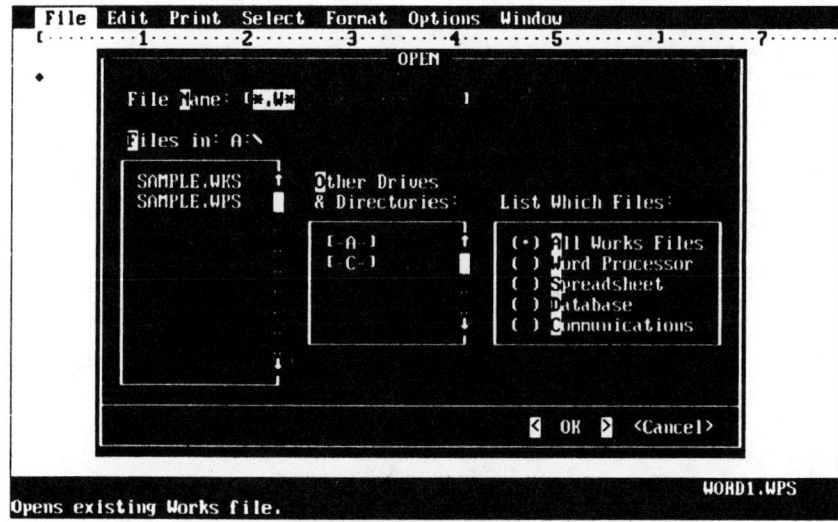

Figure 1-13

Note: Once you change the drive, it will remain the drive that *Works* uses to **Open** or **Save** files until you change the drive again or exit from *Works*.

Now that we have selected the correct drive, let's select the file named: **SAMPLE.WPS**.

1. **TAB** to the Files In List Box or press **ALT+F**.
2. Press the **DOWN ARROW** key once to select the first item in the list.

   The name of the highlighted file is entered in the File Name Text Box.

3. If the first item is not **SAMPLE.WPS**, keep pressing the **DOWN ARROW** until **SAMPLE.WPS** is highlighted.

As each file is highlighted, its name appears in the File Name Text Box.

4. Press **ENTER** when **SAMPLE.WPS** is highlighted.

Once we've entered **SAMPLE.WPS** as the file name, we can tell *Works* that it's OK to Open the file. Since there are only two buttons on this OPEN Dialog Box, no letters in either Button are bold. Since **<OK>** is the Button in highlighted brackets, if we press the **ENTER** key we will tell *Works* it's OK to open the file. If we were to decide we did not want to open the file, we could press the **ESC** key to cancel the command or we could **TAB** to the **<Cancel>** Button and press **ENTER**.

1. Press the **ENTER** key to tell Works it's OK to open the file.

The previously saved file, **SAMPLE.WPS** should appear on the screen.

Note: If you prefer, you may use the **TAB** method to move the cursor to the **<OK>** Button and then press the **ENTER** key.

Saving a File The first step in any task you do with *Works* will be to create a new file or to open an existing file. We have covered both of these tasks in this chapter. Then you will create or modify the document, spreadsheet, or database using the commands discussed in the remaining chapters of this book. Anything you do after you create or open the file is stored only in the computer's memory. Nothing is changed or added to the file on your disk until you explicitly save the new information in this file.

Since anything stored on a disk is contained in a file, the File menu also contains the **Save** commands. *Works* has two different commands that can be used to save a file. The **Save** command is used to save previously saved files using the existing file name. The **Save As...** command is used to save a file using a *new* name. We'll save the file we just opened, using a new name.

1. Activate the Menu bar.
2. Pull down the File menu.
3. Select the **Save As...** command by using the **DOWN ARROW** key to highlight the command or by typing the letter **A**.

The SAVE AS Dialog Box is opened (Figure 1-14).

Notice that the *Current Drive* is the drive that we selected when we opened the file. A highlight bar is on the file name, which is **SAMPLE.WPS**.

Changing Information in a Text Box We will call our new file **FIRST.WPS**. Information in a Text Box such as the File Name Box can be edited, but the simplest way to change something as short as a file name is to retype the entire text.

1. Type the new file name without any extension:

FIRST

Use any combination of uppercase and lowercase letters that you wish.

Rules for Naming a File

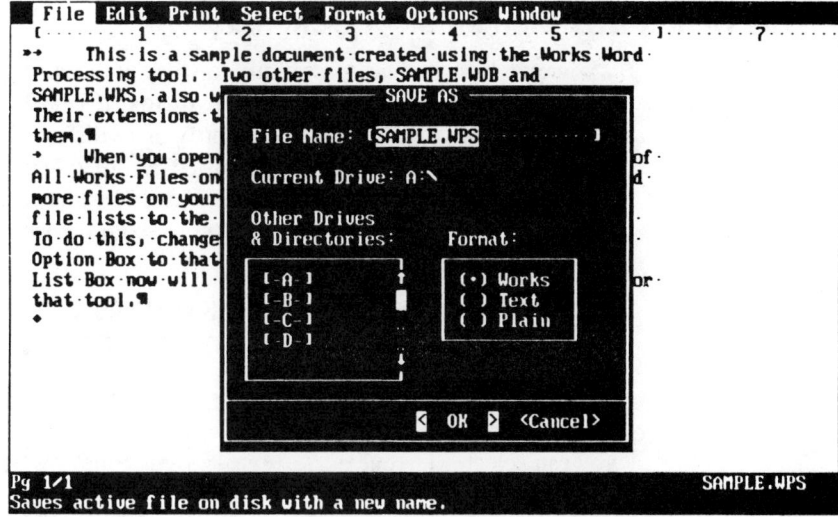

Figure 1-14

Works adds its word processing extension, **.WPS**, to the file name. The file will be saved as **FIRST.WPS** on your diskette; *Works* also changes the name in the File Name Text Box to **FIRST.WPS** as soon as you press the **ENTER** key.

2. Press the **ENTER** key.

Rules for Naming a File

We suggested a name for your first file. We tried to select a name that would help us recognize the file if we wanted to use it again in a week or two. Selecting meaningful file names is difficult because *Works* must follow the eight-letter limit on file name length imposed by DOS. *Works* allows us to add our own three-letter extension if we choose. However, as discussed earlier, if we let Works add the extensions we will be able to use its file listings when we want to open previously created files.

DOS also limits the acceptable characters in file names to letters, digits, and the following special characters:

@ ! # $ % ^ & ( ) _ - { } " ~ `

File names may *not* include a blank space.

Some acceptable file names are:

ACCTS-NY   NEW_EMP   BUDGET1   88BUDGET

Can you tell what's wrong with the following names?

INVENTORY   *SALES*   NEW EMP

The Five Dialog Box Elements—A Summary

By now you have had an opportunity to work with four Dialog Boxes, and in the process you have used Option Boxes, List Boxes, Text Boxes, and Buttons. You should be starting to recognize and identify these different elements when you see them in a Dialog Box that you haven't used before. Of course you will have many more opportunities to practice using them as we look at each of the tools in *Works*, but for now let's summarize what we know about the similarities and differences among them.

Characteristics of the Five Dialog Box Elements

	Option Boxes	List Boxes	Text Boxes	Check Boxes	Buttons
No. of options you can select at one time	one	one	one	*	one
One option is selected by default	always	never	sometimes	sometimes	always
No. of ways you can select or change options	two	one	two (sometimes)	two	two

*Each check box can be selected or not. A group of similar check boxes often appear together. More than one of these may be selected simultaneously.

Selecting Options

	Either	Or
Option Boxes	**TAB** to box; use an **ARROW** key to move the mark to the option you want	Press **ALT** plus the bold letter in the option you want
List Boxes	**TAB** to box; use the **UP** or **DOWN ARROW** key to highlight the option you want and then press **ENTER**	Press **ALT** plus the bold letter in the box name; use the **ARROW** keys to highlight the option you want and then press **ENTER**
Text Boxes	**TAB** to box; type the information in the box and press **ENTER**	Select the information from a List Box (only possible in some Dialog Boxes)
Check Boxes	**TAB** to the Check Box and press the Space Bar (you may toggle an option both on and off this way)	Press **ALT** plus the bold letter in the option (you may toggle the option both on and off this way)
Buttons	**TAB** to the Button you want and press **ENTER**	Press **ALT** plus the bold letter in the Button you want (this will not work with the **<Cancel>** Button, but you may press **ESC** to cancel a command)

If you are wondering why you haven't used Check Boxes yet, remember that not every Dialog Box contains all five elements. Check Boxes do not appear in as many Dialog Boxes as the other elements because their purpose is to let you tell the program to combine the effects of two or more related options, and that is not practical with many tasks. Check Boxes are most common in Dialog Boxes that deal with **Format** menu commands, because when you format a page you need to be able to combine options such as boldfacing and underlining. We will look at formatting in the Spreadsheet and Database tools in Chapters 3 and 4, and in the Word Processor tool in Chapter 6, so you will have an opportunity to use Check Boxes.

The Educational Version of Microsoft Works for the PC

The *Works* program included with this book is the educational version, rather than the full retail version. The two versions are very similar; most of the differences relate to size. The educational version fits neatly on one 5 1/4 in. disk or one 3 1/2 in. disk, while the full version takes up eight 5 1/4 in. disks. Missing from the educational version are features such as macros and files that allow you to take advantage of the special features of a wider range of printers. These features enhance the program but are not necessary for mastery of the basic tasks.

One task not available in the educational version is the ability to Spell Check a document using the Word Processor tool. Spell checking is a common feature of word processors that lets the program find misspelled words and even suggest possible corrections. However, in order to do this, spell checking programs compare the words in your document with the words on a dictionary that they provide. These dictionaries take up considerable space on the disk and therefore could not be included on the one disk-educational version.

Similar space limitations mandated that the onscreen Help information and Tutorial features of the full *Works* program be eliminated from this version. However, these features have not been eliminated from the Menus—the menus in the educational version are identical to those in the regular version. As a result of this, you will see an *ERROR* message when you attempt to access the Help, Tutorial, or Spell check files (Figure 1-15).

To see this message:

1. Activate the Menu Bar.
2. Open the **Window** Menu.
3. Select **Help Index**.

   When you see these "error" messages, remember that the Help, Tutorial, and Spell files were removed from the educational version intentionally—their absence is not due to an error in your disk!

4. Press **ENTER** to remove the error box from the screen.

As we have mentioned earlier, another difference between the retail and educational versions of *Works* is that the retail version contains a setup procedure that helps you specify the type of printer and monitor that you are using. With the educational version, different procedures are used to give *Works* this information. We have already discussed how to change the color settings to obtain better screen displays. In the next chapter you will learn how to specify the text printer that you

Introduction to Computing with Microsoft Works

Figure 1-15

are using. Finally, in Chapter 6 when we begin creating charts, you will learn how to specify the printer and screen display used for producing graphics.

The educational version of *Works* also limits the size of the files you can create with each tool. The maximum file size for a word processed document is 25K, which is approximately ten pages of the types of documents you will create in the word processor projects. The database and spreadsheet each are restricted to 32 columns and 256 rows, which is about one hundredth of the size they can reach with the full version of the program. However, none of these size restrictions interferes with the types of exercises normally used when learning a new program. Moreover, if you purchase the full-size version of *Works*, you still can use all of the documents, spreadsheets, and databases created with the educational version.

Exiting from Works

We've taken a quick first look at *Works*. If you want to take a break, this might be a good time. If not, continue with the next chapter. To exit from *Works*:

1. Activate the Menu Bar.
2. Pull down the **File** menu.
3. Select **Exit**.

   A DOS prompt should appear on the screen. If, however, you have typed anything on the word processing screen that was not saved, *Works* will open a Dialog Box and ask you if you want to *Save the changes* made. To exit *without* saving the changes, press the **ALT** key, and then the letter, **N**.

Conventions and Notations Used in This Text

In this chapter we've provided complete instructions for activating the menus and selecting commands. For the rest of this book we will be less specific about this one task. We will tell you the choices to make *without* giving detailed instructions. For example, if the instruction is:

Select File/Exit

It means:

- Press the **ALT** key.
- Type the **bold** letter in the menu name given (Fil**e**), or use the **ARROW** keys to move to the menu name and press the **ENTER** key.
- Type the **bold** letter in the command name given (**E**xit), or use the **UP** and **DOWN ARROWS** to move the highlight to the command name and press the **ENTER** key.

If you are making choices in a Dialog Box and it is necessary to hold down the **ALT** key while typing the **bold** letter, this will be indicated by a **+**. For example, if an instruction says:

ALT+A

It means:

- Press the **ALT** key and hold it down while you are pressing the letter **A**.

Most instructions that you are to follow will be numbered. All keys to be pressed, commands, and file names will be in large **bold** print. Specific text that you are to type either will be in large **bold** print, or if it is a long block of text, will be enclosed within a box. *Works'* responses to your actions and other text that you will see on the screen will also be highlighted by the use of a large size typeface. Some examples of these conventions are shown below:

1. Press the **DOWN ARROW** key twice.
2. Type: **Estimate:**

    The field name, *Estimate:* will appear at the top of the Work Area.

Conclusion

In this chapter we've looked briefly at the physical components of your computer system and some of the related terminology. You've also had an opportunity to practice the basic DOS commands necessary to independently manage your disks—**FORMAT, DISKCOPY, COPY,** and **DIR**. This information was preparatory to our main goal of learning *Works*.

We've also taken a first look at the *Works* interface—a *Works* screen, some of the commands that you'll be using, and how to work with the frequently displayed Dialog Boxes. Don't worry if you haven't mastered all of these tasks. We'll review the commands and procedures as we use them in the various tools.

This chapter also may be used as a reference for file naming limitations and the basic procedures required in using the menus and Dialog Boxes.

Key Terms

The following important terms and commands have been introduced and explained in this chapter:

Hardware	Software	System Unit
CPU	Disk	Disk drive
Boot the System	Current Drive	Cursor
Toggle	Load a program	DOS

DOS commands

FORMAT	DISKCOPY	DIR
COPY	DEL	

Works—parts of the screen:

Menu Bar	Work Area	Status Line
Message Line		

Works—parts of the Dialog Box:

Dialog Box	Option Box	Button
Text Box	Check Box	List Box

Works commands:

File/New	File/Open	File/Save
File/Exit		

Chapter 2
The Word Processor: An Introduction

In this chapter you will learn how to:

- Create a word processor file.
- Enter text.
- Use simple editing commands to delete, insert, and replace text.
- Copy and move text.
- Save and retrieve files.
- Print a document.

What is a Word Processor?

A word processor is a tool that allows you to create letters, memos, reports, or any documents consisting mainly of text. The advantage of the word processor over the typewriter or pen and paper is the ease with which documents can be edited, reformatted, and enhanced. Paragraphs can be copied, moved, deleted, or inserted with only a few keystrokes. The current date can be entered and changed automatically to reflect the date the document is printed. Pages can be numbered—and renumbered—automatically. Page lengths, margins, and paragraph indentations can be changed quickly.

Many word processors may be used with other types of programs to create personalized form letters, or to insert graphs or sections of spreadsheets in the middle of documents. Since *Works* combines word processing, database, and spreadsheet functions in one program, this integration of materials between tasks is facilitated, as you will see in Chapter 5.

This chapter will introduce you to the basic word processing skills—creating, editing, saving, and printing a document. Then we'll give you a taste of the more advanced features of the powerful word processor in *Works*.

Creating a New Word Processor Document

From the Main Menu If you have just started *Works*, the NEW Dialog Box should be on the screen. **Word Processor**, the first option, should be marked. Press the **ENTER** key to create a new word processor file.

36 The Word Processor: An Introduction

> *Note:* If you have not started *Works*, see the instructions in the introductory chapter.

From Works If you did not exit *Works* after the last activity, select **File/New** to open the NEW Dialog Box. Press the **ENTER** key to create a new word processor file.

The Word Processor Screen

We took a quick look at the word processor screen in the last chapter. Now let's look at some of the parts more closely (Figure 2-1).

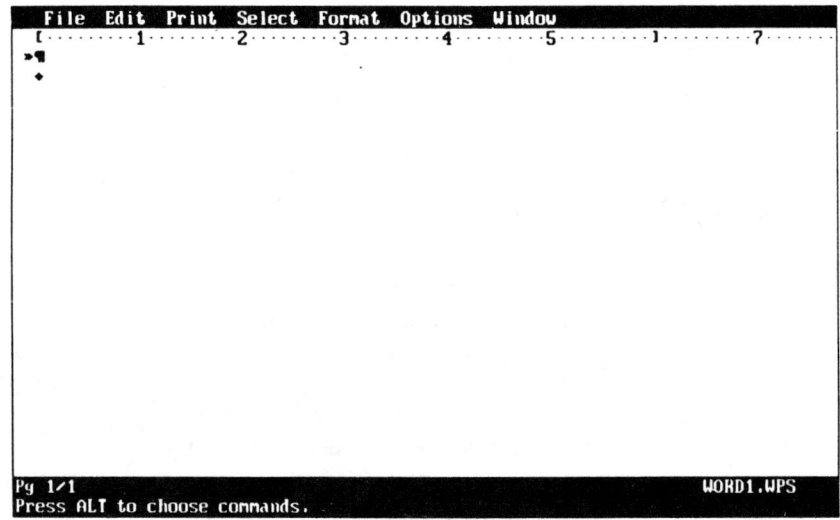

Figure 2-1

The Menu Bar As with all *Works* tools, the top line on the screen is the Menu Bar. Here's how to take a closer look at the word processor menu choices:

1. Select **File**. We've already looked at the **File** options. They remain the same in each of the *Works* tools.
2. Use the **RIGHT ARROW** to pull down the **Edit** menu. Press the **DOWN ARROW**. Look at the Message Line for a description of the highlighted command.
3. Pull down the other menus and look at the Message Line as you highlight each command to see what the *Works* word processor can do with a document.
4. Press the **ESC** key when you have finished looking at the menus.

The Status and Message Lines—Keeping Track of Your Progress

The Status Line, on the bottom of the screen, provides information about your document. In the word processor, the first piece of information tells both the current page location of the cursor and the total number of pages in the document. The right-hand side of the Status Line tells the name of the current document. *Works* automatically names the first word processor document **WORD1.WPS**, the second one, **WORD2.WPS**, and so on. We'll change the document's name to a more meaningful one when we save it.

The Message Line currently gives us a hint about how to perform a task *Works* thinks we might want to do—choose a command. Once we're involved in a command, more specific prompts or instructions will appear on the Message Line.

The Work Area

The top line of the Work Area contains a ruler that can help keep track of the cursor. Each dot on the ruler represents a column; every tenth column is indicated by a number. The ruler begins at the left margin. *Works*, like most programs, comes with predetermined settings called **default settings**. Most of the defaults can be changed from within the program. Among the word processor defaults are left and right margins of 1.3 in. and 1.2 in. and tab settings at .5 in. intervals. The space between the left and right brackets ([and]) on the ruler indicates the current line length. The default line length is 60 characters and the brackets are at the margins. If you indent the current paragraph from the margins, the brackets are moved to indicate these indentations. If you change the default tab settings, these also will be indicated on the ruler.

The flashing dash on the line beneath the ruler is the cursor. The cursor indicates where the text that you type will appear.

The >> symbol at the beginning of the top line indicates the beginning of the document. The same symbol appears at the beginning of each page of a multipage document. The diamond on the following line is the symbol for the end of a document. The cursor is the only thing between the beginning and end of document symbols at this time, because we have not yet begun to enter any text.

These are the only symbols typically displayed on the screen. As you enter text, other symbols are inserted in the text, but they remain hidden unless you select **Options/Show All Characters**.

Word Processor Project No. 1
Debbie's Letter

Let's practice entering text by typing an informal letter. Debbie's friend, Susan, has heard that she is taking an introductory computer course and has asked her for some information on application programs. We will enter, edit, and print Debbie's response to her friend.

While completing this project, you will:

- Type a rough draft of the letter.
- Learn to move around the screen.
- Delete and insert text.
- Save the letter.
- Print the letter.

Below is a copy of Debbie's first draft, followed by instructions for entering it. If you notice mistakes as you type a word, press the **BACKSPACE** key until you erase the incorrect characters. Then retype the word. Don't worry about mistakes that you don't notice until you have passed them. We'll learn how to correct them shortly.

Remember to read the instructions before you enter each segment of the letter.

Today's Date

Dear Susan,

   This is the first letter I've written on the Works Word Processor. I haven't mastered it yet, but can see how much time and energy it will save -- if I don't get too carried away editing my reports and letters.

   The word processor appears to be easy to use. You can edit the document by deleting text, or by moving and copying paragraphs. The best part is that when you insert or delete text, the rest of the document reformats around the change. No more retyping a twenty page paper because you add two paragraphs to page one!

   Microsoft Works is an integrated program. It includes word processor, spreadsheet, database and communications components. Each is a tool within one program, instead of a separate program. Therefore, once I learned how to use the word processor, the database screen looked familiar. What's more, most of the menu options were the same.

   I also like the way you can move back and forth between several word processing documents, or even word processing documents, databases and spreadsheets. I plan to use the word processor and database together to send personalized bills to my painting clients.

   Hope this has been helpful. If you use Works, let me know how you like it.

                      Debbie

Entering Text— Directions for Entering the Letter

Uppercase Letters

To type an uppercase letter, press the **SHIFT** key and, while holding it down, type the letter. Do *not* press the **CAPS LOCK** key to type a single capital letter. Once

Entering Text—Directions for Entering the Letter 39

CAPS LOCK is turned on, all of the letters that you type are capitalized until **CAPS LOCK** is turned off. If the letters *CL* appear on the Status Line, you have turned **CAPS LOCK** on. Press the **CAPS LOCK** key again to turn **CAPS LOCK** off.

1. Type today's date. Capitalize the first letter of the month.

   Since the date is the only information that we want on the first line, press the **ENTER** key. The cursor should move down to the left margin of the next line.

Including Blank Lines

Try to press the **DOWN ARROW** key. Nothing happens, except that *Works* will beep, indicating that you are attempting to do something that is not allowed. In order to move the cursor down, leaving a blank line, you must press the **ENTER** key.

2. Press the **ENTER** key three times, to leave three blank lines.
3. Type: **Dear Susan,**

   Press the **ENTER** key twice.

The Tab Key

The **TAB** key can be used to indent paragraphs or to type text in columns. We will press the **TAB** key once at the beginning of each paragraph to indent the text to the first tab stop. *Works* automatically sets tab stops at equal intervals across the line. We will use these default settings in this exercise.

4. Press the **TAB** key to indent the first line of the paragraph.

Word Wrap

Entering text is the computer-age term for typing the document. However, one of the major changes from old-fashioned typewriters, is that you do *NOT* press the **ENTER** key at the end of the line in the middle of a paragraph.

The word wrap feature of *Works* automatically will bring the cursor down to the start of the next line when you reach the right margin. If you reach the right margin in the middle of typing a word, the part of the word that you have typed will be brought down to the beginning of the next line as you complete it.

When you reach the end of a paragraph, press the **ENTER** key to move the cursor to the next line. Similarly, when you type an inside address, salutation, or any other text that does not take up the whole line, press the **ENTER** key.

5. Now type the first paragraph *without* pressing the **ENTER** key at the end of each line. Press the **ENTER** key twice at the end of the paragraph.
6. Repeat the procedure in steps 4 and 5 to type the remaining paragraphs.
   - Notice what happens in the middle of the third paragraph when the cursor reaches the bottom of the screen.

Note: The *Works* word processor has a sophisticated paragraph format system. For example, we could set the paragraph format so that *Works* skips one line and indents to the first tab each time we press the **ENTER** key. This is an advanced skill, beyond the scope of this chapter.

7. Press the **TAB** key six times to indent the closing. Type: **Debbie**
8. Press the **ENTER** key.

How Works Scrolls the Screen

As you probably noticed as soon as you began typing on the last line of the work area, the text automatically scrolled so that the cursor and last line moved from the bottom to the middle of the screen. This jump will occur whenever you edit or enter text on the last line of the screen. When you move the cursor through previously entered text to the borders of the screen, only one line at a time scrolls off.

Moving Around the Screen To read parts of the document that have scrolled off the screen, or to edit text, you must move the cursor. The four **ARROW** keys can be used to move the cursor one character or row at a time. However, there are a number of ways to move the cursor more quickly.

Let's try moving around the screen.

1. Press the **UP ARROW** once or twice. Now, hold down the **UP ARROW** until the cursor reaches the beginning of the document.
2. Use the **ARROW** keys to move the cursor under the **D** in **Dear**.

Note: Since the cursor can be moved only to parts of the screen containing text (or the hidden characters indicating such things as blank lines), the **UP** and **DOWN ARROWS** may move through the text in ways you don't expect.

3. Press the **PGDN** (Page Down) key until the cursor moves to the end of the document. Now press **PGUP** to return to the beginning.
4. There is a faster way to move to the end of the document—press **CTRL+END**. What effect does **CTRL+HOME** have?
5. We've used shortcuts for moving up and down the screen. There are also fast ways of moving across a line. Use the **ARROW** keys to move the cursor to the middle of a line of text. Press the **END** key. Then press the **HOME** key.
6. Now use the **CTRL+RIGHT ARROW** to move across the line one word at a time. What does **CTRL+LEFT ARROW** do?

Here's a summary of the key movements you've been using.

Key	Movement
ARROW keys	One space or row in the direction of the arrow
CTRL+RIGHT ARROW	Beginning of next word
CTRL+LEFT ARROW	Beginning of previous word
HOME	Beginning of line
END	End of line
PGUP	Up one screen
PGDN	Down one screen
CTRL+HOME	Beginning of document
CTRL+END	End of document

Editing a Document

Deleting Text

The **BACKSPACE** key typically is used to delete text immediately after you enter it, since it deletes text to the left of the cursor.

The **DEL** (delete) key can be used to delete text at the cursor position. Let's delete the words *and energy* from the first paragraph of the letter. (The words to be deleted are highlighted in Figure 2-2).

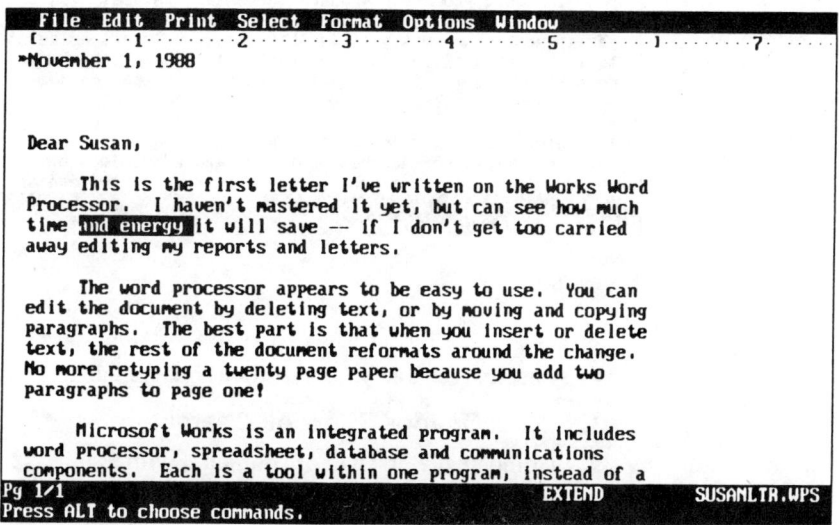

Figure 2-2

1. Put the cursor under the *a* in *and*.
2. Press the **DEL** key until *and energy* and the space that follows it are deleted.
3. Notice that as soon as you delete enough letters so that the first word on the next line fits, it will move back up to the line from which you are deleting characters. In fact the entire document is instantly respaced to take up the area left by the deleted characters. When you edit a document, word wrap keeps moving words to the next or previous line, in order to maintain full lines of text.

Did You Let Word Wrap Work?

Did your paragraph word wrap to fill in the space left when you deleted *and energy*? Often, when people first use word processors, they press the **ENTER** key at the end of lines within a paragraph. Each time you press the **ENTER** key, *Works* enters a paragraph code. If there are paragraph codes at the end of lines in the middle of paragraphs, word wrap will not work correctly when you revise the letter.

42 The Word Processor: An Introduction

Figure 2-3

Let's check to see that your letter does not contain any extra paragraph endings.

1. Select **Options/Show All Characters**.
2. Compare the first half of your letter with Figure 2-3. Notice that spaces are indicated by dots and tabs by arrows. Each time that you pressed the **ENTER** key, a paragraph sign was inserted.
3. Look at your screen and make sure that there are no paragraph signs in the middle of paragraphs.

    Move the cursor under any extra paragraph symbols, and press the **DEL** key to remove them.

While all characters still are displayed, delete the word *Microsoft* from the beginning of paragraph three (we will insert it at a different place in the letter shortly):

1. Move the cursor under the *M* in *Microsoft*.
2. Press the **DEL** key until *Microsoft* and the space after it are deleted. The rest of the paragraph remains indented because the tab symbol remains.
3. Select **Options** again. The mark preceding **Show All Characters** indicates that this command previously has been activated (Figure 2-4). Select this command again in order to deactivate it. The extra characters will be removed from the screen.

Now that you know how to toggle **Show All Characters** on and off, use this option as you wish when entering and editing text.

Inserting Text

Anything that you type in the middle of existing text is automatically inserted into the text. The only trick to inserting text is to make sure that the cursor is immediately *after* the point at which you want to insert text. For example, to insert the word

Editing a Document

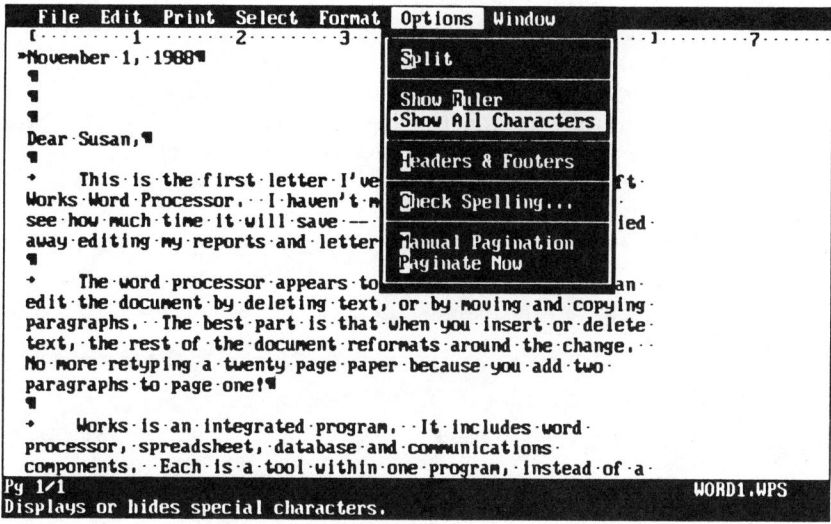

Figure 2-4

Microsoft before *Works* in the first sentence of the first paragraph, do the following:

1. Move the cursor to the *W* in *Works*.
2. Type: **Microsoft**

   Press the **SPACE BAR** once.

   Microsoft is inserted into the text and the rest of the lines in the paragraph are adjusted. (See Figure 2-5 for an illustration of the paragraph with the inserted text highlighted.)

3. Try adding the words **or inserting** in paragraph two, between the words *deleting* and *text*. Remember to add a space after **inserting**.

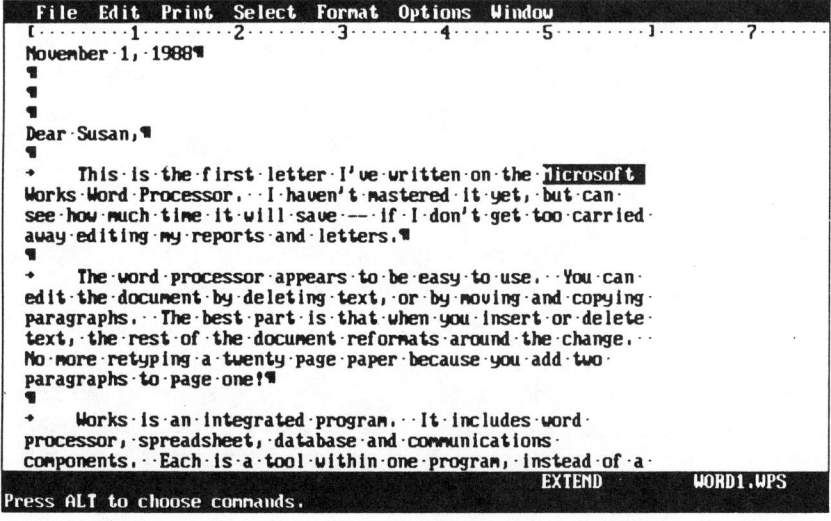

Figure 2-5

Replacing Text

Sometimes, instead of adding or deleting text, you want to correct a typographical error, or replace one word with another. Some word processors include an overwrite or replace mode that allows you to substitute newly entered characters for existing ones. *Works* is always in *INSERT* mode. Therefore, to replace text, you must both delete the unwanted characters and insert the correct ones.

When Debbie reread her letter, she remembered her former English teacher's comments on the difference between *can* and *may*. So she decided to replace *can* with *may* the two times it occurs in the document. To do this:

1. Move the cursor to the *c* in *can* in the second paragraph.
2. Press the **DEL** key three times to delete *can*.
3. Type: **may**
4. Repeat steps 1-3 to replace the word *can* with the word **may** in the next to the last paragraph.

We've learned the three basic ways of editing text. We'll learn a faster way to delete multiple characters while working on the next project. Right now, compare your letter with the edited version shown on the next page. Use the editing procedures you've learned to correct any typing errors.

Saving a Document as a File

When we enter text, two things happen—the text appears on the screen and it is stored in the computer's main memory, or **RAM (Random Access Memory)**. When we edited our document, the text was reorganized in RAM and then the screen was redrawn to reflect the changes. Since information is stored in RAM temporarily, let's save our letter on our exercise disk.

Anything saved on a disk is stored in a **file**. The file includes the text that you have entered, plus all of the formatting information that will enable *Works* to display and print the document according to your instructions. Since we are saving our document in a file, the **Save** command is located on the File menu.

1. Select **File/Save**.

   Does the Dialog Box look familiar? When you select the **File/Save** command, *Works* checks to see if the file has been saved previously. If this is the first time the file is being saved, the **SAVE AS** Dialog Box is opened because *Works* assumes that you want to save the file using a more meaningful name than **WORD1.WPS** (Figure 2-6).

   A highlight bar is on the file name.

   The only highlighted characters on the screen are the brackets around <*OK*>. If you pressed the **ENTER** key now, the file would be saved on the drive listed under current drive, using the name **WORD1.WPS**.

   If you have not exited from *Works* since you changed the drive to the one containing your exercise diskette, skip steps 2-5 and see step 6 for directions for naming the file. If you started *Works* at the beginning of this chapter, your formatted exercise disk is probably in a drive other than the one indicated. Let's review how you use the List Box under the **Other Drives & Directories** heading to change drives.

2. Press **ALT+O** (the letter O, not zero).

Saving a Document as a File 45

> Today's Date
>
> Dear Susan,
>
> This is the first letter I've written on the Microsoft Works Word Processor. I haven't mastered it yet, but can see how much time it will save — if I don't get too carried away editing my reports and letters.
>
> The word processor appears to be easy to use. You may edit the document by deleting or inserting text, or by moving and copying paragraphs. The best part is that when you insert or delete text, the rest of the document reformats around the change. No more retyping a twenty page paper because you add two paragraphs to page one!
>
> Works is an integrated program. It includes word processor, spreadsheet, database and communications components. Each is a tool within one program, instead of a separate program. Therefore, once I learned how to use the word processor, the database screen looked familiar. What's more, most of the menu options were the same.
>
> I also like the way you may move back and forth between several word processing documents, or even word processing documents, databases and spreadsheets. I plan to use the word processor and database together to send personalized bills to my painting clients.
>
> Hope this has been helpful. If you use Works, let me know how you like it.
>
>   Debbie

3. Press the **DOWN ARROW** key once to highlight the first choice.
4. Use the **UP** and **DOWN ARROW** keys, if necessary, to move the highlight to the name of the drive that contains your exercise disk.
5. Press the **ENTER** key.

Once the correct drive is indicated, the cursor returns to the File Name Text Box, and all you need to enter is the new file name.

6. Type the new file name: **Susanltr**

The Word Processor: An Introduction

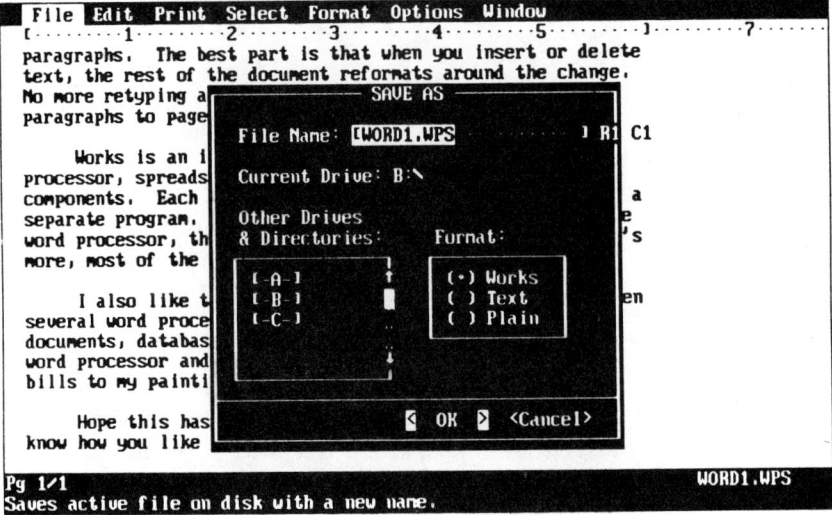

Figure 2-6

Note: The file name **Susanltr** includes the name of the person to whom we are sending the letter and an abbreviation to indicate that the document is a letter. When you save a document, you'll have to think about what name will be meaningful to you if you use the document again in a week or two, yet will not be longer than the eight characters allowed by DOS.

---

7. Press the **ENTER** key.
   - Remember that *Works* adds its word processor extension, **.WPS** to the file name. The file will be saved as **SUSANLTR.WPS** on your diskette.
   - Any combination of upper- and lowercase letters may be used when typing file names. However, when *Works* displays the file name in Dialog Boxes that you use after this, it will appear in all uppercase letters.
   - Two changes will occur to the Status Line. While the file is being saved, the percentage saved will appear on the left side of the line. After the file has been saved, the new file name will appear on the Status Line.

Note: The **File/Save As...** command can also be used to save a new file. After selecting **File/Save As...** follow steps 2 through 7 above.

Printing a Document

We're finally ready to print our letter. To pull down the Print menu to see what our options are, select **Print**.

The Print menu is divided into three sections (Figure 2-7). The top and bottom sections are identical in the three *Works* tools we will be using. The center box includes options that are specific to the word processor. Note that each command

Selecting the Text Printer   47

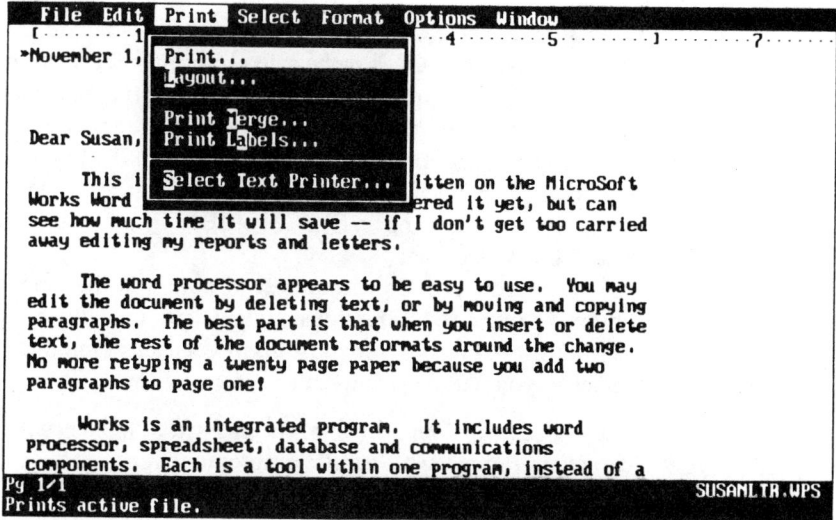

Figure 2-7

is followed by an ellipsis, indicating that a Dialog Box requesting further information will appear when the command is selected.

Selecting the Text Printer Since this is the first time we are using *Works* to print, we will make sure that the correct printer has been selected. Select **Select Text Printer**. The SELECT TEXT PRINTER Dialog Box (Figure 2-8) will be displayed.

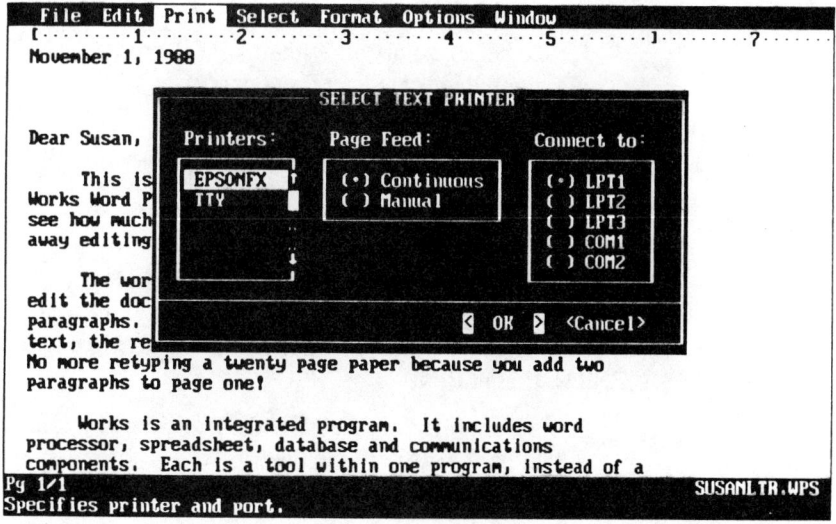

Figure 2-8

The following are descriptions of the options, followed by instructions for changing them.

Printers: There are only two printers from which to choose. The highlight bar indicates that **EPSONFX** is the selected printer. **TTY** is a general printer designation that will allow you to print a copy of a text file, but you may not be able to take advantage of your printer's special fonts, sizes, and styles.

If you are using another model EPSON or an IBM Graphics printer, experiment with both the **EPSONFX** and **TTY** settings to see which gives you a better printout. If you are not using an EPSON or IBM Graphics printer, you probably should select the **TTY** printer.

Page Feed: The **Continuous** feed option is the default selection. Keep this option if paper is fed continuously into the printer with no intervention on your part. Select **Manual** feed if you must insert each sheet into the printer. If this option is selected, you will be prompted to enter new sheets of paper.

Connect to: Your printer is attached to a computer port, or slot at the back of the computer. If you have a parallel printer (and most are), it can be attached to **LPT1**, **LPT2**, or **LPT3**. Serial printers can use **COM1** or **COM2**. Your printer probably is attached to **LPT1**. The default setting is **LPT1** because this is most commonly used. If your document does not print using the **LPT1** setting, consult your printer manual to find out whether your printer requires a serial or parallel port. Then follow the directions below to select the parallel or serial ports one at a time, until one works.

If all of the default selections are accurate, press the **ENTER** key and move to the Print section of this chapter.

If you need to change some of the settings, follow these directions:

1. To change the printer to **TTY**, press the **DOWN ARROW** once.
2. If your printer requires **Manual** Page Feed, press **ALT+A**, or use the **TAB** key to move to the Page Feed Option Box and press the **DOWN ARROW** key.
3. To select a port other than **LPT1**, press the **ALT** key together with the highlighted character for your port, or **TAB** to the Connect To Option Box and use the **DOWN ARROW** key.
4. When all of the changes have been made, press the **ENTER** key.

Print

Select **Print/Print**. The Dialog Box shown in Figure 2-9 will be displayed. The three text boxes in this box are common to all of the tools. The last item is different in the other tools. We are going to use the default settings currently displayed in the PRINT Dialog Box.

1. Before selecting the **<Print>** Button, make sure that your printer is ready to print. Check to see that:
   - the printer is turned on
   - the printer is on-line
   - the paper is correctly aligned in the printer
2. Since the **<Print>** Button is in highlighted brackets, it is the active Button. Press the **ENTER** key to print the document.

Selecting the Text Printer

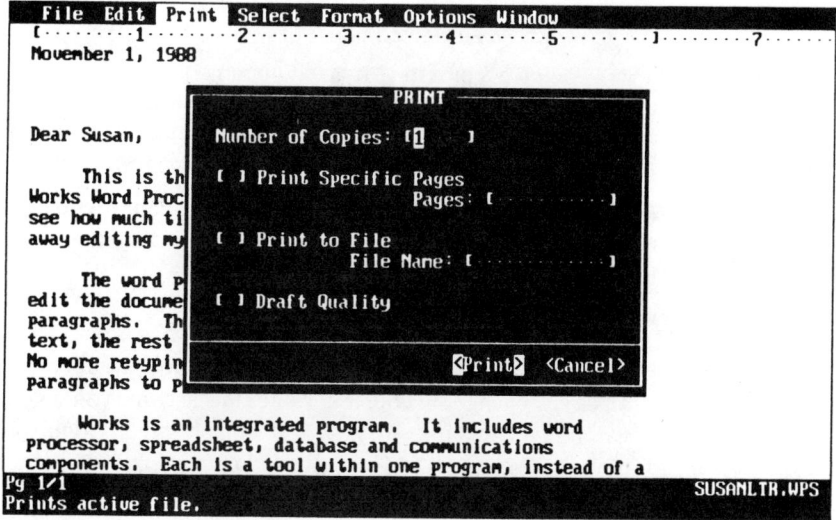

Figure 2-9

- Your document should be printed. *Page - 1* will appear at the bottom of the page because one of the default settings under **Print/Layout** adds a line at the bottom of each page, called a **footer**, which automatically numbers the pages. We will look at, and change, some of the **Print/Layout** settings in Project No. 2.

Word Processor Project No. 2
Paul's Letter

Paul has just planned the calendar for his piano students. He wants to send a simple note to the parents telling them about the schedule for their children's theory classes and recitals.

While creating Paul's letter, you will review the basic word processing skills learned in Project No. 1, as well as learn some of the more sophisticated and quicker methods of editing and formatting documents available using the *Works* word processor. Specifically, you will review how to:

- Enter text.
- Make simple editing changes.
- Save a document.
- Print a document.

You also will learn how to:

- Remove documents from the computer's memory.
- Use **CAPS LOCK** while entering text.
- Select a block of text.
- Delete a selected block of text.
- Use **UNDO** to retrieve deleted text.
- Copy a selected block of text.

- Move a selected block of text.
- Save a previously saved document.
- Print a document without a footer.

Creating a New Word Processor Document

We need an empty screen on which to begin Paul's letter. Since we are finished with our letter to Susan, let's remove it from the computer's memory by using another command from the File menu, **File/Close**.

1. Select **File/Close**.

Notice that the **Close** command is not followed by an ellipsis. If you have not made any changes to your letter since the last time you saved it, the **Close** command will be executed immediately and a blank screen (Figure 2-10) will appear. If you have made changes to your letter, a Dialog Box asking if you want to save changes to **SUSANLTR** will appear:

2. Press the **ENTER** key if you wish to save the changes; or,
3. Select **<No>** to close the file without saving the changes.

If your screen is different than Figure 2-10, you have opened or created other files. Keep selecting **File/Close** until the screen resembles Figure 2-10. After the files are closed, we are ready to create a new file, as we did at the beginning of this chapter.

Figure 2-10

Note: As many as eight files may be active at one time, so it is possible to create a new file without closing the current files. However, it is a good practice to close any files that you are not using.

Directions for Entering the Text 51

1. To display the NEW Dialog Box, select **File/New**.
2. Select **Word Processor**.

Below is a copy of Paul's first draft of his letter to parents, followed by instructions for entering it.

Dear Parents,

  Time to begin another year of piano lessons! Hope everyone's summer was a good one. We have already discussed the time for your child's individual lessons. The times and locations of this year's other events are listed at the end of this page.

  As we discussed, this year I will be holding small group theory classes once a month in addition to the weekly individual piano lessons. There is no extra fee for these sessions. I hope your child will be able to attend.

  The children will also give a recital at the end of the year.

THEORY CLASS

Day:	First Sunday of each month
Time:	5:00 - 6:00 p.m.
Place:	Simpson Room
	Whitney Hall

RECITAL

Date:	Wednesday, June 13
Time:	7:30 - 9:00 p.m.
Place:	Green Room
	Tamany Hall

  I'm looking forward to another year of working with you and your child.

                               Paul Harrison

Directions for Entering the Text

1. Type the salutation and first three paragraphs of the letter using the same procedures you used to type Debbie's letter. Remember *not* to press the **ENTER** key in the middle of paragraphs.
2. Follow the directions below to enter:

THEORY CLASS

Day:	First Sunday of each month
Time:	5:00 - 6:00 p.m.
Place:	Simpson Room
	Whitney Hall

The Word Processor: An Introduction

Using Caps Lock

1. Press the **CAPS LOCK** key once to turn **CAPS LOCK** on. When **CAPS LOCK** has been activated, the letters *CL* will appear on the Status Line.
2. Make sure you have pressed **ENTER** twice after the last paragraph.
3. Type: **THEORY CLASS**
4. Press the **CAPS LOCK** key again to turn **CAPS LOCK** off. Remember **CAPS LOCK** is a toggle key. Press it once to turn it on, and a second time to turn it off.
5. Press the **ENTER** key twice.

More About Using Tabs

The information about the theory class is set up in two columns. The **TAB** key is used to align the columns. We will use *Works'* default tabs, which have been set at regular intervals, every five spaces.

1. Press the **TAB** key once to indent the word **Day** to the first tab stop. Type: **Day**:
2. Press the **TAB** key twice. Type the remainder of the line. Press the **ENTER** key.
3. Repeat the process to enter the remainder of the theory class and recital information.

Hint: Some of the lines require a different number of **TABS** so that the second column will be correctly positioned. Figure 2-11 shows the last part of our letter with **Options/Show All Characters** selected. Each **TAB** is indicated by an arrow. To use Figure 2-11 as a guide for entering the rest of the letter, press the **TAB** key once for each arrow shown.

If you press the **TAB** key too many times, use the **BACKSPACE** key to delete the extra **TABS**. You may find it useful to turn on **Options/Show All Characters** while you are typing this part of the letter to see how *Works* formats your columns.

```
 File  Edit  Print  Select  Format  Options  Window
[·········1·········2·········3·········4·········5·········]·········7······
 →   The children will also give a recital at the end of the
year.¶
¶
THEORY CLASS¶
¶
 →     Day:→→     First Sunday of each month¶
 →     Time:→     5:00 - 6:00 p.m.¶
 →     Place:→    Simpson Room¶
 →     →     →    Whitney Hall¶
¶
RECITAL¶
¶
 →     Date:→     Wednesday, June 13¶
 →     Time:→     7:30 - 9:00 p.m.¶
 →     Place:→    Green Room¶
 →     →     →    Tamany Hall¶
¶
 →   I'm looking forward to another year of working with you
and your child.¶
¶
 →     →     →     →     →   Paul Harrison¶
Pg 1/1                                              WORD1.WPS
Press ALT to choose commands.
```

Figure 2-11

4. Type the final paragraph and closing of the letter. Figure 2-11 can help you determine how many times to **TAB**.

Proofreading and Saving a Document

1. Move the cursor to the beginning of the letter.
2. Proofread it, comparing it to the copy at the beginning of the project. Use the procedures that we learned earlier to delete, insert, or replace text as needed.

Hint: If the spacing between paragraphs is incorrect, you may delete or add blank lines.

To delete a blank line, move the cursor to the extra paragraph symbol and press **DEL**.

To insert a blank line, move the cursor to the first character following where the blank line should be and press **ENTER**.

To insert a tab, move the cursor to the position immediately following where the tab should be, and press **TAB**.

Before we edit the letter further, let's save it. Then if you get lost in the editing process, you always can open the file containing the original version and try again!

1. Select **File/Save**.
2. The SAVE AS Dialog Box will be displayed, since this is the first time we have saved this document. If you have not exited *Works* since completing Project No. 1, the current drive should be set correctly as the drive containing your exercise disk.

   - If the drive is incorrect, press **ALT+O**, highlight the correct drive, and press **ENTER**.

     Type the file name: **schedltr**

     Press **ENTER**.

     or

   - If the drive is correct, the highlight bar should already be positioned in the File Name Text Box. Simply type the file name: **schedltr**

     Press **ENTER**.

Before Paul had an opportunity to revise and send his letter, his plans for the coming year changed. He decided to break the theory class into two groups, and to offer two recitals a year. In order to emphasize the recitals, he wants to discuss them before the theory class lessons. He also realized that he had left some information, such as the starting date of the lessons, out of his letter. Since his letter is getting longer, he has decided to delete a sentence. When finished, Paul's new letter will look like the following:

Dear Parents,

Time to begin another year of piano lessons! All lessons will begin the week of September 26th. We have already discussed the time for your child's individual lessons. The times and locations of this year's other events are listed at the end of this page.

As we discussed, this year I will be holding small group theory classes once a month in addition to the weekly individual piano lessons. There is no extra fee for these sessions. I hope your child will be able to attend.

The children will also give two recitals, one in January and one in June.

RECITALS

    Date: Sunday, January 29
    Time: 7:30 - 9:00 p.m.
    Place: Green Room
              Tamany Hall

    Date: Wednesday, June 13
    Time: 7:30 - 9:00 p.m.
    Place: Green Room
              Tamany Hall

THEORY CLASS -- 6 - 9 years of age

    Day: First Sunday of each month
    Time: 5:00 - 6:00 p.m.
    Place: Simpson Room
              Whitney Hall

THEORY CLASS -- 10 years of age and older

    Day: Second Sunday of each month
    Time: 5:00 - 6:00 p.m.
    Place: Simpson Room
              Whitney Hall

I'm looking forward to another year of working with you and your child.

                        Paul Harrison

Another Look at Editing Text   We can make these changes using the same techniques we used to make the simple editing changes to Debbie's letter. However, most of these changes involve *blocks*

Another Look at Editing Text

of text instead of just a few characters. In *Works*, most text manipulation and enhancement requires that you first select the block of text, and then work with the selected block.

Selecting Text

There are several methods that you can use to tell *Works* with which part of the text you want to work. The general procedure we will use is:

- Move the cursor to the beginning of the area that needs work.
- Press the **F8** key. (*Works* calls **F8** the **EXTEND** key.)
- Use the **ARROW** keys to **EXTEND** the highlight.
- Do what you want to do to the highlighted text.
- Cancel the highlight by pressing any **ARROW** key.

Caution: It is extremely important that you **Cancel** the highlight *before* you begin typing new text. If some of the text on the screen is highlighted, and you type any character, that character will replace the entire highlighted text. If this happens accidentally, select **Edit/Undo** *before* pressing any other keys.

Let's try selecting some text.

1. Move the cursor under the *T* in *Time*, the first word in the first paragraph.
2. Press **F8**. Notice that the word EXTEND appears on the Status Line.
3. Press the **RIGHT ARROW** key a few times—each key press should highlight one letter.
4. Now press the **DOWN ARROW** key. The highlight will be extended down one line.
5. Press the **LEFT ARROW** key a few times. Now press the **UP ARROW**. The extent of the highlight should be reduced.
6. As long as the word EXTEND remains on the Status Line, any of the cursor movement keys can be used to change how much of the text is highlighted.
7. Press the **END** key to extend the highlight to the end of the line. Now press the **HOME** key.
8. Do you remember what the **CTRL+RIGHT ARROW** and **CTRL+LEFT ARROW** key combinations do? Try them and see what they do to the highlight.

Note: Unlike some word processors, with *Works* the highlight can be extended to the left and above the position the cursor was in when **F8** was pressed. The only requirement is that the original cursor position be at one end of the text to be selected.

Solving Problems in Selecting Text

What happens if you start to select text, and then you change your mind? Let's see how to **CANCEL** the text selection that you just made without doing anything to the selected text.

1. Press the **ESC** key. The word EXTEND should disappear from the Status Line.
2. Press any **ARROW** key. The highlight bar should disappear, and the cursor should return to the screen.

Now let's see what we can do if we accidently replace highlighted text with another character.

1. Select the text highlighted in Figure 2-12. If you need help, here's how to do it: Move the cursor back to the first letter of the first paragraph. Press the **F8** key. Press the **DOWN** and **RIGHT ARROW** keys until the entire paragraph is highlighted.
2. Type: **a** The first paragraph of the letter should disappear and be replaced by an *a*.
3. Select **Edit/Undo**. The original paragraph will return.

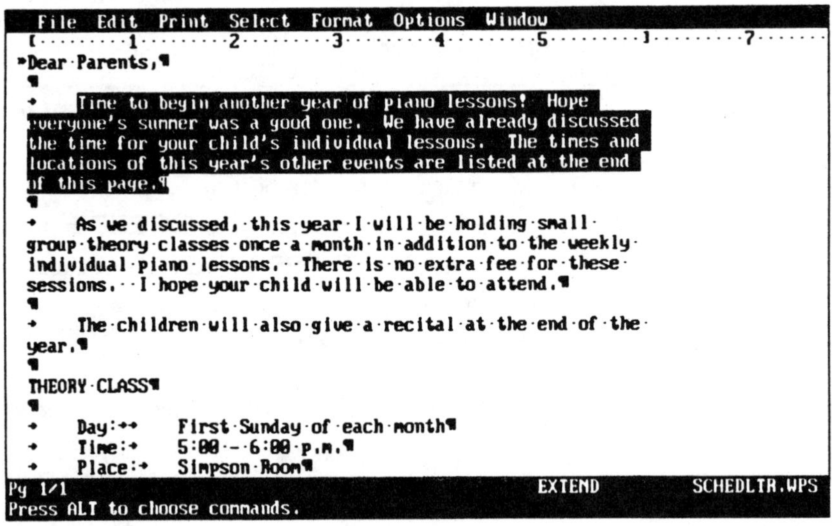

Figure 2-12

Now that we know how to select text, and how to overcome errors that may occur in the process, let's get back to revising Paul's letter.

Deleting a Block of Text

The first thing Paul wants to do is to delete the sentence: *Hope everyone's summer was a good one.*

We could do this by moving the cursor to the *H* in *Hope* and pressing the **DEL** key until the entire sentence was deleted, but we're less likely to cause an error if we select the sentence, make sure we've highlighted the correct text, and then delete it. This procedure is also faster once you get used to it.

1. Move the cursor to the *H* in *Hope*.

Another Look at Editing Text

2. Press the **F8** key to let *Works* know that you are ready to **EXTEND** the highlight.

3. How do you want to highlight the sentence? Using the methods we've learned, you could highlight one letter at a time, or one word at a time, or move down a line and then use the **LEFT ARROW** key to remove the extra highlight (Figure 2-13).

4. Press the **DEL** key. The text will disappear from the screen.

5. If you did not highlight the space after the sentence, use the **DEL** key to remove the extra spaces.

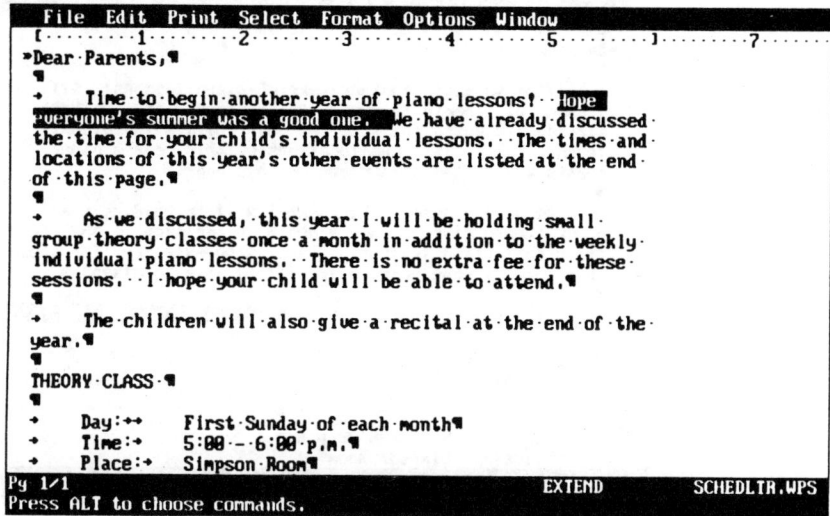

Figure 2-13

Now let's insert the sentence that tells parents when lessons are to begin.

1. Move the cursor to the beginning of the second sentence, the *W* in *We*.
2. Type:

All lessons will begin the week of September 26th.

Did you notice that the new sentence replaced the sentence that we removed? Do you know how we could have accomplished that more quickly?

We'll practice a faster way of replacing text with new text. Since Paul's students are giving two recitals instead of one, we need to edit paragraph three. We want to replace:

The children will also give a recital at the end of the year.

with:

The children will also give two recitals, one in January and one in June.

Follow the directions below to make this change in one procedure. Since the first five words remain the same, select the rest of the sentence, and then type in the new ending.

1. Move the cursor to the word *a*.
2. Press the **F8** key. **EXTEND** the highlight to the rest of the paragraph (Figure 2-14).
3. Type the new sentence ending: **two recitals, one in January and one in June.**

    As soon as you type the first letter, the highlighted sentence fragment should disappear.
4. Press the **ENTER** key to end the paragraph.

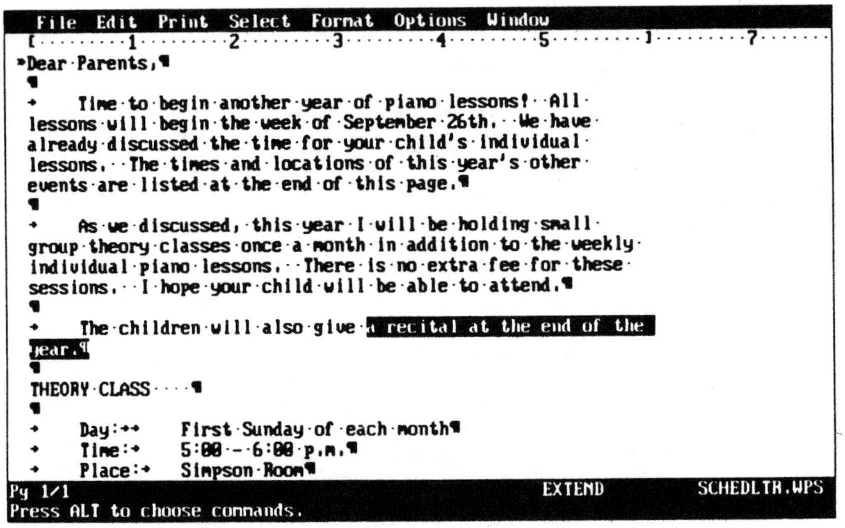

Figure 2-14

Our next editing task is to provide the information about the second theory class and second recital schedules. One advantage of using a word processor is that it allows us to reuse text that we've already typed. Let's **copy** the original theory class and recital sections of the letter and then edit them to make the few changes necessary.

Copying Text

Since we know how to select text, copying text is easy. All we need to do is:

- **Select** the text to be copied.
- Choose **Edit/Copy**.
- **Move** the cursor to the new location.
- Press the **ENTER** key.

If you want to experiment, use these general directions and the illustration of the revised letter to copy and revise the information on the theory class. For more help, follow the instructions below:

Another Look at Editing Text   59

1. **Select** the entire theory section as shown in Figure 2-15. Notice that we have selected the blank line at the end of the theory section, since we will want a blank line at the end of our new section.

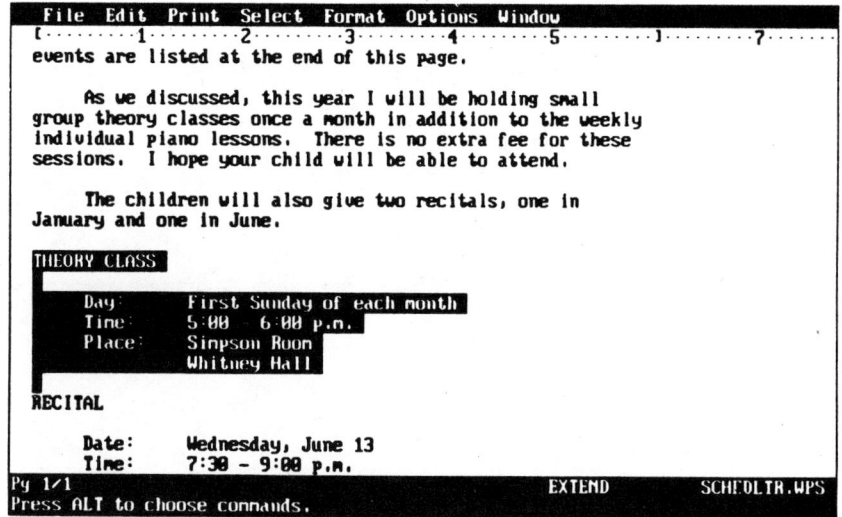

Figure 2-15

2. Choose **Edit/Copy**.

    Works provides the following instructions on the Message Line for continuing or cancelling the task:

    Select new location and press ENTER or ESC to cancel.

    Check that you have highlighted the correct information. If you have not, press the **ESC** key to cancel.

3. If the theory section has been highlighted, move the cursor under the *R* in *RECITAL*, since this is the new location for the copied text. Press the **ENTER** key.

4. To differentiate between the two theory classes, we must type the information on age groups after each class. See Figure 2-16 for the correct information.

Hint: You may have some trouble adding the information. The cursor movement keys can only move the cursor to parts of the screen that contain characters or codes (the hidden characters that represent spaces, tabs, and new paragraphs, etc.). Use the **ARROW** and/or **END** keys to move the cursor to the space immediately after *THEORY CLASS*. Press the **SPACE BAR** and type the text to be added.

The Word Processor: An Introduction

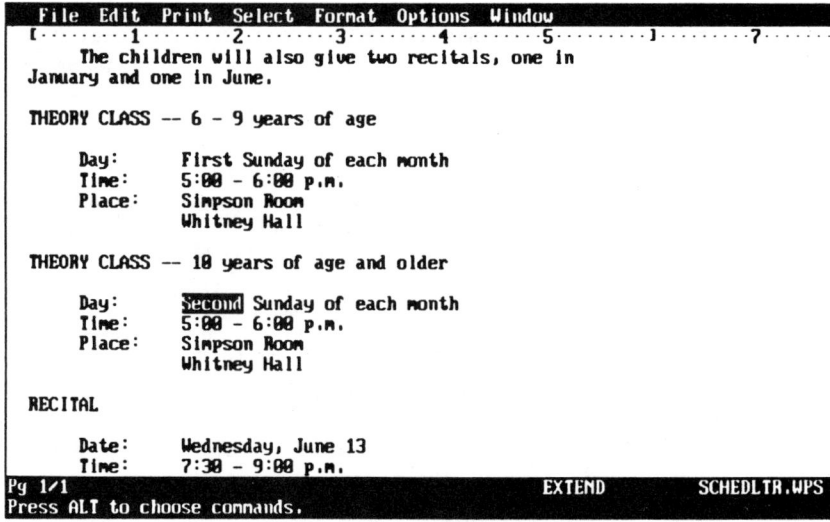

Figure 2-16

5. Change the meeting day for the second theory class to that indicated by the highlighted word in Figure 2-16 by deleting *First* and replacing it with:

   Second

6. Before we copy the information on the recital section, let's select **Options/ Show All Characters**, so that we can see exactly what we're doing.

7. Now use the same procedure that we used previously to copy the date, time, and location from the original recital section.

   Be sure to copy the TAB code before the word *DATE*. Otherwise the date will not be lined up correctly. See Figure 2-17 for the screen as it should look after the text has been selected.

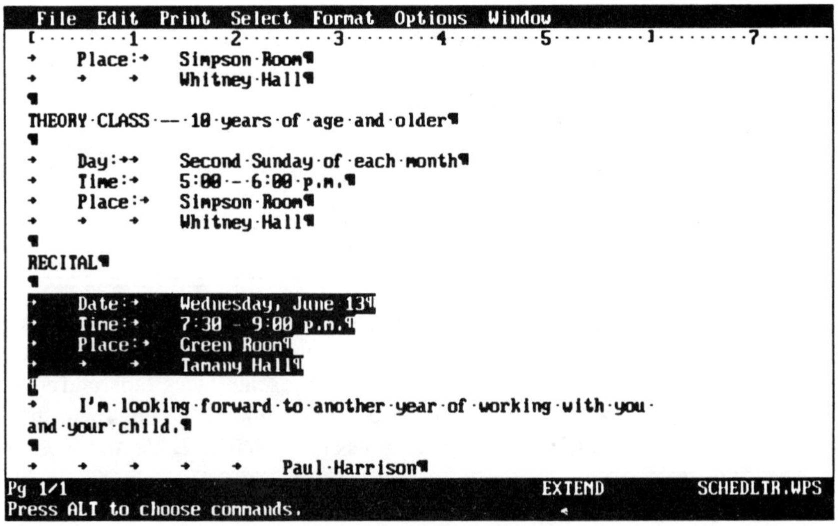

Figure 2-17

Saving a Document for a Second Time 61

8. To correct the recital information:
   a. Add an **S** to the end of the word *RECITAL*.
   b. Change the *Date:* entry for the first recital to:

   Sunday, January 29

Moving Text

Our remaining editing task is to move the information about the recitals before the theory class schedules. In *Works* the procedure for moving text is almost identical to that for copying text. The only procedural difference is that the **Edit/Move** command is used in place of the **Edit/Copy** command. Text that is moved appears only in the new location while copied text appears in the original and new locations.

Try to move the two recital dates before the theory class schedules on your own or follow the instructions below:

1. Select the entire recitals section.
2. Choose **Edit/Move**.
3. Move the cursor to the space above the first *THEORY CLASS* heading.
4. Press the **ENTER** key.
5. Adjust the spacing as necessary.
6. Compare your document with the copy of the revised document and make any corrections needed.

Saving a Document for a Second Time

Let's save the letter with our corrections. Since we have already saved this document once, we have two choices:

- We can save the document using the same name; or
- We can save the document using a new name.

In this instance we will save the document using the *same* name. Typically, you do not want to keep multiple revisions of the same document — this wastes space on the disk and, if you go back to the document after a few days, you may accidentally retrieve a document without the right changes.

However, sometimes you are not sure if you prefer your edited or original version. At other times you may want to use your original as a **template**—the frame of a document that may be used over and over with some modifications or additions.

In either of these cases, or if you are using this book in a course and your instructor wants to see copies of both the original and edited documents, you would use **File/Save As...** to save the document using a new name. Instructions for both of these options follow.

To save the file using the *same name*:

1. Select **File/Save**.

   Works automatically will replace the previously saved file with the revised text.

To save the file using a different name:

1. Select **File/Save As...**

   The SAVE AS Dialog Box appears. The current file name is highlighted.

The Word Processor: An Introduction

2. Type the new file name that you wish to use. Refer to the file naming rules, to make sure that your new file name is valid.

Note: If you use an invalid file name, *Works* will give you an error message indicating that the name is invalid.

3. Press the **ENTER** key.

Printing a Document

1. Print a copy of Paul's letter using the default settings.

   It should not be necessary to select a text printer, since you checked the text printer settings when you printed Debbie's letter. Once printer settings have been selected, *Works* retains them.

Notice that as in Debbie's letter, the footer, *Page - 1*, appears on the bottom of the letter. One of *Works'* default settings is to print the page number at the bottom of each page. However, since this is only a one page letter, Paul has decided to remove the footer.

Changing the Layout of a Printed Document

The **Print/Layout** command is used to change the top, bottom, left, and right margins of your document, and to change the headers and footers printed on each page. To remove the page number footer:

1. Select **Print/Layout**. The LAYOUT Dialog Box will be displayed.
2. Press the **ALT** key to highlight a character in each option. Figure 2-18 shows the Dialog Box as it appears after the **ALT** key has been pressed.

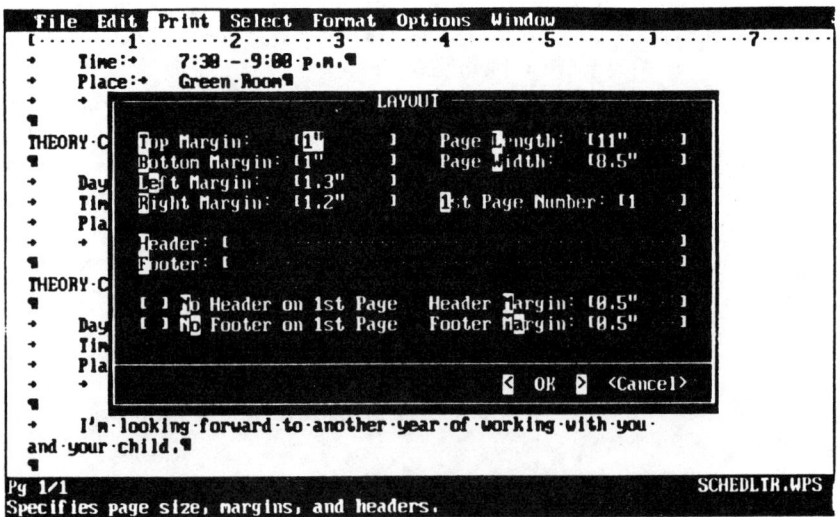

Figure 2-18

3. Press **ALT+F** to move the highlight to the Footer Text Box.
4. Press the **SPACE BAR** once. The footer text will be eliminated.
5. Press the **ENTER** key to accept the new page layout.
6. Select **Print/Print**.
7. Press the **ENTER** key to print using the default settings.

Note: As indicated on the Message Line, press the **ESC** key if you wish to cancel printing.

Conclusion

This chapter has introduced you to the basic word processing tasks: creating, editing, saving, and printing a document. In addition you were introduced to some of the more advanced concepts that demonstrate the power of *Works*. We moved from editing character by character to selecting and working with blocks of text. The procedures followed should provide the basis for further exploration of the word processor and of the other *Works* tools. For example, the process of selecting a block of text and then acting upon it with a command is the first step in many of the more advanced word processing activities. We will also use the same procedure in some of the database and spreadsheet activities that you will do later in this book.

Commands that we used also will be expanded upon when we work with the other tools. For example, the main part of the LAYOUT Dialog Box remains constant throughout the *Works* tools, and the procedure we used in this chapter to delete the footer could be used to change the header or footer in a spreadsheet or database.

Key Terms

The following important terms and commands have been introduced and explained in this chapter:

Default settings	Print/Print	Edit/Undo
Word wrap	RAM	File/Close
Template	Footer	Edit/Copy
File/New	F8-EXTEND	Print/Layout

Options/Show All Characters

Print/Select Text Printer

Independent Word Processor Project No. 1

1. Enter the letter shown on the next page.
    a. After you type the information on the **Green Room**, copy the block of information so that it appears again immediately below itself. Figure 2-19 shows the highlighted block, which is ready to be copied.
    b. Edit the block so that it includes the information for the **Blue Room**.

c. Copy the information for the **Blue Room** immediately below itself. Edit the block so that it contains the information on the **Starr Room**.
2. Proofread the letter. Use the editing techniques you have learned to correct any errors.
3. Save the letter on a disk.
4. Produce a printed copy of the letter.

September 5, 1988

Paul Harrison
123 Strawberry Lane
Ann Arbor, Michigan 48108

Dear Mr. Harrison,

Dean McCartney has forwarded your letter regarding rental of a recital hall to me. There are several rooms that are available for small private recitals. Below is a list of the rooms, their seating capacity, and rental fee. If you are not familiar with the rooms, please feel free to call my office to arrange a tour.

When you decide which room is appropriate for you, send me a list of the rooms and dates you wish to reserve. As our facilities are heavily used during peak recital times, please include three possible dates for each recital and indicate all acceptable rooms.

      Room: Green Room
      Hall: Tamany Hall
      Seating Capacity: 50
      Fee: $100

      Room: Blue Room
      Hall: Tamany Hall
      Seating Capacity: 40
      Fee: $80

      Room: Starr Room
      Hall: Hopper Hall
      Seating Capacity: 40
      Fee: $80

Sincerely yours,

Lucy S. Diamond
Assistant Dean

Figure 2-19

Independent Word Processor Project No. 2

1. Type Paul's resume as shown on next page.
2. Proofread the resume. Use the editing techniques you have learned to correct any errors.
3. Make the following revisions to the resume:
   a. Insert the area code **(313)** before Paul's telephone number.
   b. Delete the words *Junior Division* in the Westchester Music Camp entry.
   c. Insert the following text between *Massachusetts* and *September, 1981* in the entry for the University of Massachusetts.
      Major—Education, Minor—Music,
   d. In the first item under experience, change: Second Grade Teacher to
      Elementary School Teacher
   e. Insert a blank line before each of the headings:
      EXPERIENCE, EDUCATION, PERSONAL INTERESTS, REFERENCES AVAILABLE UPON REQUEST.

Hint: Place the cursor immediately *after* the desired location of the blank line, and press the **ENTER** key.

---

   f. Move the entire *EDUCATION* section of Paul's resume above the *EXPERIENCE* section.
4. Save the resume as **INDROJ2**.
5. Print a copy of the resume.

Paul Harrison
123 Strawberry Lane
Ann Arbor, Michigan 48108
Telephone: 345-6789

EXPERIENCE

Second Grade Teacher, Little Falls, New York, September 1985 - June 1987

Accompanist, Ross-Spaulding Music School, Scarsdale, New York, September 1980 - June 1981

Assistant Counselor, Westchester Music Camp, Junior Division, White Plains, New York, summer 1981

Participant, Interlochen Music Camp, Interlochen, Michigan, summers 1978, 1979

Participant, Westchester Music Camp, White Plains, New York, summers 1974 - 1977

EDUCATION

Graduate Student, University of Michigan School of Music, Ann Arbor, Michigan, September 1987 - present

B.A., University of Massachusetts, Amherst, Massachusetts, September 1981 - June 1985

PERSONAL INTERESTS

Piano, computers, photography

REFERENCES AVAILABLE UPON REQUEST

6. A copy of the completed resume appears on the next page. Compare your document with it and make any necessary corrections.

Paul Harrison
123 Strawberry Lane
Ann Arbor, Michigan 48108
Telephone: 345-6789

EDUCATION

Graduate Student, University of Michigan School of Music, Ann Arbor, Michigan, September 1987 - present

B.A., University of Massachusetts, Major--Education, Minor--Music, Amherst, Massachusetts, September 1981 - June 1985

EXPERIENCE

Elementary School Teacher, Little Falls, New York, September 1985 - June 1987

Accompanist, Ross-Spaulding Music School, Scarsdale, New York, September 1980 - June 1981

Assistant Counselor, Westchester Music Camp, White Plains, New York, summer 1981

Participant, Interlochen Music Camp, Interlochen, Michigan, summers 1978, 1979

Participant, Westchester Music Camp, White Plains, New York, summers 1974 - 1977

PERSONAL INTERESTS

Piano, computers, photography

REFERENCES AVAILABLE UPON REQUEST

Chapter 3
The Spreadsheet: An Introduction

In this chapter you will learn how to:

- Move around the spreadsheet.
- Enter labels, numbers, and formulas.
- Use one of *Works'* built-in functions.
- Copy the contents of one cell to another cell or to a range of cells.
- Change the appearance of lables and values.
- Change the width of cells.
- Save and print the spreadsheet.

What is a Spreadsheet?

A spreadsheet is an organized way to keep track of a lot of numerical information. Usually this information is financial, and oftentimes this information changes quickly. For those who are in business settings, spreadsheets have become an indispensable tool. For individuals who are involved with groups doing fund raising or budgeting, a spreadsheet is invaluable. And for just day-to-day home budgets or vacation planning, a spreadsheet can be quite useful.

In this chapter we are going to take a first look at the *Works* spreadsheet. You will become familiar with some of the key vocabulary words used and will have the opportunity to practice entering data into several spreadsheets. Along the way, you will begin to use the menus found on the Spreadsheet tool in *Works*.

Starting a Spreadsheet File

From the Main Menu If you have just loaded *Works* into your computer, the familiar Main Menu screen should appear. The second option in the NEW Dialog Box is Spreadsheet, and the <New> Button is enclosed in highlighted brackets. The message in the bottom left corner of the screen informs us that making this choice *Creates new Works file*. Move the cursor to **Spreadsheet** and press **ENTER**.

From Works If you already are using *Works* and want to use the Spreadsheet tool, then select **File/New** to open the NEW Dialog Box. Move the cursor to **Spreadsheet** and press **ENTER**.

70   The Spreadsheet: An Introduction

The Spreadsheet Screen

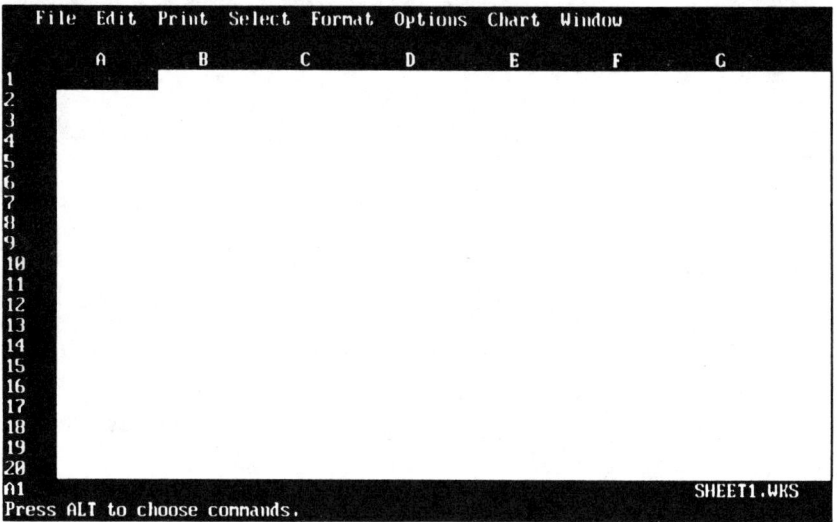

Figure 3-1

The Menu Bar Across the top of the spreadsheet screen (Figure 3-1) is the Menu Bar. Note how similar it is to the Menu Bar in the word processor. As you would expect, this Menu Bar provides us with the spreadsheet options. You may select a menu choice as you have done earlier by pressing the **ALT** key to highlight one letter in each of the menu options, and then either type the highlighted letter in the option you wish to select or use the **ARROW** keys and press **ENTER**.

The Formula Bar Below the Menu Bar is the Formula Bar, which is blank at the moment. As you will see shortly, this area serves as a "holding zone" when we enter information into our spreadsheet. When we type in information, it appears in the Formula Bar first so that we have the opportunity to examine it and make corrections before we "send" it off to its designated cell. You will see this in action in a few moments.

Column Names Below the Formula Bar is the row of **column names**. There are 32 columns in the spreadsheet; only columns A through G currently are displayed on your screen. To see additional columns, press the **RIGHT ARROW** key until you see the columns to the right. When you are done, press the **HOME** key to bring you back where you started.

Row Numbers In the left margin of the spreadsheet are the **row numbers**. There are 256 rows in the spreadsheet; only rows 1 through 20 currently are displayed on your screen. To see the subsequent rows, press the **DOWN ARROW** key until you see the rows below row 20. When you are done, press the **CTRL+HOME** key to bring you back where you started.

The Status Line At the bottom of the screen is the Status Line. In the far left corner of the Status Line is the cell address *A1*. A **cell** is where a column and a row intersect, such as *A1*, or *D35*, or *F18*. The cell shown on the Status Line is known as the **Active Cell**, which is the cell where information currently is being entered into the spreadsheet.

In the far-right-hand corner of the Status Line is the name of the current spreadsheet, **SHEET1.WKS**. *Works* automatically names the first new spreadsheet **SHEET1.WKS**, the second one **SHEET2.WKS**, and so on. You may give the spreadsheet a more meaningful name when you save it.

The Message Line At the very bottom of the screen is the Message Line. This line, which presently says *Press ALT to choose commands*, is where *Works* sends you messages as you enter and modify information. Sometimes these messages will tell you about the options that you have, and sometimes these messages will tell you what to do if you have a problem.

Moving Around the Spreadsheet Screen

Do you remember trying to move the cursor around the word processor screen before you had entered any text or blank lines? The program wouldn't let you do it. Once you had entered text, however, there were a number of ways to move the cursor around the screen. One of the differences between that screen and the spreadsheet screen is that it is possible to move the cursor around the spreadsheet screen before you enter any information. You've already used the **RIGHT** and **DOWN ARROW** keys to see beyond the first seven columns and the first 20 rows, and you used the **HOME** key and the **CTRL+HOME** key combination to bring the cursor back to cell *A1*.

As you probably already have guessed, there are several keys and key combinations that you can use to move around the spreadsheet screen quickly and efficiently. There are differences, however, in the way some keys will move the cursor around a blank screen and around a screen that has data entered into cells. For now let's take a look at those cursor movement keys that achieve the same results on both an empty and a full spreadsheet. Then, after we have entered some information in the first project, we'll take another look at moving around the spreadsheet screen.

When you move around a spreadsheet, usually you do so in one of three ways: **cell-to-cell**, **screen-to-screen**, or with **global movement**. We will save looking at the global movement key combinations until we have entered information in some cells, because as long as the screen is blank the program treats cell *A1* as both the beginning and the end of the spreadsheet file.

Cell-to-cell movement is accomplished by using the **ARROW** keys on your keyboard. Each one of these keys has an arrow pointing in a particular direction. Pressing these keys will move the cursor one cell in the direction of the arrows.

Screen-to-screen movement is accomplished by using some of the special keys on your keyboard. These keys, and the movements that they perform, are listed below:

KEYS	MOVEMENT
PGDN	Down one screen (20 rows)
PGUP	Up one screen (20 rows)
CTRL+PGDN	Right one screen
CTRL+PGUP	Left one screen

Entering Labels and Values

When we enter information into a spreadsheet, we will enter either text, numbers, or formulas. Those who use spreadsheets refer to text as **labels** and to numbers and formulas as **values**.

Labels Labels in spreadsheets are what we ordinarily refer to as words. They are used to identify the information that we will be putting into the spreadsheet. Labels can appear anywhere on the spreadsheet but are often used across the top of the spreadsheet as column headings or down the left-hand side of the spreadsheet. You will use labels in both ways as we do the projects in this chapter.

When we type labels they are automatically **left justified**. This means that the label starts at the left edge of the cell. We will learn later how to change this justification, should we choose to do so. Also, *Works* automatically places a quotation mark in front of any label. You will not see the quotation mark in the cell itself, but it appears in the Formula Bar. This quotation mark is known as a preceding label indicator, and it signifies that the contents of the cell constitute a label rather than a value. You cannot see the quotation mark in the cell itself, but you can see it in the Formula Bar when the contents of the cell are displayed there.

Values Values in spreadsheets are what we ordinarily refer to as numbers or formulas. Values may be used for all mathematical computations, such as addition, subtraction, multiplication, and division. When we type a value into a cell, it is unformatted, but then if we so choose we can add symbols such as dollar signs or percent signs by formatting the cell. The numbers not only are unformatted when we enter them, but also are automatically **right justified**. This means that they are automatically placed on the right of each cell.

Practice Exercise No. 1

Before we begin with a "real" project, let's just practice entering some labels and values on a spreadsheet. A blank spreadsheet should be on the screen. If it is not, select **File/New/Spreadsheet**.

Entering Labels
1. Use the **RIGHT** and **DOWN ARROW** keys to move the cursor to cell *B3*.
2. Type: **Monday** and press **ENTER**.

Entering Labels 73

Notice that the word *Monday* appears in the Formula Bar with a quotation mark preceding it, even though you did not type this. The quote symbol is the indicator that *Works* automatically adds to show that a label has been entered in the cell.

3. Move the cursor to cell *C3* and begin typing the following labels. This time, after you type each label, press the **RIGHT ARROW** key instead of **ENTER**. This will enter the information in the cell and then move your cursor over to the next available cell in one step.

CELL	LABEL
C3	**Tuesday**
D3	**Last Year**

4. Let's try entering the name of a month as the label in cell *E3*. Type: **January** and press **ENTER**.

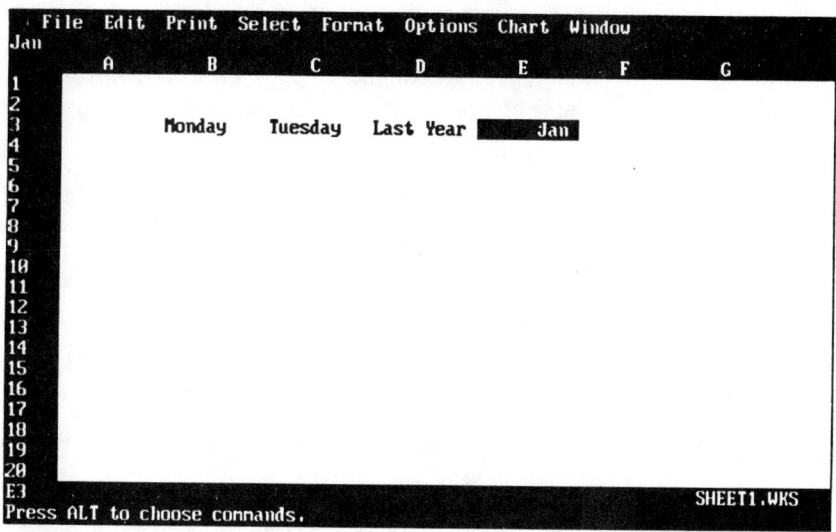

Figure 3-2

Notice that something unusual happens (Figure 3-2). The word *January*, which seems as if it should be a normal label, doesn't look like the other labels we have entered. First of all, *January* has been shortened to just the first three letters, *Jan*. In addition, the word *Jan* is **right justified** in the cell and it is *not* preceded by a quote symbol in the Formula Bar.

If you try entering **February** in cell *F3* and **March** in cell *G3*, you will notice that what happened with January happens with the names of all months. Only the first three letters of the month appear, the label is right justified in the cell, and there is no preceding quote symbol in the Formula Bar. The reason for all of this is that one of the default settings in *Works* tells the program to treat months as values rather than as labels. *Works* enters them with a special Time/Date format that includes right justification and that assigns a numerical value to them. You will not see numbers on the screen when you enter the name of a month in a cell, but if you include that cell in a mathematical computation, you can find out what number value it was assigned.

If you want the entire name of a month to appear in a cell, you have to tell *Works* to treat it as a conventional label and not as a special Time/Date value. *Works* uses a quotation mark to indicate a label, so if you type a quote before you type the name of a month, the program will accept the month as a label. Let's try this now.

1. Move the cursor to cell *E4*.
2. Type: **"January** and press **ENTER**.

   Notice how this entry has the same characteristics as the conventional labels in cells *B3*, *C3*, and *D3*. It is left justified, there is a quote symbol preceding it in the Formula Bar, and all the letters you typed are visible in the cell.

Entering Values When we enter a value in a *Works* spreadsheet, we really are entering the "absolute value" in that cell. In other words, we are entering only the numbers or formulas that will generate the value in that cell. Then, after all of the values have been entered, we can **format** them so that anyone looking at the spreadsheet can tell by their appearance what they represent, such as currency or percentages. We will learn how to format cells as we complete the two projects in this chapter, but for now let's just enter some numbers and formulas and see how the unformatted values appear.

1. In cell *B6* type: **200**
2. In cell *C6* type: **287.89**
3. In cell *D6* type: **1,234.56**

   Note how the **,** does *not* appear

4. In cell *E6* type: **=C6+D6**

   Note how this formula permits us to *add* the values in two cells.

5. In cell *F6* type: **=E6*2**

   Note how this formula permits us to *multiply* the value in cell *E6* times 2.

6. In cell *B8* type: **=B6/3**

   Note how this formula permits us to *divide* the value in cell *B6* by 3, and that the new value includes six decimal places.

7. In cell *C8* type: **1988**

   Suppose you wanted to use the year 1988 as a label for a row or column of information. Can you guess how you would tell *Works* to treat 1988 as a label rather than as a value? Let's try that next.

8. In cell *D8* type: **"1988** and press **ENTER**.

Note how the numbers now are left justified. If you have entered all of the values and labels correctly, your spreadsheet should resemble Figure 3-3.

Now that we have tried these introductory exercises, let's begin with our first project. If you want to take a break now, select **File/Exit**. You will see a Dialog Box that asks you if you want to *Save changes to: SHEET1.WKS?* Since we were just practicing, there is no need to save this spreadsheet, so you want to select the **<No>** Button. Either press **ALT+N** or **TAB** to the **<No>** Button and press **ENTER**. When you are ready to continue, restart *Works* and select **Spreadsheet** from the NEW Dialog Box.

Concepts

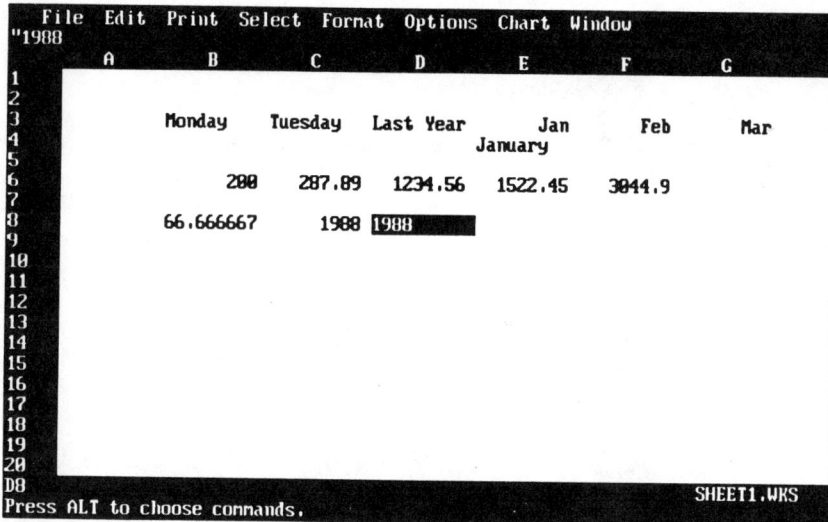

Figure 3-3

If you wish to continue with the following project now, select **File/New**. Be aware that throughout Project No. 1 we will be referring to **SHEET1.WKS** and your spreadsheet will be **SHEET2.WKS**.

Spreadsheet Project No. 1
Budgeting Expenses

Let's try setting up our first spreadsheet. In this project, we will set up a simple budget that could be used to keep track of your monthly expenses. While completing this project you will:

- Review entering labels and values.
- Review the differences between labels and values.
- Correct errors.
- Enter formulas.
- Copy from one cell to another.
- Change the alignment of the contents of a cell.
- Change the appearance of values.
- Save the spreadsheet.
- Print the spreadsheet.

The completed budget spreadsheet is shown in Figure 3-4.

Concepts The first part of setting up any spreadsheet is to set up the labels that will identify the values to be entered. First we will enter labels across the top of the spreadsheet, and then we will enter labels in column A.

The Spreadsheet: An Introduction

```
File  Edit  Print  Select  Format  Options  Chart  Window
     A         B         C        D        E        F        G
1
2
3             My First Budget
4             September - November, 1988
5
6             Monthly    Sept     Oct      Nov      1st Q    1st Q
7   Expenses  Budget     Actual   Actual   Actual   Budget   Actual
8
9   Rent      $150       $135     $135     $135     $450     $405
10  Food      150        185      136      135      450      456
11  Clothing  50         75       45       100      150      220
12  Utilities 75         83       65       75       225      223
13  Phone     35         46       45       42       105      133
14  Train     100        84       100      65       300      249
15
16  Total     $560       $608     $526     $552     $1,680   $1,686
17
18
19
20
A1                                                       BUDGET1.WKS
Press ALT to choose commands.
```

Figure 3-4

Entering Labels

1. Move the cursor to cell B3; type: **My First Budget**

   (Do not worry if you make a mistake while you are typing. You will learn how to correct mistakes shortly.)

2. Press the **DOWN ARROW** key to move to cell *B4*.

3. Type: **September - November, 1988** and press **ENTER**.

4. Move the cursor to cell *A7*; type: **Expenses.** Then press the **RIGHT ARROW** key (Figure 3-5).

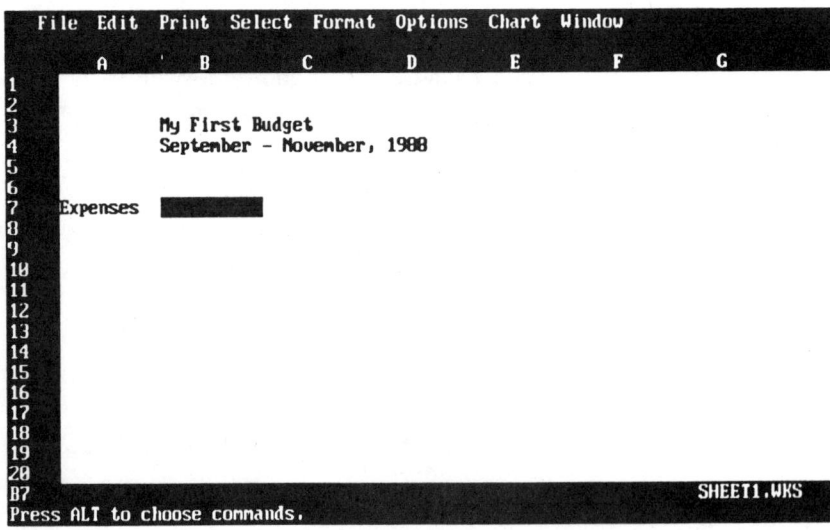

Figure 3-5

Entering Labels

> *Note:* There are several column headings that are rather long in our spreadsheet. The default in *Works* is to make all columns 10 positions wide; therefore, some of our headings will be too long for our columns. To avoid some of the problems that will arise, when we have two word column headings, we will type the first word in one cell and the second in the cell directly below it. In this way, we will be able to keep our columns as narrow as possible. See Figure 3-6 for an illustration of what we are about to do. Use your **ARROW** keys to move from cell to cell.

5. Type: **Monthly** in cell *B6* and **Budget** in cell *B7*.
6. In cell *C6* type: **"Sept** and in *C7* type: **Actual**

> *Note:* It is important to type the quotation mark in front of the month, because we do not want to accept *Works'* abbreviations for the months.

7. In cell *D6* type: **"Oct** and in cell *D7* type: **Actual**
8. In cell *E6* type: **"Nov** and in cell *E7* type: **Actual**
9. In cell *F6* type: **1st Q** and in cell *F7* type: **Budget**

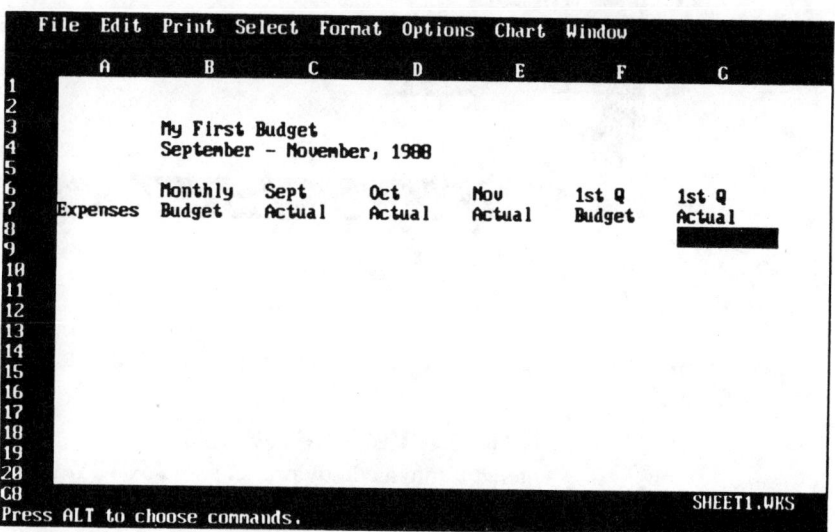

Figure 3-6

10. Type: **1st Q** in cell *G6* and **Actual** in cell *G7*.
11. Move your cursor to cell *A9*, and in cells *A9*, *A10*, *A11*, *A12*, *A13*, and *A14*, type the names of the different expense categories listed below. After typing each one, press the **DOWN ARROW** key.

The Spreadsheet: An Introduction

The names are:

Rent

Food

Clothing

Utilities

Phone

Train

Then move to cell *A16* and type:

Total

When you are done, your spreadsheet should resemble Figure 3-7.

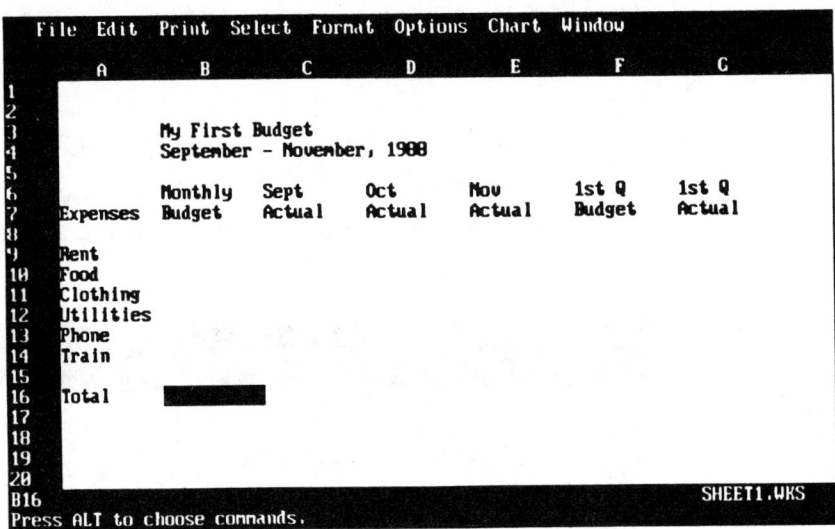

Figure 3-7

Correcting Errors There are several ways to correct errors you make while entering information. They are:

1. Use the **BACKSPACE** key to erase what you are typing *before* you have entered it into a cell by pressing an **ARROW** key or **ENTER**.

2. Move your cursor to the cell in which you have made the mistake. Type the correct text and then press **ENTER**. The information you just typed will replace the incorrect information.

3. Move your cursor to the cell in which you have made the mistake, and press **F2** to access *Works' EDIT* mode. When you do this, the word *EDIT* will appear on the Status Line, and the message *Edit Formula* will appear on the Message Line.

   When this happens, the cell contents are available to you on the Formula Bar as if you had just typed them. You may use your **BACKSPACE** key to

Entering Values

79

erase incorrect characters, or you may use your **ARROW** keys to move your cursor to the location in which you would like to change information and then delete and insert the necessary characters.

Entering Values Now it's time to enter some numerical information into our spreadsheet. Remember that numbers are referred to as values by *Works*, and will be right justified by the program as they are entered. That is, the numbers that you enter will be pushed over to the right of each cell.

The Monthly Budget expenses in cells *B9* through *B14* are:

Rent	150	*Utilities*	75
Food	150	*Phone*	35
Clothing	50	*Train*	100

1. Move your cursor to cell *B9* and enter **150**. Then press the **DOWN ARROW** key.
2. Enter **150** for Food in cell *B10* and press the **DOWN ARROW** key.
3. Continue to do this for the remaining values in column B. See Figure 3-8.

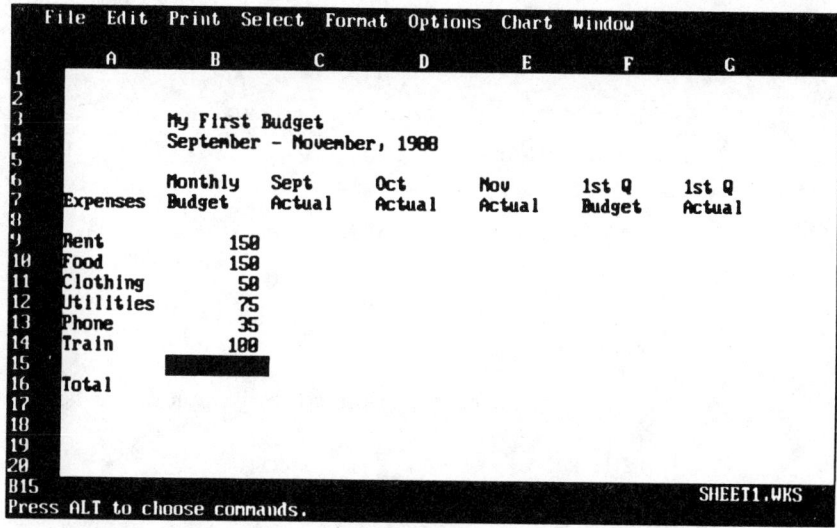

Figure 3-8

The actual expenses for September (cells *C9* through *C14*) are:

Rent	135	*Utilities*	83
Food	185	*Phone*	46
Clothing	75	*Train*	84

1. Enter **135** in cell *C9* and press the **DOWN ARROW** key.
2. Enter **185** in cell *C10* and press the **DOWN ARROW** key.
3. Enter the remaining values in cells *C11* through *C14* (Figure 3-9).

The Spreadsheet: An Introduction

```
 File  Edit  Print  Select  Format  Options  Chart  Window
        A       B       C       D       E       F       G
 1
 2
 3            My First Budget
 4            September - November, 1988
 5
 6            Monthly  Sept    Oct     Nov     1st Q   1st Q
 7  Expenses  Budget   Actual  Actual  Actual  Budget  Actual
 8
 9  Rent      150      135
10  Food      150      185
11  Clothing   50       75
12  Utilities  75       83
13  Phone      35       46
14  Train     100       84
15
16  Total
17
18
19
20
C15                                                  SHEET1.WKS
Press ALT to choose commands.
```

Figure 3-9

As you have done for columns B and C, type in the values for columns D and E. The actual expenses for October (cells *D9* through *D14*) and November (cells *E9* through *E14*) are:

	Oct Actual	Nov Actual
Rent	135	135
Food	136	135
Clothing	45	100
Utilities	65	75
Phone	45	42
Train	100	65

If you have done this correctly, your spreadsheet should resemble Figure 3-10.

Moving Around a Spreadsheet Now that we have filled several cells with information, let's take another look at moving the cursor around the spreadsheet screen. If you try moving the cursor from cell to cell and from screen to screen with the keys that we discussed earlier in the chapter, you will find that they achieve the same results as they did when the screen was blank. Now, however, we also can use the global movement keys. Let's try some of these now.

1. Use the **ARROW** keys to move your cursor to cell *E14* if it is not there already.
2. Press the **HOME** key. As you probably expected, this returns the cursor to column A of the same row (i.e., cell *A14*).
3. Now press the **END** key. The cursor moves to cell *G14*, although you might have expected it to stop in cell *E14* since E is the last column with an entry

Entering a Formula

81

```
 File  Edit  Print  Select  Format  Options  Chart  Window
         A         B         C         D         E         F         G
1
2
3              My First Budget
4              September - November, 1988
5
6              Monthly    Sept       Oct        Nov        1st Q      1st Q
7    Expenses  Budget     Actual     Actual     Actual     Budget     Actual
8
9    Rent      150        135        135        135
10   Food      150        185        136        135
11   Clothing  50         75         45         100
12   Utilities 75         83         65         75
13   Phone     35         46         45         42
14   Train     100        84         100        65
15
16   Total
17
18
19
20
E15                                                                SHEET1.WKS
Press ALT to choose commands.
```

Figure 3-10

in row 14. The **END** key, however, always moves the cursor to the last column which contains an entry in any row.

4. Press **CTRL+HOME**. Even though there is no information in cell *A1*, the program considers it the beginning of the spreadsheet. Where does the cursor go when you press **CTRL+END**?

Just as the **END** key moves the cursor to the last column that contains an entry in any row, **CTRL+END** moves the cursor to the intersection of the last row that contains any data and the last column that contains any data.

Here's a summary of the key movements we've been trying:

KEY	MOVEMENT
HOME	To column A of the current row
END	In the current row, to the right-most column that has data in it on any row
CTRL+HOME	To cell *A1*
CTRL+END	To the intersection of the last filled row and the last filled column in the spreadsheet

Entering a Formula

Typing Cell Addresses into a Formula

A **formula** in *Works* permits us to enter a relationship into a cell. For example, to see the *1st Q Budget* amount for *Rent* in cell *F9*, take the value for one month's rent, which is in cell *B9*, and multiply it by 3, since there are three months in the first quarter. Here's how to do this:

1. Move the cursor to cell *F9*.
2. In cell *F9*, type: **=B9*3**

The Spreadsheet: An Introduction

Notice how the formula appears at the top left of your screen in the Formula Bar. If you see that you have made a mistake, use your **BACKSPACE** key to erase what you have typed and then type it again.

Note: The equal sign (=) tells *Works* that the contents of this cell constitute a formula, and the asterisk (*) is the symbol for multiplication. It is important to begin every formula with an equal sign, because otherwise *Works* will treat the entry as a label. Even if you type a number instead of a cell address (i.e., 150 instead of B9), as soon as you type the symbol for the arithmetic operator (+ for addition, - for subtraction, * for multiplication or / for division), *Works* will think the entry is a label unless it has the equal sign at the beginning to signify a formula.

---

3. Press **ENTER**.

   If you have done this correctly, the value *450* automatically appears in cell *F9* (Figure 3-11).

```
File  Edit  Print  Select  Format  Options  Chart  Window
B9*3
      A        B         C          D         E         F          G
 1
 2
 3           My First Budget
 4           September - November, 1988
 5
 6           Monthly   Sept       Oct        Nov       1st Q      1st Q
 7  Expenses Budget    Actual     Actual     Actual    Budget     Actual
 8
 9  Rent     150       135        135        135       450
10  Food     150       185        136        135
11  Clothing 50        75         45         100
12  Utilities 75       83         65         75
13  Phone    35        46         45         42
14  Train    100       84         100        65
15
16  Total
17
18
19
20
F9                                                              SHEET1.WKS
Press ALT to choose commands.
```

Figure 3-11

4. Now enter the formula **=B10*3** into cell *F10*.
5. Enter the formula **=B11*3** into cell *F11*.
6. Enter the formula **=B12*3** into cell *F12*.
7. Enter the formula **=B13*3** into cell *F13*.
8. Enter the formula **=B14*3** into cell *F14* (Figure 3-12).

Using Pointing to Enter a Formula

As you were doing this, you may have begun to wonder why you were typing what is basically the same formula over and over. Since spreadsheets are designed to save

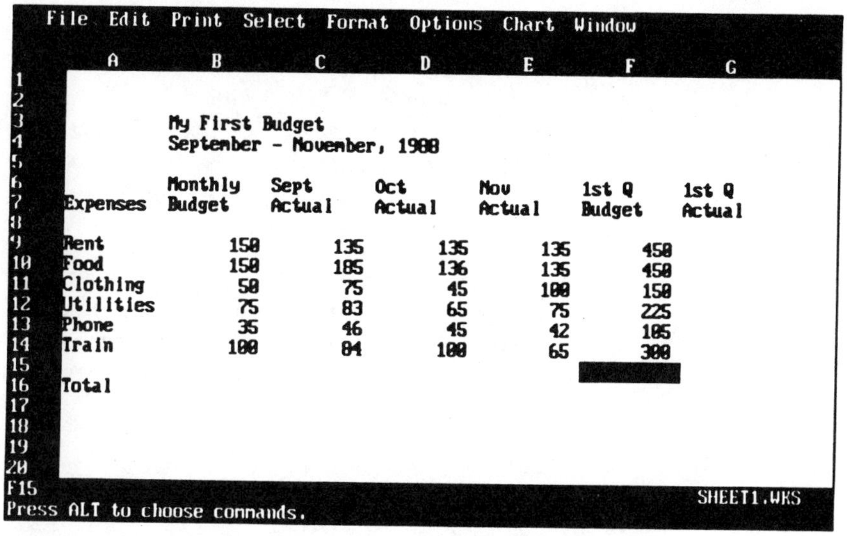

Entering a Formula

Figure 3-12

you from such repetitive typing, we will show you one way to begin to use some of the time-saving features built into *Works*.

Rather than *typing* the formula, we will type part of the formula and use our cursor to **point** to the other information that we wish to include. Specifically, we still will type the mathematical symbols (= and +), but *each time* a cell address should be added to the formula, we will move the cursor (and thus point) to the cell rather than typing the cell name. Here's how to do this:

1. Begin with your cursor in the cell where the formula is to go. Move your cursor to cell *G9*.

2. Begin the formula with an equal sign (=) so that *Works* will know that you are entering a *value*, not a label. Type: **=**

3. Now use the **LEFT ARROW** key to move the cursor over to cell *C9* (September), the first cell that we want to add in our formula. Notice that the word *POINT* has appeared at the bottom of your screen (Figure 3-13).

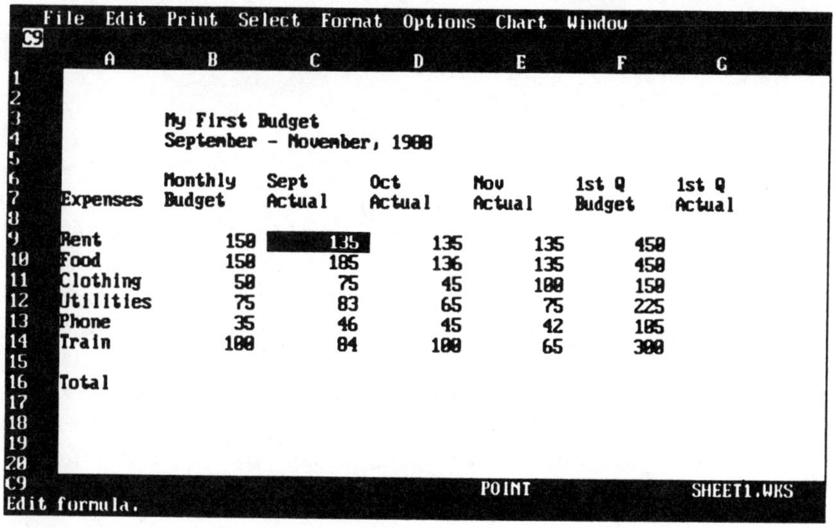

Figure 3-13

4. Type a plus sign (+). This tells *Works* that you are going to add something else to the formula. The cursor automatically will move back to cell *G9* and *Works* will wait for you to continue.

5. Move the cursor to cell *D9* (October). Type: + Again, your cursor automatically will move back to cell *G9* and *Works* will wait for you to continue.

6. Now move the cursor to cell *E9* (November). This time press **ENTER**, and watch your total automatically appear (Figure 3-14).

The formula for cells *G10*, *G11*, *G12*, *G13*, and *G14* is exactly the same as the one in cell *G9*, except that the rows are different. Therefore, you should repeat the same sequence of steps to enter a formula into each of these cells.

Notice that the ability to point the cursor provides you with three benefits:

- Speed
- Accuracy
- The ability to see exactly what cells are being used in the formula(s) that you are creating.

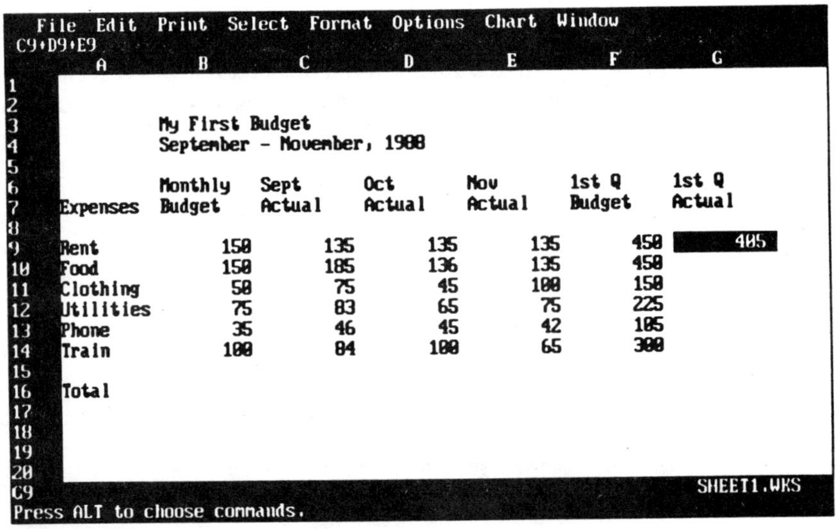

Figure 3-14

Copying Cells

Sometimes we have information in one part of our spreadsheet that could be used in other cells. For example, the first formula at the top of column F is really the same formula that was used all the way down that column. The only difference is that the formula has been **adjusted** to reflect the actual *row* that it is in. (The formula in cell *F9* is =*B9*3*. The formula in cell *F10* is =*B10*3*. The formula in cell *F11* is =*B11*3*.)

This is also true for the formulas in column G. So even though pointing at cells is a vast improvement over typing and retyping the information, we now would like to proceed one step further and make entering formulas even easier.

Copying Cells   85

In this operation, we will create one formula to total our Monthly Budget allocations (cell *B16*), and then we will **COPY** this formula across to the other columns on the spreadsheet. Let's try!

1. Move the cursor to cell *B16*.
2. Type in the following formula:

    a. Type an equal sign (=) and move the cursor to cell *B9*. Then type a **+**. The cursor returns to cell *B16*.

    b. Move the cursor to cell *B10* and type a **+**. The cursor returns to cell *B16*.

    c. Move the cursor to cell *B11* and type a **+**. The cursor returns to cell *B16*.

    d. Move the cursor to cell *B12* and type a **+**. The cursor returns to cell *B16*.

    e. Move the cursor to cell *B13* and type a **+**. The cursor returns to cell *B16*.

    f. Move the cursor to cell *B14*. Check to see that your formula is correct. If it is, press the **ENTER** key. The cursor returns to cell *B16*, where the value *560* now is displayed.

If you have done this correctly, your spreadsheet should resemble Figure 3-15.

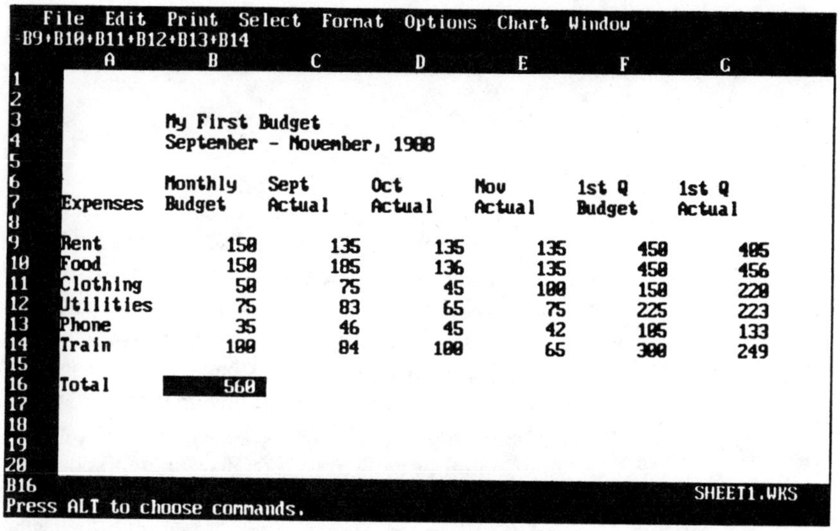

Figure 3-15

3. Select **Edit/Copy**.

    The Message Line says *Select new location and press ENTER or press ESC to cancel.*

4. Since we want the exact same formula in cell *C16*, move the cursor to cell *C16*. Press **ENTER**.

    Notice that the formula has been correctly copied over to column C and that the cell references have been *relatively adjusted* by *Works*.

5. Select **Edit/Copy** again.

The Spreadsheet: An Introduction

6. Move the cursor to cell *D16* and press **ENTER**.
7. Repeat these steps for cells *E16*, *F16*, and *G16*.

If you have done this correctly, your spreadsheet should resemble Figure 3-16.

```
 File  Edit  Print  Select  Format  Options  Chart  Window
=G9+G10+G11+G12+G13+G14
       A         B         C         D         E         F         G
 1
 2
 3           My First Budget
 4           September - November, 1988
 5
 6           Monthly   Sept      Oct       Nov       1st Q     1st Q
 7  Expenses Budget    Actual    Actual    Actual    Budget    Actual
 8
 9  Rent     150       135       135       135       450       405
10  Food     150       185       136       135       450       456
11  Clothing  50        75        45       100       150       220
12  Utilities 75        83        65        75       225       223
13  Phone     35        46        45        42       105       133
14  Train    100        84       100        65       300       249
15
16  Total    560       608       526       552      1680      1606
17
18
19
20
G16                                                           SHEET1.WKS
Press ALT to choose commands.
```

Figure 3-16

Relative cell adjustment is an extremely useful spreadsheet feature. Often we will develop one formula, and then discover that it will work quite well for the rest of the relationships in a specific column or row. Although this will not always be true, it does work frequently enough that it is worth understanding, so that you may learn how to use the **Edit/Copy** command easily and comfortably.

Relative cell adjustment works because the program really is adding up cells according to where they are in relationship to the cell in which the formula appears. That is, the formula in cell *G9* really says to add up the values in the cells that are two, three, and four cells to its left. If we were to copy that formula down column G, the same *relationship* would be copied into each of the other rows. We will discuss how to create a formula that does not adjust when copied when we take another look at the Spreadsheet tool in Chapter 6.

Formatting Labels and Values

Earlier, we observed that labels in this spreadsheet are all left justified. It would be nice if we could line them up above the values in their respective columns. Also, since we are dealing with currency, we might wish to have some dollar signs on the budget. Changes to both the appearance and the alignment of the labels and values in a cell are made using the **Format** command. Here's how to do this.

Formatting Labels

First, we need to identify the specific cells to be formatted. Next, we must decide which format we would like to have. This process will introduce us to a new

Formatting Labels and Values

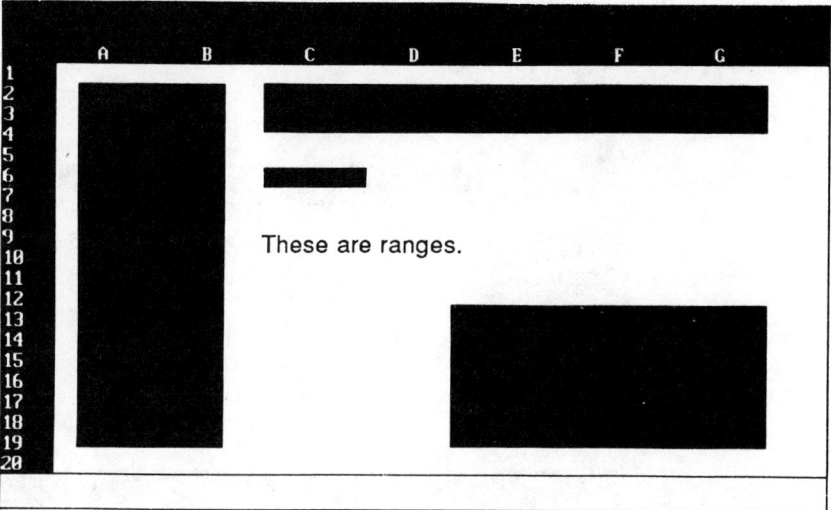

Figure 3-17

vocabulary word, the word **range**. In a spreadsheet, a range is one cell or a rectangular block of cells (Figure 3-17).

In addition to being able to format one cell at a time, we can format a range of cells, by selecting the range first, and then specifying how to format it. This is similar to selecting a block when using the word processor. In fact, to select a range, we use function key **F8**, just as we selected a block of text in the word processor.

1. Move the cursor to cell *B6* and press **F8**.

   Notice that the word *EXTEND* appears on the Message Line. *EXTEND* means that *Works* is waiting for us to define the range with which we are going to work.

2. Use your **ARROW** keys to **EXTEND** the highlight across to column G and then down to row 7. Notice that the far-left corner of the Status Line says that the range has been defined as *B6:G7* (Figure 3-18).

Note: Remember that if you start to **EXTEND** the highlight and then change your mind, you can press the **ESC** key to quit the EXTEND mode.

3. Select **Format/Style** (Figure 3-19).
4. Select **Right** in the Alignment Option Box and press **ENTER**. The labels all should be right justified.

Formatting Values

Values also may be formatted to change their alignment in the cells, but typically values in a spreadsheet remain right justified. Instead, we use the **Format** command to change their appearance. The procedure to do this is almost the same as the one

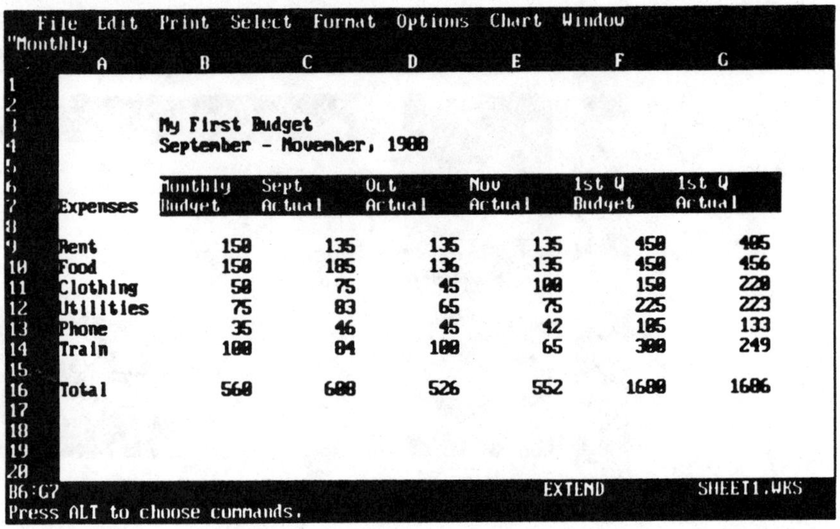

The Spreadsheet: An Introduction

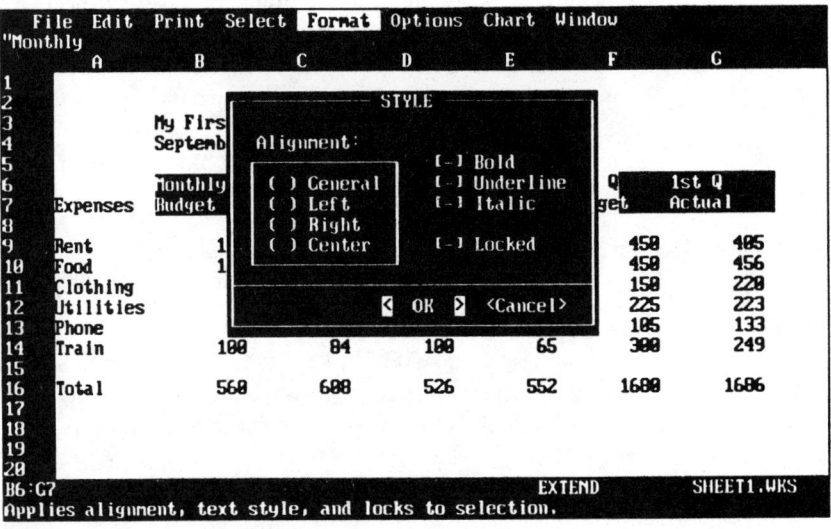

Figure 3-18

Figure 3-19

to change the label justifications. First you have to indicate the range that you are interested in changing, and then you have to tell *Works* how you would like to format that range. In this example, we would like to format all of the values in rows 9 and 16 with dollar signs. Here's how to do it:

1. Move the cursor to cell *B9*.
2. Press **F8** and **EXTEND** the highlight for all of the values in row 9.
3. Select **Format/Dollar**.

   The DECIMALS Dialog Box permits you to choose how many decimals you would like to include after each value.

Save and Save As... 89

4. Type: the number **0** and press **ENTER**.
5. Move the cursor to cell *B16*. Then press **F8** and **EXTEND** the highlight to cell *G16*.
6. Select **Format/Dollar**.
7. Type: **0** in the DECIMALS Dialog Box and press **ENTER** (Figure 3-20).

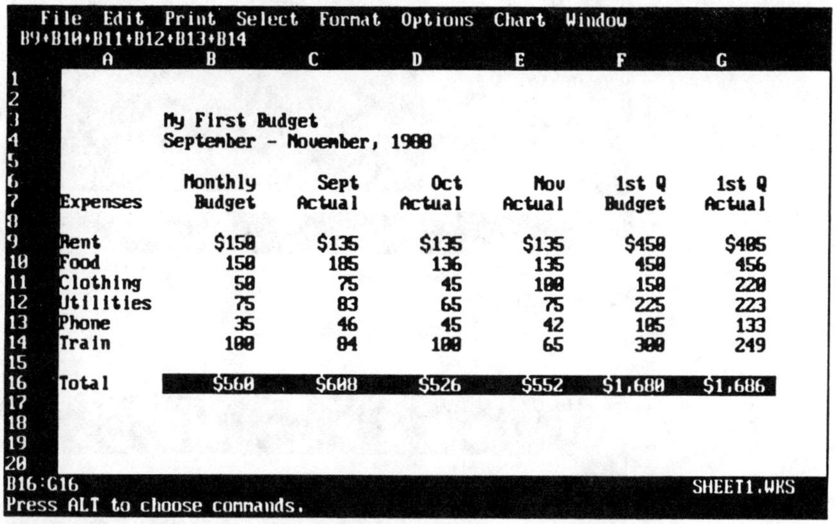

Figure 3-20

Save and Save As... As you have learned, it is important to save your work fairly frequently. The usual advice is to save your work every 15 minutes, so that if you should make a serious mistake, or if the power should fail, you will not lose all your work. Let's save our spreadsheet.

1. Select **File/Save**.

    The SAVE AS Dialog Box appears because this is the first time we are saving this spreadsheet, and *Works* assumes that we want to give it a more meaningful name than **SHEET1.WKS** (Figure 3-21).

2. If the Current Drive entry is not the drive containing your exercise disk, there are two ways to save the file on the correct drive. The first method is the one you used in the first two chapters. You selected the appropriate drive from the Other Drives and Directories List Box and then typed the new file name in the File Name Text Box. You may also use the procedure described below.

    If you are saving your data in Drive A, type: **A:BUDGET1**

    If you are saving your data in Drive B, type: **B:BUDGET1** (Figure 3-22).

Note: This procedure does not permanently change the current default drive.

90   The Spreadsheet: An Introduction

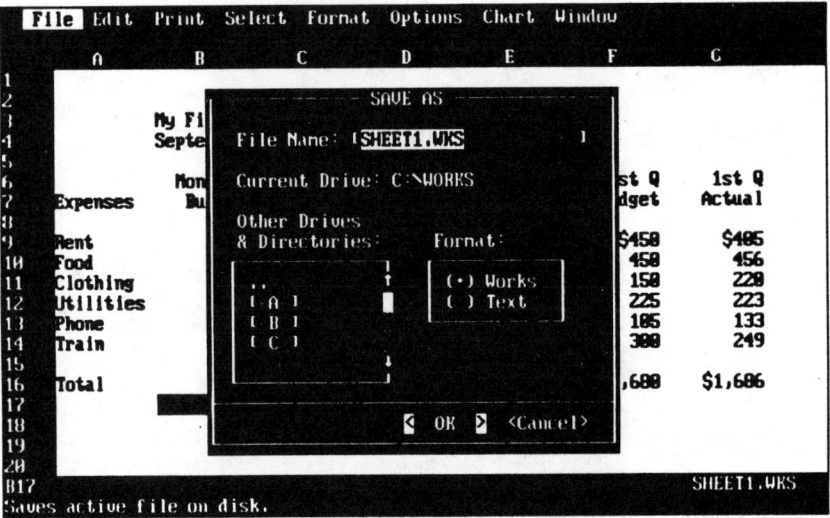

Figure 3-21

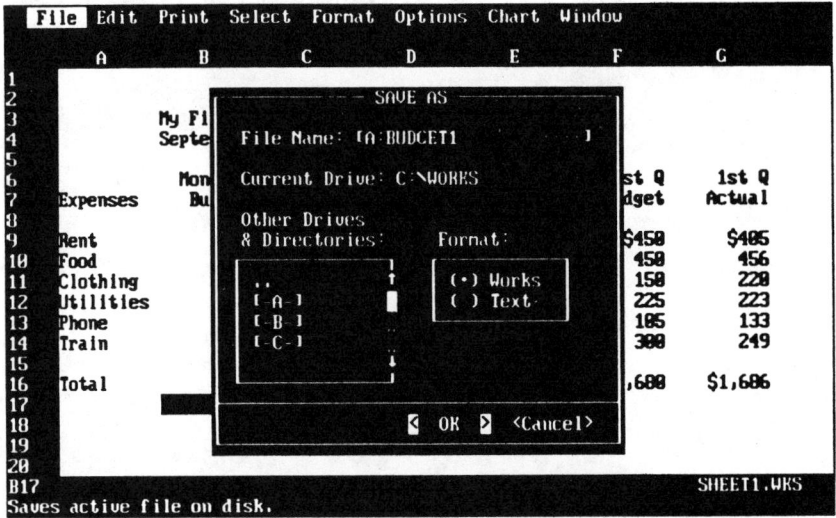

Figure 3-22

Note: We type the drive name and the name of the file, but we do *not* type the file extension. The spreadsheet extension (**.WKS**) will be added automatically by *Works*.

3. Press **ENTER**.

Caution: From here on, each time you save your file using **File/Save**, it automatically will be saved as **BUDGET1.WKS** on the drive that you chose.

Printing the Spreadsheet

Should you wish to change the name of your file again (or the drive on which it will be saved), you will have to Select **File/Save As...** to do so.

Printing the Spreadsheet There are many options available to you within the Print menu. For the moment, however, we will ignore most of them and just print out our newly created spreadsheet, **Budget1.Wks**. Here is how to do that:

1. We have to tell *Works* which range of cells we would like to print.
   a. Move the cursor to cell *A1*.
   b. Press **F8** and **EXTEND** the highlight to cover cells *A1* through *G16*.
2. Select **Print/Set Print Area**.

   This sends a signal to *Works* telling it that the range of cells that you have highlighted is the area to be printed when the **Print** command is given.
3. Select **Print/Print**.

   This will cause the PRINT Dialog Box to appear on your screen. We will use the default selections provided by *Works* (Figure 3-23).

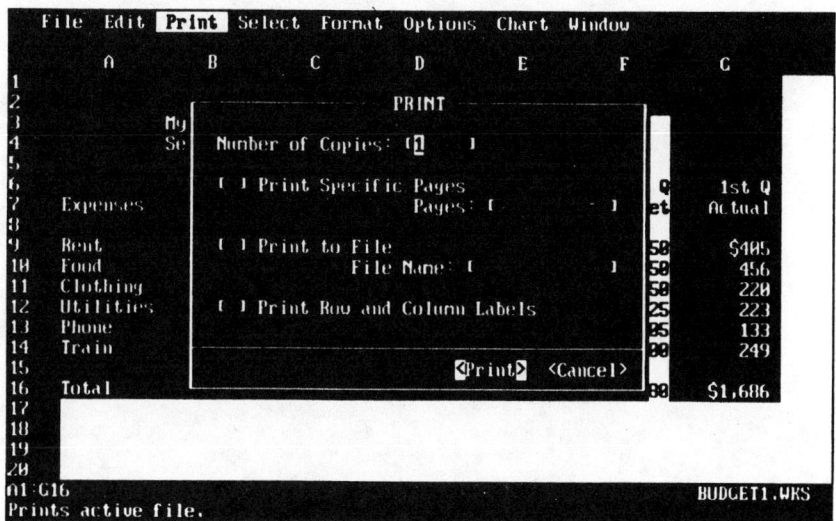

Figure 3-23

4. Make sure that your printer is on and on-line, and that the paper is aligned properly.
5. Press **ENTER** and watch the magic!

There is one problem when you print this spreadsheet, which is that it is too wide to fit on a standard piece of paper. So *Works* automatically divides it into chunks and prints it out on two pages. You probably aren't happy with the way this looks, however. One way to get around this problem is to change the margins for printing. Follow these steps to print your entire spreadsheet on one piece of paper:

92 The Spreadsheet: An Introduction

Note: It is not necessary to use **Print/Set Print Area**, since we are using the same part of the spreadsheet that we printed most recently. Once a print area has been set, that area will be printed each time you print this spreadsheet until you set the print area again or close the spreadsheet without saving it If you save the spreadsheet after setting a print area, the print area will be saved also.

1. Select **Print/Layout**.

    This will cause the LAYOUT Dialog Box to appear on your screen (Figure 3-24).

    You should recognize this Dialog Box as the one you used to change the footer of your document in the word processor chapter.

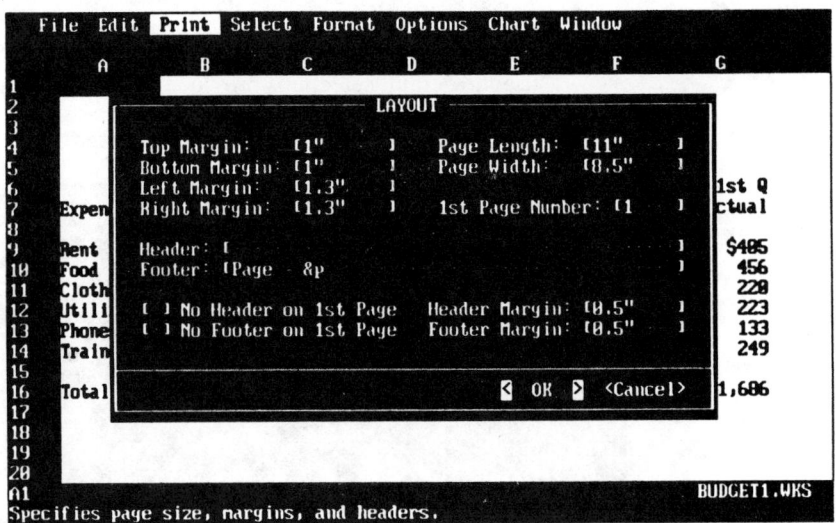

Figure 3-24

2. **TAB** down to the Left Margin Text Box or press **ALT+E** to move to the Left Margin Text Box.
3. Type: **0.5"**
4. Now change the Right Margin Text Box to **0.5"**
5. Press **ENTER**.
6. Select **Print/Print**.

Spreadsheet Project No. 2
Monitoring Travel Expenses

In the first spreadsheet project you had a chance to see how a spreadsheet can be used and to begin working with some of the menu options for this tool. In this second

Starting the Spreadsheet File 93

project, we would like to set up a simple *Travel Expense Form*, which could be used to keep track of either vacation expenses or work-related travel expenses. Many of the concepts are similar to the ones covered in the first project, so you will get more practice with the procedures you have used thus far. There are several new concepts and commands as well, however. While completing this project you will review how to:

- Enter labels and values, including formulas.
- Correct errors.
- Change the alignment of the contents of a cell.
- Change the appearance of values.
- Save a spreadsheet.
- Print a spreadsheet.

You also will learn how to:

- Change the width of a column.
- Copy from one cell to a range of cells in the same row or column.
- Use a function to calculate values.
- Erase the contents of a cell.

The spreadsheet you will create is shown in Figure 3-25.

```
File  Edit  Print  Select  Format  Options  Chart  Window
         A         B       C       D       E       F       G       H       I
 1
 2
 3                         Travel Expense Report
 4     Categories   Sun    Mon     Tues    Weds    Thur    Fri     Sat     Total
 5
 6     Air Fare            358.00                                          358.00
 7     Car Rental          49.00   49.00   49.00   49.00   49.00           245.00
 8     Hotel               68.00   68.00   68.00   68.00   68.00           340.00
 9     Breakfast           4.50    4.75    4.25    5.25    4.35            23.10
10     Lunch               5.75    5.15    6.15    3.75    5.25            26.05
11     Dinner              18.00   16.35   22.25   18.55   15.75           90.90
12     Local Travel        8.75    4.50    3.75    12.00   8.00            37.00
13     Miscellaneous       6.00    7.50    6.25    5.15    4.50            29.40
14
15     Daily Total  0.00   518.00  155.25  159.65  161.70  154.85  0.00    1,149.45
16
17
18
19
20
A1                                                                    TRAVEL1.WKS
Press ALT to choose commands.
```

Figure 3-25

Starting the Spreadsheet File If you already are using *Works*, then select **File/New**. If not, start Works and then select **Spreadsheet/New**. Notice that *Works* gives this new spreadsheet the name **SHEET2.WKS**. This is because we have not exited from the program since we used **SHEET1.WKS**.

The Spreadsheet: An Introduction

Entering the Labels and Values

As is always the case when we set up a new spreadsheet, our first activity will be to enter the labels, so that we will know what the spreadsheet is all about. Remember that if you make a mistake while entering a label, just use the **BACKSPACE** key to correct what you have typed. If you do not catch your mistake in time, you may always retype the label and then enter it into the cell again.

1. In cell *C3*, type: **Travel Expense Report**
2. In cell *A4*, type: **Categories**
3. In cells *B4* through *I4*, enter the following:

> **Sun**
> **Mon**
> **Tues**
> **Weds**
> **Thur**
> **Fri**
> **Sat**
> **Total**

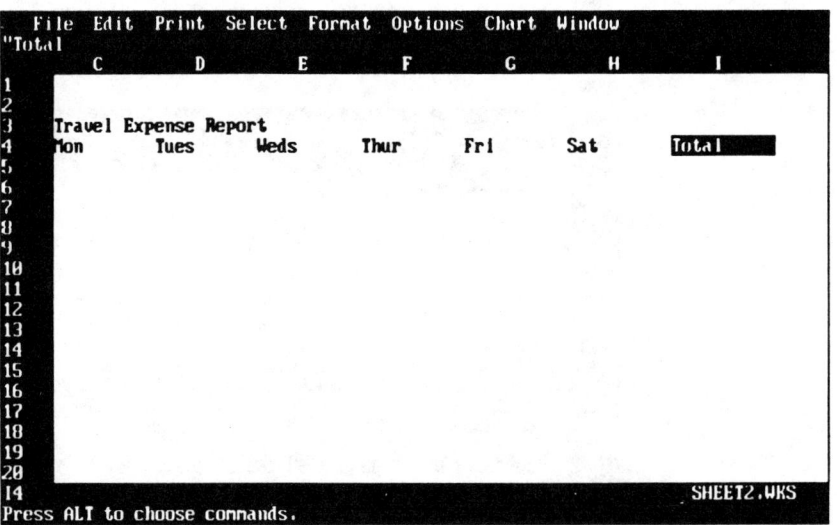

Figure 3-26

Note: These labels run horizontally across your spreadsheet, beyond the width of the screen, causing it to scroll right. This means it is impossible to read all of the labels at one time. In a moment we will correct this problem by adjusting the width of the labels.

Changing Column Widths

4. Enter the following labels in cells A6 through A13:

   Air Fare
   Car Rental
   Hotel
   Breakfast
   Lunch
   Dinner
   Local Travel
   Miscellaneous

   When you are done, your spreadsheet should resemble Figure 3-27. (Don't worry about the fact that some of the labels in column A are too wide to fit in the column; we will fix this problem in a moment.)

5. Select **File/Save**.

6. If you are saving your data in Drive A, type: **A:Travel1** and press **ENTER**.

   If you are saving your data in Drive B, type: **B:Travel1** and press **ENTER**.

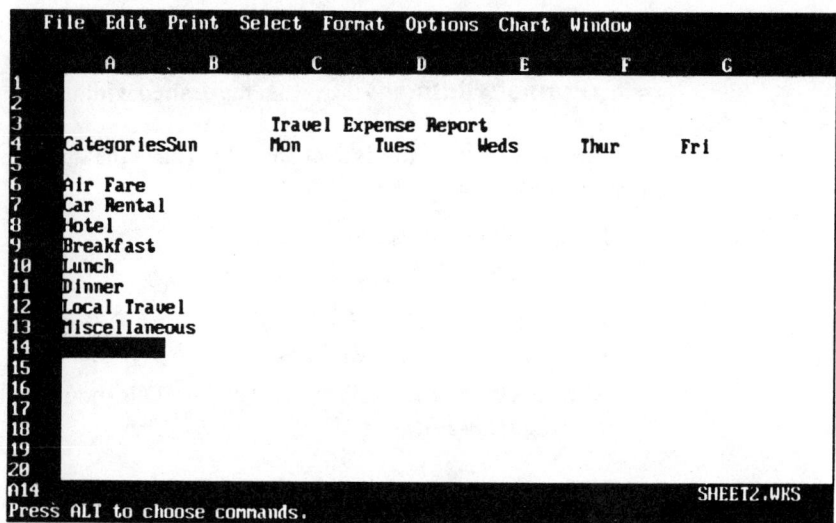

Figure 3-27

Changing Column Widths We have two problems on our hands; some labels are too wide for the column they are in, and other labels cannot be seen. We need to use the **Format/Width** command. Here goes:

1. Place your cursor in column A on the widest label.

2. Select **Format/Width**.

   The default width is *10*. To fit the widest of these labels in column A, and to leave one extra space between it and column B, increase the width by four.

The Spreadsheet: An Introduction

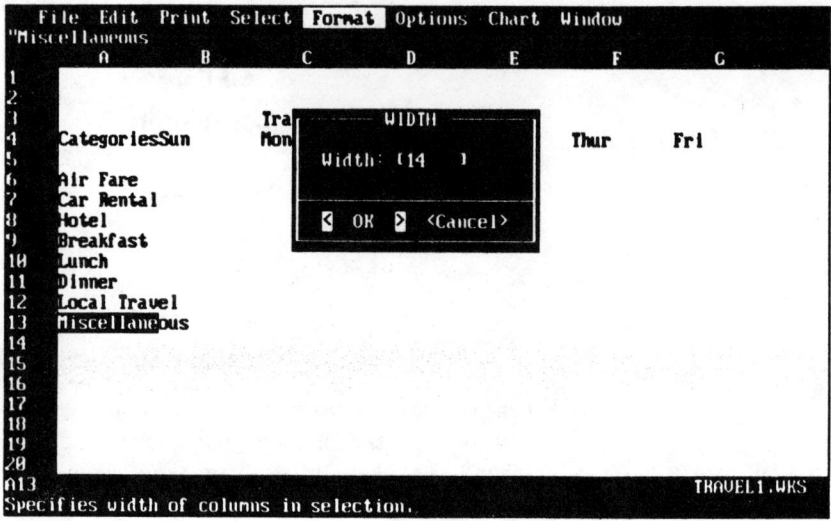

Figure 3-28

3. Type: **14** and press **ENTER** (Figure 3-28).

We would like to make columns B through I narrower, so that we can see all of them at one time. One way to do this is to move the cursor to each column in turn, select **Format/Width**, and then enter the desired width. This will work; it just takes time.

A second way to do this is to change them all at the same time. To try this, follow along below:

1. Move your cursor to cell *B4*.
2. Press **F8** and **EXTEND** the highlight to *I4*.
3. Select **Format/Width**.
4. Type: **7** and press **ENTER**.
5. Press the **HOME** key. Now all of the labels should be visible on your screen (Figure 3-29).

Right Justifying Labels

While we are thinking about the labels, let's also **right justify** them, in anticipation of adding values to the cells.

1. Move the cursor to cell *B4*. Press **F8**.
2. **EXTEND** the highlight to cell *I4*.
3. Select **Format/Style**.
4. Select **Right** and press **ENTER**.

Entering Values

For this part of the exercise, we will add some values and then learn a few shortcuts.

In column C (*Mon*) enter the following:

Entering Values

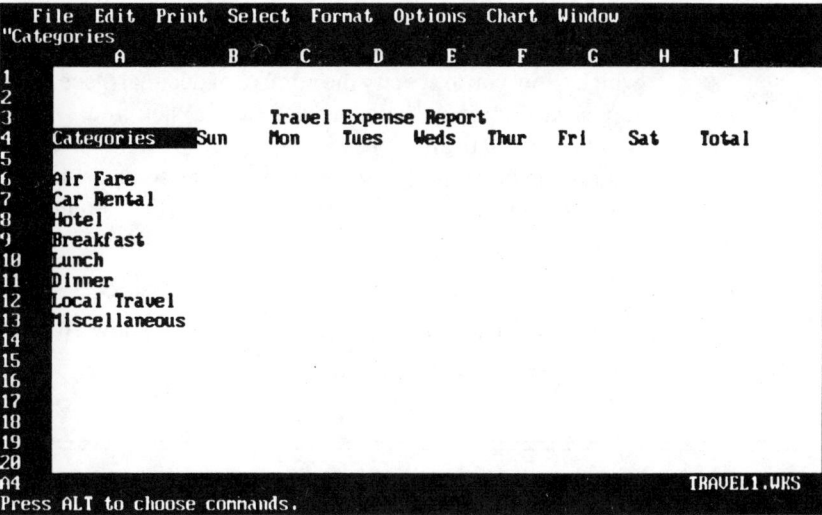

Figure 3-29

Air Fare	358
Car Rental	49
Hotel	68
Breakfast	4.5
Lunch	5.75
Dinner	18
Local Travel	8.75
Miscellaneous	6

We have a problem! Our numbers are not lining up correctly, with the decimal point in the right location (Figure 3-30).

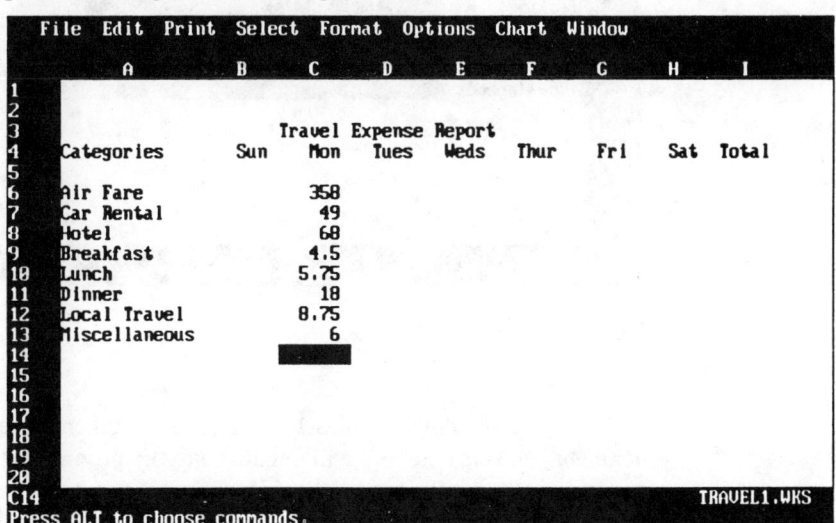

Figure 3-30

The Spreadsheet: An Introduction

This is because the default format for values is to enter them with whatever number of decimal places you type. Works has five other value formats, however, which allow you to specify the number of decimal places and also what the numbers represent (currency, percentages, etc.). When you select one of these formats, Works automatically types in the specified number of decimal places, so your values line up properly. Since we are going to be using uneven dollar amounts in some of our work on this spreadsheet, let's format the entire spreadsheet now, so that as we enter our values, each will appear with the same number of decimal places.

1. Move your cursor to cell *B6* and press **F8**.
2. **EXTEND** the highlight over to *I6* and down to *I13*.
3. Select **Format/Comma**.

Note: We did *not* select **Format/Dollar** for a very specific reason. If we had done so, every single value would have had a dollar sign ($) in front of it. Such formatting is very hard to read. For that reason, we often select **Format/Comma** when we are working with dollars.

---

4. The default for the Number of Decimals is *2*. Press **ENTER** to accept that. Notice the improvement (Figure 3-31)!

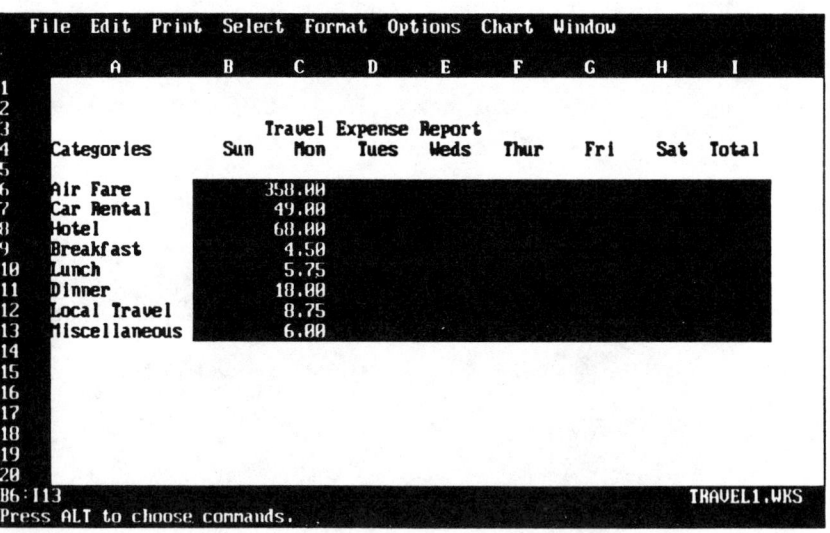

Figure 3-31

Before we enter more values, let's think for a moment. It seems likely that the car rental bill and the hotel bill will remain constant throughout the week, since the car costs a certain flat fee every day, as does the base cost for the hotel room. Let's see how we can enter that information once and then just reuse it whenever necessary.

Using Formulas and Functions   99

1. Move the cursor to cell *C7* and press **F8**.
2. **EXTEND** the highlight to cell *G7*.
3. Select **Edit/Fill Right**.

We could have used the **Edit/Copy** command outlined earlier in the chapter, but that method copies the contents of a cell to only one other cell at a time. When we need to copy the contents of a cell to a range of adjacent cells in the same row, **Edit/Fill Right** is much more efficient.

Notice that the number *49* appears (correctly formatted) in cells *C7* through *G7*. Now we will do the same thing to enter the Hotel information in cells *C8* through *G8*.

1. Move the cursor to cell *C8* and press **F8**.
2. **EXTEND** the highlight to cell *G8*.
3. Select **Edit/Fill Right**.

Enter the remaining values for Tuesday through Friday:

	Tues	*Weds*	*Thur*	*Fri*
Breakfast	**4.75**	**4.25**	**5.25**	**4.35**
Lunch	**5.15**	**6.15**	**3.75**	**5.25**
Dinner	**16.35**	**22.25**	**18.55**	**15.75**
Local Travel	**4.50**	**3.75**	**12.00**	**8.00**
Miscellaneous	**7.50**	**6.25**	**5.15**	**4.50**

SAVE your spreadsheet again. It should resemble Figure 3-32.

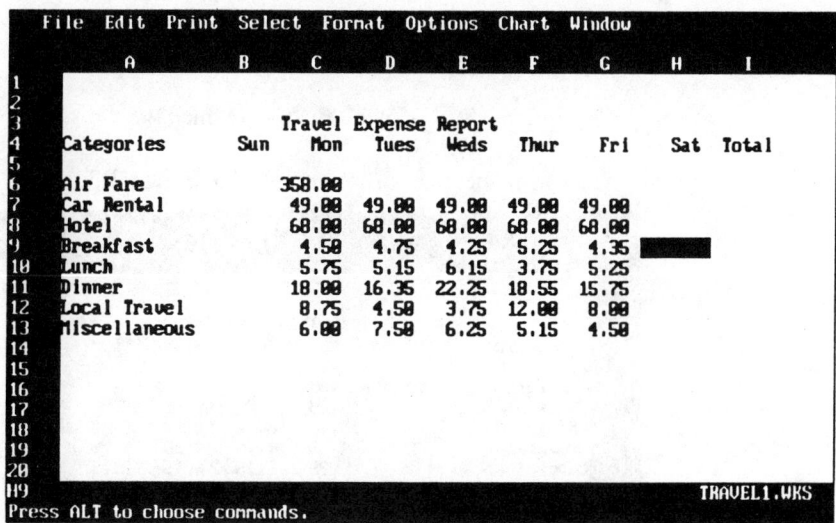

Figure 3-32

Using Formulas and Functions The purpose of developing this spreadsheet was so that we could quickly keep track of our Travel Expenses. Daily and weekly totals are essential if we are to do this. Column I already is labeled *Total* to provide us with our weekly totals. Type the

100 The Spreadsheet: An Introduction

label **Daily Total** in cell *A15*, to indicate that row 15 will provide us with that information.

Now we could use a formula in cell *B15* that will provide us with the daily totals. Once we have that, we can copy it across for the rest of the week.

Our goal is to add up the range of cells from *B6* through *B13*. One way to do this is to create a formula as we did before, by using the POINT method. A quicker way is to use one of the 57 **functions** found in *Works*.

A function is a built-in calculation or formula, and by using it we avoid having to type in the arithmetic operator (+, -, *, /). To use a function we type its name, and then tell it what values to act upon. For example, we will use the SUM function to add up this column of numbers.

Note: The word **SUM** must be preceded by an equal sign (=) so that *Works* recognizes that we are about to enter a formula, not a label.

---

1. Move the cursor to cell *B15* and type the formula:

   =SUM(B6:B13)

2. Press **ENTER**.

This formula tells *Works* to add the range of information from cell *B6* through cell *B13*. A zero (*0*) should appear in cell *B15*, since there presently is no data in that column.

3. Move the cursor to cell *I6* and type the formula:

   =SUM(B6:H6)

4. Press **ENTER**.

The number *358.00* should appear, since we did spend 358.00 for an airplane ticket on Monday.

The spreadsheet now should resemble Figure 3-33.

```
 File  Edit  Print  Select  Format  Options  Chart  Window
=SUM(B6:H6)
           A         B       C       D       E       F       G     H    I
 1
 2
 3                        Travel Expense Report
 4   Categories    Sun     Mon     Tues    Weds    Thur    Fri   Sat  Total
 5
 6   Air Fare             358.00                                          358.00
 7   Car Rental            49.00   49.00   49.00   49.00   49.00
 8   Hotel                 68.00   68.00   68.00   68.00   68.00
 9   Breakfast              4.50    4.75    4.25    5.25    4.35
10   Lunch                  5.75    5.15    6.15    3.75    5.25
11   Dinner                18.00   16.35   22.25   18.55   15.75
12   Local Travel           8.75    4.50    3.75   12.00    8.00
13   Miscellaneous          6.00    7.50    6.25    5.15    4.50
14
15   Daily Total    0
16
17
18
19
20
I6                                                                TRAVEL1.WKS
Press ALT to choose commands.
```

Figure 3-33

Using Formulas and Functions 101

To copy the formula in *B15* across row 15, perform the following steps:

1. Move the cursor to cell *B15* and press **F8**.
2. **EXTEND** the highlight to *I15*.
3. Select **Edit/Fill Right**.

Row 15 was not formatted in the previous steps, so while this range is highlighted let's format the values.

1. Select **Format/Comma**.
2. Format the values with **2** decimal places.

To copy the formula in *I6* down column I, perform the following steps:

1. Move the cursor to cell *I6*, press **F8**.
2. **EXTEND** the highlight to cell *I15*.
3. Select **Edit/Fill Down**.

Just as **Edit/Fill Right** allows us to copy from one cell to a range of adjacent cells on the same row, **Edit/Fill Down** allows us to copy from one cell to a range of adjacent cells in the same column, quickly and efficiently.

Column I is filled with values, except for cell *I15*, which now has a series of ###### symbols in it. This is because the number in cell *I15* is too wide for the cell. When we make the column wide enough, the number will be displayed properly.

1. With your cursor still in column I, select **Format/Width**.
2. Type: **9** and press **ENTER**.

   Now your spreadsheet should resemble Figure 3-34.

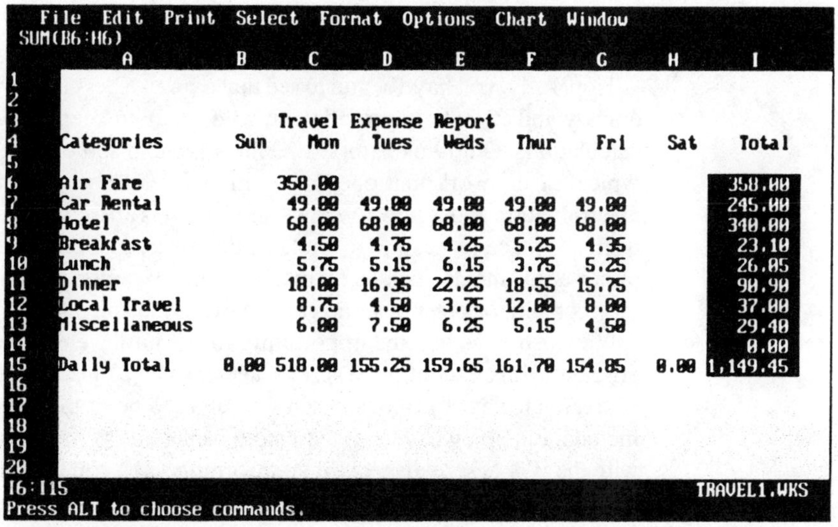

Figure 3-34

The *0.00* is displayed in cell *I14* since the formula is adding all blank values. Let's erase the contents of cell *I14* so the spreadsheet looks cleaner. The **Edit/Clear**

The Spreadsheet: An Introduction

command can be used to erase the contents of the cell containing the cursor. It also can be used to erase a range of cells that has been highlighted using **F8**.

1. Move your cursor to cell *I14*.
2. Select **Edit/Clear**.
3. **SAVE** your spreadsheet.

Printing the Spreadsheet As before, there are many options available to you within the Print menu. For the moment, however, we will ignore most of them, and just print out our newly completed spreadsheet, **TRAVEL1.WKS**. Here is how to do that:

1. Specify the range of cells to be printed. Move your cursor to cell *A1* and press **F8**.
2. **EXTEND** the highlight to cells *A1* through *I15*.
3. Select **Print/Set Print Area**.
4. Select **Print/Layout**.
5. Change the left margin to: **0.5"**
6. Change the right margin to: **0.5"**
7. Press **ENTER**.
8. Select **Print/Print**, and press **ENTER** to accept the print defaults.

Conclusion

This chapter has provided you with an introduction to the spreadsheet module found in *Works*. For many people, the concepts of setting up a spreadsheet are new and sometimes seem unfamiliar for a while.

Hopefully, you have begun to see that a spreadsheet is a powerful tool, which can quickly and efficiently provide you with a way to keep track of complex financial calculations. Our two examples, while simple in some respects, in many ways are typical of the work that one does with a spreadsheet. There is always the initial determination about how the rows and columns are to be labeled. Then one usually begins to place values and formulas into the spreadsheet. Finally, there are all of the minor adjustments such as formatting cells to better present the information that they contain, or erasing some cells to clean the spreadsheet up a bit.

You also have had the opportunity to see how we can become more and more efficient with our continued spreadsheet mastery. Initially we had to type in the cell addresses for our formulas. Then we began to point to the cells that we wished to include. Finally, we were able to incorporate one of the many functions that come with the *Works* spreadsheet into our formulas. As you have seen, each one of these steps provides us with greater power for less work.

Independent Spreadsheet Project No. 1

Key Terms

The following are the important terms and commands that have been introduced and explained in this chapter:

Formula Bar	Cell	Active Cell
Label	Value	Pointing
Range	Function	Edit/Copy
Edit/Fill Right	Edit/Fill Down	Format/Style
Format/Width	Format/Comma	Format/Dollar
Left Justify	Right Justify	Print/Set Print Area
Relative Cell Adjustment		

Independent Spreadsheet Project No. 1

In this first independent project, you will set up a simple spreadsheet that will enable you to determine the cost of purchasing some sporting goods for a community athletic program. The completed spreadsheet resembles Figure 3-35.

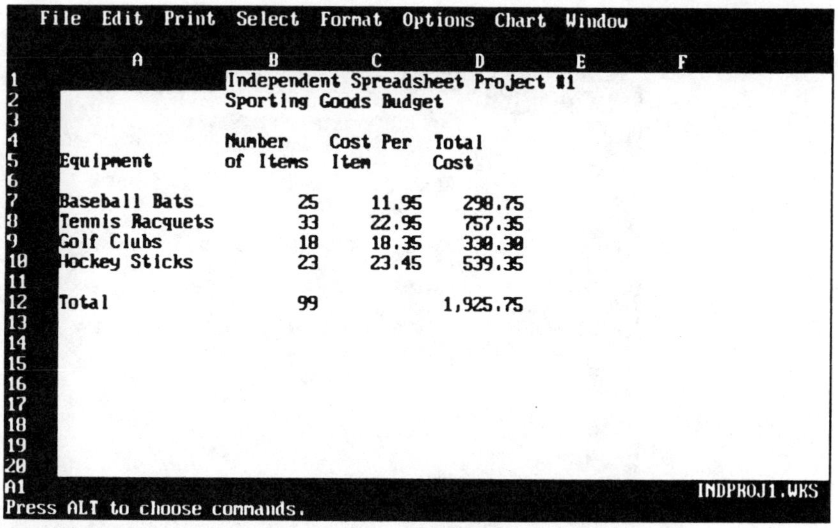

```
 File  Edit  Print  Select  Format  Options  Chart  Window
        A         B         C         D         E         F
 1               Independent Spreadsheet Project #1
 2               Sporting Goods Budget
 3
 4               Number   Cost Per  Total
 5   Equipment   of Items Item      Cost
 6
 7   Baseball Bats    25    11.95    298.75
 8   Tennis Racquets  33    22.95    757.35
 9   Golf Clubs       18    18.35    330.30
10   Hockey Sticks    23    23.45    539.35
11
12   Total            99             1,925.75
13
14
15
16
17
18
19
20
A1                                              INDPROJ1.WKS
Press ALT to choose commands.
```

Figure 3-35

Here are some hints to help you complete the project:

1. Be sure to type in all of your labels first. You will probably find that column A needs to be widened to accommodate the labels.
2. Enter the values in columns B and C for rows 7 through 10.
3. Enter a formula in cell *B12* that will total the number of items to be purchased. Copy this formula to cell *D12*.

4. Enter a formula in cell *D7* that will generate the result of the Number of Items times the Cost Per Item.

5. Either continue to enter this formula for the remaining cells in column D, or use the **Edit/Copy** or the **Edit/Fill Down** commands to copy the formula in cell *D7* to the other cells.

6. If you choose to do so, you could format some of the values so that they appear with dollar signs, and you might wish to format the labels at the top of columns B, C, and D so that they are more directly above the values in those columns. Suit yourself!

7. Save the spreadsheet as **INDPROJ1.WKS**.

8. Print out a copy of your spreadsheet.

Independent Spreadsheet Project No. 2

In this second project, we are going to put together a spreadsheet that will reflect a departmental budget for two years' worth of expenses. The supervisor wishes to have the budget reflect the percent of change for each category, in addition to the actual dollar differences. When you are done, your spreadsheet should resemble the one depicted in Figure 3-36.

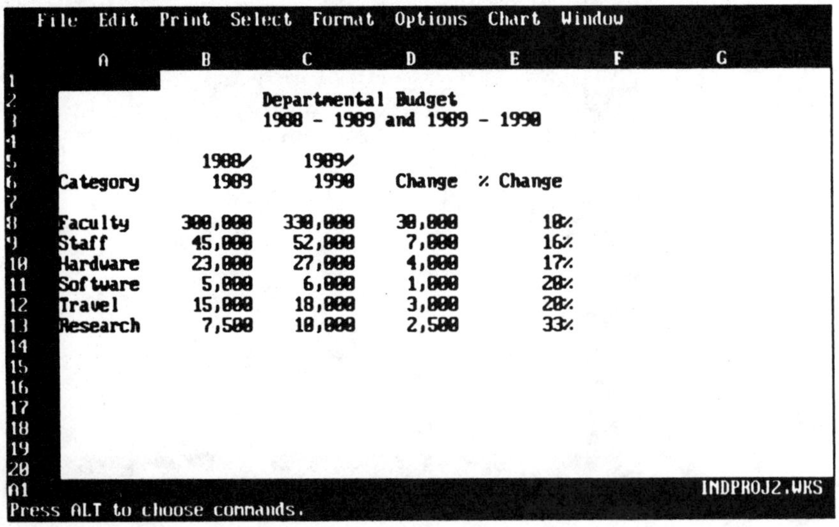

Category	1988/1989	1989/1990	Change	% Change
Faculty	300,000	330,000	30,000	18%
Staff	45,000	52,000	7,000	16%
Hardware	23,000	27,000	4,000	17%
Software	5,000	6,000	1,000	20%
Travel	15,000	18,000	3,000	20%
Research	7,500	10,000	2,500	33%

Departmental Budget
1988 - 1989 and 1989 - 1990

Figure 3-36

Here are some hints to help you complete the project:

1. First type in all of the column headings and the labels that will be needed in column A. You will have to widen column A so that they all will fit. Also, if you wish to use the dates 1988, 1989, and 1990 as labels, you should be sure to precede them with a quote symbol in the cells in which they are not followed by a slash.

Independent Spreadsheet Project No. 1

2. Next, enter the values for columns B and C.
3. Then enter a formula for cell *D8* that reflects the difference between the amounts being spent in 1989/1990 and 1988/1989.
4. When you are sure that the formula is correct, copy it down column D.
5. Next, enter a formula that reflects the percent of change. This can be done by dividing the actual amount of the change by the original amount. In this case the original amount is the 1988/1989 figure.
6. When you are sure that the formula is correct, copy it down column E.
7. Now format the values in columns B, C, and D so that they all have commas in them and no decimal points.
8. Next, format the values in column E so that they are percents with no decimal points.
9. If you wish to be fancy, you could format all of the labels above columns B, C, D, and E so that the labels are right justified.
10. Finally, save your spreadsheet as **INDPROJ2.WKS**, and print out a copy of it.

Chapter 4  The Database Manager: An Introduction

In this chapter you will learn how to:

- Design a database file.
- Enter information into the database.
- View information in the database.
- Change the width of the fields displaying information.
- Search for information in the database.
- Print information in the database.

What is a Database?

A database is an organized way to keep track of a lot of information. One of the most familiar examples might be the telephone book, in which we are able to access data about particular individuals in a quick and efficient fashion. In addition, we often have data for the groups that we belong to, the various colleges or jobs to which we are applying, the names of all of the records or stamps in our collection, or the names of all of the clients to whom we are giving piano lessons or whose houses we are painting.

A database, although in some respects similar to a spreadsheet, is in many ways quite different. If the work that we are doing has a great deal of numerical information in it, and if there are lots of relationships among that information, then a spreadsheet is the logical tool for us to be using. However, if we are dealing primarily with people, and the streets they live on, and the cities and states within which they live, then a database is the correct choice. In addition, a good database also can become an important part of your word processing and spreadsheet work.

Starting a Database File

From the Main Menu If you have just loaded *Works* into your computer's memory, the familiar Main Menu screen should appear. The third option on the screen is **Database** and the

107

The Database Manager: An Introduction

<New> Button is in highlighted brackets. The Message Line states that by selecting this option you will create a new *Works* file. Move your cursor down to **Database** and press **ENTER**.

From Works If you already are using *Works*, select **File/New** to open the NEW Dialog Box. Then select **Database** and enter the tool.

Designing a Database

When we begin to use a database, the first thing that we must decide is what information we wish to include. Thinking about Paul's piano students and Debbie's painting clients might help us to see this more clearly. Let's consider Paul's data needs first.

Database Project No. 1
Paul's Piano Students

While completing this project you will:

- Design a database for Paul's students.
- Enter information about them.
- View the information in the database.
- Edit information.
- Change the width of the fields displaying the information.
- Search for specific information.
- Print the database.

When Paul contemplates setting up a database, he begins to think about the kind of information he would like to have about each student. Probably he would like to have their names, addresses, and phone numbers, as well as the day and hour of their scheduled lessons. He might also include the names of their brothers and sisters, and the names of their parents. And if he were going to try to keep track of how the students came to him, he might wish to record whether it was through his advertising campaign, his most recent concert, or a referral from a friend.

Each one of these different categories is known in the world of database management as a **field**. So a partial list of fields for Paul might include the following:

First Name:

Last Name:

Address:

City:

State:

Zip:

A Tour of the Form Design Screen

Phone:

Siblings:

Mother's Name:

Father's Name:

Lesson Day:

Lesson Time:

Referred by:

An entire collection of these fields for one individual is called a **record**. Each record includes a full set of fields, some (or all) of which have information in them.

The entire set of records for Paul's piano students is called a **file**.

There can be no database until we first define the fields to be included. Therefore, the *Works* database takes us directly to the DESIGN screen, where we have the opportunity to define our fields. Let's look at the DESIGN screen (Figure 4-1).

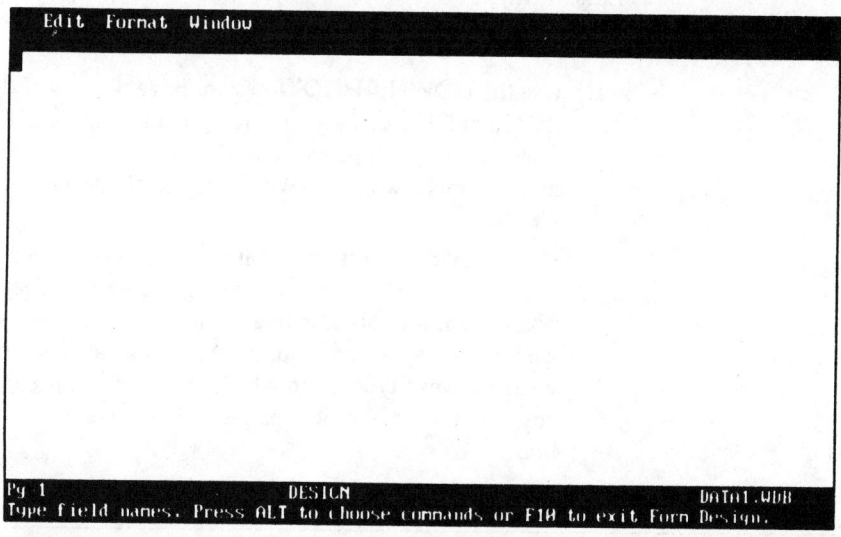

Figure 4-1

A Tour of the Form Design Screen Across the top of the DESIGN screen is the Menu Bar. Notice that it resembles much of what you already have seen when you were using the word processor and the spreadsheet. As you would expect, the Menu Bar provides us with some of the options available within the database. You may enter any of these menu choices as you have done earlier. Press the **ALT** key, which will highlight one letter on each of the menus, and then either press the bold letter in the menu name or use the **ARROW** keys and press **ENTER**.

At the bottom of the screen is the Status Line. In the far left corner of the Status Line we are told that we are on *Pg 1*. In the center of the Status Line is the word *DESIGN*. In the far right-hand corner of the Status Line (as you might expect) is the name of the current database, **DATA1.WDB**.

As we have seen with both the word processor and the spreadsheet, *Works* automatically will give your new file (in this case your new database file) a name, until you select **File/Save** for the first time and name it yourself.

The Database Manager: An Introduction

At the very bottom of the screen is the Message Line. This line, which presently says *Type field names. Press ALT to choose commands or F10 to exit Form Design*, will send you messages as you enter and modify information.

Entering Field Names

Entering field names onto the DESIGN screen is quite simple. We would like to start setting up the database that Paul is going to use to keep track of his piano students. Rather than be fancy about it now, we just quickly will set up the most fundamental parts of the database. We will include the name of each of his students, their phone number, and the day when they take their lessons.

Here are the field names that we need:

First Name:

Last Name:

Phone Number:

Lesson Day:

Now, let's enter these field names onto our database.

1. Use the **DOWN ARROW** key to move the cursor down a few lines from the top of DESIGN screen, and type the first field's name with a colon (:) after it. It is very important that you always type a colon after entering a field name, as this is what tells *Works* that the field name is complete. Type: **First Name:**

   Notice that the words appear at the top of your screen, on what we called the Formula Bar when we were using the spreadsheet (Figure 4-2). At this point, the information is in a similar holding zone on the database, where we have the opportunity to review it and to change it if we choose. Review what you have typed, and when you are done, use your **DOWN ARROW** key to enter the first field name and to move your cursor down one or two lines.

Note: Just as in the Spreadsheet tool, information can be entered from the Formula Bar onto the screen by pressing the **ENTER** key or an **ARROW** key. We will press the **DOWN ARROW** key as a shortcut; it will position the cursor for the next field.

---

2. Now we would like to enter the second field. Type in the following, and then use your DOWN ARROW key when you are done.

   Last Name:

Reminder: Be sure to type a colon at the end of the field name.

---

3. Let's add the third field. Type:

   Phone Number:

Entering Field Names 111

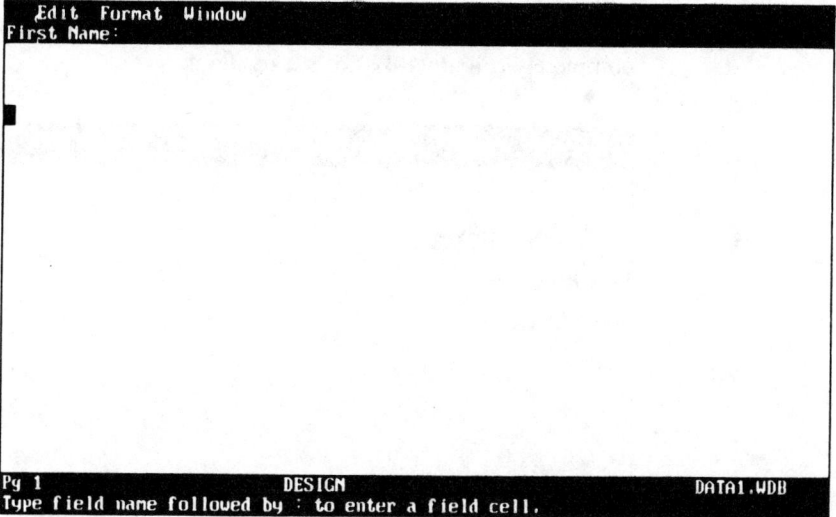

Figure 4-2

Use your **DOWN ARROW** to move the cursor down a few lines.

4. Let's add the final field. Type:

Lesson Day:

Follow this by a **DOWN ARROW**, even though you are not going to enter any more field names at the moment (Figure 4-3).

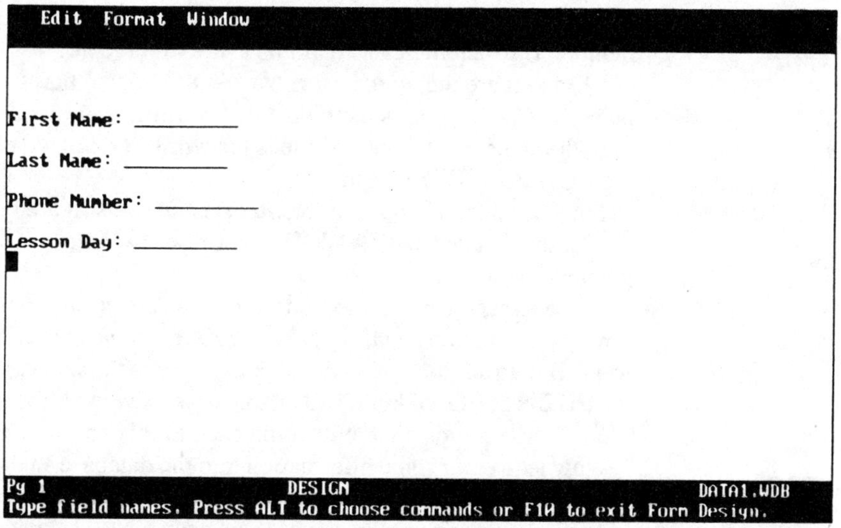

Figure 4-3

5. Since we are done entering field names, press function key **F10**.

Entering Data You probably noticed that as soon as you press **F10** that your whole screen changed completely (Figure 4-4). Let's take a look.

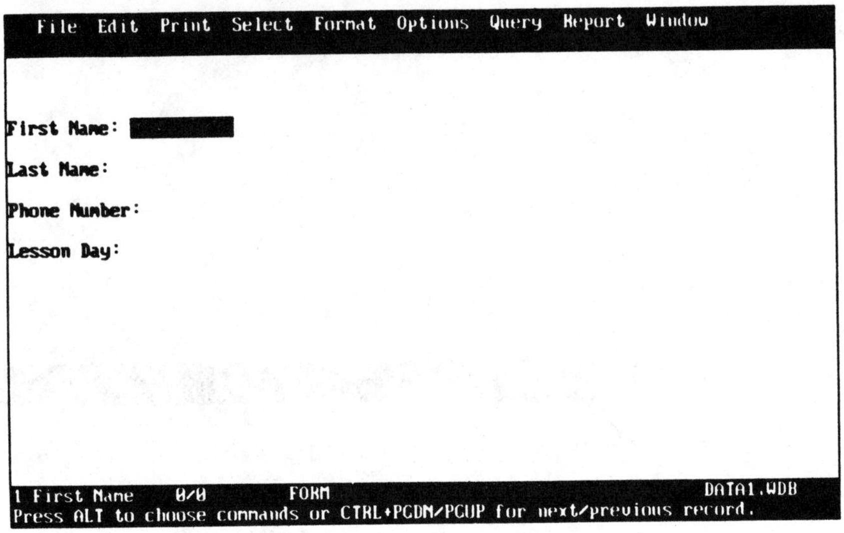

Figure 4-4

The Menu Bar is much more extensive than it was before. There are options such as **File**, **Edit**, and **Format**, which we have seen repeatedly, as well as some new ones such as **Query** and **Report**.

Your cursor is at the top of the screen, and there is a large space marked off next to the field *First Name:*.

The Status Line provides us with quite a bit of information. On the far left is the number *1*, which indicates that this is the first record.

Next to it are the words *First Name*, to indicate that the field that is presently being filled with data is the field *First Name:*.

In the center of the Status Line is the word *FORM*, which tells us that we are in the *FORM ENTRY* screen.

Finally, on the far right of the Status Line, we still are being told that we are in the database called **DATA1.WDB**, since we have not yet saved this database and given it a new name.

The Message Line at the bottom of the screen provides us with the (by now) familiar instruction that if we press the **ALT** key we may select commands from the Menu Bar. In addition, we are told that the use of the **CTRL** key, in conjunction with the **PGDN** or **PGUP** keys, will enable us to examine information on either the next or previous records. (We will come back to this option in a few moments.)

Now let's enter some information into the database so that we can begin to get a feel for how it works. When you enter the information for each field, it will appear in the holding zone at the top of the screen first. Use the **BACKSPACE** key to correct any typing errors, and then press your **DOWN ARROW** key to enter the information at the field and to move down to the next field.

After you enter the information for the fourth field, however, press **ENTER** instead of the **DOWN ARROW**, so that you don't move immediately to the next record.

Entering Data 113

> ***Note:*** Don't worry for now if you notice errors after information is entered at a field. (We will discuss editing data a little further on in the chapter.)

Here is the information for the first record:

1. First Name: **Peter**
   Last Name: **McCarthy**
   Phone Number: **764-8765**
   Lesson Day: **Monday**

When you have finished, your screen should resemble Figure 4-5.

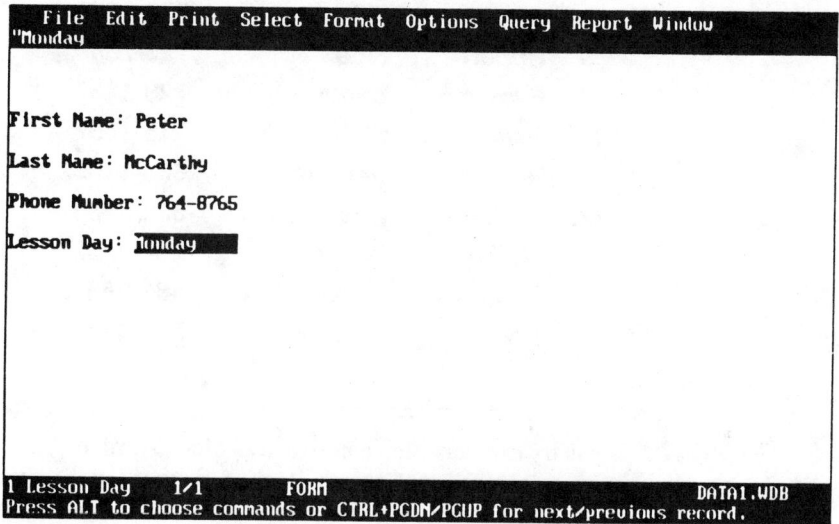

Figure 4-5

Now press your **DOWN ARROW** key to move to the next record. The data for the next four students is listed below:

2. First Name: **Deborah**
   Last Name: **Jones**
   Phone Number: **764-1234**
   Lesson Day: **Tuesday**

3. First Name: **Billy**
   Last Name: **Williams**
   Phone Number: **861-7896**
   Lesson Day: **Wednesday**

4. *First Name:* **Marcy**
   Last Name: **McAllister**
   Phone Number: **764-1424**
   Lesson Day: **Thursday**

5. *First Name:* **Aric**
   Last Name: **Press**
   Phone Number: **764-8765**
   Lesson Day: **Monday**

Now enter the information for the rest of Paul's piano students:

	First Name	Last Name	Phone Number	Day
6.	George	Hackett	725-1465	Tuesday
7.	Jennifer	Skinner	725-8796	Monday
8.	Robert	Fine	723-7659	Wednesday
9.	Eva	Betka	723-1237	Thursday
10.	Sam	Siebert	235-1987	Friday
11.	Ronald	Henkoff	636-1965	Monday
12.	Barbara	Rosen	632-5436	Tuesday
13.	William	Lipinski	237-4532	Monday
14.	Tom	Morganthau	681-8907	Thursday
15.	Noelle	Gaffney	576-4378	Friday

Note: If you try to enter a first name such as Marc, April, or June, *Works* assumes you are entering a month, and enters only the first three letters of the name (Mar, Apr, Jun). To enter the name, or partial name, of a month as text, type a quote before the rest of the entry (e.g., **"Marc**, etc.). (See the Practice Exercise in the Spreadsheet chapter.)

Saving a Database The data in your database is precious and is worth saving on a regular basis. Let's do so now.

1. Select **File/Save**. Since this is the first time that you are saving data, notice that the SAVE AS Dialog Box appears (Figure 4-6). Just as with the word processor and the spreadsheet, Works assumes that the first time you save a file, you will want to give it a name other than the one that has been assigned by the program, in this case, **DATA1**.

   Each time you first save data in a *new* database, the SAVE AS Dialog Box will appear to let you rename the database. Once you have done so, if you select **File/Save** to save additional data, *Works* will save the data using the name that you have provided and will replace the preceding version of the file.

Viewing Records in the Database 115

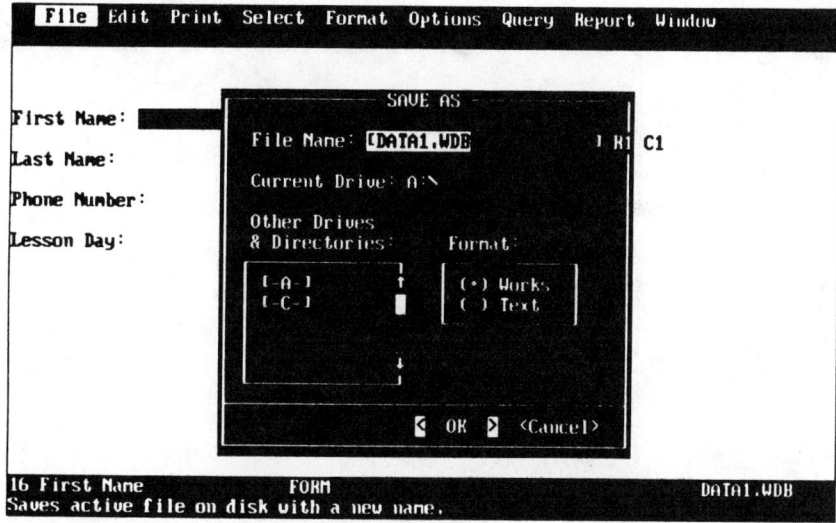

Figure 4-6

2. Make sure that the Current Drive indicates the name of the drive containing your data disk (*A:* or *B:*). If it doesn't, select the correct drive from the Other Drives & Directories List Box.
3. For our file name, we will use **PIANO**. Works automatically will add the extension **.WDB** (*Works* Data Base) to the file name. Type: **PIANO**
4. Press **ENTER**.

Viewing Records in the Database When we set up a database in *Works*, we initially are using the database in what is known as *Form View*. Each record (remember, that means a set of information about a particular individual) is displayed as a separate form, and may be viewed simply by using a combination of keys. To move to the *previous* record in *Form View*:

1. Press the **CTRL** key, and while holding it down, press the **PGUP** key. **CTRL+PGUP** will move you back through the database, so that you may see one or several of the previous records. Try this now, until you are looking at the first record in the database, that of **Peter McCarthy** (Figure 4-7).

To move to the *next* record in *Form View*:

1. Be sure that you have Peter McCarthy's form on your screen. Now, press down the **CTRL** key, and while holding it down, press down the **PGDN** key. **CTRL+PGDN** will move you forward through the database, so that you may see one or several of the next records. Try this now until you have reached Noelle Gaffney's record (Figure 4-8).

Warning: When you reach the end of the database in *Form View*, it is possible to continue past it by continuing to press **CTRL+PGDN**. If you do this now, you will be able to look at lots of blank records. You have not done anything wrong; you just have reached the end of the database.

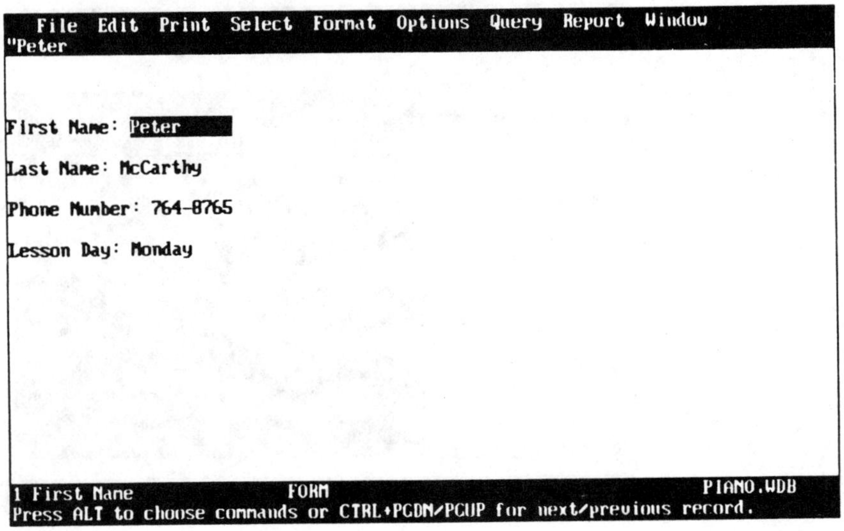

The Database Manager: An Introduction

```
 File  Edit  Print  Select  Format  Options  Query  Report  Window
"Peter


First Name: Peter
Last Name: McCarthy
Phone Number: 764-8765
Lesson Day: Monday





1 First Name              FORM                              PIANO.WDB
Press ALT to choose commands or CTRL+PGDN/PGUP for next/previous record.
```

Figure 4-7

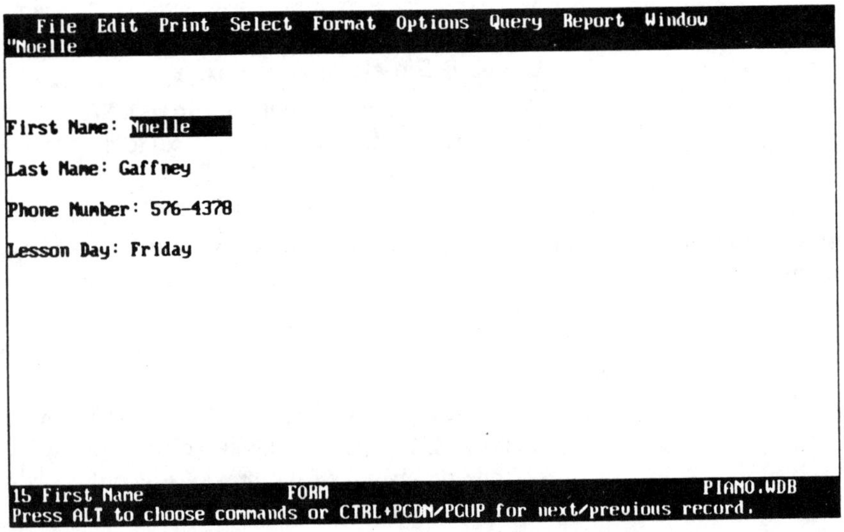

```
 File  Edit  Print  Select  Format  Options  Query  Report  Window
"Noelle


First Name: Noelle
Last Name: Gaffney
Phone Number: 576-4378
Lesson Day: Friday





15 First Name             FORM                              PIANO.WDB
Press ALT to choose commands or CTRL+PGDN/PGUP for next/previous record.
```

Figure 4-8

To move to the *very first record* in *Form View*:

1. As you may have expected, there is a quicker way to move to the very beginning of your database. Just press **CTRL+HOME**, and you will return instantly to the first record in the database, that of Peter McCarthy. Try this now.

To move to the *very last record* in *Form View*:

1. Press **CTRL+END**. Notice that it takes you to the record *after* the final one in your database, in anticipation that you might wish to enter some additional information.

Changing from List View to Form View

2. Press **CTRL+PGUP** to view the final record.

Using List View to View Records

Works also provides us with the ability to see many records at once, in a list, in what is known as *List View*. It is easy to do this. Follow along.

1. Select **Options/View List**. Your screen should resemble that shown in Figure 4-9. Notice that the cursor is on the same field and record as it was in *Form View*.

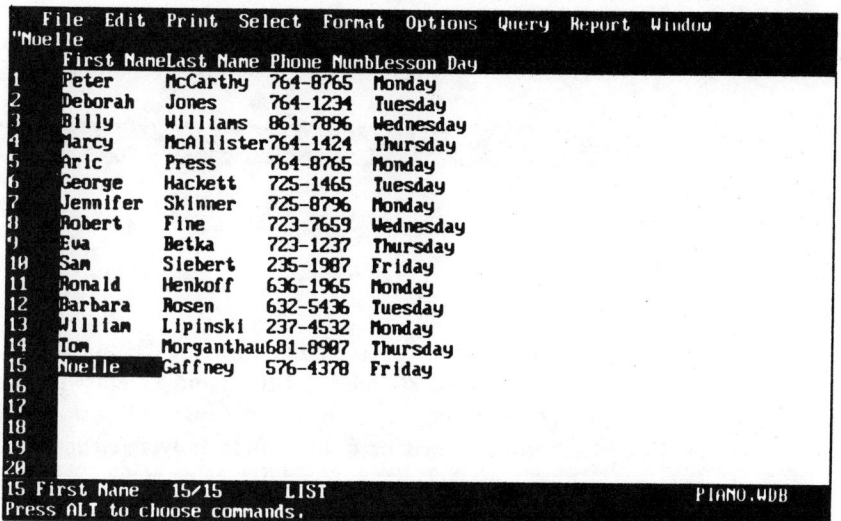

Figure 4-9

The *List View* mode of the database in many ways resembles the *Works* spreadsheet that you used earlier. Many of the keys used to move the cursor and many of the menu choices in *List View* are the same as those used in the spreadsheet.

Changing from List View to Form View Occasionally, you may wish to look at one record in more detail while you are using *List View*. Here's how:

1. Move your cursor to any field in the record that interests you. Let's move to the *First Name* field in *Aric Press's* record to see how this works.
2. Press function key **F9**. Notice that the form has appeared (Figure 4-10).

You may use **F9** at any time to move from the *List View* to the *Form View* and back.

3. Press **F9** to return to *List View*.

Note: Just as the spreadsheet only displays 20 rows on the screen at one time, so does *List View* permit us to view only 20 records at one time. The number of fields visible at any one time is also limited.

The Database Manager: An Introduction

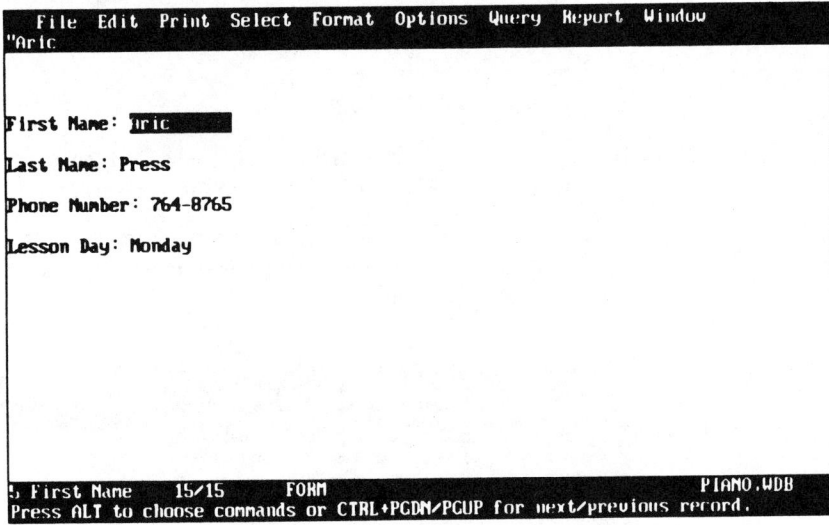

Figure 4-10

Moving Around The List

The keys used to move around *List View* are the same as those used to move around the spreadsheet. A summary of these movements follows. For a more detailed explanation see the section Moving Around a Spreadsheet in Chapter 3.

Record-to-record or **field-to-field** movement is accomplished by using the **ARROW** keys on your keyboard. Each one of the four arrows points in a particular direction. Pressing these keys will move the cursor in their respective directions.

Screen-to-screen movement allows you to jump an entire screen by pressing one of the special keys on your keyboard or a combination of keys. These keys or key combinations, and the movements that they perform, are listed below:

Keys	Movement
PGDN	Down one screen (20 records)
PGUP	Up one screen (20 records)
CTRL+PGDN	One screen to the right
CTRL+PGUP	One screen to the left

Sometimes you want to move from the beginning to the end of a record or of your file. Special keys or key combinations can be used to accomplish these **global movements**.

Keys	Movement
CTRL+HOME	Beginning of database
CTRL+END	End of database (*Note:* End of the database is defined as the intersection of the right-most field containing any data and the last record containing any data.)
HOME	First field in the current record

Changing Field Width in List View

END — Last field in the current record (*Note:* Last field is defined as the right-most field that contains information for any record, even if that field is blank for the current record.)

Changing Field Width in List View

While *List View* is certainly an improvement in one way, since we can view many of the records in our database at one time, it also has some problems. One problem is that the various fields in the database are all smashed together on the screen. While the information is visible, it is rather difficult to read it clearly. Let's see what we can do to improve this. The procedure for changing the width of a field is identical to the one we used earlier when changing cell width in the spreadsheet.

Note: It is also possible to change the width of a field in *Form View*. However, we will not look at that procedure until we do the second database project.

---

1. Move your cursor to the field you wish to widen. (Let's use the *First Name* column as an example.)
2. Now select **Format/Width**.
3. Notice that the default is 10, just as it was in the spreadsheet. Let's make it 15. Type in **15** (Figure 4-11) and press **ENTER**.

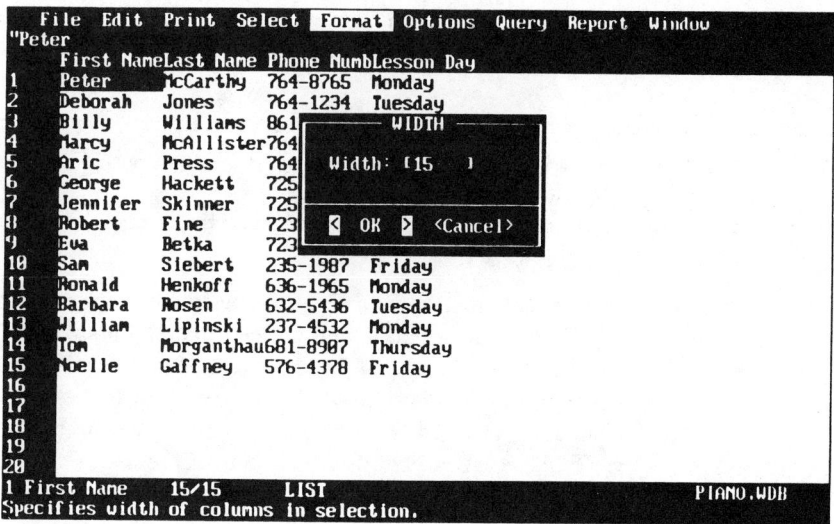

Figure 4-11

4. Now increase the width of the other fields to **15**, so that your database resembles Figure 4-12.

The Database Manager: An Introduction

```
 File  Edit  Print  Select  Format  Options  Query  Report  Window
"Monday
      First Name      Last Name      Phone Number     Lesson Day
 1   Peter           McCarthy        764-8765         Monday
 2   Deborah         Jones           764-1234         Tuesday
 3   Billy           Williams        861-7896         Wednesday
 4   Marcy           McAllister      764-1424         Thursday
 5   Aric            Press           764-8765         Monday
 6   George          Hackett         725-1465         Tuesday
 7   Jennifer        Skinner         725-8796         Monday
 8   Robert          Fine            723-7659         Wednesday
 9   Eva             Betka           723-1237         Thursday
10   Sam             Siebert         235-1987         Friday
11   Ronald          Henkoff         636-1965         Monday
12   Barbara         Rosen           632-5436         Tuesday
13   William         Lipinski        237-4532         Monday
14   Tom             Morganthau      681-8907         Thursday
15   Noelle          Gaffney         576-4378         Friday
16
17
18
19
20
1 Lesson Day    15/15    LIST                              PIANO.WDB
Press ALT to choose commands.
```

Figure 4-12

5. Save your database using **File/Save As...** Call it **PIANO2**.

Editing Data One of the challenging aspects of database management is keeping a database current and accurate. Since the data in a database frequently changes, it is important that you be able to edit this data quickly and comfortably. You also need a simple way to correct mistakes that you may have made when initially entering the data. The methods for editing data are the same as those used in the spreadsheet. Let's see how we'd edit some of the data in Paul's database.

Note: The same procedures are used to edit data in both *Form View* and *List View*. We will edit data just in *List View*.

After entering the data, Paul reviewed the index cards on which he previously kept student information and noticed that Deborah's telephone number is really 784-1234 instead of 764-1234 as you have entered in your database. Since the telephone number is short, it would be easy to simply move the cursor to the field containing Deborah's telephone number, type the entire number and press the **ENTER** key. However, *Works,* as you may remember from Chapter 2, has a special editing key that allows you to change part of an entry without retyping the whole thing. Let's try this method.

1. Move the cursor to the field containing **Deborah Jones'** telephone number.
2. Press **F2**, the **EDIT** key.

   The cursor now appears in the Formula Bar at the end of the entry, and on the Status Line we are told that we are in *EDIT* mode (Figure 4-13).

Editing Data 121

```
 File  Edit  Print  Select  Format  Options  Query  Report  Window
"764-1234
         First Name      Last Name     Phone Number    Lesson Day
 1   Peter           McCarthy        764-8765         Monday
 2   Deborah         Jones           764-1234         Tuesday
 3   Billy           Williams        861-7896         Wednesday
 4   Marcy           McAllister      764-1424         Thursday
 5   Aric            Press           764-8765         Monday
 6   George          Hackett         725-1465         Tuesday
 7   Jennifer        Skinner         725-8796         Monday
 8   Robert          Fine            723-7659         Wednesday
 9   Eva             Betka           723-1237         Thursday
10   Sam             Siebert         235-1987         Friday
11   Ronald          Henkoff         636-1965         Monday
12   Barbara         Rosen           632-5436         Tuesday
13   William         Lipinski        237-4532         Monday
14   Tom             Morganthau      681-8987         Thursday
15   Noelle          Gaffney         576-4378         Friday
16
17
18
19
20
2 Phone Number               LIST               EDIT            PIANO2.WDB
Edit formula.
```

Figure 4-13

3. Use the **LEFT ARROW** key to move the cursor under the digit that we wish to change (the *6*),
4. Type the correction: **8**
5. Press the **DEL** key to delete the *6* and press **ENTER**.

Note: The data has been changed in the database as well as on the screen. Therefore, if you press **F9**, you will notice that the data has been changed in *Form View* as well.

If you are in *Form View* return to *List View* so that you can quickly scan the data. Look carefully at the records in your list to see if you entered any data incorrectly. Then follow the general directions below to make the necessary changes.

If the amount of data in the field is *small* or most of it is incorrect:

1. Move your cursor to the information that you wish to change.
2. Retype the new information and press **ENTER**.

If the data entry to be changed is long and you only want to change one or two characters or add or delete characters:

1. Move your cursor to the field you wish to edit.
2. Press the **EDIT** key (function key **F2**).
3. You now can move your cursor to the part of the information that you wish to change, and then retype it. Delete any remaining incorrect information. Use your **ARROW** keys to move the cursor, just as you have done previously when you were editing with the spreadsheet.
4. When you are finished changing the data, press **ENTER**.

The Database Manager: An Introduction

Searching for Data Once you have assembled information in a database, the next step is to be able to use the database so that you may find specific information that you need. In Paul's case, that might mean looking for a student's phone number, or perhaps printing out a quick listing of all of his Wednesday students, or maybe printing out an alphabetical listing of his students for an upcoming recital. We will not try to do all of these right now, but they are all possible with this database once you become familiar with searching techniques.

We will work with the database called **PIANO2.WDB**. If it is not presently open, select **File/Open** to retrieve it. Then press **F9** to put it into *List View*.

Initiating a Search

1. With your database in *List View*, select **Select/Search**.
2. The SEARCH Dialog Box will appear (Figure 4-14).

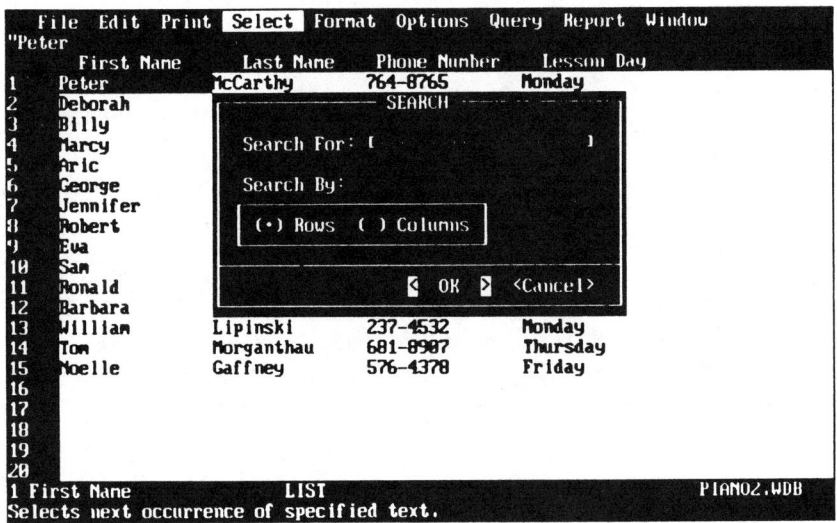

Figure 4-14

3. Type the name **Fine** in the Search For Text Box and press **ENTER**.

Note: *Works* is not case sensitive; for example, you could enter **fine** or **FINE** and it would find the data just as well.

---

4. Notice how your cursor immediately moves to the last name *Fine* (Figure 4-15).

Searching for Data 123

```
 File  Edit  Print  Select  Format  Options  Query  Report  Window
"Fine
       First Name      Last Name      Phone Number    Lesson Day
1    Peter           McCarthy        764-8765        Monday
2    Deborah         Jones           784-1234        Tuesday
3    Billy           Williams        861-7896        Wednesday
4    Marcy           McAllister      764-1424        Thursday
5    Aric            Press           764-8765        Monday
6    George          Hackett         725-1465        Tuesday
7    Jennifer        Skinner         725-8796        Monday
8    Robert          Fine            723-7659        Wednesday
9    Eva             Betka           723-1237        Thursday
10   Sam             Siebert         235-1987        Friday
11   Ronald          Henkoff         636-1965        Monday
12   Barbara         Rosen           632-5436        Tuesday
13   William         Lipinski        237-4532        Monday
14   Tom             Morganthau      681-8987        Thursday
15   Noelle          Gaffney         576-4378        Friday
16
17
18
19
20
8 Last Name      15/15      LIST                               PIANO.WDB
Press ALT to choose commands.
```

Figure 4-15

5. If you wish, you can switch to *Form View* to see his record by itself.

Note: Obviously, with only 15 records, all of which can be seen on the screen at one time in *List View*, searching for one of them is not that big a deal. However, this technique will become much more valuable as the number of records in your database increases, or as you have more fields than may be viewed on the screen at one time.

A Search for Several Records

The above method serves to help us find information about a specific individual quickly. However, what if we want to find a group of records, such as all of the Friday students? Here is how we could search for all of them:

1. With your database in *List View*, move your cursor up to Home position, by pressing **CTRL+Home**. Now select **Select/Search**.
2. The SEARCH Dialog Box will appear.
3. Type: **Friday** (Figure 4-16)
4. Press **ENTER** to let the database search by rows.
5. Notice that your cursor immediately moves to the first field containing *Friday*, which in this example is in **Sam Siebert's** record.
6. If you wish, you may switch to *Form View* to see his record by itself. Press **F9** to return to *List View*.
7. To find out the name of the next Friday student, press function key **F7**. The cursor immediately moves to *Friday* in **Noelle Gaffney's** record.
8. Continue to press **F7** until you have seen the names of all of the Friday students.

The Database Manager: An Introduction

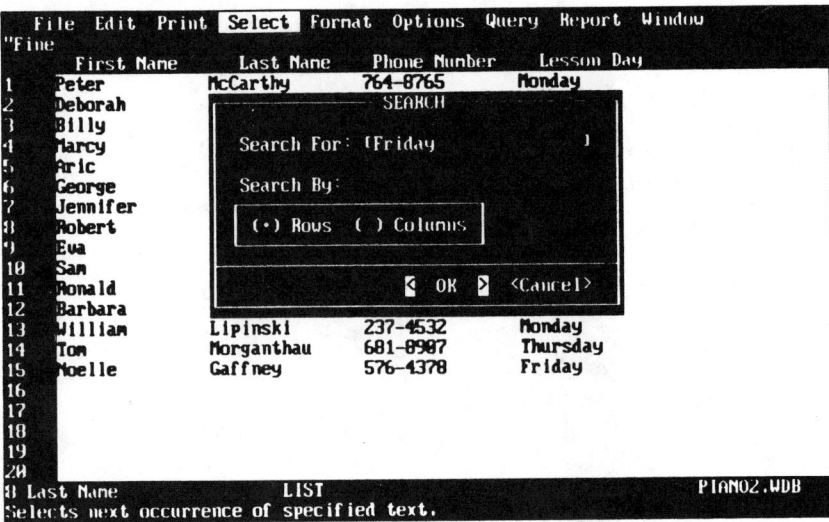

Figure 4-16

Note: When you are done, the cursor will cycle back to the first Friday student, **Sam Siebert**.

Printing Records

There are three options available to you, should you wish to print out the information in your database. The first one permits you to print a list of information. The second one permits you to print fairly intricate reports, and the third one allows you to print information from *Form View*, but you must do this in conjunction with the word processor. We'll look at the first option here and discuss creating reports in Chapter 6.

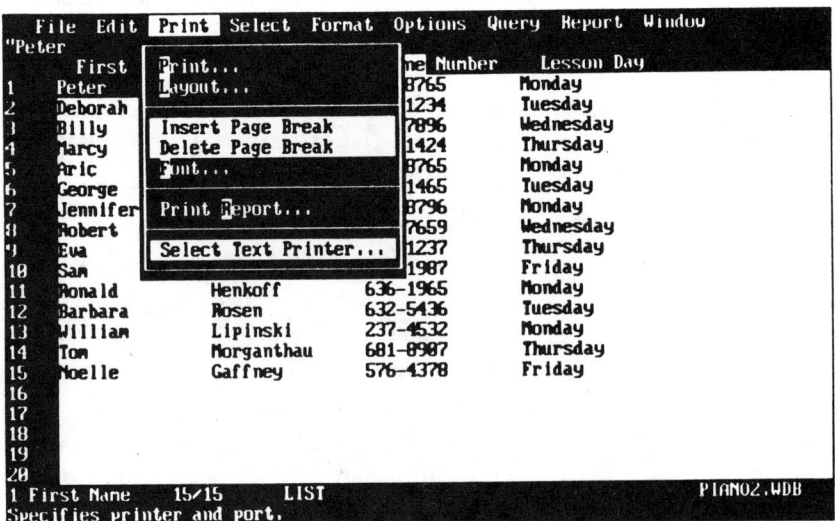

Figure 4-17

Printing Records

Here's how to print out a list of Paul's piano students:

1. Make sure that your printer is turned on, is on-line, and has paper properly aligned in it.
2. Select **Print/Select Text Printer** (Figure 4-17).
3. The SELECT TEXT PRINTER Dialog Box will appear. Just as you did earlier with the word processor and the spreadsheet, check the settings to make sure that the *Printers*, *Page Feed*, and *Connect to:* information is set correctly. Then press **ENTER**.
4. Select **Print/Layout**. The LAYOUT Dialog Box will appear (Figure 4-18). Our only interest here is to add a **header** to the list that we will print.

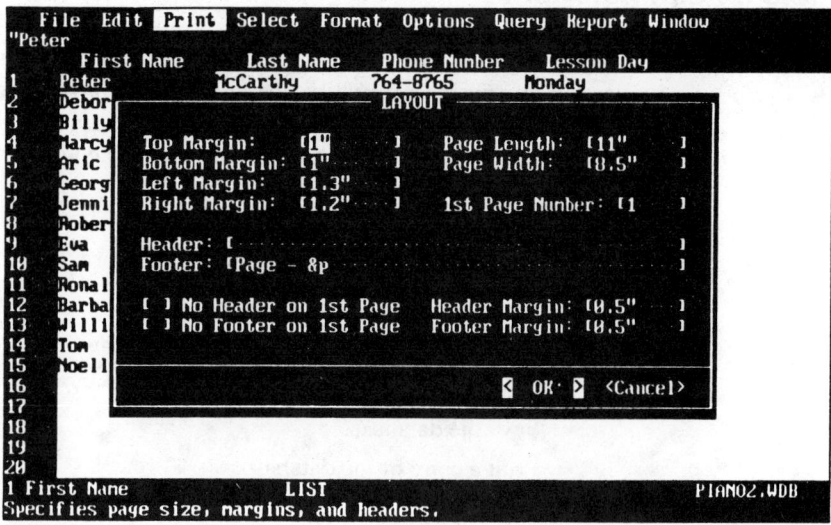

Figure 4-18

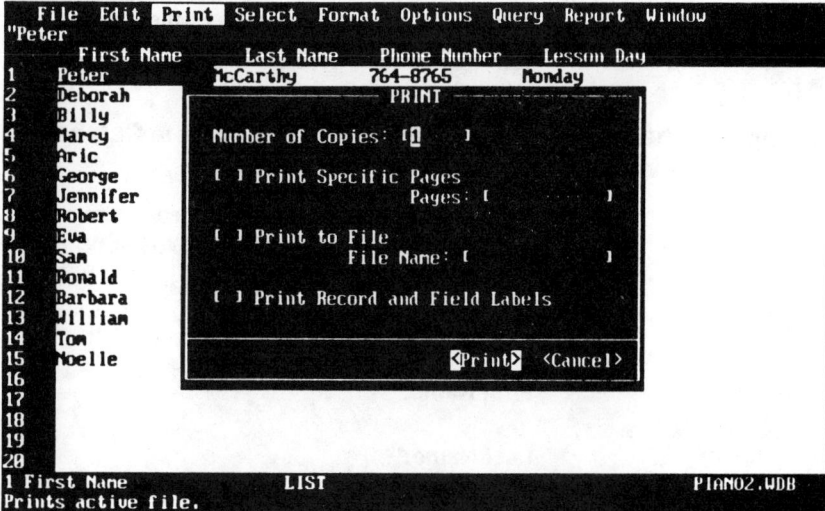

Figure 4-19

126 The Database Manager: An Introduction

5. Move your cursor to the **Header** Text Box. Then type:

   Paul's Piano Students as of 9/1/88

   Press **ENTER** when you are done.

6. Now select **Print/Print**.

7. The PRINT Dialog Box will appear (Figure 4-19). Let's just press **ENTER** and see what happens.

Database Project No. 2
Debbie's Painting Clients

As you might imagine, Debbie also has a database that she is beginning to use with her painting business. Initially, she just wants to have basic information about her clients such as their names, addresses, phone numbers, and painting estimates. However, her database and the tasks for which she wants to use it are a little more complex than those in the previous project.

While completing this project you will review how to:

- Set up the fields for the database.
- Enter information into those fields.
- Adjust the width of the fields in *List View*.
- Search for information.
- Save the database.
- Print a copy of the database.

You also will learn how to:

- Enter numbers as text data.
- Adjust the width of fields in *Form View*.
- Sort the database.
- Hide fields to print only some of the fields in the database.
- Redisplay hidden fields.

Designing the Database

1. Select **File/New**. Move the mark to **Database** and press **ENTER**.
2. The DESIGN screen should appear.
3. Enter the fields listed as they appear. Remember to type a colon (:) at the end of each field. Use the **DOWN ARROW** to enter each field name on the form and insert one line between names.

   Title:

   First Name:

   Last Name:

   Address:

Entering Data 127

        City:

        State:

        Zip:

        Phone (Home):

        Phone (Office):

        Estimate:

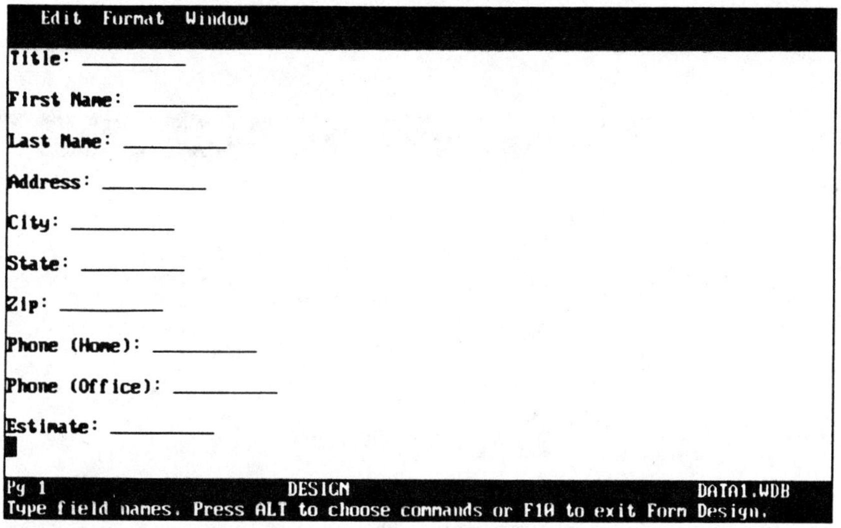

Figure 4-20

Your screen should resemble Figure 4-20.

4. Press **F10** to leave the DESIGN screen.
5. **Save** your database design. Call it **PAINT1**.

Entering Data Enter the first set of data. There are some problems, but we will fix them shortly.

Title: **Mr. & Mrs.**

First Name: **Robert**

Last Name: **Downey**

Address: **52 Wilmot Circle**

City: **Scarsdale**

The Database Manager: An Introduction

State: **NY**

Zip: **10583**

Phone (Home): **(914) 725-8907**

Phone (Office): **(212) 234-7865**

Estimate: **1400**

If you have done this correctly, your screen should resemble Figure 4-21.

We are unable to see the word *Circle* in the *Address* line, as well as the last four digits in each of the two phone numbers. We will correct these problems, but first let's take a look at some less obvious problems with the way the data was automatically entered by *Works*.

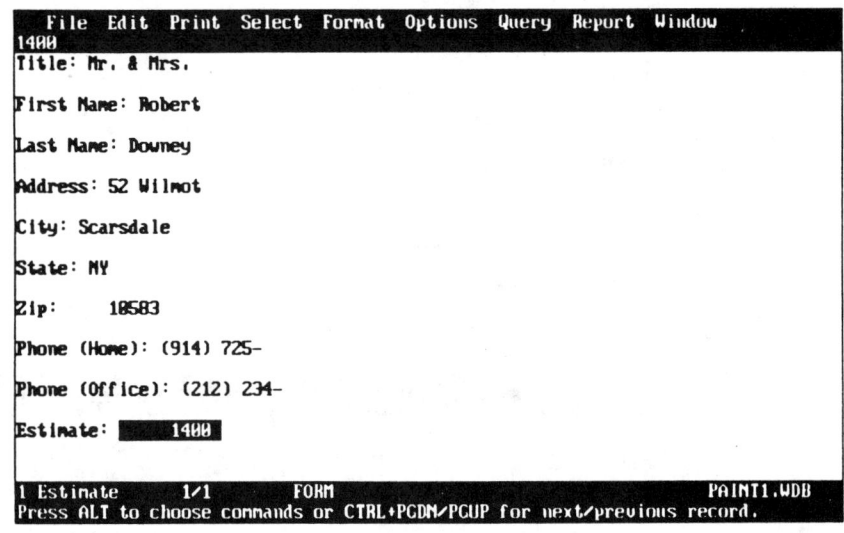

Figure 4-21

Entering Numbers as Text

When entering data, you simply typed the information and didn't worry about whether it contained letters, numbers, or both. *Works* does differentiate, however. It considers all of the entries except *Zip* and *Estimate* as text, while *Zip* and *Estimate* are considered to be numeric entries since they contain only numerals.

1. Using the **UP ARROW** key, move the cursor to the *State: NY* field. Notice that the name of the state is left justified, or positioned toward the left side of the screen.

2. Now move the cursor to the *Zip: 10583* field and notice the position of the zip code. See Figure 4-22.

    The zip code is right justified because all numeric entries are automatically right justified. Notice that the same is true for *Estimate*. There are other

Entering Data

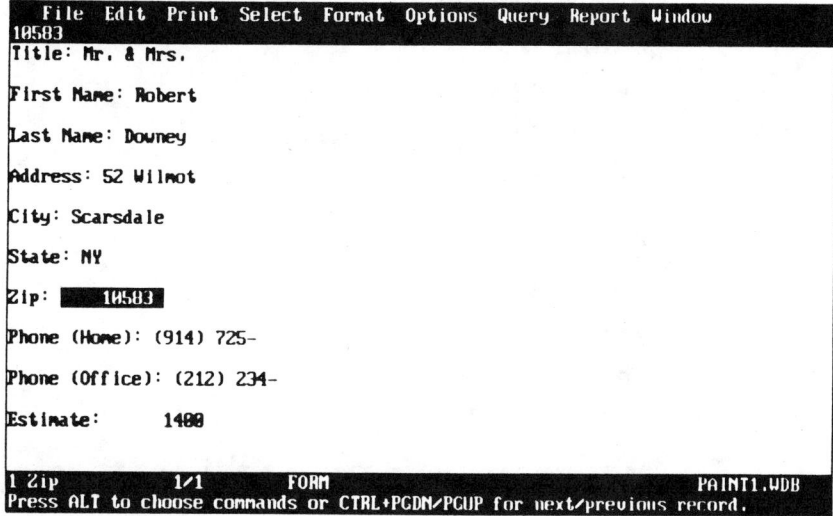

Figure 4-22

ways in which *Works* treats numeric data differently from text. Some of these differences would have serious consequences for the zip code data. For example, if you attempt to enter a zip code beginning with a zero, such as 03456, *Works* will eliminate the leading zero and enter 3456.

3. Let's try that now. With your cursor on the *Zip* field, type: **03456**

   Press **ENTER** and notice what happens. (Figure 4-23).

   To enter numeric data as text, we must type a quote before the rest of the entry (**"03456**). As in the spreadsheet tool, the quote allows *Works* to recognize a string of numerals as text instead of numeric data.

4. With your cursor still on the *Zip* field, retype the original zip code with a quote preceding (**"10583**) it and press **ENTER**. Notice how it becomes left justified.

Note: Do not change the *Estimate* field because we want to keep the number in this field as a numeric value. We don't want it to be considered as text. You may also be wondering why the telephone numbers are considered to be text and are already left justified. *Works* will understand the telephone number to be text and not a numeric value because it is not just a string of numbers, but contains a hyphen and a set of parenthesis.

When you have finished, your screen should match Figure 4-24.

130 The Database Manager: An Introduction

Figure 4-23

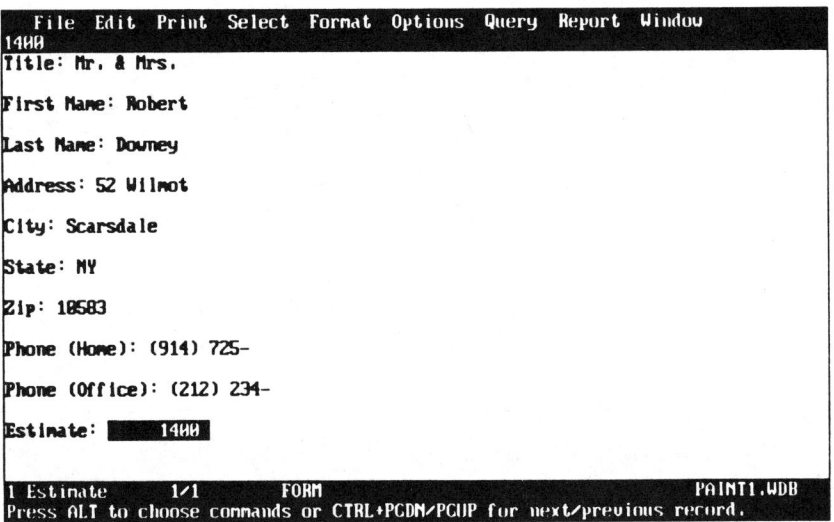

Figure 4-24

5. **SAVE** your database now.

Changing Field Width in Form View Now let's look at the screen again and notice that we are unable to see part of the address as well as part of the telephone number fields. In the interest of saving space, the program automatically assigns a field width of 10 to each database field, just as it assigns a width of 10 to each cell in the spreadsheet tool. You should be aware that the information you typed is really there, but is not visible on the screen.

Changing Field Width in Form View

Sometimes a field width of 10 is fine, but in several cases it is not sufficient. Let's see how we can fix this.

1. We must return to DESIGN mode to change the form, so select **Options/Define Form** (Figure 4-25).

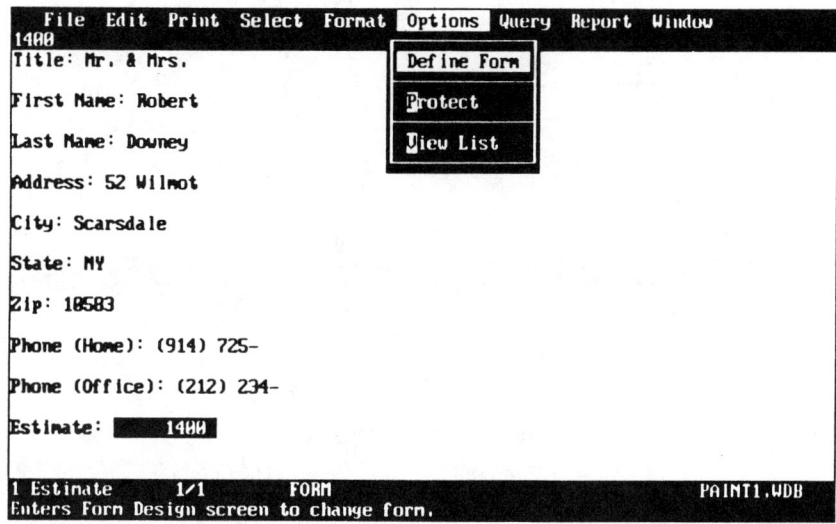

Figure 4-25

2. Move your cursor to the *Address:* field. The field is highlighted, which tells us that we can proceed (Figure 4-26).

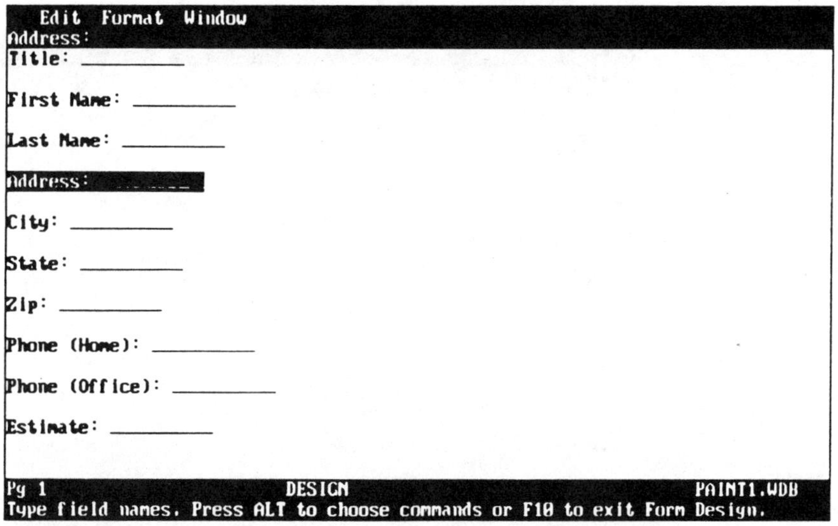

Figure 4-26

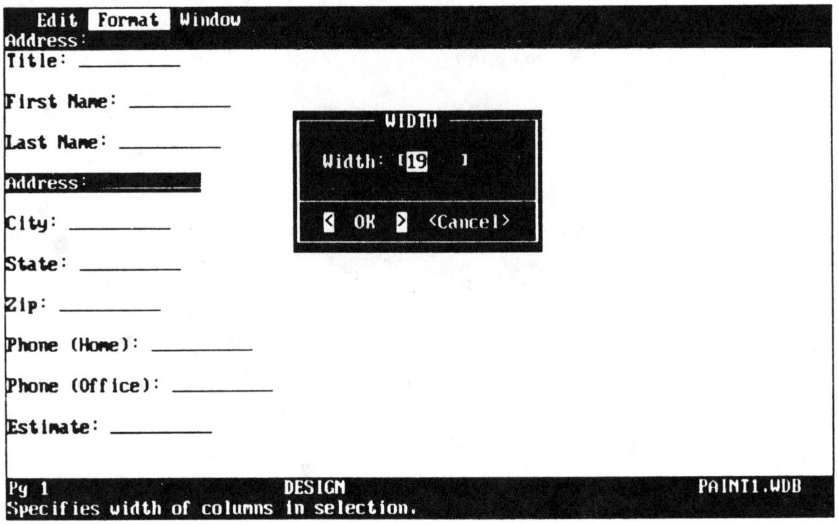

The Database Manager: An Introduction

[Screenshot of form with WIDTH dialog box showing Width: 19, OK / Cancel buttons]

Figure 4-27

3. Select **Format/Width**.

   When the WIDTH Dialog Box appears, you are told that the present width is *19* (Figure 4-27). This is perplexing, until we realize that the program is counting both the *characters* in the field name and the *10 spaces* allotted for the contents of the field. To be safe, let's make the field width for *Address* 30. Type in **30** and press **ENTER**.

4. The field widths for both *Home* and *Office* phones each appeared to be too short by four. Move your cursor to the respective fields, and add *four* to their present widths. Your screen now should resemble Figure 4-28.

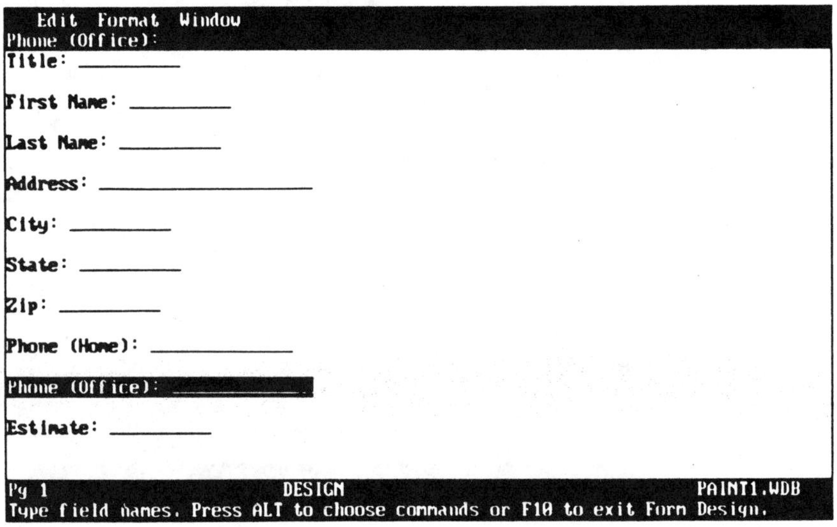

[Screenshot of form with Phone (Office) field highlighted]

Figure 4-28

Changing Field Width in Form View 133

5. If you press **F10** when you are done, it will return you to the first record in the database, the one for **Mr. and Mrs. Downey**. You should be able to see all of the information for each of the fields, correctly displayed on the screen (Figure 4-29).

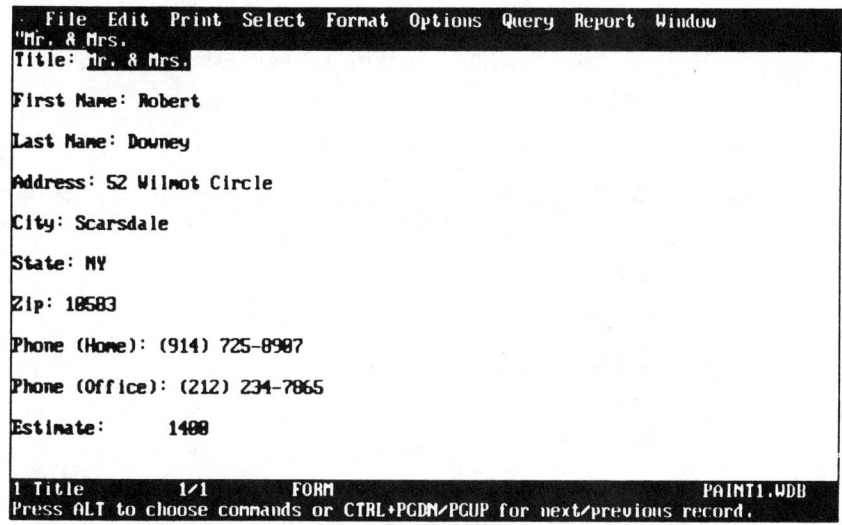

Figure 4-29

6. Now, use either your **DOWN ARROW** key or **CTRL+PGDN** to move on to the next record. Type in the information for Debbie's next customer as listed below.

Caution: When you change the width of a field it remains changed when you enter subsequent records. However, each time you fill in the *Zip* field, you must always type a quote first so that the entry will be treated as text.

Title: **Dr. & Mrs.**
First Name: **Peter**
Last Name: **Brody**
Address: **456 Gilbert Street**
City: **South Salem**
State: **NY**
Zip: **"10590**
Phone (Home): **(914) 763-7676**
Phone (Office): **(212) 654-8765**
Estimate: **1200**

The Database Manager: An Introduction

Oops! There is a slight problem. We are not able to see the last letter in South Salem. So, let's change the form width one more time.

1. Select **Options/Define Form**.
2. Move the cursor to the field for *City*.
3. Now select **Format/Width**.
4. Change the width to **18** and press **ENTER**.
5. Press **F10** to return to your record, and the data should be displayed correctly (Figure 4-30).

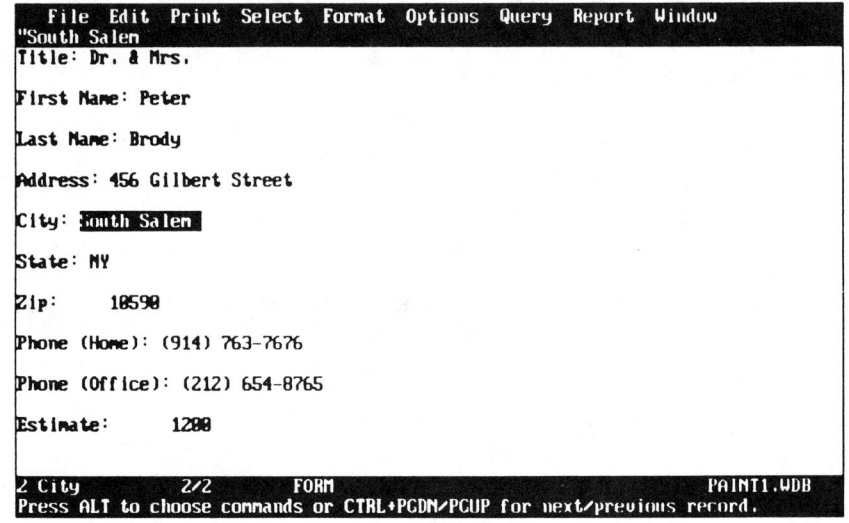

Figure 4-30

Now we can continue.

Title: **Ms.**	*Title:* **Mr. & Mrs.**
First Name: **Gloria**	*First Name:* **Jerome**
Last Name: **Penberthy**	*Last Name:* **Adams**
Address: **Snake Hill Rd.**	*Address:* **15 Martine Ave. # 3M**
City: **Yorktown Heights**	*City:* **White Plains**
State: **NY**	*State:* **NY**
Zip: **10598**	*Zip:* **10608**
[Don't forget the quote ("10598)]	*Phone (Home):* **(914) 681-5674**
Phone (Home): **(914) 764-3201**	*Phone (Office):* **(212) 345-7689**
Phone (Office): **(914) 681-1000**	*Estimate:* **400**
Estimate: **1800**	

Changing Field Width in Form View

Title: **Mr. & Mrs.**
First Name: **Robert**
Last Name: **McDonald**
Address: **43 Lakeshore Drive**
City: **South Salem**
State: **NY**
Zip: **10590**
Phone (Home): **(914) 763-9008**
Phone (Office): **(914) 681-1635**
Estimate: **1200**

Title: **Dr.**
First Name: **Susan**
Last Name: **Lippman**
Address: **Whipporwill Drive**
City: **Darien**
State: **CT**
Zip: **06820**
Phone (Home): **(203) 224-6785**
Phone (Office): **(203) 224-3425**
Estimate: **800**

Title: **Mr. & Mrs.**
First Name: **John**
Last Name: **Fischer**
Address: **P.O. Box 1118**
City: **Tarrytown**
State: **NY**
Zip: **10456**
Phone (Home): **(914) 592-7683**
Phone (Office): **(914) 592-3425**
Estimate: **400**

Title: **Mr. & Mrs.**
First Name: **James**
Last Name: **Patterson**
Address: **Sheridan Hill Drive**
City: **Greenwich**
State: **CT**
Zip: **06830**
Phone (Home): **(203) 744-3489**
Phone (Office): **(203) 687-6745**
Estimate: **2500**

Oops!! Once again, our field widths need to be adjusted. You probably noticed, as you entered your data, that **Yorktown Heights** was too long to fit at the *City* field. So return your cursor to the record for **Ms. Gloria Penberthy** and refer to the instructions given on the preceding pages to correct the width. When you press **F10** again your screen should resemble Figure 4-31.

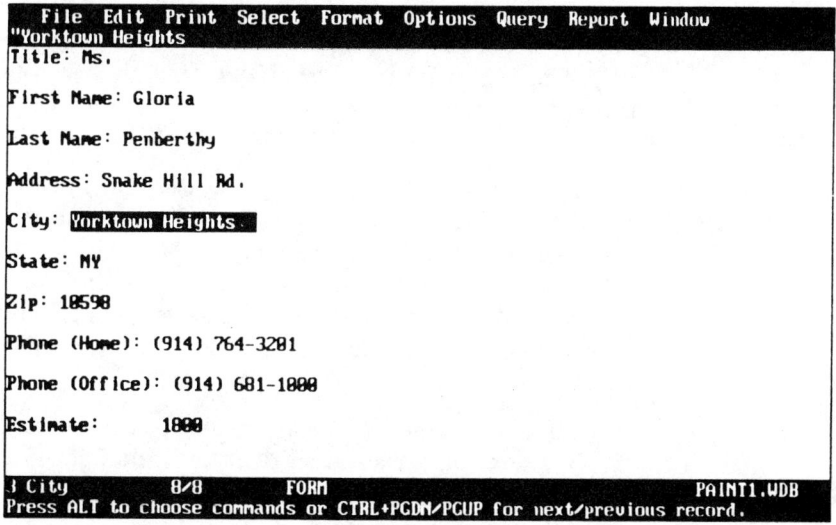

Figure 4-31

The Database Manager: An Introduction

Now add the last two records.

Title: **Ms.**
First Name: **Suzanne**
Last Name: **Miller**
Address: **96 Summer Hill Rd.**
City: **Bedford**
State: **NY**
Zip: **10542**
Phone (Home): **(914) 234-3916**
Phone (Office): **(212) 654-8765**
Estimate: **5000**

Title: **Mr. & Mrs.**
First Name: **William**
Last Name: **Tippett**
Address: **Fox Hollow Run**
City: **Bedford**
State: **NY**
Zip: **10542**
Phone (Home): **(914) 234-7821**
Phone (Office): **(212) 650-6734**
Estimate: **300**

Viewing Records in the Database

As you might remember, there are two ways for us to view the data in our database. The first method is for us to move between the records in *Form View*, using **CTRL+PGUP** and **CTRL+PGDN**.

A more effective way to find data, especially as the size of your database grows, is to use the **Select/Search** command. This command can be used in either *List View* or *Form View*. We will use **Select/Search** in *List View* so that we can see more of our database at one time and get a better feeling for what the command is doing. Let's also move our cursor to the beginning of the database so that our searches will begin with the first record.

1. Move to the first record in the file.
2. Press **F9**.

Note: Although we changed the widths of some of the fields earlier when we were in *Form View*, this is *not* reflected in *List View* (Figure 4-32). For most tasks such as entering and editing data, moving the cursor and adding enhancements, changes made on one screen are reflected on the other. However, for other attributes, such as field width, *Works* treats *List View* and *Form View* as two separate database entities that may be formatted differently.

Changing Field Width in List View

Let's change some field widths now. The usual rule when working with a database such as this, which uses columns to display its information (just as when using a spreadsheet), is to make each column one character wider than the widest entry in it. This permits you to have some space between each column, which makes the list easier to read. More than one extra character per column is wasteful, however, because the blank space limits the number of columns you can see on the screen at one time.

1. Let's make the *Title* column two characters wider. Move your cursor to the *Title* column and select **Format/Width**. Change this width to **11**.
2. The *Address* column is clearly too narrow. Move to the *Address* column, and select **Format/Width**. Experiment with this until you have found a width that is one character wider than the widest entry.

Searching for Data

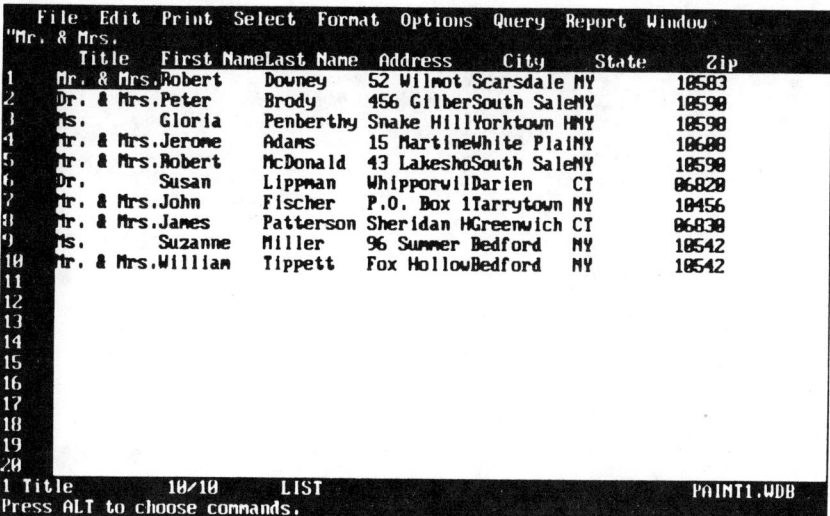

Figure 4-32

Note: Selecting widths for columns of numeric data is trickier than for text columns. In numeric columns, the minimum width at which the number will be displayed as entered is equal to one space more than the widest entry because *Works* reserves one space for a percent sign or parenthesis. Additional spaces are required if you format the data for currency, comma, etc. These factors will not affect our database as the only numeric data is unformatted.

---

3. When we encounter the *State* column, we have a somewhat different problem. That is, the column is actually too *wide* for the entries in it. Move your cursor into the *State* column, and then reduce the width so that it is only one character wider than the widest entry, the heading, *State*.

4. Adjust the widths of the remaining columns so that each is one character wider than its widest entry.

5. Move your cursor across the columns, and make sure that all of them have been changed correctly. Your screen should resemble Figure 4-33.

6. After you have done this, Save the database, but let's use **File/Save As...** so that you can give this file the new name **PAINT2**.

Searching for Data

As we discovered earlier, it is quite easy to search for data, especially if we take advantage of the **F9** key to move us back and forth between *List View* and *Form View*, and the **F7** key, which permits us to continue a search.

1. Using the **PAINT2.WDB** database, make sure that you are in *List View*.

2. Move your cursor to Home position. Now, select **Select/Search** and enter the words **South Salem** into the Search For Text Box.

   Remember *Works* is not case sensitive, so you could type **south salem** and it would find the data just as well (Figure 4-34).

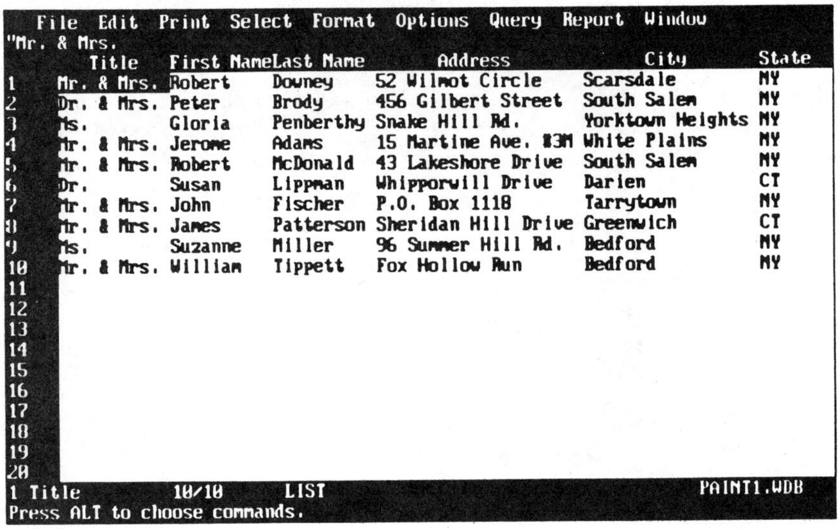

The Database Manager: An Introduction

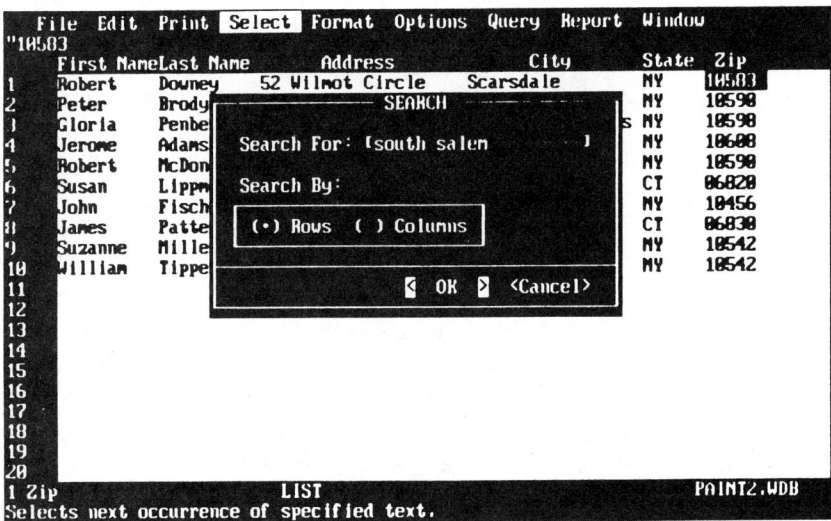

Figure 4-33

Figure 4-34

3. When the cursor moves to the words *South Salem* for *Peter Brody*, remember that you may see his entire record by pressing **F9** or using the **ARROW** keys to scroll to the fields not currently visible. If you have switched to *Form View*, switch back to *List View* by pressing **F9** again.

4. Now, press **F7** to find out about the next client in **South Salem**. Again, you could use **F9** or the **ARROW** keys to learn more about the **McDonald** family.

Sorting Records Another way to find groups of related records is to sort the database. A database may be sorted into alphabetical or numerical order, using the contents of any field in the

Sorting Records 139

database. A second and third field by which to sort also may be selected, but these only sort records that have identical entries in the first sort field. For example, when sorting by *Last Name*, *First Name* typically is chosen as a second sort field so that records containing the same *Last Name* can be sorted in a logical order.

Once the **Sort** command is issued, all following commands, such as **Print**, act upon the sorted database. Furthermore, when you save the file, it is saved in its sorted order. If you wish to maintain both the sorted and unsorted files, use **File/Save As...** to save the sorted file with a new name.

Let's sort the database by the *Zip* field, so that our list will be in order for mailing purposes.

1. Select **Query/Sort**.

    The SORT Dialog Box will be displayed (Figure 4-35). *Works* has placed the name of the first field in the database, *Title*, into the 1st Field Text Box, because people frequently want to sort a database on the first field.

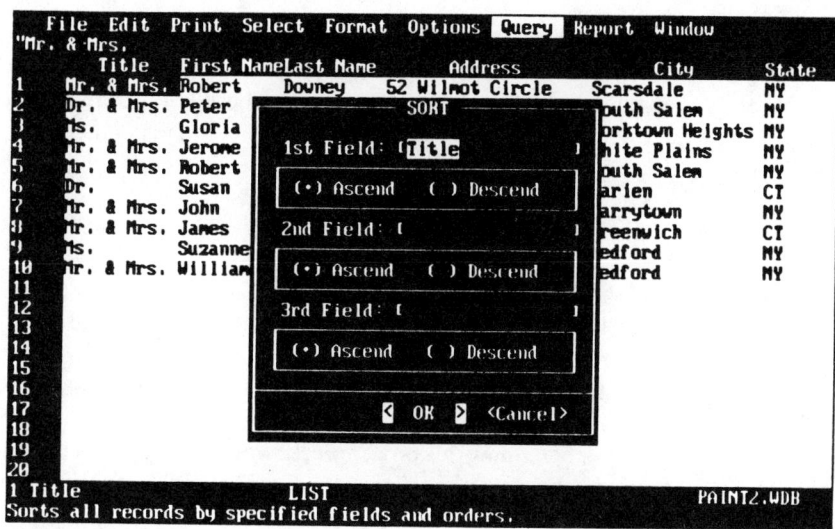

Figure 4-35

2. Type: **Zip**

    It is possible to sort in descending order and/or to select a second and third field, but we do not wish to do this.

3. Press the **ENTER** key to accept the other default options.

Note: *Works* will sort all text entries first and then all numeric entries. If you omitted the " before some of the zip codes when you entered them, they will appear at the end of the list. Edit those entries to include the ".

---

4. Use **File/Save As...** to save the sorted database with the name **PAINT3**.

Printing Records

Here's how to print out a copy of Debbie's Painting Clients:

1. Make sure that your printer is turned on, is on-line, and has paper aligned in it properly.
2. We will print the list as it appears in **PAINT2.WDB**, so use **File/Open** to retrieve **PAINT2.WDB**.
3. Select **Print/Select Text Printer**, and check that the settings in the SELECT TEXT PRINTER Dialog Box are correct.
4. Select **Print/Layout**, and enter the header:

    Debbie's Painting Clients 11/15/88

    Press **ENTER** when you are done.
5. Select **Print/Print** and press **ENTER**.

Notice that because the database is so wide, we actually have printed it in *three* separate sections. The **Print** program automatically breaks the data into more manageable chunks for us and then prints it on consecutive pages, just as it does with a spreadsheet that is too wide for one piece of paper. One way to avoid this situation is to print only some of the fields for each record. This is done by hiding some of the fields from the list.

Hiding Fields in List View

You will remember that earlier we changed the width of some of the fields in *List View* by using **Format/Width**. *Works* permits us to make a field from 0 to 79 characters wide. If we set the width at **0**, the information remains in the program's memory, but the field disappears from the screen. This is known as **hiding a field** from *List View*, and it is simple to do. You always should **SAVE** *your database before* beginning this procedure, however, as that will make it easier to redisplay the fields when you want them back. So, **SAVE PAINT2** and then follow along so that you can print a useful list of Debbie's clients on one piece of paper.

First we need to decide which fields to hide and which to have on a printout. Let's print the *Title*, *Last Name*, *Phone (Home)*, and *Phone (Office)* fields. That means we will have to hide the *First Name*, *Address*, *City*, *State*, *Zip*, and *Estimate* fields.

1. Move the cursor to the *First Name* field in any record.
2. Select **Format/Width**.
3. Type **0** in the Width Text Box (Figure 4-36).
4. Press **ENTER**, and the *First Name* column will be gone from your screen (Figure 4-37).
5. Now move the cursor to the *Address* field.
6. Select **Format/Width**.
7. Type: **0** and press **ENTER**.

Hiding Fields in List View 141

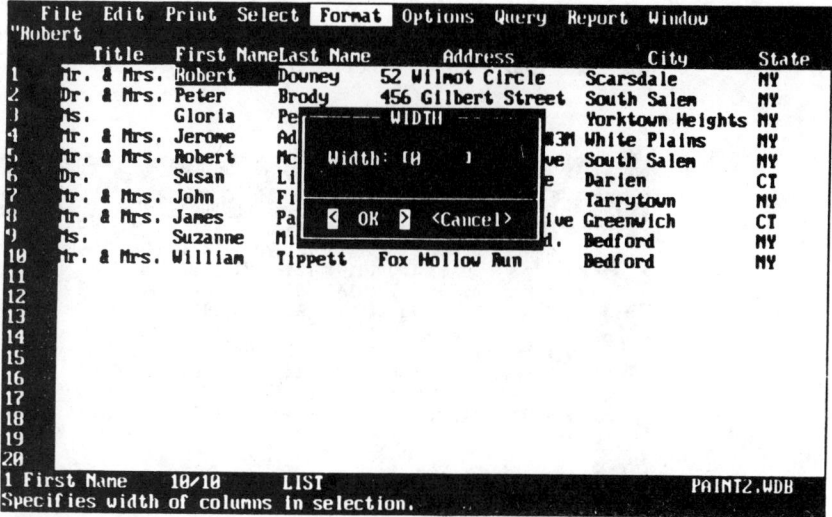

Figure 4-36

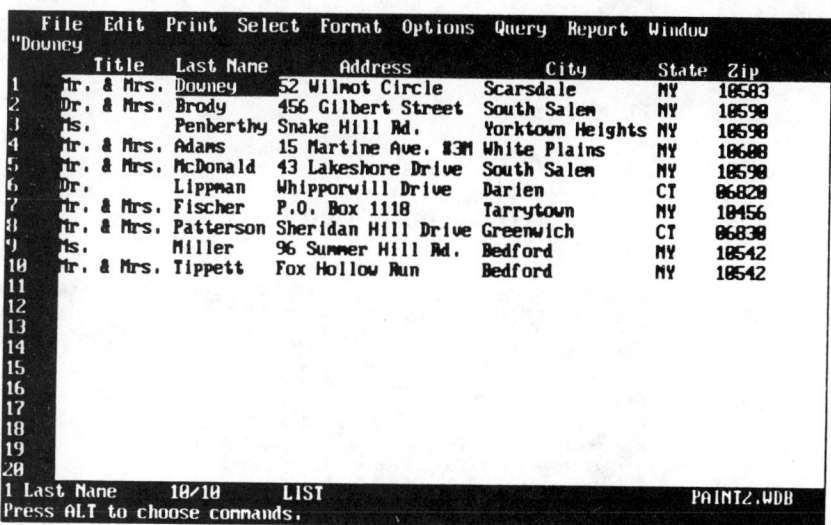

Figure 4-37

8. Repeat these steps with the other four fields that we want to hide. When you are finished, your screen should resemble Figure 4-38.
9. Save the database using **File/Save As...** Call it **PAINT4**.
10. Now we are ready to print the condensed version of Debbie's client list.

By this time you should be able to complete the printing process with ease, but if you need to check a step along the way you always can refer back to the directions given earlier in this chapter.

Redisplaying Hidden Fields in List View Obviously the option to hide fields is a great help if you don't need information from more than a few fields in your printed list. What if you accidentally saved the condensed list without changing the file name, however, and you realize that you

The Database Manager: An Introduction

need to get some or all of the hidden fields back? Follow the steps below to **redisplay** the fields that we have hidden from the List Screen.

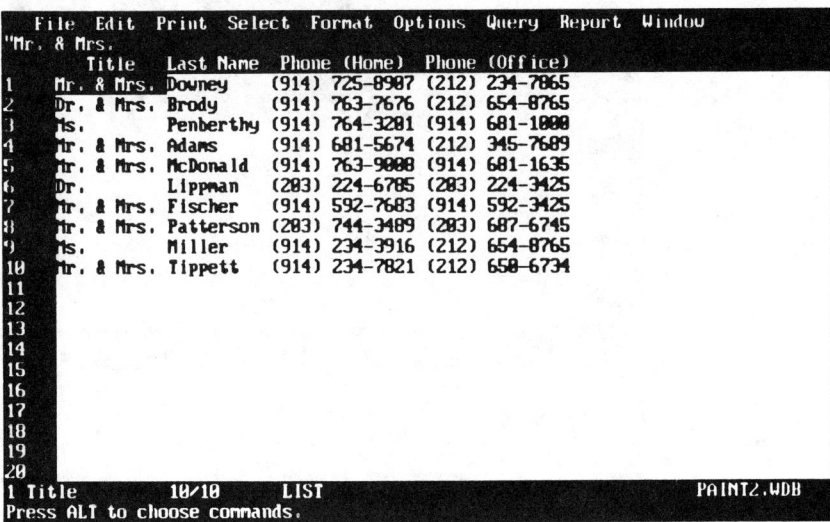

Figure 4-38

1. Select **Select/Go To** (Figure 4-39).

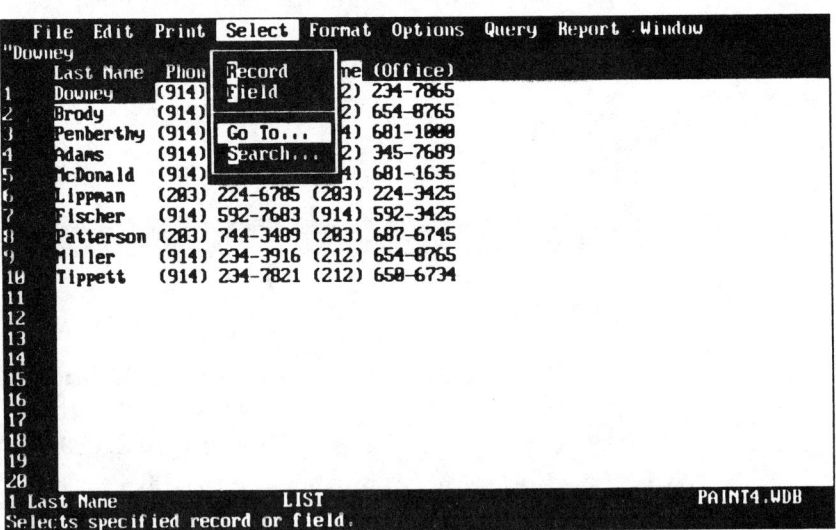

Figure 4-39

Notice that the GO TO Dialog Box appears. This is a Dialog Box that we haven't seen before, but the methods of making selections within it are the same as with any other Dialog Box in *Works*.

Redisplaying Hidden Fields in List View

2. Select the *First Name* field, as this is the first field that we will redisplay (Figure 4-40).

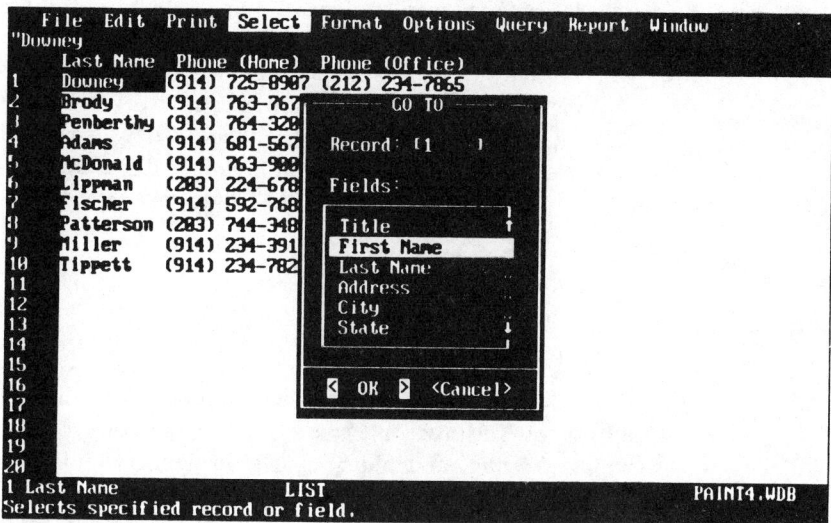

Figure 4-40

3. Now select **Format/Width**.
4. We need to enter a width of 11 in order both to fit the information in the *First Name* field and to leave one blank space between it and the next field. Type **11** and press **ENTER**.
5. Repeat these steps in order to redisplay the *Address* field. When you reach the step of entering a width in the Width Text Box, type: **20**

Notice that when you press **ENTER** the list includes these two fields just as they were before you hid them. Obviously, if you repeat these steps with each hidden

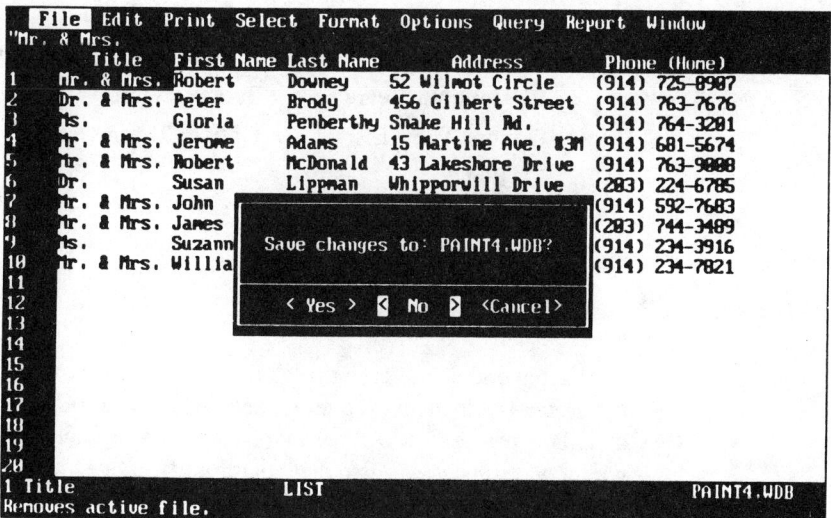

Figure 4-41

field, you will be able to return the list to its original size. There are two problems with redisplaying fields in this way, however. As you may have noticed, you have to remember how wide the field was before you hid it, so that when you redisplay it the information won't run into the next field. In addition, the procedure becomes tedious when you have to redisplay several fields. This is why it is important that you *not* save the changes to a database in which you have hidden fields *unless* you save the database under a new file name. If you need to hide fields just for one printout, and don't plan to save the condensed list, be sure that when you close the database or exit from *Works* you highlight the **<No>** Button in the Dialog Box (Figure 4-41) that asks you if you want to save the file.

Conclusion

A **database** is an interesting, powerful tool, once you begin to master some of its intricacies. The procedures we used in the previous project, such as changing field widths, sorting, and hiding and redisplaying fields do not change the basic information in the database, but they do allow us to manipulate that information so that we may view and print only the records and fields we need. As you have seen, many of these procedures resemble techniques that you encountered in the Word Processor and Spreadsheet tools of *Works*. With continued use of a database, it should become a comfortable and very useful part of your computer expertise.

Key Terms

The following important terms and commands have been introduced and explained in this chapter:

Field	Record	File
Database	Form View	List View
Hidden Field	F10-Exit Form	F9-List/Form View
F7-Continue Search	Format/Width	Select/Search
Options/View List	Options/Define Form	Query/Sort
F2-Edit		

Independent Database Project No. 1

As you have seen earlier in this chapter, the essence of using a database is to set up the proper fields, then to enter the data, and then to be able to search for the needed data. This first project will permit you to set up the necessary fields, change the field widths when necessary, and then search and retrieve the information you desire. The data for this exercise is printed below:

Independent Database Project No. 1

Sue	Hutchinson	632-1768	Thursday
Bob	Cohn	681-7432	Thursday
Paul	Keating	234-7645	Wednesday
Robert	Huse	682-9134	Friday
Phil	Humber	576-3482	Wednesday
Daniel	Shapiro	234-7693	Friday
Michael	Brown	763-2387	Thursday
Jean	Seligmann	234-9012	Tuesday
Mary	Hager	563-1827	Friday

1. Set up the fields in your database.
2. Enter the information for the nine individuals into the database.
3. Save the database as **INDPRO1**.
4. Switch to *List View* and change the widths of any fields that are not at least one space wider than the widest item in that field. When you are done, your database might resemble Figure 4-42.

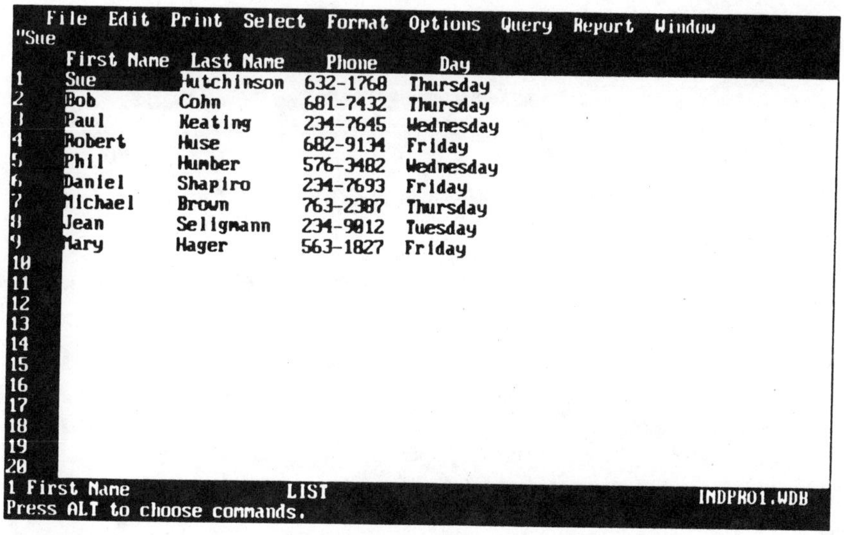

Figure 4-42

5. Save your database again, and then print out a copy.
6. Try doing several searches. See if you can get *Works* to identify all of the students who are taking lessons on Thursday. What happens if you type **234-** in the Search For Text Box? The results will probably surprise you. *Works* finds the character string that you type anywhere in any field in the database.

Independent Database Project No. 2

Using the procedures we have covered in this chapter, set up a database that will include the names, addresses, and phone numbers of ten of your friends. Make sure that you adjust the field widths in both *Form View* and *List View* so that the data in each field may be seen. Be sure to save your data, and then try printing a copy of it.

Chapter 5
Integrating Works: An Introduction

In this chapter you will learn how to:

- Use the **Window** menu to move between several active files.
- Copy information from a database to a word processor document.
- Copy information from a spreadsheet to a word processor document.

When you purchased *Works*, someone may have mentioned to you that you were buying an "integrated software package," which at that time, may have meant little or nothing to you. Now, however, that you have seen the word processor, spreadsheet, and database, it is time to think about that concept again.

The first advantage of an "integrated software package" is that the menus and procedures for the separate components that it includes are quite similar, and in some cases, identical. As you have seen, the *Works* **File** commands are identical in the word processor, spreadsheet, and database. In each of them the File menu contains the commands **New**, **Open**, **Save**, **Save As**, **Save All**, **Close**, **DOS**, and **Exit**.

Many of the other menus in the three tools are similar, and all of them operate in the same way. You select a menu heading and press **ENTER** to pull down a menu of commands and options. Once you make a selection, the procedures are often quite similar, and so too are the Dialog Boxes that are used. This consistent menu and interface structure contributes to increased speed both in using the individual applications and in mastering their concepts.

Another advantage of an integrated software package has to do with the way in which the files created with the separate tools may be used together. Usually, when you purchase software, the procedure to use your word processor files together with your database and your spreadsheet files is quite complicated. Sometimes it leaves people very frustrated. With an integrated software package, it is simple and comfortable to use files that have been created with the separate tools together, for in reality, the tools are different aspects of the same program.

You will find that the word processor is often the base of operations for integrating information from the various tools. It is frequently useful to include part of a database, spreadsheet, or chart (graph created from spreadsheet data) in a document that you are creating using the word processor. In addition, the word processor can be used to create form letters or mailing labels using information from the database.

148 **Integrating Works: An Introduction**

In this chapter, we are going to take a first look at how integration functions in Works while creating three projects. You will begin to get a sense of the power that is really yours because you have purchased an integrated software package.

Integrated Project No. 1
Using Information from a Database
in a Word Processor Document

Debbie needs to send short notes to her two painting clients in Bedford. She would like to quickly look up their names and addresses in her database and copy that information into her word processor, so that she may include that information in her notes.

In the process of creating Debbie's note you will review how to:

- Open files.
- Search for information in a database.
- Use the **Edit/Copy** command.
- Edit word processor documents.

You also will learn how to:

- Use the **Window** menu to switch between files.
- Use **Select/Record** to select an entire database record.
- Copy information from a database to a word processor document.

Opening More Than One File at a Time There are several steps to the process of using files in an integrated fashion. The first step, and the one that always begins the conversation, is for you to open or create the files that you wish to use. Let's begin this process.

1. Start *Works*, and enter the Word Processor to create a new *Works* file. As is always the case, you will be told that you are creating a file named **WORD1.WPS**. This file will function as our **DESTINATION** file during this project.

2. Select **File/Open**.

    If the drive name that follows *Files in:* in the OPEN Dialog Box is not the drive containing your exercise disk, then highlight the correct name (*A* or *B*) from the *Other Drives & Directories* List Box and press the **ENTER** key.

    If *All Works Files* is not the marked option in the List Which Files Option Box, mark it and press the **ENTER** key. Your screen should resemble Figure 5-1, although there may be some differences in the list of *Works* files saved on your disk.

3. Select **PAINT2.WDB**.

    This file, which will function as our **SOURCE** file, contains all of the names, addresses, and phone numbers of Debbie's painting clients.

    The file **PAINT2.WDB** should appear on your screen.

Opening More than One File at a Time

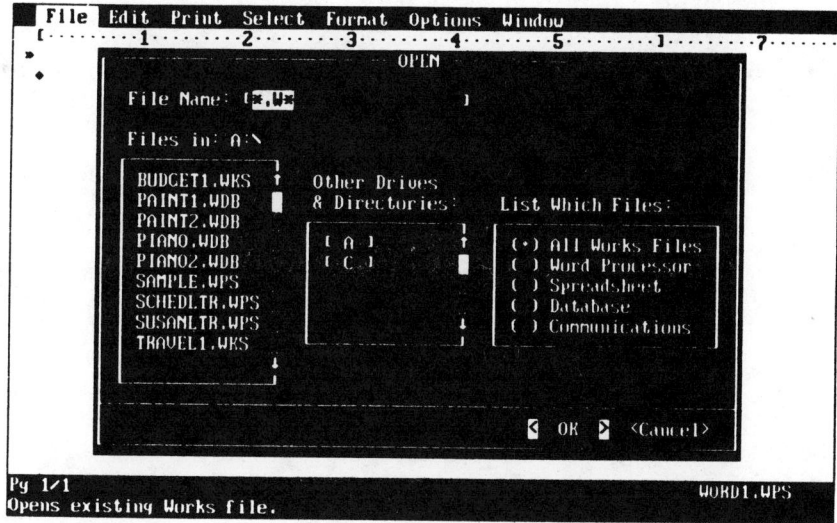

Figure 5-1

You have now opened two files; the first one is the word processor file (DESTINATION file), **WORD1.WPS**, to which we will copy the information, and the second one is the database file (SOURCE file), **PAINT2.WDB**, which contains the information to be copied.

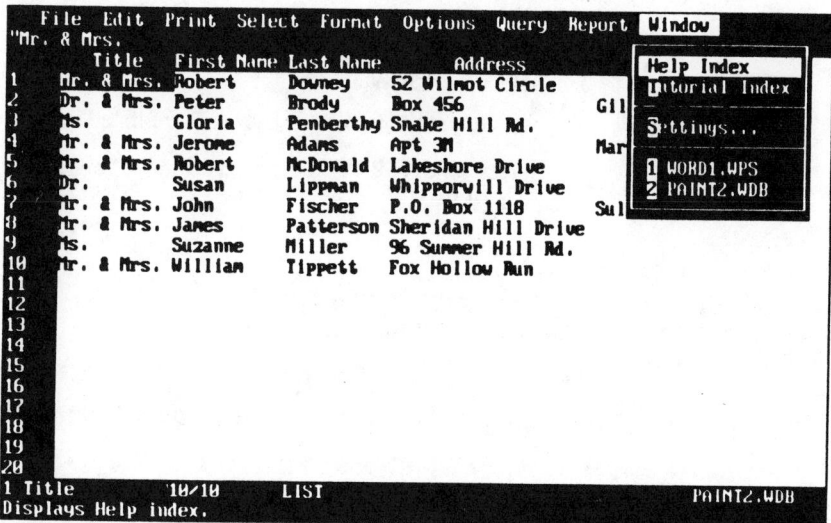

Figure 5-2

Using the Window Command to Switch Between Files

Now that you have opened two files, how do you use them?

1. Select **Window**.

   The menu lists the two open files (Figure 5-2).

2. Select **WORD1.WPS** by moving the cursor down to **WORD1.WPS** and pressing **ENTER**, or by typing the highlighted number **1** preceding the file name.

   The word processor file is displayed (Figure 5-3).

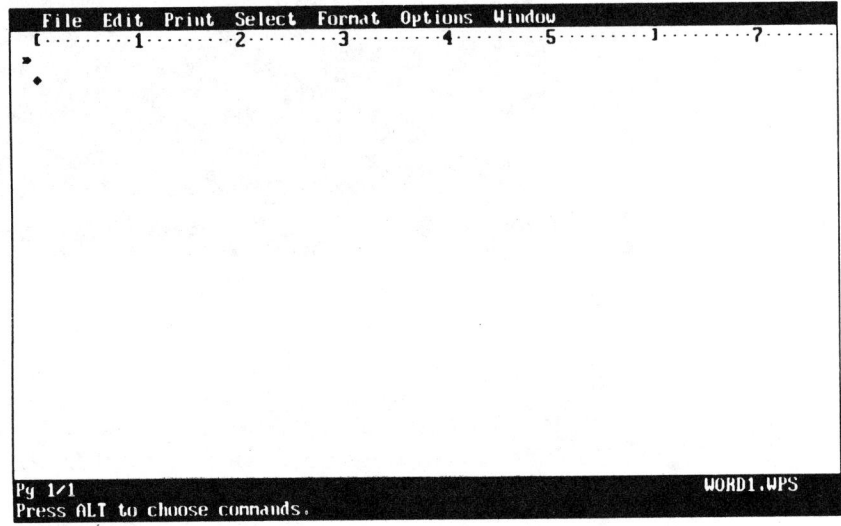

Figure 5-3

3. Select **Window** again.

   Notice that the two open files still are listed in the bottom box in the menu.

4. Select **PAINT2.WDB**, and you will be back into your database file instantly!

Copying from the Database to the Word Processor

Now that we've practiced moving between files, let's see how to use information from Debbie's database in her letter.

1. Choose **Select/Search** and enter **Bedford** in the Search For: Text Box.

   The cursor moves to the word *Bedford* in Suzanne Miller's record (Figure 5-4).

2. Choose **Select/Record**. The **Select/Record** command is used to highlight the entire record that includes the field currently containing the cursor.

   The entire record for Suzanne Miller is highlighted (Figure 5-5).

3. Select **Edit/Copy**.

Copying from the Database to the Word Procesor 151

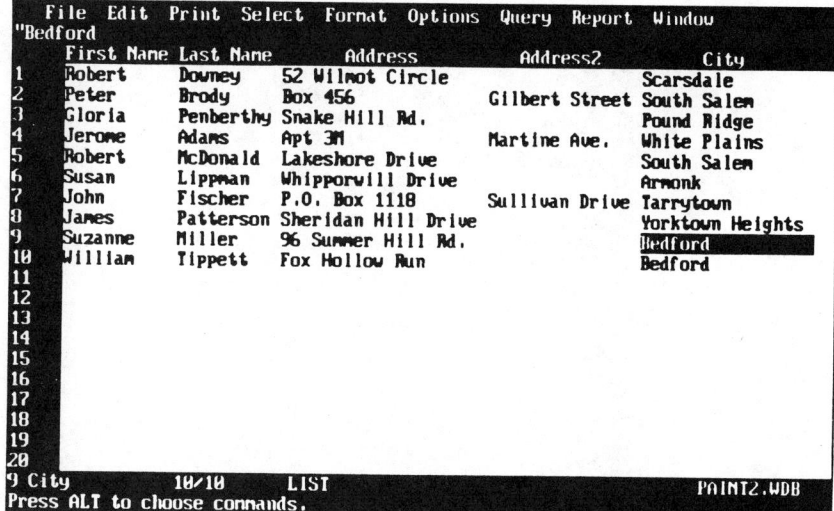

Figure 5-4

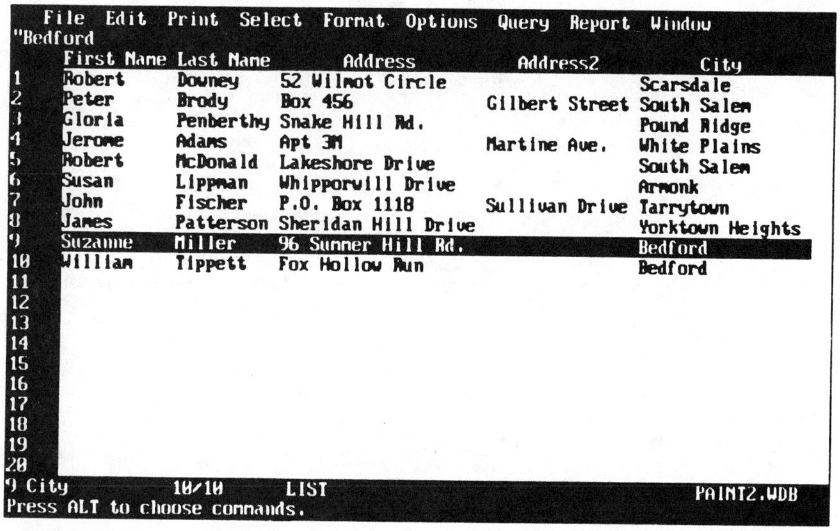

Figure 5-5

Even though only *Bedford* remains highlighted, (Figure 5-6), when you specify a new location the entire section that you had highlighted will be copied there.

The Message Line tells us to *Select a new location and press ENTER or press ESC to cancel.*

DO *NOT* PRESS **ENTER** YET! WE WISH TO SWITCH BACK TO THE WORD PROCESSOR FILE BEFORE COPYING THIS DATA.

152 Integrating Works: An Introduction

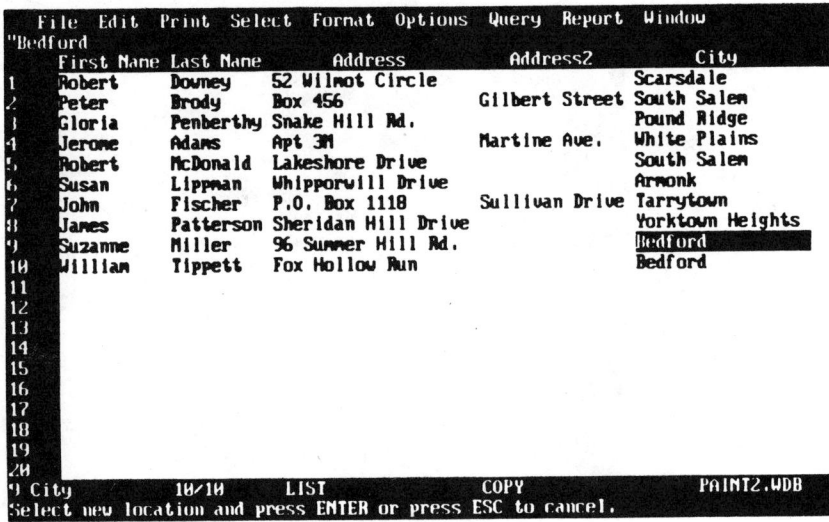

Figure 5-6

4. Select **Window/WORD1.WPS**.
5. When **WORD1.WPS** appears on the screen, press **ENTER**. Suzanne Miller's complete database record will be copied to your document (Figure 5-7).

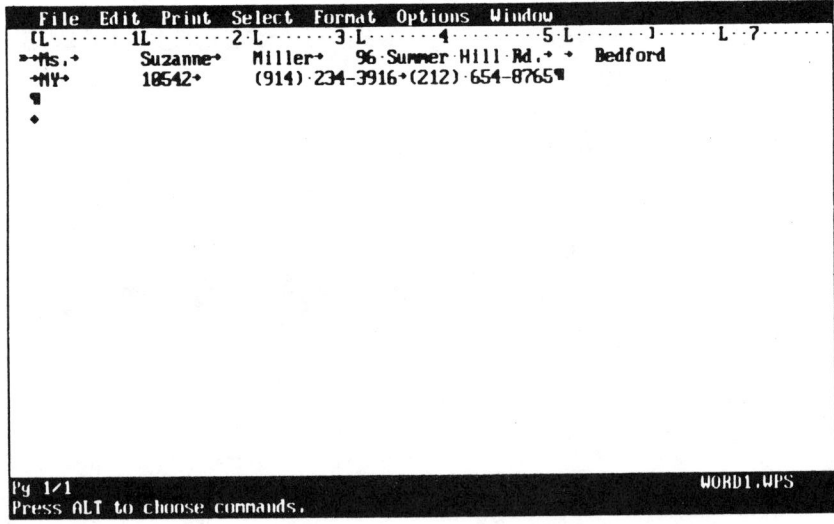

Figure 5-7

Note: In Figure 5-7, **Options/Show All Characters** had been selected, so the tab, space, and paragraph symbols were displayed.

Reformatting Copied Information

6. If the tab symbols are *not* displayed on your screen, select **Options/Show All Characters** so that your screen resembles Figure 5-7.

Reformatting Copied Information

You might be wondering why the information is separated by tabs. Data in databases and spreadsheets is stored in rows and columns. When this information is copied to the word processor, *Works* inserts a tab between each column.

The problem for us right now is that the information that we wish to have is on the screen, but it is not displayed in quite the style that we would have chosen.

At this point, there are two options. One option is to retype Suzanne Miller's address, and then to delete the database information that contains all the tab symbols. The second option is to edit the information so that it is in the desired form. *Choose one* of these methods now. Directions for editing the information follow.

1. Press the **DEL** key to delete the initial tab.
2. Delete the tab symbol between *Ms.* and *Suzanne*.
3. Press the **SPACE BAR** once to insert a space between *Ms.* and *Suzanne*.
4. Repeat steps 2 and 3 to delete the next tab, and then insert a space between *Suzanne* and *Miller*.
5. Move the cursor to the tab symbol following *Miller*.
6. Press the **ENTER** key to move the rest of the line down to the next line.
7. Delete the initial tab.
8. Move the cursor to the tab following *Summer Hill Rd.* and press the **ENTER** key to move the rest of the data down one line.

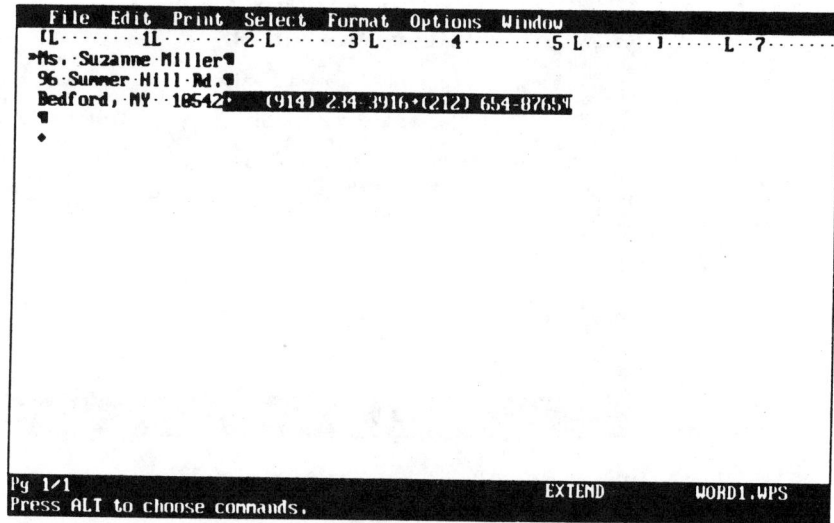

Figure 5-8

Integrating Works: An Introduction

9. Delete tab symbols, and insert spaces and commas until the final line of the address says:

   Bedford, NY 10542

   followed by Suzanne's telephone numbers.

10. There's just one more step — to remove the extra information:

    a. Move the cursor to the tab following the zip code and press **F8**. **Extend** the highlight to cover the remaining information (Figure 5-8).

    b. Press the **DEL** key.

11. If Debbie really were going to use this information, she would now type a letter to Ms. Miller and print it. We will skip these steps.

12. Save this file as **MILLER2.WPS**.

Debbie has another client in Bedford. Let's follow the same procedure to enter the address for this client.

1. Use the **File/New** command to create a new word processor file.

2. Select **Window/PAINT2.WDB**. When the **PAINT2** database is displayed, the cursor is where it was when we last saw this screen, and *Works* remembers the last search we conducted.

3. Press **F7** to repeat the last search.

   The cursor will move to the next Bedford entry, which is part of the record about the William Tippett family (Figure 5-9).

```
 File  Edit  Print  Select  Format  Options  Query  Report  Window
"Bedford
      First Name  Last Name      Address       Address2      City
1     Robert     Downey     52 Wilmot Circle                Scarsdale
2     Peter      Brody      Box 456        Gilbert Street   South Salem
3     Gloria     Penberthy  Snake Hill Rd.                  Pound Ridge
4     Jerome     Adams      Apt 3M         Martine Ave.     White Plains
5     Robert     McDonald   Lakeshore Drive                 South Salem
6     Susan      Lippman    Whipporwill Drive               Armonk
7     John       Fischer    P.O. Box 1118  Sullivan Drive   Tarrytown
8     James      Patterson  Sheridan Hill Drive             Yorktown Heights
9     Suzanne    Miller     96 Summer Hill Rd.              Bedford
10    William    Tippett    Fox Hollow Run                  Bedford
11
12
...
20
10 City         10/10    LIST                              PAINT2.WDB
Press ALT to choose commands.
```

Figure 5-9

4. Choose **Select/Record** to highlight the record.

5. Select **Edit/Copy**.

6. Select **Window/WORD2.WPS** to return to the new word processor document.

Reformatting Copied Information 155

7. Press **ENTER**. The record of the Tippett family will appear at the top of your document (Figure 5-10).

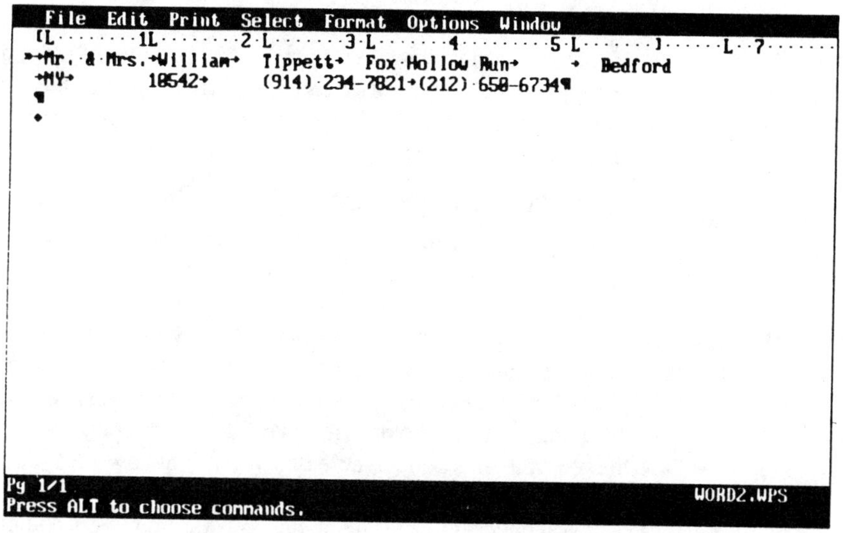

Figure 5-10

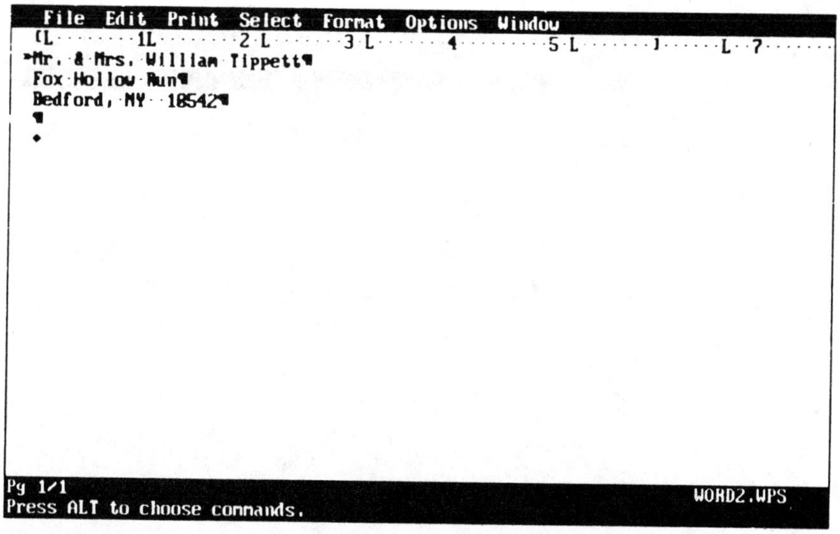

Figure 5-11

8. As you did in the letter to Suzanne Miller, either retype the information about the family, or edit the information (Figure 5-11).

9. Debbie's next step would be to type her letter to the Tippett family. We will not do this. If you want to save the file, do so using a name of your choice. (If you need to review rules for naming files, they are included in Chapter 1.)

156 Integrating Works: An Introduction

Intgrated Project No. 2
Inserting Information from a Database in
a Word Processor Document

Paul is sending a letter to his assistant, which should include the names of all of his Monday students, with their names and phone numbers. To do this, he would like to copy as much information as possible from his database into his word processor.

While completing this project you will review many of concepts learned in Project No. 1, as well as:

- Sorting a database.
- Closing files.

Managing the Files If you have just completed Project No. 1, you should close the files that you have been using before creating or opening the files for this project. *Works* will permit you to have eight files open at one time. Usually this is more than sufficient for the work that you wish to do. However, if you are spending a great deal of time using the program, it is conceivable that you might have eight files open and still want to open another one.

If you have eight files open, and you attempt to open another file or create a new one, the ERROR Dialog Box will appear on your screen. *Works* will inform you that there are *Too many files open*. At that time, you will have to use **File/Close** to close one or more of your files.

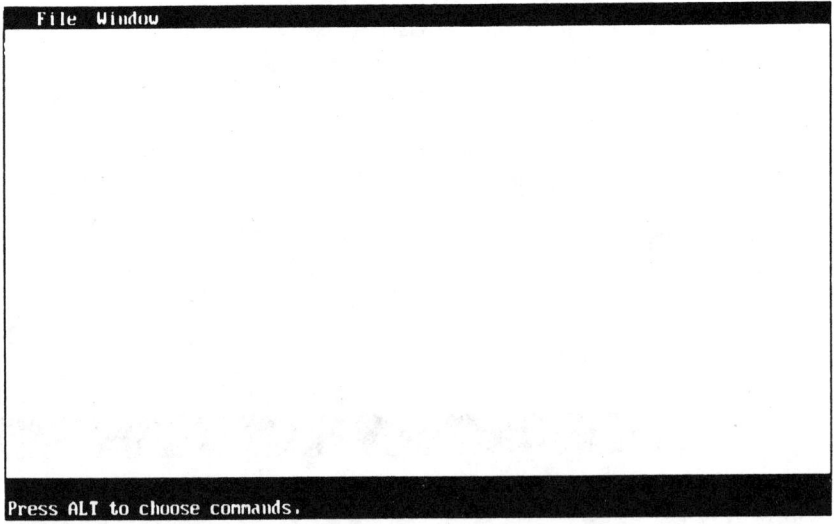

Figure 5-12

We will use **File/Close** at this time to close the files you were using in the first project.

1. Select **File/Close**.

Managing the Files 157

Works will cycle through the open files, from the last one opened to the first one opened. In each case, if you have not saved your changes, a Dialog Box will appear, asking if you want to save the changes. **TAB** to the **<No>** Button and press the **ENTER** key, or use **ALT+N** to close the file without saving the changes.

2. Continue selecting **File/Close** until all files are closed. Your screen will resemble Figure 5-12.

Now, we're ready to work on Paul's letter.

1. Select **File/Open** and open **PIANO2.WDB**. This will be our SOURCE file (Figure 5-13).

```
 File  Edit  Print  Select  Format  Options  Query  Report  Window
"Peter
      First Name     Last Name     Phone Number    Lesson Day
1    Peter          McCarthy      764-8765        Monday
2    Deborah        Jones         764-1234        Tuesday
3    Billy          Williams      861-7896        Wednesday
4    Marcy          McAllister    764-1424        Thursday
5    Aric           Press         764-8765        Monday
6    George         Hackett       725-1465        Tuesday
7    Jennifer       Skinner       725-8796        Monday
8    Robert         Fine          723-7659        Wednesday
9    Eva            Betka         723-1237        Thursday
10   Sam            Siebert       235-1987        Friday
11   Ronald         Henkoff       636-1965        Monday
12   Barbara        Rosen         632-5436        Tuesday
13   William        Lipinski      237-4532        Monday
14   Tom            Morganthau    681-8987        Thursday
15   Noelle         Gaffney       576-4378        Friday
16
17
18
19
20
1 First Name     15/15     LIST                          PIANO2.WDB
Press ALT to choose commands.
```

Figure 5-13

2. Now, create a new word processor file to serve as the DESTINATION file.

Note: If you have just started *Works*, this file will be called **WORD1.WPS**. Otherwise, it will be called **WORD3.WPS**, because we have already used **WORD1.WPS** and **WORD2.WPS**.

---

3. Enter the text which appears at the top of page 158.

George Starr
543 State St.
Ann Arbor, MI 48106

Dear George,

I am pleased to hear that you will be working with me on Mondays this year. Lessons will begin September 26th. Please call each of the parents prior to the first lesson to discuss your role in their children's musical education. Below is a list of the names and telephone numbers of the Monday students.

4. End the paragraph by pressing the **ENTER** key twice (Figure 5-14). The data from the SOURCE file will be copied at the point of the cursor.

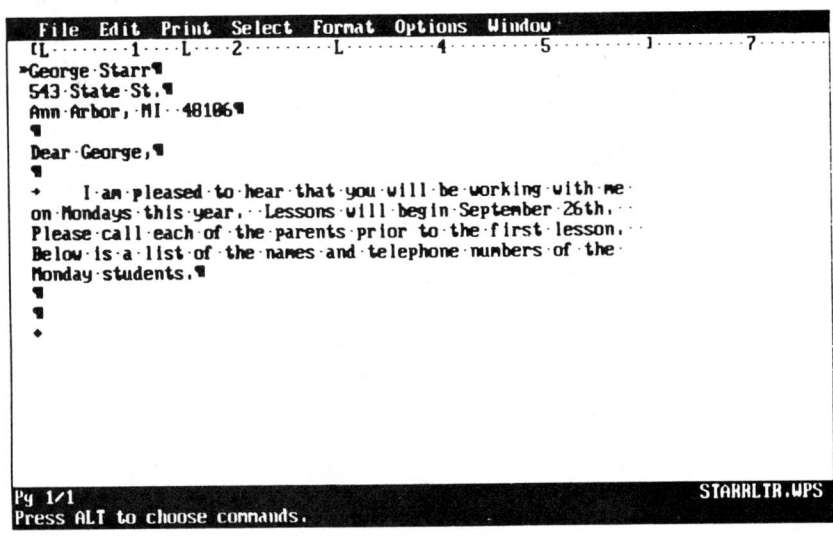

Figure 5-14

Copying from the Database to the Word Processor Now we're ready to get the information that we want to insert in our letter. We will display the database, sort it so that all of the Monday students are listed together in alphabetical order, and copy the names and phone numbers of the Monday students to our letter.

5. Select **Window/PIANO2.WDB** to display the **PIANO2** database.
6. Select **Query/Sort**.
7. Type: **lesson day** in the 1st Field Text Box.
8. Press **ALT+2** or **TAB** to the 2nd Field Text Box.
9. Type: **last name** (Figure 5-15)

    We want the records to be sorted, first by day of lesson and then by last name.

Copying from the Database to the Word Processor 159

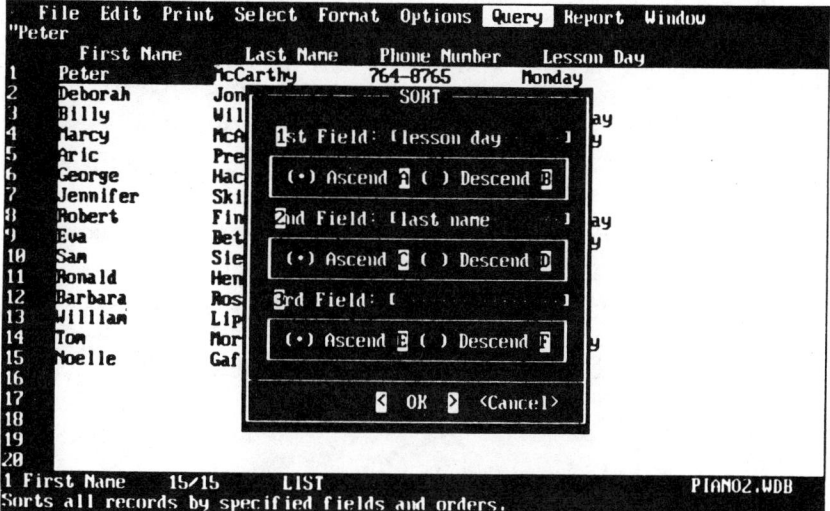

Figure 5-15

10. Press **ENTER**.
11. Choose **Select/Search**.

Note: If you have not exited *Works* since doing Project No. 1, the item searched for in that project, Bedford, will be displayed in the Search For Text Box.

12. Type: **Monday** and press **ENTER**.
13. Press the **LEFT ARROW** once to move the cursor to the phone number *636-1965*.
14. Press **F8** and use the **ARROW** keys to highlight the *First Name*, *Last Name*, and *Phone Number* fields for the Monday students (Figure 5-16).

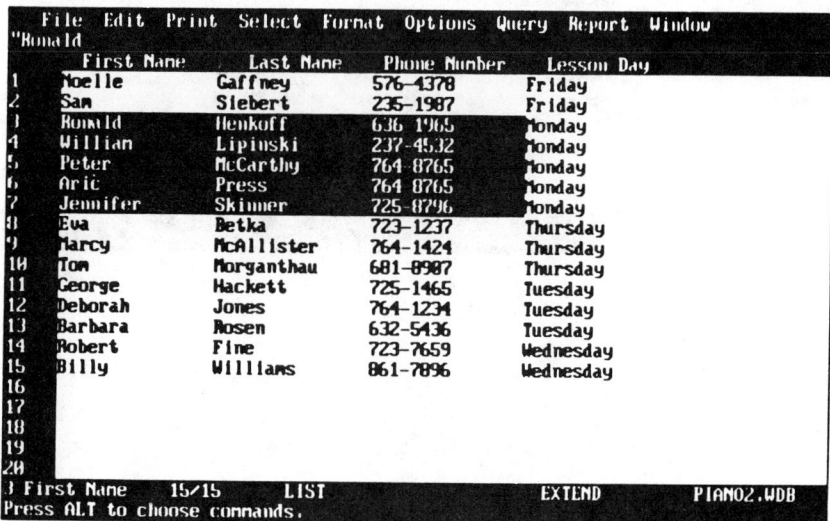

Figure 5-16

Integrating Works: An Introduction

15. Select **Edit/Copy**.
16. We wish to copy this information to our DESTINATION file. Using **Window**, select **WORD1.WPS** or **WORD3.WPS**, depending on which you used to start your letter.
17. Press **ENTER** to place the Monday students' information in the letter at the current cursor position (Figure 5-17).
18. Delete the tabs that precede each of the students' first names.
19. Move the cursor to the end of the last line.
20. Press **ENTER** to leave a blank line and then conclude your letter with the following (Figure 5-18):

```
Sincerely,



Paul
```

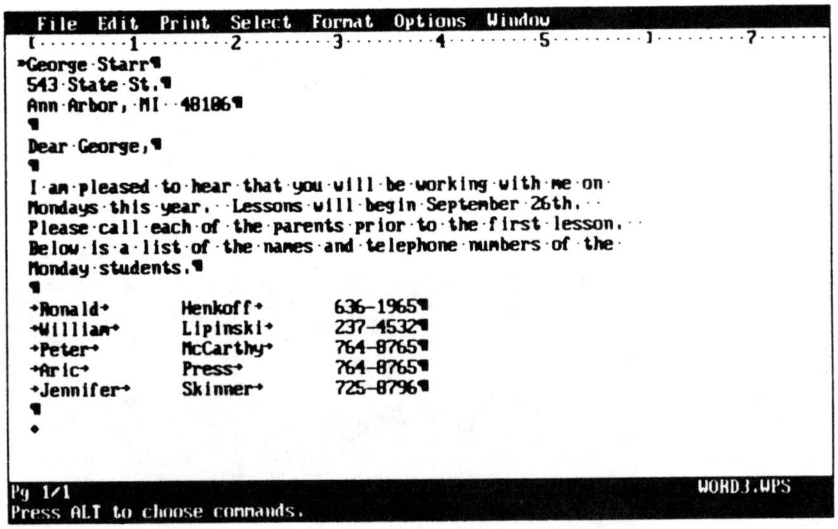

```
 File  Edit  Print  Select  Format  Options  Window
[.........1.........2.........3.........4.........5.......]......7.....
→George·Starr¶
 543·State·St.¶
 Ann·Arbor,·MI··48106¶
 ¶
 Dear·George,¶
 ¶
 I·am·pleased·to·hear·that·you·will·be·working·with·me·on·
 Mondays·this·year.··Lessons·will·begin·September·26th.··
 Please·call·each·of·the·parents·prior·to·the·first·lesson.·
 Below·is·a·list·of·the·names·and·telephone·numbers·of·the·
 Monday·students.¶
 ¶
 →Ronald→   Henkoff→    636-1965¶
 →William→  Lipinski→   237-4532¶
 →Peter→    McCarthy→   764-8765¶
 →Aric→     Press→      764-8765¶
 →Jennifer→ Skinner→    725-8796¶
 ¶
 ♦

Pg 1/1                                              WORD3.WPS
Press ALT to choose commands.
```

Figure 5-17

Managing the Files

```
 File  Edit  Print  Select  Format  Options  Window
[.........1.........2.........3.........4.........5.......].......7......
¶
Dear George,¶
¶
I am pleased to hear that you will be working with me on
Mondays this year.  Lessons will begin September 26th.
Please call each of the parents prior to the first lesson.
Below is a list of the names and telephone numbers of the
Monday students.¶
¶
Ronald→     Henkoff→      636-1965¶
William→    Lipinski→     237-4532¶
Peter→      McCarthy→     764-8765¶
Aric→       Press→        764-8765¶
Jennifer→   Skinner→      725-8796¶
¶
Sincerely,¶
¶
¶
¶
Paul¶
♦
Pg 1/1                                              WORD3.WPS
Press ALT to choose commands.
```

Figure 5-18

21. Save your finished letter, using a file name of your choice.
22. Print the finished letter.

Note: If you try printing this letter and the size of the print is smaller than normal, there is a problem with the printer selection. Try using **Print/Select Text Printer** to change the printer to **TTY**. If a problem remains, it is a result of the limited printer selections in the educational version and would not appear in the retail version.

Integrated Project No. 3
Including Information from a Spreadsheet in
a Word Processor Document

Sometimes there is information in a spreadsheet that you need to include in a word processor document. For example, we would like to include part of the budget that you prepared in Chapter 3 in a letter to your aunt and uncle. While preparing this letter you will learn how to:

- Copy information from a spreadsheet to a word processor document.
- Adjust the **Print/Layout** margins to accommodate the wider spreadsheet insert.

Managing the Files If you have not exited *Works* since completing Project No. 2, use the **File/Close** command to close all of the open files. If you need instructions for completing this task, see the beginning of Project No. 2.

Next, you need to make sure that the files that we wish to work with are open.

Integrating Works: An Introduction

1. Our SOURCE file will be the file called **BUDGET1.WKS**. Open that file now.
2. Our DESTINATION file will be a new word processor file. Create that file now.

Note: As we have seen before, the name *Works* assigns to that file will depend on how many word processor files you have created since last starting Works.

Now, let's begin with the word processor file and type a short note to precede the data from the spreadsheet.

3. Type the text for the letter:

> Dear Aunt Helen and Uncle Steve,
>
> I thought that you would get a kick out of seeing how well I am (or am not) doing with my budget this Fall. Actually, the first three months have not been too bad, and I think that December should be a somewhat less expensive month.
>
> I also thought that you would find it interesting to see how I am able to use my new Microsoft Works program to both write you a letter as well as to keep track of my finances. You would be amazed to see how easy it is for me to transfer the spreadsheet data into this letter, just by copying it from one part of my program to another. Here goes!!

4. Make sure that you press the **ENTER** key twice at the end of the letter so that the cursor is positioned correctly for the spreadsheet data that we will include.
5. Save this letter as **WILSON** on your data disk.

Copying from the Spreadsheet to the Word Processor

1. Select **Window/BUDGET1.WKS**.
2. Move the cursor to cell *A6*.
3. Press your **F8** key and **EXTEND** your cursor to highlight cells *A6* through *G16* (Figure 5-19).
4. Now, select **Edit/Copy**.
5. Move back to the Wilson letter by selecting **Window/WILSON.WPS**.
6. Press **ENTER**. As if by magic, the selected portion of the spreadsheet will appear (Figure 5-20).

Reformatting Copied Information

7. If the tab symbols are not displayed on your screen, select **Options/Show All Characters** to display them.

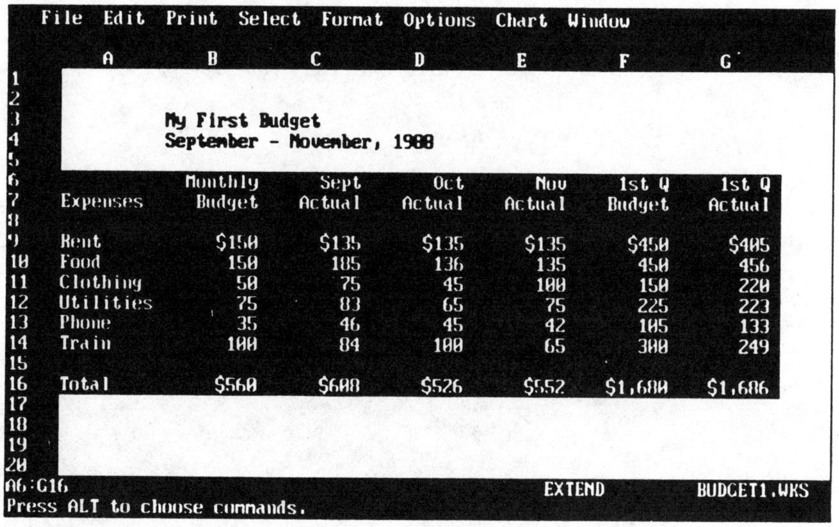

Reformatting Copied Information 163

Figure 5-19

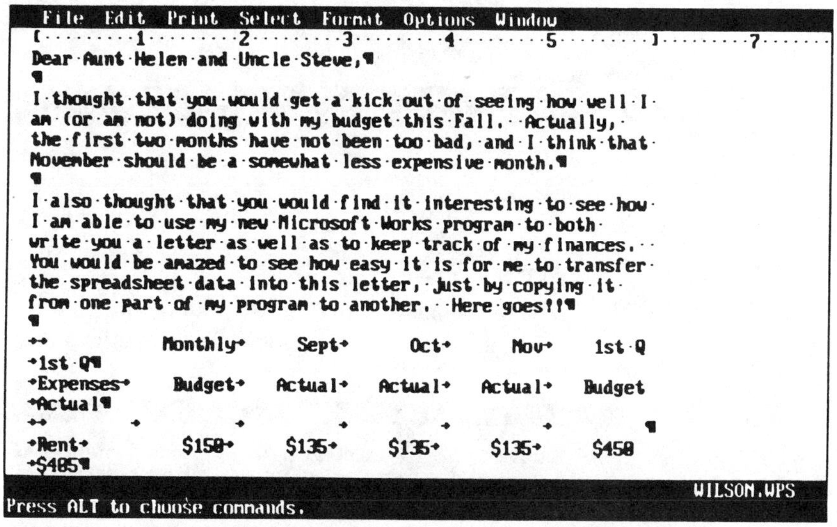

Figure 5-20

You may notice that the budget doesn't look quite the way it should. However, it is fairly easy to correct these problems. The first problem is the one most commonly encountered when spreadsheet data is integrated into a word processor document. The width of the spreadsheet section copied is wider than the line length. Therefore, the first quarter actual expenses word wrap to the next line. If you read down the first column, you will notice that the expense categories (*Rent, Food*, etc.) are mingled with the 1st quarter expenses (*$405, $456*, etc.). Since the difference in width is small, we can correct this problem by using the **Print/Layout** command to change the width of the margins (and thereby increase the length of each line of text). You have already used this technique in the spreadsheet chapter, when you decreased the margins so that the spreadsheets could be printed on one page.

Integrating Works: An Introduction

1. Select **Print/Layout**.
2. **TAB** to the Left Margin Text Box or press **ALT+E** to move the highlight to the Text Box.
3. Type the new Left Margin size: **.5"**
4. Change the Right Margin Text Box to: **.5"** (See Figure 5-21.)

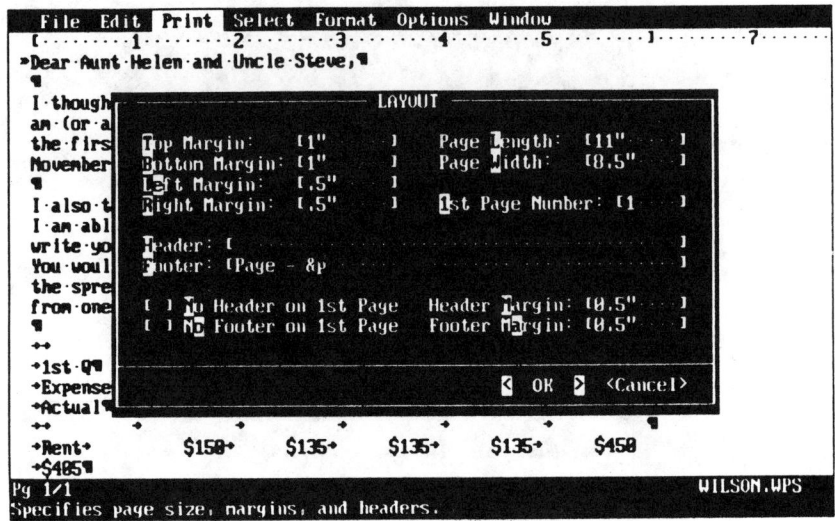

Figure 5-21

5. Press **ENTER**.

   Each spreadsheet row is now on one line, but the figures that have been formatted with dollar signs still are not aligned correctly (Figure 5-22).

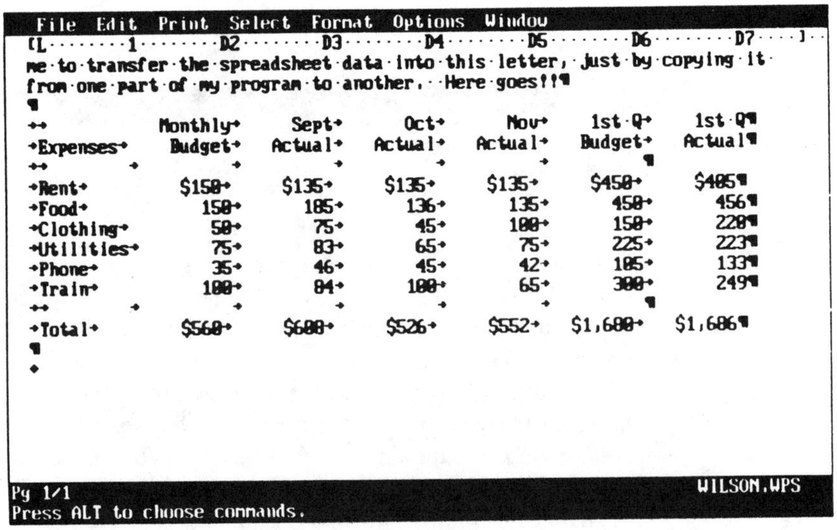

Figure 5-22

Reformatting Copied Information 165

6. Beginning with *Expenses*, delete the tab that precedes the first entry in each line (i.e., *Expenses*, *Rent*, *Food*, etc.)
7. Now, let's line up the values in the rows formatted with dollar signs.
    a. Move your cursor to the tab symbol following the word Rent.
    b. Delete the tab symbol. The cursor should now be under the $.
    c. Press the **SPACE BAR** until the **$150** is lined up with the *150* in the row below it. You will need to press the **SPACE BAR** until spaces (represented by dots) extend from the Rent entry to the dollar sign (Figure 5-23).

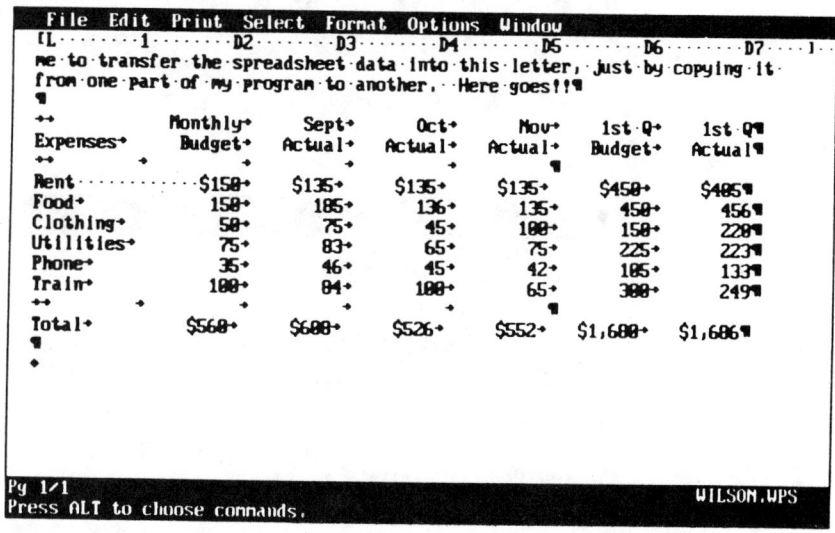

Figure 5-23

   d. Delete the tab following *$150* and enter spaces to align the next value in the line.
   e. Repeat steps a-c for the remaining entries in this line and all of the entries in the other line that is formatted for currency (the *Totals* line).

   Figure 5-24 (next page) illustrates the screen after all of the figures have been aligned.

8. Now insert a blank line at the end of the spreadsheet data and conclude your letter with the following:

As you can see, this has been a pretty good start on my new fiscal policy! It was great seeing you at Thanksgiving.

Lots of love,

Terry

```
File  Edit  Print  Select  Format  Options  Window
[L·······1······D2······D3······D4······D5······D6······D7···]
me to transfer the spreadsheet data into this letter, just by copying it
from one part of my program to another.  Here goes!!¶
¶
→→         Monthly→    Sept→     Oct→      Nov→      1st Q→    1st Q¶
Expenses→  Budget→    Actual→   Actual→   Actual→   Budget→   Actual¶
→→            →          →         →         ¶
Rent·········$150·····$135······$135······$135······$450······$405¶
Food→         150→     185→      136→      135→      450→      456¶
Clothing→     50→      75→       45→       100→      150→      220¶
Utilities→    75→      83→       65→       75→       225→      223¶
Phone→        35→      46→       45→       42→       105→      133¶
Train→        100→     84→       100→      65→       300→      249¶
→→             →         →          →          ¶
Total·········$560·····$600······$526······$552·····$1,600····$1,686¶
¶
◆

Pg 1/1                                                      WILSON.WPS
Press ALT to choose commands.
```

Figure 5-24

9. Save the file again using the same name.
10. Print Terry's letter.

Saving All Open Files When you are working with the **Window** part of *Works*, you will always have at least two files open at one time, and occasionally more than that. Sometimes, it is hard to keep track of which changes you have made, and which files you have saved when you are done changing them.

Works has a wonderful feature built into it that should help you with this problem. If you select **File/Save All**, *Works* will cycle through all of the open files, and save any of the ones that have been opened and changed, but not saved. Try this now. If nothing appears to happen, it means that you have not made any changes since the files were last changed.

Conclusion

In this chapter, we have tried to introduce you to some of the concepts used in integrating the different parts of *Works*. As you have seen, we are able to move quickly back and forth among our word processor, spreadsheet, and database files. In all three projects, we were able to copy quickly and use information from one of the SOURCE files in a DESTINATION file. While there are some more sophisticated techniques available when using the integrated aspect of *Works* (we'll learn one in Chapter 6), the ones you have learned in this chapter should provide you with a feeling for the power of *Works*!

Key Terms

The following important terms and commands have been introduced in this chapter:

    Source File   Destination File   Window/(file name)
    Select/Record   File/Save All

Independent Integrated Project No. 1

In this project, we would like you to take the **Sporting Goods Budget** that you created as an independent project at the end of Chapter 3 and integrate it into a memo that you will create now. When you are done, it should resemble Figure 5-25.

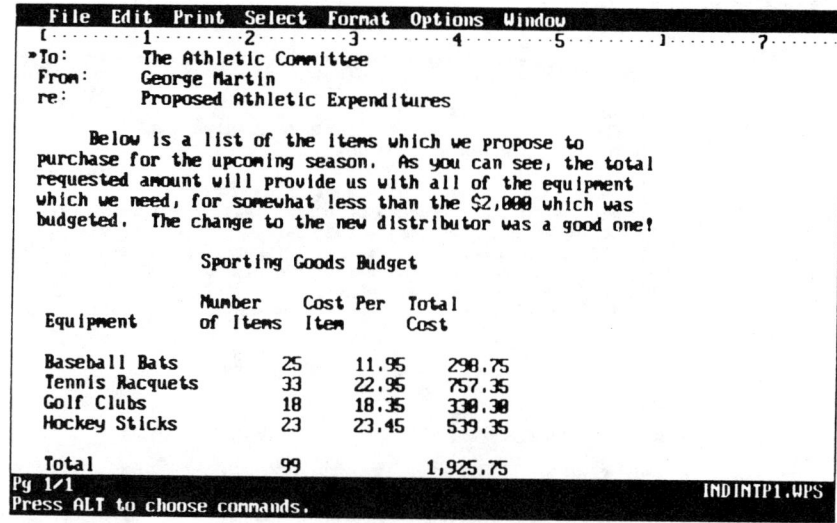

Figure 5-25

1. Open a new word processor file.
2. Open **INDPROJ1.WKS**.
3. Write the following memo:

To:	The Athletic Committee
From:	George Martin
re:	Proposed Athletic Expenditures
	Below is a list of the items which we propose to purchase for the upcoming season. As you can see, the total requested amount will provide us with all of the equipment which we need, for somewhat less than the $2,000 which was budgeted. The change to the new distributor was a good one!

168 Integrating Works: An Introduction

4. Save your file as **INDINTP1.WPS**.

5. Using **Window**, switch to the **INDPROJ1.WKS**. Highlight cells *A2* through *D13*, and then **Copy** the information over to your word processor document. Save your file again, now that it is complete.

Independent Integrated Project No. 2

Again, we are going to integrate information that was created with a spreadsheet into a memo being created with the word processor. We will write a short cover letter for the budget that was created for the computer science department. When you are done, it should resemble Figure 5-26.

```
 File Edit Print Select Format Options Window
[.........1.........2.........3.........4.........5.........]........7....
>To:       The Dean
 From:     Your faithful department chairperson
 re:       Next year's budget

 Here is the Department Budget which you requested.  I
 believe that it reflects University guidelines with regard
 to increments for Faculty and Staff.  The percent of
 additional money for Hardware, Software, Travel and Research
 is higher than the 18% that we had discussed, but I think
 that the funds are all defensible in light of the
 discussions at our last department meeting.  Thoughts?

                    Departmental Budget
                   1988 - 1989 and 1989 - 1990

               1988/    1989/
 Category      1989     1990      Change   % Change

 Faculty      300,000  330,000    30,000     18%
 Staff         45,000   52,000     7,000     16%
 Hardware      23,000   27,000     4,000     17%
Pg 1/1                                              INDINTP2.WPS
Press bold letter in menu or use DIRECTION keys and press ENTER.
```

Figure 5-26

1. Open a new word processor file.

2. Make sure that the **INDPROJ2.WKS** file from Chapter 3 is open.

3. Notice that the largest percentage of change in the budget has to do with Software, Travel, and Research.

4. Here is the memo that we would like to send along with the budget:

Independent Integrated Project No. 2

> To: The Dean
> From: Your faithful department chairperson
> re: Next year's budget
>
> Here is the Department Budget which you requested. I believe that it reflects University guidelines with regard to increments for Faculty and Staff. As you can see, the percent of additional money for Hardware, Software, Travel, and Research is higher than the 10% that we had discussed, but I think that the funds are all defensible in light of the discussions at our last department meeting. Thoughts?

5. Save this memo as **INDINTP2.WPS** and then copy the Spreadsheet from **INDPROJ2.WKS** into it.

6. Save your file again, and then print out a copy.

Chapter 6 Extending Your Knowledge with Microsoft Works

In this chapter you will learn how to:

- Enhance word processing documents by adding bold, underlining, and italics.
- Center text in a word processing document.
- Set and change tab stops in a word processing document.
- Start a new line but not a new paragraph.
- Change the spacing of part of a document from single to double.
- Modify existing spreadsheets by inserting columns.
- Create and copy formulas using absolute cell addresses.
- Hide columns so that nonadjacent parts of the spreadsheet can be printed.
- Use the MIN and MAX functions in spreadsheets.
- Copy more than one cell at a time in a spreadsheet.
- Create and modify a chart based on data in a spreadsheet.
- Modify an existing database by adding a field.
- Create simple queries of the database.
- Create and modify a report of data in a database.
- Create and print a customized form letter.

In the preceding chapters, we have taken a first look at the Word Processor, Spreadsheet, and Database tools of *Works* and the ways in which the individual tools can be used together. *Works* has many features that were not covered. In this chapter, we will take another look at each of these tools and integration. The projects will introduce some of the features not previously explored, expand on skills introduced in earlier chapters, and show you alternative ways for doing previously learned tasks.

The format of this chapter is similar to that of the previous chapters with one change. Since many different topics relating to different tools are covered, independent projects are included throughout the chapter as appropriate, rather than grouped at the end.

The Word Processor Tool

In Chapter 2 we looked at basic document preparation skills—entering, editing, saving, printing, and retrieving documents. We also explored the power of word processing by learning some advanced editing commands involving selecting blocks of text, and moving and copying. In this chapter we will learn how easy it is to enhance and customize the appearance of documents with *Works*.

Formatting Text

The appearance of the text in your word processor documents can be altered by using the Format menu commands. Text can be displayed using bold, underline, or italic, or with a superimposed strikethrough character (dashed line). In addition, individual characters or groups of characters can be printed as superscripts or subscripts. The retail version of *Works* also allows different fonts and text sizes to be used for different parts of the document. This feature is not supported in the educational version of *Works*.

The Format menu options also allow you to center, right or left justify a paragraph. *Works* defines a paragraph as text of any length followed by a paragraph mark. Each time you press the **ENTER** key, a paragraph mark is inserted in the text.

When the format is changed without first selecting existing text, all new text will appear in the new format. Previously typed text can be reformatted by selecting the text and then using the Format menu to change the format.

Extended Skills Project No. 1
Enhancing Paul's Letter

Paul wants to enhance the letter he wrote to parents in Word Processor Project No. 2 by using the bold, underline, and center options.

In this project you will learn how to:

- Bold, underline, and center existing text.
- Use shortcut keys to bypass a menu command.

Bold and underline may affect any number of characters. Therefore, the general procedure followed is:

- Select the text to be formatted.
- Select **Format/Bold**, **Format/Underline**, or **Format/Character**.
- Cancel the selected text.

Centering text is a **paragraph** format. Paragraph formats affect the entire paragraph containing the cursor. Therefore, the general steps involved are different from those used to bold and underline:

- Move the cursor anywhere in the paragraph to be centered.
- Select **Format/Center**.

Formatting Text

A copy of the enhanced letter follows. If you have not completed Word Processor Project No. 2, first enter the text that follows, *without* centering the *THEORY CLASS* and *RECITALS* titles or emphasizing text. (See Word Processor Project No. 2 for directions if necessary.)

Dear Parents,

Time to begin another year of piano lessons! All lessons will begin the week of September 26th. We have already discussed the time for your child's individual lessons. The times and locations of this year's other events are listed at the end of this page.

As we discussed, this year I will be holding small group theory classes once a month in addition to the weekly individual piano lessons. There is no extra fee for these sessions. I hope your child will be able to attend.

The children will also give two recitals, one in January and one in June.

RECITALS

Date: Sunday, January 29
Time: 7:30 - 9:00 p.m.
Place: Green Room
          Tamany Hall

Date: Wednesday, June 13
Time: 7:30 - 9:00 p.m.
Place: Green Room
          Tamany Hall

THEORY CLASS -- 6 - 9 years of age

Day: *First Sunday* of each month
Time: 5:00 - 6:00 p.m.
Place: Simpson Room
          Whitney Hall

THEORY CLASS -- 10 years of age and older

Day: *Second Sunday* of each month
Time: 5:00 - 6:00 p.m.
Place: Simpson Room
          Whitney Hall

I'm looking forward to another year of working with you and your child.

                        Paul Harrison

Extending Your Knowledge with Microsoft Works

Now we're ready to add bold, underline, and centering to the document.

1. If you have previously created Paul's scheduling letter, open the file (our suggested file name was **SCHEDLTR.WPS**).
2. To center the first section title:
   a. Place the cursor anywhere on the title *RECITALS*.
   b. Select **Format/Center**. (Figure 6.1 shows the *Format* menu.)

Note: The bold letter in "Format" is a "t", not an "F." Typing "F" will open the *File* menu.

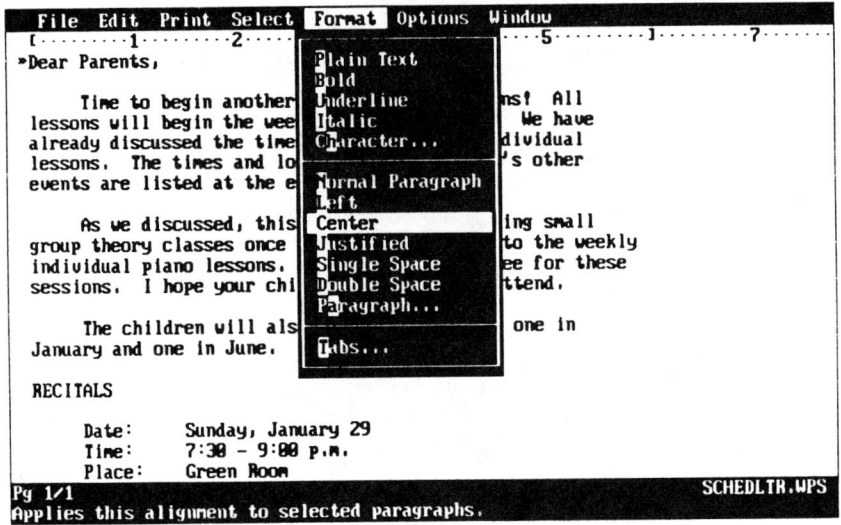

Figure 6-1

3. To bold the section title:
   a. Use the **F8** key to highlight the word that you have just centered.
   b. Select **Format/Bold**.

Caution: The highlighted text remains selected until you move the cursor. If you accidently type a character, the character will replace the highlighted text. If this happens, you may use the **Edit/Undo** command to restore the original text.

4. To underline text:
   a. Move the cursor to the *D* in *Date*.
   b. Highlight: *Date*

Formatting Text 175

> *Note:* Do not highlight the colon following *Date*.

      c. Select **Format/Underline**.

> *Note:* Bold and underlined text both will appear on the screen in bold letters. However, as you move the cursor under a formatted letter, the Status Line will contain a letter indicating what enhancement has been selected (*B*=Bold, *I*=Italic, *U*=Underline).

    5. Underline *Date*, *Time*, and *Place* each time they appear in the Recitals section.

Formatting Shortcut Keys   *Works* provides shortcut keys that enable you to perform the main formatting options in fewer steps. The shortcut keys only take the place of the Format menu commands; they do not select the text to be enhanced. Therefore, you must highlight the text before you use the shortcut keys just as you would before using the Format menu commands. The shortcut keys for the character formats and for centering paragraphs are:

Shortcut Keys	Format
CTRL+B	Bold
CTRL+U	Underline
CTRL+I	Italic
CTRL+S	Strikethrough (dashed line)
CTRL+SHIFT+=	Superscript
CTRL+=	Subscript
CTRL+SPACEBAR	Plain text
CTRL+C	Center Paragraph

    1. Use the shortcut keys to center, bold, and underline the appropriate parts of the THEORY section of Paul's letter, *except* for "First Sunday" and "Second Sunday." These will be italicized and underlined later using the **Format/Character** command. Use the sample letter at the beginning of the project to determine the parts of the letter to be enhanced.

    2. Save the letter, using the same or a new file name.

    3. Print the letter.

> *Note:* If the underlined and bold words do not print correctly, check your document to make sure that the letter has been formatted correctly. If it has been, the failure to print text enhancements is probably caused by the limited printer setups available with the educational version of *Works*.

Using the Format Character Option

The **Format/Character** option is another way of changing the style of characters. It is typically used to change their fonts (an option available only in the full version of *Works*) or their positions. However, **Format/Character** also is used when you want to enhance a character in more than one way.

To emphasize the difference between the two theory classes, we will enhance the day of each class by adding both italics and underlining:

1. Highlight: *First Sunday*
2. Select **Format/Character**.

   The CHARACTER Dialog Box (Figure 6-2) has Check Boxes in addition to the List and Option Boxes we have used previously. Check Boxes are similar to Option Boxes except that more than one item may be selected at a time.

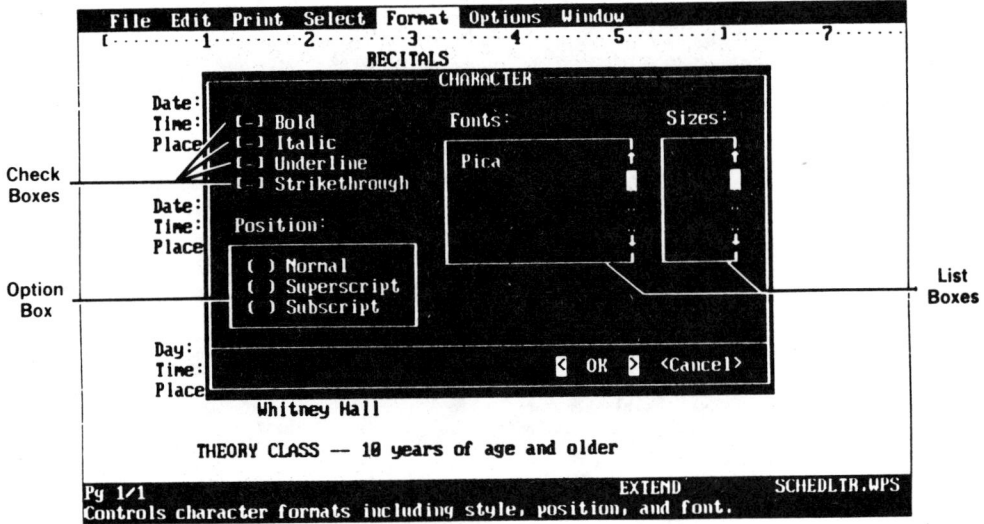

Figure 6-2

If only one character has been highlighted when the **Format/Character** command is invoked, the selections which apply to that character will be marked.

If two or more characters have been highlighted, the Check Boxes will contain a dash, indicating that they are neutral, while the Option and List Boxes will not have anything selected. The general procedure for changing an item in a Check Box from selected to nonselected or vice versa, is to **TAB** to the desired item and press the **SPACE BAR** or to press **ALT+bold letter**. Only *attributes* that you *change* will affect the highlighted text. For example, if part of the selected text already was bold and part was not, and you select underline, the entire selected text will be underlined but only those parts that originally were bold will continue to be bold.

3. To select italics and underlining, **TAB** to the Italic and Underline Check Boxes and press the **SPACE BAR** in each, or press **Alt+I** and **Alt+U** (Figure 6-3).

Formatting Text

Caution: Each Check Box is a separate Dialog Box element so you have to use the **TAB** key to move from one to the next. If you press the **DOWN ARROW** key to try to move to the next Check Box, it will have the same effect as pressing the **SPACE BAR**. It will toggle off the selection that you just made.

   4. Press **ENTER**.

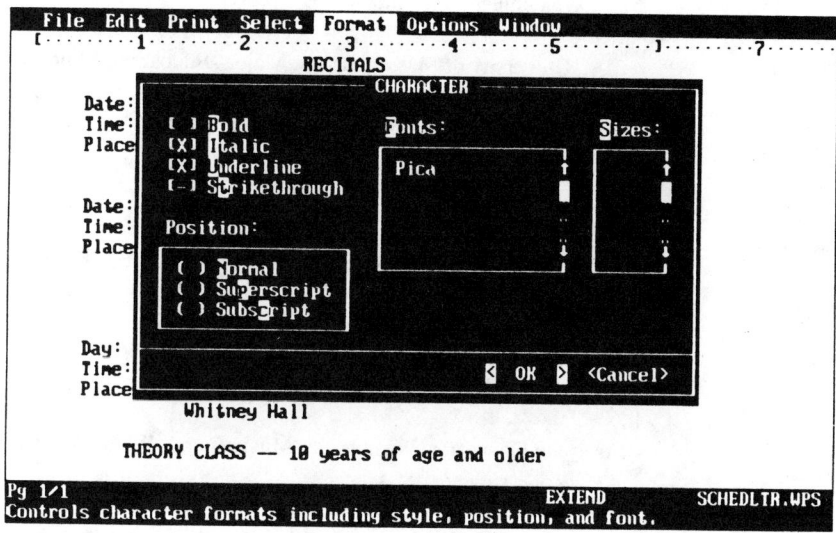

Figure 6-3

   5. Make *Second Sunday* (under the second theory class heading) underlined and italicized.
   6. Save and print your document again.

Note: Not all printers support italics, particularly with the TTY printer setup.

Independent Extended Skills Project No. 1
Enhancing Paul's Resume

Use bold, underline and centering to enhance Paul's resume (Independent Word Processing Project No. 2). Make Paul's resume resemble the following or choose enhancements of your own.

> Paul Harrison
> 123 Strawberry Lane
> Ann Arbor, Michigan 48108
> Telephone: (313)345-6789
>
> **EDUCATION**
>
> Graduate Student, University of Michigan School of Music, Ann Arbor, Michigan, September 1987 - present
>
> B.A., University of Massachusetts, Major--Education, Minor--Music, Amherst, Massachusetts, September 1981 - June 1985
>
> **EXPERIENCE**
>
> <u>Elementary School Teacher</u>, Little Falls, New York, September 1985 - June 1987
>
> <u>Accompanist</u>, Ross-Spaulding Music School, Scarsdale, New York, September 1980 - June 1981
>
> <u>Assistant Counselor</u>, Westchester Music Camp, White Plains, New York, summer 1981
>
> <u>Participant</u>, Interlochen Music Camp, Interlochen, Michigan, summers 1978, 1979
>
> <u>Participant</u>, Westchester Music Camp, White Plains, New York, summers 1974 - 1977
>
> **PERSONAL INTERESTS**
>
> Piano, computers, photography
>
> **<u>REFERENCES AVAILABLE UPON REQUEST</u>**

Extended Skills Project No. 2
Changing Tabs and Line Spacing

In Expanded Skills Project No. 1, we changed the appearance of the document by centering or enhancing the text characters. The appearance also can be changed by altering the placement of the text on the page. In Chapter 5 we used the **Print/Layout** command to change the left and right margins. In this project, we will use

Formatting Text

the **Format** command to change the spacing between lines of text and to change the placement and type of tab settings.

In this project you will learn how to:

- Set right, left, and center tabs.
- Use the **SHIFT+ENTER** keys to move the cursor to a new line without creating a new paragraph.
- Clear existing tab stops.
- Change tab stops in existing text.
- Change the line spacing.

You will also review the use of the **Print/Layout** command to change margins.

Tab Settings Each new word processor file has default tab settings at .5 inch intervals. In Word Processing Project No. 2 we used the default tabs, pressing the **TAB** key more than once in order to allow more space between columns. Instead of doing this, we can set the tab stops at the exact positions desired. In addition, we can change the alignment of the tab. The possible tab alignment settings are:

Left	Text begins at the tab; this is the default setting
Right	The cursor moves to the tab; all text is entered to the left of the tab
Decimal	Text is aligned so that the decimal point is at the tab position; if no decimal point is typed, this works the same way as a right tab
Center	Text is centered around the tab position
Leaders	A leader is a character, such as a period, which will be printed between the last character typed before pressing **TAB** and the tab stop. For example:

Word wrap.......56

The general procedure for establishing new tab settings is:

- Select **Format/Tabs**.
- Type the new position of the tab.
- If the tab is not a left tab, change the alignment to center, right, or decimal
- If a leader character is desired, select the character.

Default tab settings often are changed to create tabular columns. We will create the following portion of a letter, which includes a column chart:

Enclosed is a listing of our Personal Computer Workshop offerings for March and April. For further course descriptions or registration information, please call 323-4343.

Workshop	Program Used	Dates
Integrated	Works	3/1, 3/2
Word Processing	Word	3/11, 3/12
Spreadsheet	Excel	4/6, 4/7
Database	Javelin	4/10, 4/11

1. If you have already been using *Works*, close all open files.
2. Type the first paragraph of the preceding letter.
3. Press the **ENTER** key twice.

Now let's look at the default tab settings:

1. Select **Options/Show All Characters** so that you will be able to see the tab characters once they are used.
2. Press the **TAB** key several times. Arrows will appear indicating tab stops at .5 inch intervals.

Note: Under the default settings, .5 inches equals five spaces or characters because one inch is assumed to equal 10 characters. The reason the default unit for all settings is inches is that the number of characters per inch changes as you change fonts. By setting tabs and margins in inches, the spacing will remain consistant regardless of the font used. If, however, you would like to use a different unit of measure, the **Window/Settings** command can be used to change the units to centimeters, 10 pitch, 12 pitch, or points.

3. Press the **BACKSPACE** key to erase all of the **TAB** marks.

Setting Tab Stops

Now let's set left tabs at .5 and 2.5 inches, and a center tab at 5 inches:

1. Select **Format/Tabs**.

   The TABS Dialog Box will appear (Figure 6-4).

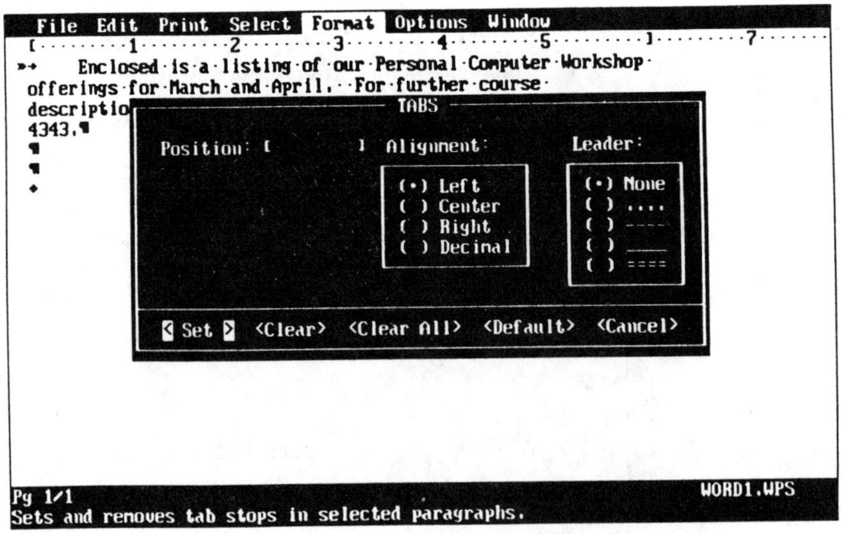

Figure 6-4

Formatting Text

                The cursor should be in the Position Text Box.

2. Type: **2.5**
3. Press **ENTER**. Since the **<SET>** Button is the active (highlighted) button, pressing **ENTER** sets the tab.

    An *L* (for left tab) now will appear on the ruler between the 2 and 3 markers.

                [..........1..........2....L....3..........4..........5..........]

4. Press the **TAB** key.

    Notice that the cursor moves directly to the new tab setting.

Note: Whenever a tab is set, *all* of the *default settings* to the left of the new setting disappear. Therefore, although a tab was set at .5 by default, it was removed when a new tab was set at 2.5 inches.

---

5. Use **Format/Tabs** to set a left tab at: **.5**
6. To set a Center Tab at 5 inches:
   a. Type: **5**

      DO NOT press the **ENTER** key.

   b. Set the Alignment to: **Center**
   c. Press **ENTER**.

    Notice that a *C* appears in place of the *5* marker.

Using the Shift+Enter Keys

Now we're ready to enter the information for the chart.

1. Make sure that all tab characters have been deleted and that the cursor is at the left margin.
2. Press the **TAB** key once. Type: **Workshop**
3. Press **TAB** again and type: **Program Used**
4. Press **TAB** again and type: **Dates**

    Notice that after you type every second letter in **Dates**, the entire entry moves back one space. This centers the entry around the tab position.

5. Press the **SHIFT+ENTER** key *two* times to end the current line and leave one blank line, without beginning a new paragraph.

Note: The **SHIFT+ENTER** key combination affects wordwrap in the same way that the **ENTER** key alone does; however, it does not end a paragraph. Since *Works* allows you to rapidly format and manipulate entire paragraphs, it is sometimes useful to use this for text such as tables that are treated as one unit. If **Options/Show All Characters** has been activated, you will see a down arrow inserted each time **SHIFT+ENTER** is pressed.

6. Use tabs to type the remaining four lines of the table. Press **SHIFT+ENTER** at the end of the first three lines. At the end of the last line, press the **ENTER** key to end the table and paragraph.

Integrated	Works	3/1, 3/2
Word Processing	Word	4/11, 4/12
Spreadsheet	Excel	6/6, 6/7
Database	Javelin	7/10, 7/11

When finished, your screen should resemble Figure 6-5.

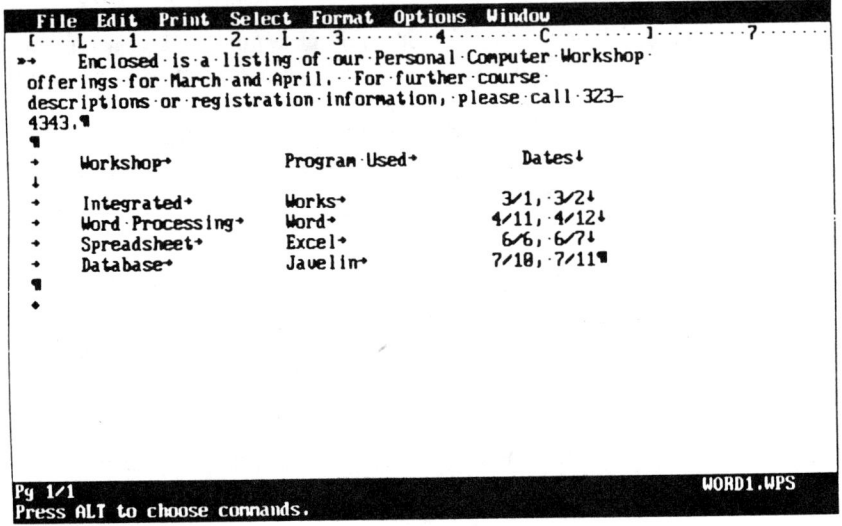

Figure 6-5

Changing Existing Tab Stops

After creating the table, you decide that you want to add a column. To do this, you need to move the *Dates* column so that there is enough room for the new column. To avoid having extra tab stops, you should clear the old tab position after adding the new tab.

1. Move the cursor anywhere in the table.
2. Select **Format/Tab**.
3. Create a **Center** tab at **4.5** inches.

    As soon as you press the **ENTER** key, the entire last column is moved so that the text is centered around the new tab position.

4. To delete the Center tab that exists at 5 inches:

    a. Select **Format/Tab**.

    b. Enter the position of the tab to be removed: **5**

    c. Select the **<CLEAR>** Button by pressing **Alt+C** or **TAB** to the **<CLEAR>** Button and press the **ENTER** key.

Formatting Text   183

5. Now add a new tab setting with the following attributes:
   Position: **6**
   Alignment: **Right**

6. Make sure that **Options/Show All Characters** has been activated. It is difficult to position the cursor correctly to add the new column unless you can see the characters indicating the current end of line.

7. Position the cursor at the end of the first line of the table (under the down arrow code). Press the **TAB** and type: **Page**

Caution: If the cursor is to the right of the down arrow code rather than under it, the tab will be entered on the line below the one it should be.

---

8. Press the **DOWN ARROW** twice to move to the next line of text.

9. Add the last column of the table. Be sure your cursor is under the down arrow code when you **TAB**.

Integrated	*Works*	*3/1, 3/2*	**4**
Word Processing	*Word*	*4/11, 4/12*	**9**
Spreadsheet	*Excel*	*6/6, 6/7*	**10**
Database	*Javelin*	*7/10, 7/11*	**11**

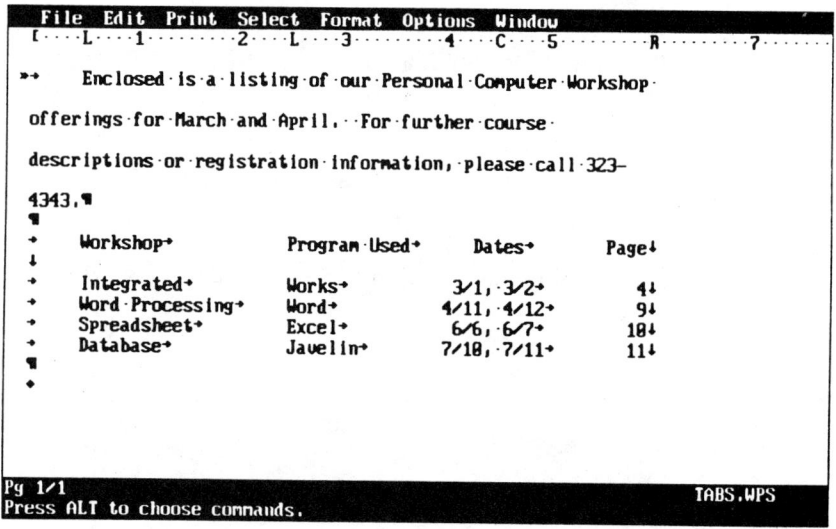

Figure 6-6

Changing the Line Spacing   After looking at your letter, you decide that it would look better if the opening paragraph were double spaced instead of single spaced. The **Format/Double Space** option can be used to change this.

1. Move the cursor anywhere in the first paragraph.

2. Select **Format/Double**.

Note: To change the format of multiple paragraphs to double spaced, use the **F8** and **ARROW** keys to select the portion of the document to be changed and then select **Format/Double**. As with the tab setting commands, if the line spacing is changed before entering text, the newly entered text will be entered double spaced. Triple or fractional line spacings can be entered using the **Format/Paragraph** command.

---

3. Save the letter using the name **TABS**.

   The finished letter with codes shown should resemble Figure 6-6 on the following page.

Independent Extended Skills Project No. 2
Using Tabs in a Letter

In the letter on the following page we will use tabs to create a tabular chart and to right justify the date and the letter closing. Use the copy of the finished letter and the instructions that follow to complete the letter.

Today's Date

Joy Watson
234 South Street
White Plains, NY 10601

Dear Ms. Watson:

 Below is a list of Caribbean tours that should fit nicely with your travel plans.

Destination	Departure Date	Duration
Aruba	8/1	5 days
St. Thomas	8/5	4 days
St. Croix	8/7	5 days
Aruba	8/11	3 days

Let me know which tour you'd like to schedule.

Sincerely yours,

Julie Winters
Travel Representative
ABC Tours

Instructions:

1. Set a **Right** tab at **6** inches.
2. Press the **TAB** key once and type today's date.
3. Leave six blank lines.
4. Type the inside address, salutation, and first paragraph.
5. Set **Left** tabs at **.5, 2.5**, and **4.5** inches.
6. Type the tour schedule using the tabs that you have just set.
7. Type the last sentence of the paragraph.
8. Clear the tab setting at **4.5** inches.
9. Type the letter closing using the right tab setting to align them at the right margin.

Note: When text is typed at a right tab, it is entered to the left of the tab until the previous tab setting is encountered. Any remaining text is then word wrapped to the next line. Therefore, it was necessary to clear the tab at 4.5 inches before typing the salutation.

10. Save and print the letter.

The Spreadsheet Tool

Our second look at the spreadsheet tool will focus on expanding your ability to use one of the most powerful features of *Works*—formulas. You'll learn to create formulas that remain constant when they are copied. You will also practice using some new functions in formulas. In addition, we'll introduce *Works'* charting capabilities that enable you to graph your spreadsheet data.

Relative and Absolute Copying

When you created spreadsheets in Chapter 3, you learned to copy a formula from one cell to other cells. *Works* automatically adjusted the cell addresses in the formula so that the relationship between the cell containing the formula and the cells making up the formula remained constant. This automatic procedure is referred to as **relative cell adjustment**. Sometimes, however, you do not want the cell addresses to adjust. You can stop a cell address from adjusting when you copy the formula containing it to another cell location by making the reference to the cell address **absolute** when you create the formula. An absolute cell address reference is indicated by dollar signs preceding the row and column names (e.g., *$A$1*).

Extended Skills Project No. 3
Relative and Absolute Copying

We are going to revise the budget that you created as the first project of the spreadsheet chapter. Currently, the spreadsheet contains the budget and actual figures for three months and totals for the first quarter. The budget and actual totals for the first quarter are very close, but we want to see if the percentage of the total spent in each category is the same for the budget and actual figures. In order to do this, we will create new formulas including absolute cell addresses and see what happens when we copy these formulas. We will also rearrange the spreadsheet to make room for the new formulas and print part of the spreadsheet.

In this project you will learn how to:

- Insert columns into an existing spreadsheet.
- Create formulas containing absolute cell addresses.
- Hide columns so that nonadjacent parts of the spreadsheet can be printed.

First let's get the worksheet ready for the new formulas.

1. Open the file **BUDGET1.WKS**.

Note: If you have not created this spreadsheet, follow the instructions for Project No. 1 in the spreadsheet chapter.

2. Move the cursor anywhere in column G.

Inserting Columns We want to insert a blank column between columns F and G so that we can place the percents for the 1st quarter budget figures immediately to the right of the totals.

3. Choose **Select/Column**.

Note: **Select/Column** is used instead of **F8** and the **ARROW** keys because we must select the entire column and this would be too tedious using **F8** and the **ARROW** keys. If only part of a column is selected, the **Insert** command, which we will use next, cannot be selected from the Edit menu (Figure 6-7). If cells from more than one column have been highlighted, **Select/Column** selects the columns containing each of the highlighted cells.

4. Select **Edit/Insert**. One column will be inserted to the left of the selected column.

Relative and Absolute Copying

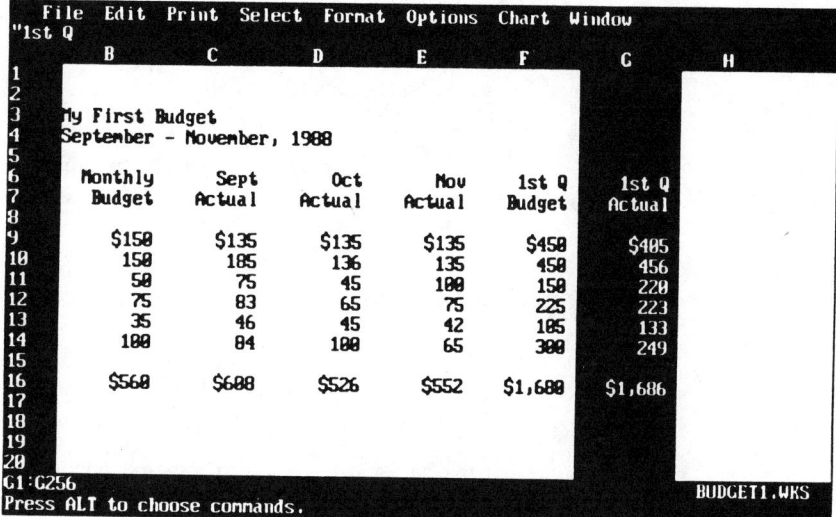

Figure 6-7

Hint: Some hints for using the **Edit/Insert** command are:

- The **Edit/Insert** command can be used to insert rows or columns immediately to the left or above the highlighted row(s)/column(s).

- In the preceding task the **Edit/Insert** command inserted one column because we had highlighted only one column. If you want to insert two columns/rows, you must first select two columns/rows, etc.

Caution: **Edit/Insert** inserts a row/column the entire width/length of the spreadsheet. This can cause damage if there is data in a part of the spreadsheet that is not visible on the screen that should *not* have a row/column inserted into it.

Creating Absolute Cell Address References

Before we create the new formulas using absolute cell referencing, let's look at the formulas already in the spreadsheet.

1. Move the cursor to the cell containing the total Monthly Budget figures (cell *B16*). Look at the formula in the Formula Bar. It should read:

   =B9+B10+B11+B12+B13+B14

2. When we created the spreadsheet we entered the formula in cell *B16* and copied it across the row. Move the cursor across row 16 and look at each formula. Each formula adds the cells above it. Therefore, the contents of the formula have been adjusted to reflect the column being added.

Let's look at the content of the new formulas that we want to create. Do *NOT* enter the formulas on the spreadsheet yet. We want to create a formula in cell *G9* that will divide the budgeted figure for the rent by the total budget so that we can determine

Extending Your Knowledge with Microsoft Works

what percentage of the total was budgeted for rent. Then we want to copy the figure to the rest of the expense items in the column to determine what percentage of the total was budgeted on food, clothing, etc.

The formula for cell *G9* should be:

budgeted rent/total budget
or
F9/F16

The formula for cell G10 should be:

budgeted food/total budget
or
F10/F16

Notice that the cell address used in the first part of the formula, the expense category, should be different for each formula, but in each case the cell address of the divisor remains the same—cell *F16*. When we create the formula for the rent percentage, therefore, we must tell *Works* that the divisor must remain constant or **absolute**. To do that we will use the **Reference** or **F4** key when creating the formula. Follow the directions below to see how this works.

1. Move the cursor to *G9*.
2. Start the formula by typing: **=**
3. Move the cursor to cell *F9* and then type a / to indicate division. The cursor will return to cell *G9*.
4. Move the cursor to cell *F16*. The Formula Bar should read: *=F9/F16*
5. Press the **F4** function key *one* time and watch how the formula changes. It now should read:

=F9/$F$16

The $ preceding the column and row names indicates that both the column and the row will remain absolute when the formula is copied.

Caution: The **F4** key is a toggle key. If it is pressed one time, dollar signs are inserted before the row and column designations ($F$16). If it is pressed multiple times, the $ may precede only part of the cell address ($F16 or F$16) or disappear completely. Continued key presses repeat the cycle. Therefore, it is important to check that the dollar sign precedes both the row and column. If it does not, continue pressing **F4** until it does.

When the $ precedes only part of the cell address, the cell reference is part absolute and part relative. When mixed cell addresses are copied, part adjusts while part remains the same. These mixed references will not be used in this book.

---

6. Press the **ENTER** key. Your screen now should resemble Figure 6-8.

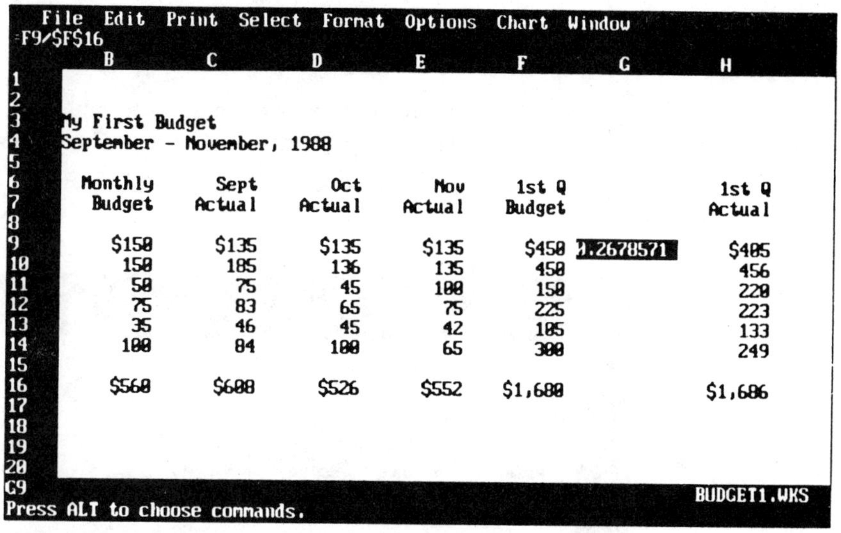

Relative and Absolute Copying

Figure 6-8

> *Note:* Cell address references can also be made absolute by typing the **$** before the column and row names.

Now we can use the **Edit/Fill Down** command to copy the formula to the rest of the column.

7. Highlight cells *G9* to *G16*.
8. Select **Edit/Fill Down**.
9. Move the cursor to each of the cells into which the formula was copied and watch the Formula Bar. Notice that the first cell address in the formula adjusts while the absolute portion of the formula does not change (Figure 6-9).

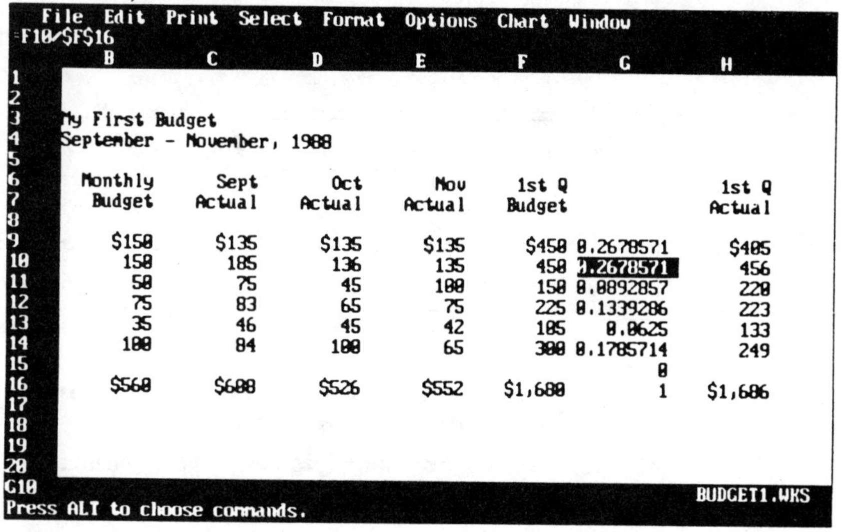

Figure 6-9

We want to create a similar formula for the *1st Quarter Actual* figures in column I.

10. Follow the procedure above to create a formula to determine the percentage of the actual expenditures spent on rent. Create this formula in cell *I9*.
11. Copy the formula to cells *I10* through *I16* (Figure 6-10).

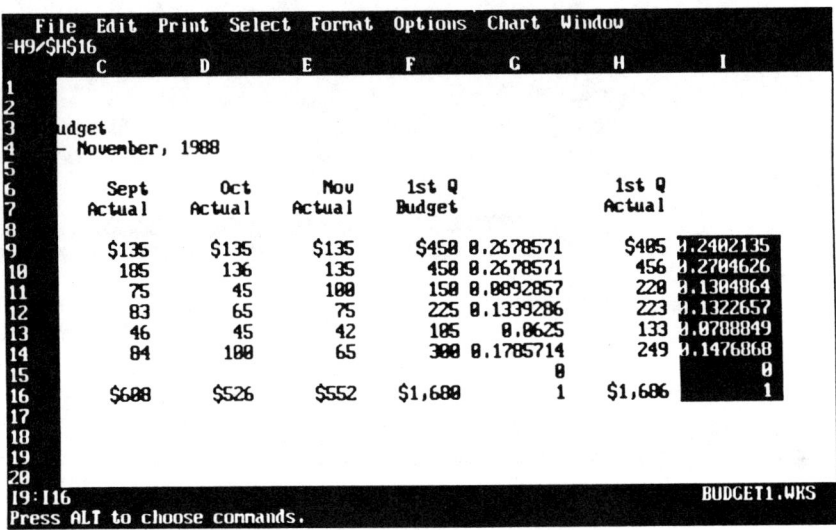

Figure 6-10

The only steps that remain are to improve the appearance of the spreadsheet and to save and print it.

12. Highlight cells *G15* to *I15*. Select **Edit/Clear** to remove the formulas from the blank row.
13. **Format** the figures in the two new columns for **Percent, 2** decimal places.

Hint: Remember to select the cells you want to format first.

Note: You will need to format each column separately since they are not adjacent.

14. Type the title **Budget Percents** in cells *G6* and *G7* and **Actual Percents** in cells *I6* and *I7*.
15. Use the **Format/Style** command to change the alignment for *Budget Percents* and *Actual Percents* to: **Right** (Figure 6-11).

Relative and Absolute Copying 191

```
 File  Edit  Print  Select  Format  Options  Chart  Window
"Actual
        D         E         F         G         H         I         J
1
2
3
4    , 1988
5
6        Oct       Nov      1st Q    Budget     1st Q    Actual
7       Actual    Actual    Budget   Percents  Actual   Percents
8
9       $135      $135      $450     26.79%    $405     24.02%
10       136       135       450     26.79%     456     27.05%
11        45       100       150      8.93%     228     13.85%
12        65        75       225     13.39%     223     13.23%
13        45        42       105      6.25%     133      7.89%
14       100        65       300     17.86%     249     14.77%
15
16      $526      $552    $1,680    100.00%  $1,686    100.00%
17
18
19
20
16:17                                                        BUDGET1.WKS
Press ALT to choose commands.
```

Figure 6-11

Note: The titles *Budget Percents* and *Actual Percents* do not appear to be right justified when compared to the percentages that appear in the same column. In *Works* when right justification is selected, a space is left on the far right side of the cell that is filled only if the value includes a percent sign or a right parenthesis (which is used to indicate negative numbers in some formats).

---

16. **Save** the spreadsheet using the name: **Budget2**

Hiding Columns If we want to print the spreadsheet, we will have a problem fitting it on a standard-size piece of paper even if we change the margins as we did in the spreadsheet chapter. However, we can obtain a printout of parts of the spreadsheet—the expense categories, monthly budget figures, 1st quarter totals, and percents—by hiding the columns that we do not want to include. The procedure for doing this is similar to that used in Database Project No. 2. Make sure that you have saved the current spreadsheet and then complete the following instructions.

1. Highlight one cell each in columns *C*, *D* and *E* (Figure 6-12).
2. Choose **Format/Width**.
3. Type **0** in the Width Text Box.
4. Press **ENTER**. Columns C, D, and E will no longer be visible on the screen. The cursor also will not be visible since it was in a hidden column (Figure 6-13). Press the **RIGHT** or **LEFT ARROW** key until the cursor is visible.
5. To print the document:
    a. Highlight the cells to be printed, *A3* through *I16*.
    b. Select **Print/Set Print Area**.
    c. Select **Print/Print**.

Extending Your Knowledge with Microsoft Works

```
 File  Edit  Print  Select  Format  Options  Chart  Window
"Sept
      A          B         C         D         E         F         G
 1
 2
 3        My First Budget
 4        September - November, 1988
 5
 6                 Monthly    Sept      Oct       Nov       1st Q     Budget
 7     Expenses   Budget    Actual    Actual    Actual    Budget    Percents
 8
 9     Rent       $150      $135      $135      $135      $450      26.79%
10     Food        150       185       136       135       450      26.79%
11     Clothing     50        75        45       100       150       8.93%
12     Utilities    75        83        65        75       225      13.39%
13     Phone        35        46        45        42       105       6.25%
14     Train       100        84       100        65       300      17.86%
15
16     Total      $560      $600      $526      $552    $1,680     100.00%
17
18
19
20
C6:E6                                                EXTEND    BUDGET2.WKS
Press ALT to choose commands.
```

Figure 6-12

```
 File  Edit  Print  Select  Format  Options  Chart  Window
      A          B         F         G         H         I         J
 1
 2
 3        My First Budget
 4        September - November, 1988
 5
 6                 Monthly    1st Q     Budget    1st Q     Actual
 7     Expenses   Budget    Budget   Percents   Actual    Percents
 8
 9     Rent       $150      $450     26.79%     $405      24.02%
10     Food        150       450     26.79%      456      27.05%
11     Clothing     50       150      8.93%      228      13.85%
12     Utilities    75       225     13.39%      223      13.23%
13     Phone        35       105      6.25%      133       7.89%
14     Train       100       300     17.86%      249      14.77%
15
16     Total      $560    $1,680    100.00%    $1,686    100.00%
17
18
19
20
C5:E5                                                          BUDGET2.WKS
Press ALT to choose commands.
```

Figure 6-13

6. It is possible to redisplay the hidden columns. However, this is time consuming. If you want to continue working on this file, the easiest way to return to the entire spreadsheet is to open the spreadsheet that we saved immediately before hiding columns:

   a. Select **File/Open**.
   b. Select **BUDGET2.WKS**.

      You will be prompted:

      File is already open. Ok to lose changes?

   c. Press **ENTER** and the last saved version of **BUDGET2.WKS** will appear.

More About Functions

In the spreadsheet chapter we used the SUM function to total a range of figures. *Works* provides 57 functions designed to perform statistical, mathematical, financial, logical, date, and special computations that help you to rapidly analyze data. In the following project you will learn two more functions: MIN and MAX.

Extended Skills Project No. 4
More Functions

In Spreadsheet Project No. 1 and Extended Skills Project No. 3 you created a simple budget and then used formulas to calculate information about the budget. Formulas were used to total expenses for each month and to calculate the quarterly amount and percentage of the total budgeted and actual expenses for each of several categories. Since the *Works* Spreadsheet tool makes calculating so quick, it's easy to manipulate the data to obtain more information. For example, we're going to find the minimum and maximum amounts spent in each category and use them to see what a "starvation" and "high-spender" budget might look like.

While completing this project, you will learn to:

- Use *Works* functions to find the minimum and maximum of a group of values.
- Use pointing to enter the range on which the function is acting.
- Copy a range of cells.
- Use **Edit/Fill Down** to copy more than one formula.
- Work with an area of the spreadsheet that is too large to fit on the screen at one time.

In the process of completing the project, we will also review and extend our use of some of the commands learned in the spreadsheet chapter.

Figure 6-14 shows what the part of the spreadsheet that will contain the new calculations should look like when you have finished the project.

Using More of the Spreadsheet First we will set up new columns to contain our calculations. Then we will find the minimum and maximum values for each expense category, and finally we will find a total budget if only the minimum or only the maximum is spent on each item.

1. Open **BUDGET2.WKS** if it is not already open.
2. To copy the category titles to a new part of the spreadsheet:
   a. Highlight cells *A7* through *A16*.

Note: You already know how to select cells by pressing **F8** and then using the arrow keys to **EXTEND** the highlight. An alternative method is to place the cursor in a cell at one end of the range, press the **SHIFT** key and keep it depressed while using the **ARROW** keys to extend the highlight. The word *EXTEND* does *NOT* appear on the Message Line when this method is used, but the same result is achieved.

```
 File Edit Print Select Format Options Chart Window
=SUM(C21:C26)
      A         B         C         D         E         F         G
10 Food         150       185       136       135       450       26.79%
11 Clothing     50        75        45        100       150       8.93%
12 Utilities    75        83        65        75        225       13.39%
13 Phone        35        46        45        42        105       6.25%
14 Train        100       84        100       65        300       17.86%
15
16 Total        $560      $600      $526      $552      $1,600    100.00%
17
18             Low       High
19 Expenses    Budget    Budget
20
21 Rent        $135      $135
22 Food        135       185
23 Clothing    45        100
24 Utilities   65        83
25 Phone       42        46
26 Train       65        100
27
28 Total       $487      $649
29
C28                                                      BUDGET2.WKS
Press ALT to choose commands.
```

Figure 6-14

   b. Select **Edit/Copy**.

   c. Move the cursor to *A19* and press **ENTER**.

   d. Move the cursor down the A column until you see that all of the expense categories have been copied to cells *A19* through *A28*.

Our spreadsheet no longer fits vertically on one screen. Therefore, periodically we will need to scroll the screen so that the part of the spreadsheet with the information relevant to the current task will be visible.

   3. First, move the cursor so that rows 6 to 25 are visible on the screen (Figure 6-15).

   4. Enter the title **Low Budget** in cells *B18* and *B19* and **High Budget** in cells *C18* and *C19* (Figure 6-16).

The Min, Max, and Sum Functions and Pointing

In the spreadsheet chapter you entered a function by typing it in the cell. First you had to type = to inform *Works* that you were entering a formula rather than a label. Then you typed the function, which in Chapter 3 was **sum**. You typed the range of cells inside parentheses, and you included a colon (:) just like the one that appears in the Message Line whenever a range of cells has been highlighted (ie. C9:E9). The colon is very important in selecting a range, because it **anchors** the starting point of the highlight in a particular cell. When we enter a function in this project, we will type part of it and then use pointing to highlight the range on which the function will act. This will enable us to actually see the range and, therefore, it is less likely that we will accidently include the wrong cells.

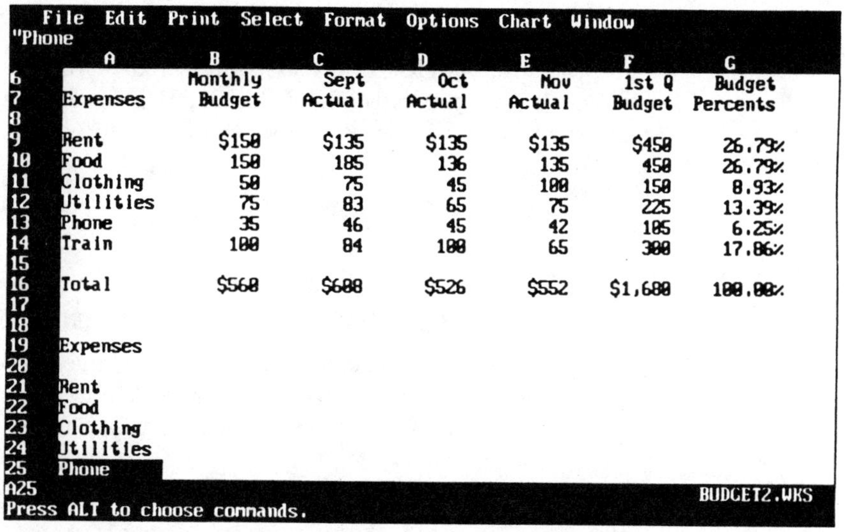

More About Functions

[Figure 6-15: Spreadsheet screen showing BUDGET2.WKS with Monthly Budget, Sept Actual, Oct Actual, Nov Actual, 1st Q Budget, and Budget Percents columns; Expenses rows include Rent, Food, Clothing, Utilities, Phone, Train, and Total. Below is a second Expenses section with Rent, Food, Clothing, Utilities, Phone. Status line reads "Press ALT to choose commands."]

Figure 6-15

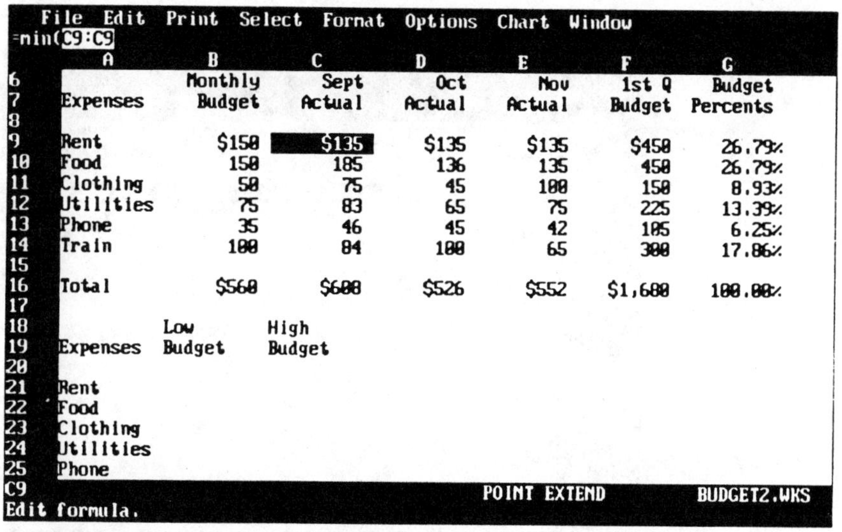

[Figure 6-16: Same spreadsheet with cell C9 ($135) highlighted; formula bar shows =min(C9:C9; headings "Low Budget" and "High Budget" appear above the second Expenses list. Status line reads "Edit formula." with POINT EXTEND indicator.]

Figure 6-16

5. Move the cursor to cell *B21*.

6. Start the function by typing: **=min(**

We want to find the minimum of the Sept., Oct., and Nov. Actual Rent expenditures.

7. Move the cursor to cell *C9*.

The word *POINT* will appear on the Status Line indicating that you are using pointing.

8. Press the **:** (colon) to anchor the pointer.

A colon and the current cell, *C9*, will be added to the formula indicating that the selected range so far is the cell *C9* (Figure 6-16).

Extending Your Knowledge with Microsoft Works

Once the pointer has been **anchored**, the cursor key can be moved to highlight a larger range of cells. As discussed in the spreadsheet chapter, a range is any rectangular group of cells. The word EXTEND appears on the Status Line as an indication that *Works* is waiting for you to extend the highlight and select a range of cells.

9. Use the **RIGHT ARROW** key to extend the range to cells *D9* and *E9* (Figure 6-17).
10. Type: **)** to complete the formula entry.
11. Press the **ENTER** key. The value *135* should appear in cell *B21*.

    In this case all of the cells in the range contained the same value. If they had not, the lowest value would appear in the cell containing the MIN function. We'll see how this works when we copy the formula to other expense categories.

12. Beginning in cell *C21*, use the procedure described above to create a formula for the maximum value contained in the same three cells. The formula should begin: **=MAX(**

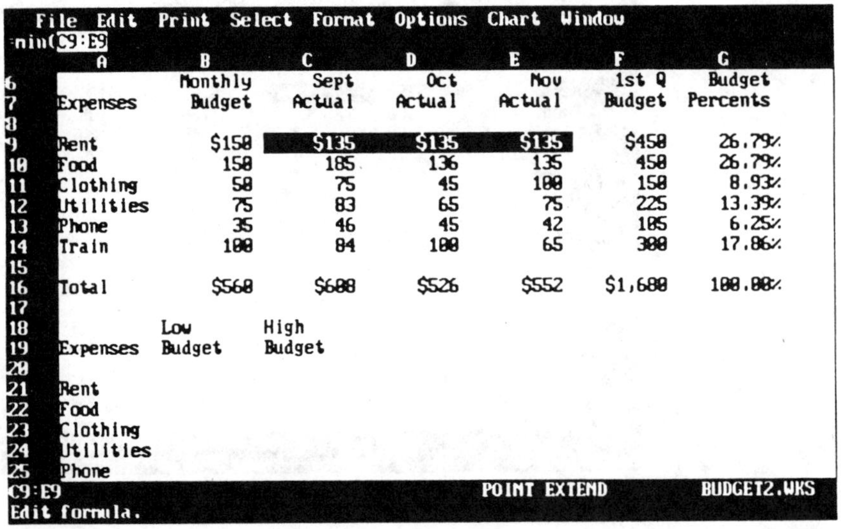

Figure 6-17

Next we'll copy the MIN and MAX functions to the remaining expense categories and find the High and Low Budget totals.

13. Highlight the area containing cells *B21* through *C26*.
14. Select **Edit/Fill Down** (Figure 6-18).

    Remember that when part of the screen is highlighted, any command you select will act upon the entire highlighted area. Since two columns were highlighted, the **Edit/Fill Down** command copied the contents of the first cell in each column to the rest of that column.

More About Functions

```
 File  Edit  Print  Select  Format  Options  Chart  Window
=MIN(C9:E9)
         A         B        C        D        E        F       G
 11  Clothing      50       75       45      100      150     8.93%
 12  Utilities     75       83       65       75      225    13.39%
 13  Phone         35       46       45       42      185     6.25%
 14  Train        100       84      100       65      300    17.86%
 15
 16  Total       $560     $600     $526     $552   $1,600   100.00%
 17
 18              Low      High
 19  Expenses    Budget   Budget
 20
 21  Rent        135      135
 22  Food        135      185
 23  Clothing     45      100
 24  Utilities    65       83
 25  Phone        42       46
 26  Train        65      100
 27
 28  Total
 29
 30
B21:C26                                             BUDGET2.WKS
Press ALT to choose commands.
```

Figure 6-18

15. Move the cursor into the cells to which you copied the formula.

    Notice that the formulas have been adjusted.

16. Now, let's use the **SUM** function and pointing to find the total for the low budget.

    a. Move the cursor to cell *B28*.

    b. Type: **=SUM(**

    c. Move the pointer to cell *B21*.

    d. Type a **:** to anchor the pointer.

    e. Use the **DOWN ARROW** to extend the highlight so that it includes the range *B21:B26* (Figure 6-19).

```
 File  Edit  Print  Select  Format  Options  Chart  Window
=sum(B21:B26
         A         B        C        D        E        F       G
 11  Clothing      50       75       45      100      150     8.93%
 12  Utilities     75       83       65       75      225    13.39%
 13  Phone         35       46       45       42      185     6.25%
 14  Train        100       84      100       65      300    17.86%
 15
 16  Total       $560     $600     $526     $552   $1,600   100.00%
 17
 18              Low      High
 19  Expenses    Budget   Budget
 20
 21  Rent        135      135
 22  Food        135      185
 23  Clothing     45      100
 24  Utilities    65       83
 25  Phone        42       46
 26  Train        65      100
 27
 28  Total
 29
 30
B21:B26                             POINT EXTEND   BUDGET2.WKS
Edit formula.
```

Figure 6-19

Extending Your Knowledge with Microsoft Works

    f. Type a **)** and press **ENTER**.

    g. Copy the formula from *B28* to *C28*.

Now you can see how much your monthly budget would be if you always spent the least amount possible. Notice how much lower it is than the lowest actual total in the three-month period. Similarly, the "high-spender" budget is $41 higher than the total in September, the most expensive month for actual spending.

The only remaining tasks are to enhance the appearance of the spreadsheet and to save and print it.

17. Use **Format/Style** to change the alignment of the labels *Low Budget* and *High Budget* to right justified.
18. Use **Format/Dollar** to format the *Rent* figures and the *Total* figures to a dollar format with **0** decimals (Figure 6-20).
19. **Save** the spreadsheet.
20. **Print** only the new section of the spreadsheet (cells *A18* through *C28*).

Figure 6-20

Independent Extended Skills Project No. 3
Using Absolute Cell Addressing and Statistical Function
to Summarize Spreadsheet Data

In Spreadsheet Project No. 2 you developed a travel expense report. Let's assume that the person administering the travel budget wants to develop guidelines for the amount of money allowed for meals. Therefore, you must create a new section of your spreadsheet that will contain information on the minimum, maximum, and average amounts of money spent on meals. Specifically, you will calculate the minimum, maximum, and average amounts of money spent on each meal, the total

More About Functions 199

if only the minimum, maximum, or average amounts are spent, and the percent spent on each meal in the average budget. A copy of the finished addition to the spreadsheet (Figure 6-21) and general instructions for completing it follow.

```
File  Edit  Print  Select  Format  Options  Chart  Window
         A          B       C       D       E       F       G       H       I
 6  Air Fare              358.00                                          358.00
 7  Car Rental             49.00   49.00   49.00   49.00   49.00          245.00
 8  Hotel                  68.00   68.00   68.00   68.00   68.00          340.00
 9  Breakfast               4.50    4.75    4.25    5.25    4.35           23.10
10  Lunch                   5.75    5.15    6.15    3.75    5.25           26.05
11  Dinner                 18.00   16.35   22.25   18.55   15.75           90.90
12  Local Travel            8.75    4.50    3.75   12.00    8.00           37.00
13  Miscellaneous           6.00    7.50    6.25    5.15    4.50           29.40
14
15  Daily Total    0.00  518.00  155.25  159.65  161.70  154.85    0.00  1,149.45
16
17                                          Avg
18                 Min     Max     Avg    %Total
19  Breakfast     $4.25   $5.25   $4.62   16.49%
20  Lunch          3.75    6.15    5.21   18.68%
21  Dinner        15.75   22.25   18.18   64.91%
22
23  Total        $23.75  $33.65  $28.01   ████
24
25
E23                                                              TRAVEL_B.WKS
Press ALT to choose commands.
```

Figure 6-21

1. Open **Travel1.WKS**. If you did not create this file in the Spreadsheet chapter, follow the instructions in spreadsheet Project No. 2.
2. Copy the labels, *Breakfast, Lunch,* and *Dinner* from cells *A9:A11* to cells *A19:A21*.
3. In cell *A23*, type: **Total**
4. In cell *E17*, type: **Avg**
5. Move the cursor to cell *B18* and add the following labels:

Cell	Label
B18	MIN
C18	MAX
D18	AVG
E18	%TOTAL

   Your spreadsheet should resemble Figure 6-22

6. Use the MIN, MAX and AVG functions in cells *B19, B20,* and *B21* to calculate the minimum, maximum, and average amounts spent on breakfast for Monday- Friday.

Note: We have not used the AVG function before. It works in the same way as the minimum and maximum functions do. Just type AVG instead of MIN or MAX. Check your figures against those in Figure 6-21.

Extending Your Knowledge with Microsoft Works

```
 File  Edit  Print  Select  Format  Options  Chart  Window
"%Total
         A        B      C      D      E      F      G     H        I
 4   Categories  Sun    Mon    Tues   Weds   Thur   Fri   Sat    Total
 5
 6   Air Fare          358.00                                    358.00
 7   Car Rental         49.00  49.00  49.00  49.00  49.00        245.00
 8   Hotel              68.00  68.00  68.00  68.00  68.00        340.00
 9   Breakfast           4.50   4.75   4.25   5.25   4.35         23.10
10   Lunch               5.75   5.15   6.15   3.75   5.25         26.05
11   Dinner             18.00  16.35  22.25  18.55  15.75         90.90
12   Local Travel        8.75   4.50   3.75  12.00   8.00         37.00
13   Miscellaneous       6.00   7.50   6.25   5.15   4.50         29.40
14
15   Daily Total  0.00 518.00 155.25 159.65 161.70 154.85  0.00 1,149.45
16
17                              Avg
18              Min    Max    Avg    %Total
19   Breakfast
20   Lunch
21   Dinner
22
23   Total
E18                                                         TRAVEL1.WKS
Press ALT to choose commands.
```

Figure 6-22

7. Use **Edit/Fill Down** to copy these functions to the lunch and dinner rows.
8. Use the SUM function in cell *B23* to find the total of the minimum amounts spent for each meal.
9. Copy this function to cells *C23* and *D23*.
10. In cell *E19* calculate the value of the average amount spent on breakfast (cell *D19*) divided by the total of the average amounts spent on all three meals (cell *D23*).

```
 File  Edit  Print  Select  Format  Options  Chart  Window
=D19/$D$23
         A        B      C      D      E      F      G     H        I
 4   Categories  Sun    Mon    Tues   Weds   Thur   Fri   Sat    Total
 5
 6   Air Fare          358.00                                    358.00
 7   Car Rental         49.00  49.00  49.00  49.00  49.00        245.00
 8   Hotel              68.00  68.00  68.00  68.00  68.00        340.00
 9   Breakfast           4.50   4.75   4.25   5.25   4.35         23.10
10   Lunch               5.75   5.15   6.15   3.75   5.25         26.05
11   Dinner             18.00  16.35  22.25  18.55  15.75         90.90
12   Local Travel        8.75   4.50   3.75  12.00   8.00         37.00
13   Miscellaneous       6.00   7.50   6.25   5.15   4.50         29.40
14
15   Daily Total  0.00 518.00 155.25 159.65 161.70 154.85  0.00 1,149.45
16
17                              Avg
18              Min    Max    Avg    %Total
19   Breakfast   4.25   5.25   4.62   0.1649
20   Lunch       3.75   6.15   5.21
21   Dinner     15.75  22.25  18.18
22
23   Total      23.75  33.65  28.01
E19                                                         TRAVEL1.WKS
Press ALT to choose commands.
```

Figure 6-23

Setting up Works to Display Graphics 201

Hint: Because you want to copy this formula to the lunch and dinner rows, the entry for the *Total* of the average meal prices (cell *D23*) must be absolute. That way it will remain constant when the formula is copied (Figure 6-23).

11. Copy the formula to cells *E20* and *E21*.
12. **Format** the cells for currency and percents as indicated in Figure 6-21. **Format** the remaining values for **Fixed**, **2** decimal places.
13. Right justify the column headings (*Min*, *Max*, *Avg*, and *Avg %Total*).
14. Save the spreadsheet using the name **TRAVEL_B**.
15. Print just the new section of the spreadsheet.

Charting

In Extended Skills Projects No. 3 and No. 4 we took the budget we created in the spreadsheet chapter and used some additional formulas and functions to get a better feel for the monthly changes in spending. Often the best way to get a better understanding of the patterns in spreadsheet data is by creating a picture—or chart—of the data. *Works* makes this task easy by creating charts for you. Once the chart is created, you can easily enhance or edit it. More importantly, since the chart is attached to the spreadsheet, changes made to the spreadsheet are instantly reflected in the chart.

Some computer setups do not have the ability to display graphics. If the computer you are using cannot display graphics, skip Extended Skills Project No. 6.

Setting up Works to Display Graphics

All of the work we have done so far in *Works* involved the use of text characters. Charts, however, are displayed on your screen and printed using graphics characters. The type of information that *Works* must supply to your computer monitor or printer to display graphics figures depends on the type of monitor and printer that you have. The retail version of *Works* contains a setup program that asks the user some questions and then uses the responses to set itself up so that graphics can be used with the monitor and printer in use. In the educational version, we have to do the setup ourselves. Many of you will not be able to print the graphs because the **TTY** printer selection cannot be used to print graphics. However, by following the directions below you should be able to display the graphs on your monitor providing that the monitor you are using is able to display graphics.

The first step is to determine the graphics capability of your system, which depends upon the type of graphics card that your computer contains. The graphics card is found in the system unit of your computer. Two computers that look the same to you may contain different graphics cards. Some monochrome or LCD monitors may not have any graphics card and therefore may be able to display only text. *Works* contains setups to work with the following graphics cards:

Extending Your Knowledge with Microsoft Works

CGA	Color Graphics Adapter
EGA	Enhanced Graphics Adapter
MCGA	Monochrome Graphics Adapter
HERCULES	Hercules Monochrome Graphics Adapter
TANDY	Tandy Graphics Adapter

The best way to determine the one that best matches the type of monitor and graphics card that you are using is to ask someone—your instructor, the assistants in the computer lab, or the salesperson from whom you bought your computer. If these people are not available, check the manuals that came with your computer. If all else fails, use the instructions below to set up the computer to work with first one graphics card and then another until one works. If your computer is an IBM PC or XT, try the CGA setup first. For an IBM System 2 start with the EGA setup. For a monochrome monitor try the MCGA and HERCULES setups first. Even if your system has a different graphics card than those indicated above, one of the setups may still be close enough to work.

Once you determine the type of graphics card your system has, or you have made a reasonable first guess, you must tell *Works*. The *Works* system disk comes with five special programs, called screen drivers, which help your computer understand the information *Works* sends it when it wants to display a graph. Until we finish the setup, however, *Works* doesn't know which of these drivers to use with your computer. You have to pick one, based on the type of graphics card you have, and then give it a new name that will enable *Works* to recognize it as the driver to use with your computer. This sounds complicated, but we will walk you through it, and the charts you will be able to display as a result will make it worthwhile.

If You Are Using Works from a Floppy Disk

If you are using *Works* from a floppy disk, follow the instructions below. If you installed *Works* on your hard (fixed) drive, skip to the section on hard drives. The renaming procedure is done using DOS commands rather than *Works* commands. Refer to the introductory chapter of this manual if necessary while completing the instructions.

1. Boot the computer, or exit from *Works* so that you have an *A>* prompt on the screen.
2. Put the *Works* disk into the A drive and close the door.
3. Now we'll check to make sure that the files we want are on the disk, by obtaining a directory of the special driver programs:
   a. Type: **dir *.gsd** (you may use upper- or lowercase letters) and press **ENTER**.
   b. Your screen should resemble Figure 6-24. Notice that the first part of each file contains the name of one of the graphics cards we listed above. Each file also contains the extension, gsd, which is an abbreviation for graphics screen driver.
4. Now let's rename the file containing the graphics screen driver appropriate for your monitor and card.
   a. If you are using a CGA card, type:

   rename cga.gsd screen.gsd

Setting up Works to Display Graphics

```
A:\>dir *.gsd

 Volume in drive A has no label
 Directory of   A:\

CGA      GSD     4825   9-22-87   6:10p
HERCULES GSD     5113   9-22-87   6:11p
EGA      GSD     1765   9-22-87   6:10p
MCGA     GSD     2485   9-22-87   6:11p
TANDY    GSD     2739   9-22-87   6:12p
        5 File(s)      5120 bytes free

A:\>
```

Figure 6-24

    b. For an EGA card, type:

        rename ega.gsd screen.gsd

    c. For a HERCULES card, type:

        rename hercules.gsd screen.gsd

    d. For a MCGA card, type:

        rename mcga.gsd screen.gsd

    e. For a TANDY card, type:

        rename tandy.gsd screen.gsd

5. Press the **ENTER** key.

Now you're ready to start creating charts. In step 5 of Extended Skills Project No. 5 you will display your first chart. If the chart does not appear on your screen, check to make sure that you followed the directions in Project No. 5 correctly. If you did, exit from *Works*, rename **screen.gsd** back to its original name, and repeat the procedure above renaming a different file as **screen.gsd**. Skip the next section and continue with Extended Skills Project No. 5.

If You Have Installed Works on Your Hard Disk

If you have installed *Works* on your hard disk, follow the directions below. The renaming procedure is done using DOS commands rather than *Works* commands. Refer to the introductory chapter of this manual if necessary while completing the instructions.

1. If you have not yet turned on the computer, boot the computer, and when you have a *C>* prompt type: **cd\works**

If you are currently using *Works*, exit from *Works*. You should have a **C:>WORKS** prompt on the screen. If you do not, type: **cd\works**

204   **Extending Your Knowledge with Microsoft Works**

> *Note:* The preceding instruction assumes that you installed *Works* in a subdirectory named "**works**," as Chapter 1 suggests. If you installed *Works* in a subdirectory with a different name, substitute that name for the word "works" in the preceding command.

2. Now we'll check to make sure that the files we want are in the Works subdirectory by obtaining a directory of the special driver programs:

    a. Type: **dir *.gsd** (you may use upper- or lowercase letters)

    b. Your screen should resemble Figure 6-25. Notice that the first part of each file contains the name of one of the graphics cards we listed above. Each file also contains the extension, gsd, an abbreviation for graphics screen driver.

```
C:\>cd\works

C:\WORKS>dir *.gsd

 Volume in drive C has no label
 Directory of  C:\WORKS

CGA       GSD     4825   9-22-87   6:10p
HERCULES  GSD     5113   9-22-87   6:11p
SCREEN    GSD     1765   9-22-87   6:10p
MCGA      GSD     2485   9-22-87   6:11p
TANDY     GSD     2739   9-22-87   6:12p
        5 File(s)     473888 bytes free

C:\WORKS>
```

Figure 6-25

3. Now let's rename the file containing the graphics screen driver for your monitor and card.

    a. If you are using a CGA card, type:

    rename cga.gsd screen.gsd

    b. For an EGA card, type:

    rename ega.gsd screen.gsd

    c. For a HERCULES card, type:

    rename hercules.gsd screen.gsd

Charting

        d. For a MCGA card, type:

                rename mcga.gsd screen.gsd

        e. For a TANDY card, type:

                rename tandy.gsd screen.gsd

    4. Press the **ENTER** key.

Now you're ready to start creating charts. In step 5 of Extended Skills Project No. 5 you will display your first chart. If the chart does not appear on your screen, check to make sure that you followed the directions in Extended Skills Project No. 5 correctly. If you did, exit from *Works*, rename **screen.gsd** back to its orignal name, and repeat the procedure above renaming a different file as **screen.gsd**.

Extended Skills Project No. 5
Charting Your Monthly Expenditures

In this project we will create a bar chart showing the September, October, and November expenditures for Food, Clothing, Utilities, and Phone as included in the **BUDGET1.WKS** spreadsheet.

While completing this project, you will learn:

- Some of the terminology relating to charts.
- How to use the *Works* speed charting generator to create a chart.
- How to select the part of the spreadsheet to be used for the *X*-axis labels.
- How to add a legend and titles to the chart.
- How to name and save a chart.
- How *Works'* charts change when the values of the cells they were created from changes.

Before we create the chart we should review some basic terminology. **Chart** is another word for graph. In charts, bars, lines, pies, and points on a grid are used to show the relationships within or among sets of data. We will create the bar chart shown in Figure 6-26. This chart has a horizontal and a vertical axis. The horizontal axis is called the **X-axis**. In most bar charts, the *X*-axis shows the way in which we have classified the data being charted. Our *X*-axis categories are the expense categories—food, clothing, utilities, and phone. The vertical axis, or **Y-axis**, is used to measure each of the items being charted. Notice that the chart consists of four clusters of bars, one for each expense category noted on the *X*-axis. Each cluster of bars contains three bars—one representing the September expenditure, one for October, and one for November. A **legend** at the bottom of the chart indicates which bar represents which series of data. The data for each month is called a **Y-series**. Therefore, the values from September form the 1st *Y*-series, October values form the 2nd *Y*-series, and November values form the 3rd *Y*-series.

Now let's create the chart.

If you are still at the DOS prompt,

    1. Load *Works*.

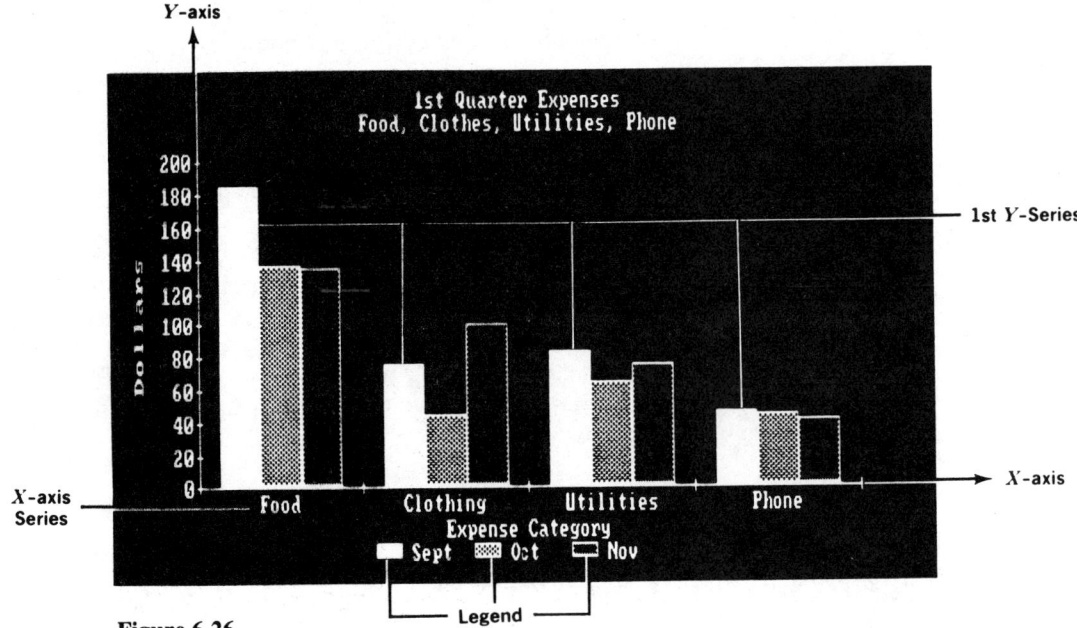

Figure 6-26

2. Open **BUDGET1.WKS** which you created in the first project in the spreadsheet chapter.

   If you did not create **BUDGET1.WKS**, use the instructions in Spreadsheet Project No. 2 to create it.

   You also may use **BUDGET2.WKS**. **BUDGET2** has more data than **BUDGET1**. Therefore, your screen will look different from the figures presented in this chapter, but the differences will not affect the chart that we will create.

Creating a Speed Chart

In *Works* you may create a chart from scratch by specifying the content of each X- and Y-axis series, or you may highlight a range of your spreadsheet and let *Works* create a **speed chart** from the data in the highlighted range. Depending on the type of data in the selected range, the speed chart will contain only the graphed data, or the data plus the X-axis labels and a legend. We will use speed charting to enter the data only on our chart.

Only two steps are required to create a speed chart—highlighting the data to be included and selecting the command to create a new chart.

3. Highlight the September, October, and November actual expenditures for food, clothing, utilities, and phone (Figure 6-27).

4. Select **Chart/New** (Figure 6-28).

   The CHART screen should appear. The Work Area of the screen remains the same, but the Menu Bar now contains the commands used to create and use charts. The word *CHART* now appears on the Status Line.

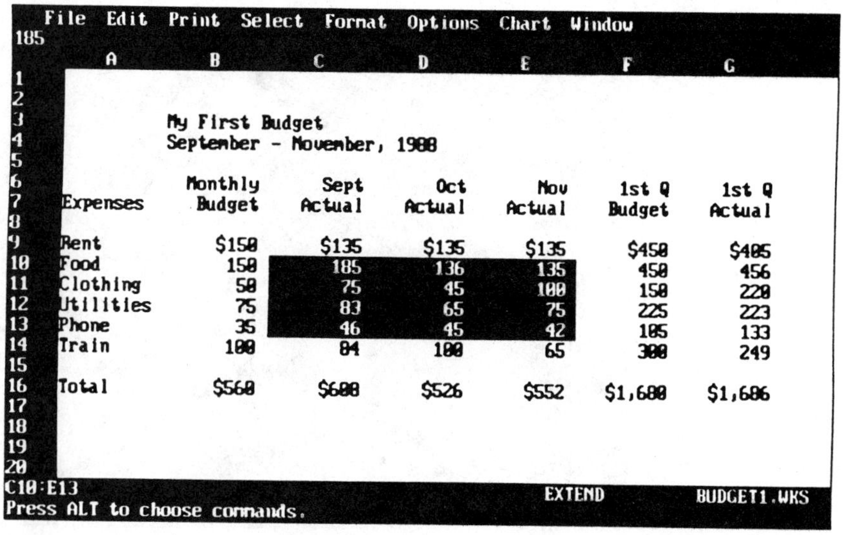

Charting   207

Figure 6-27

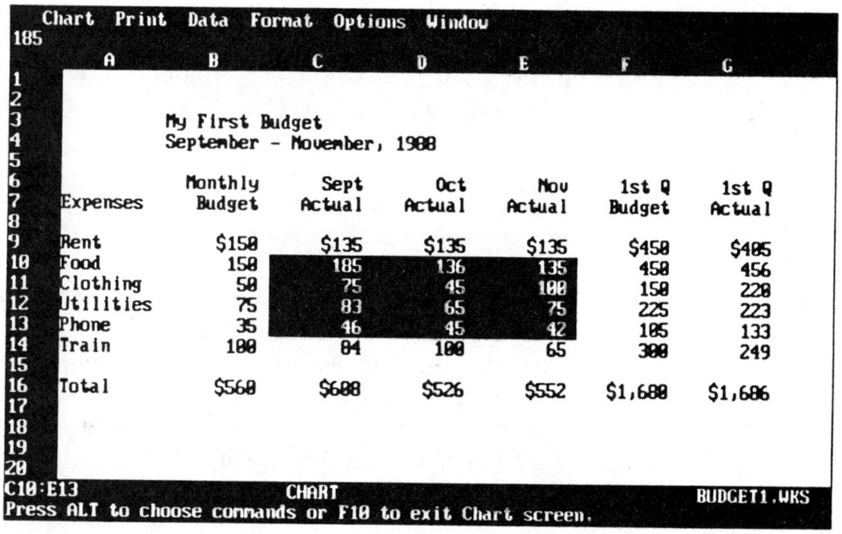

Figure 6-28

5. Select **Chart/View** to see your chart (Figure 6-29).

Works has instantly charted all of the data that you highlighted. We just need to add some labels and a legend to make the chart clearer. *Works* speed charting is so flexible, in fact, that if our spreadsheet had been arranged differently, *Works* would have added the X-axis labels and legend. For example, if the labels that we want to use for the X-axis and the legend had been located in the row and column adjacent to the data we charted, we could have selected them when we selected the data to be charted and the speed chart would have included this information. (See Extended Skills Individual Project No. 4 for an example of how this works.) One of the

208 **Extending Your Knowledge with Microsoft Works**

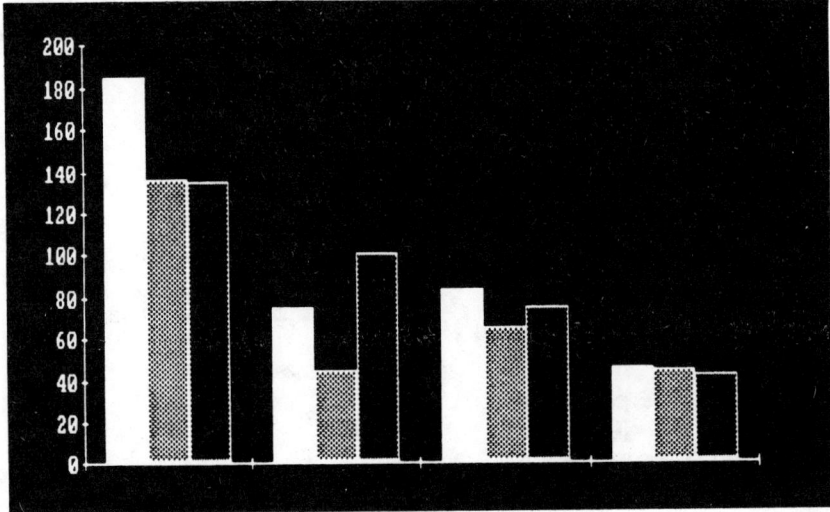

Figure 6-29

strengths of speed charting is that if the information you want to chart is *not* located in a single range on your spreadsheet, you can modify the chart to add the extra information. Let's take a closer look at the chart that *Works* created before we add a legend and labels to make the chart clearer.

6. Press *any key* to return to the CHART screen.

Using Figure 6-29 and the information on your screen, we can compare values and see how the information was charted. For example, the first bar on the left is a little over 180. This corresponds to the food expenditure for September. The next two bars measure a little over 130 and therefore must correspond to the October and November expenditures for food. Therefore, we can see that the first cluster contains the values from the first highlighted row—food—and each highlighted column contributed one bar to the cluster. This tells us that we want to use the row labels (the expense categories) as our *X*-axis categories and the columns as our *Y*-axis categories. Let's see how to include this information on our graph.

1. Highlight the four expense category labels in cells *A10:A13*.
2. Select **Data/X-Series**.
3. Select **Chart/View** or press the shortcut key, **SHIFT+F10**, to view your chart (Figure 6-30).

Caution: If you accidently press just the **F10** key when you attempt to use the shortcut key combination **SHIFT+F10**, you will exit the CHART screen and return to the original spreadsheet screen. If you want to get back to the CHART screen, select **Chart/Define**.

The highlighted labels have been added to the chart.

Charting

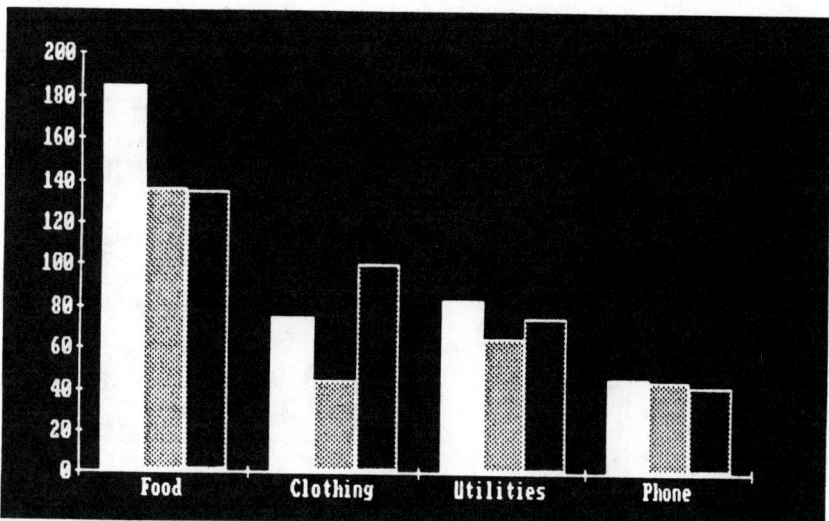

Figure 6-30

Note: On some low-resolution screens some of the letters in the longer labels may not be visible. They are still in memory. If you cannot see all of the letters in the labels and your chart currently is displayed in color, select **Options/Format for B&W**. The monochrome screen may have a higher resolution, enabling it to display more of the letters.

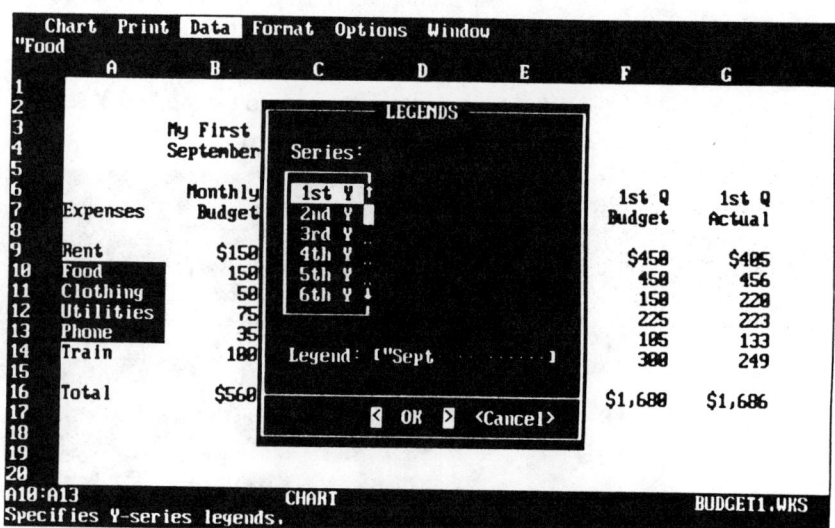

Figure 6-31

4. To create a legend for the chart:
   a. Select **Data/Legends...**

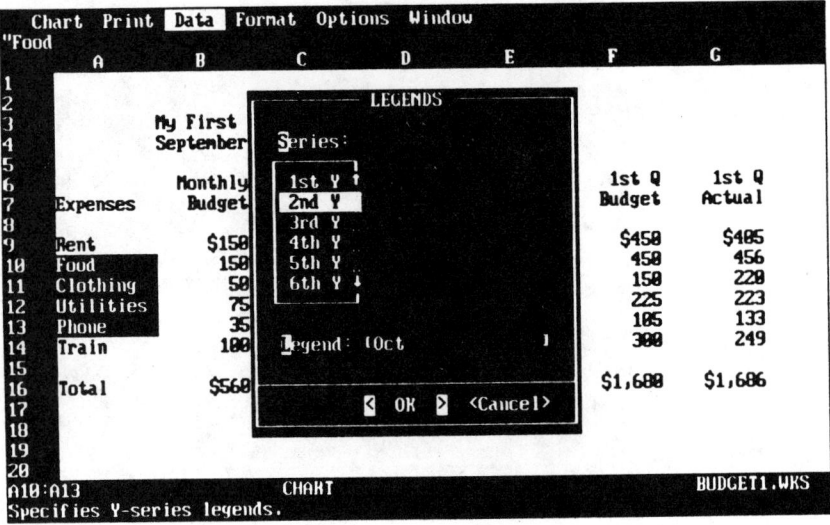

Figure 6-32

 b. Make sure the **1st Y** listing in the Series List Box is highlighted.

 c. Press **ALT+L** or **TAB** to the Legend Text Box, type: **Sept** and press **ENTER**.

 d. View the chart. Notice that the legend for *Sept* has now been added to the chart.

 e. Return to the CHART screen.

 f. Select **Data/Legends...**

 Notice that when *1st Y* is highlighted in the Series List Box, the corresponding label, *"Sept* appears in the Legend Text Box (Figure 6-31).

 g. Use **Oct** as the legend for the **2nd Y** series (Figure 6-32). Press **ENTER**.

 h. Enter **Nov** as the legend for the **3rd Y** series.

5. View the chart (Figure 6-33).

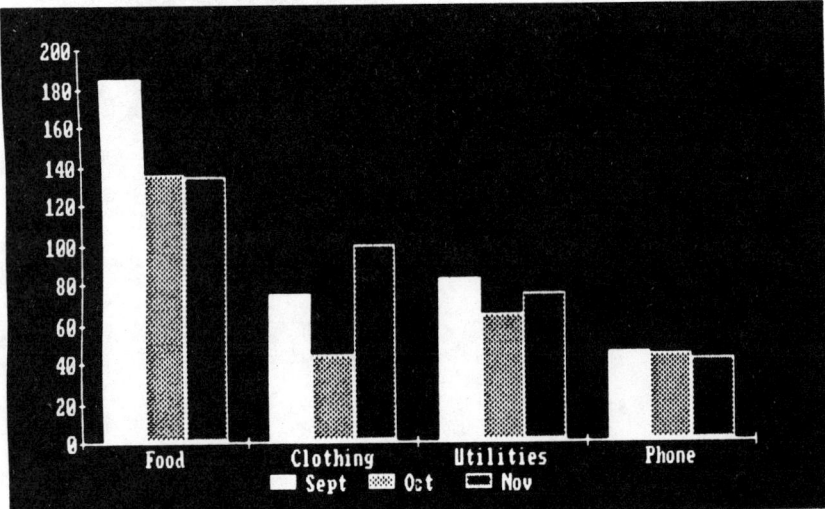

Figure 6-33

Charting   211

Now that we've added the *X*-axis labels and the legend, you can see how easy it is to get a feel for your data by using a chart. The relatively high amounts of money spent on food in September and clothing in November stand out. It is also clear that after relatively high spending in September, expenses were limited in October and then began to drift up again in November. We could make these interpretations fairly easily because we knew this was a chart of expenditures for three months. However, this information is not yet included on the chart. Let's just add a few titles so that the contents of the chart will be clear to someone not knowing anything about the content of the related spreadsheet.

6. Select **Data/Titles** from the CHART screen menu.
7. Complete the Text Boxes in the TITLES Dialog Box with the following information:

Chart Title:	**1st Quarter Expenses**
Subtitle:	**Food, Clothes, Utilities, Phone**
X-Axis:	**Expense Categories**
Y-axis:	**Dollars**

Note: If you fill a Text Box, the text scrolls to the left allowing you to type additional text. Each title may contain as many as 40 characters (Figure 6-34).

---

8. Press **ENTER**.
9. View your graph.

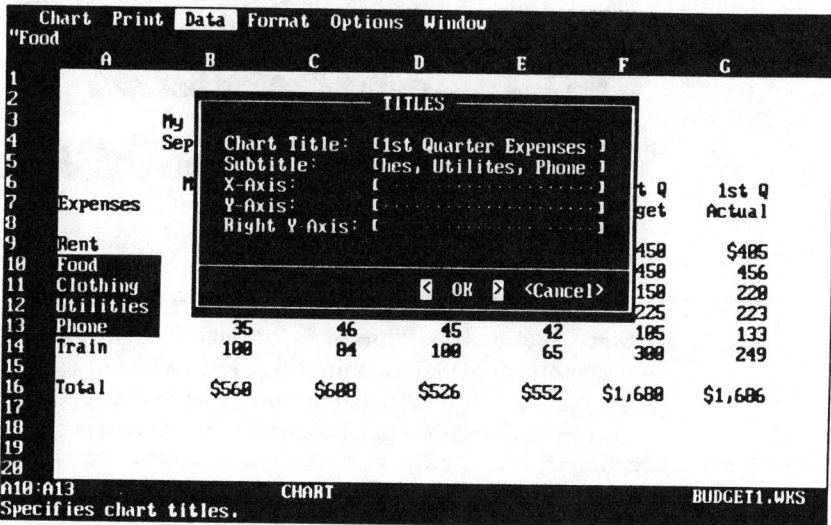

Figure 6-34

We've finished our first chart. Let's name and save the chart and then try to print it, if it's possible to do so with your printer.

Extending Your Knowledge with Microsoft Works

Naming and Saving a Chart

1. Open the **Chart** menu.

   Look at the bottom of the menu, which currently lists Chart1. This section of the menu is similar to the bottom section of the **Window** menu, with which you already are familiar. The **Window** menu lists all open files and lets you move among them. The **Chart** menu lists all the charts that have been generated for the active spreadsheet (up to a maximum of eight) and lets you change the one that is active or current. Since we have generated only one chart so far, it is the only one listed. The mark next to it indicates that it is the current chart.

   If you saved your spreadsheet now, the chart you created would be saved as **chart1**. However, you may give it a different name that will make it easier to identify on the Chart menu. This name will not appear on the chart itself.

2. Select **Charts**.
3. Use **ALT+N** or **TAB** to the Name Text Box.
4. Type a name for your chart: **Expense Bar** (Figure 6-35)

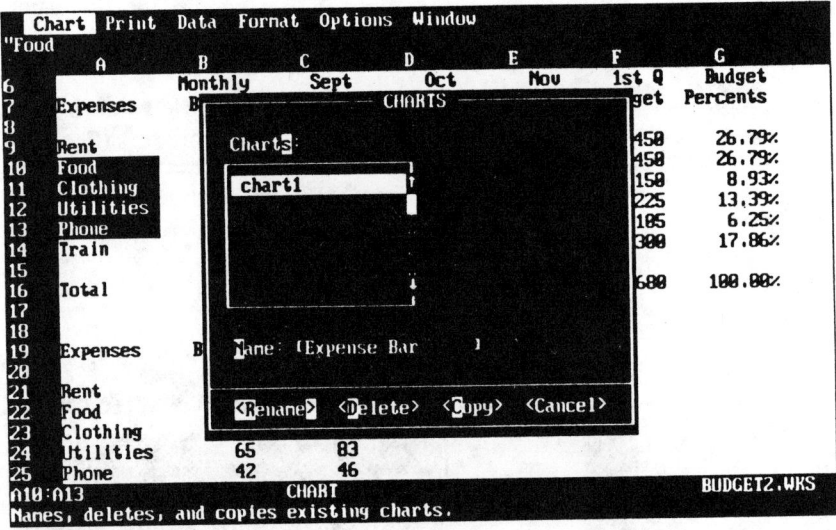

Figure 6-35

Note: Since the chart name is used only for identification on *Works* menus, it does not need to conform to DOS file naming rules. For maximum usefulness, the name should be 15 characters or less so that the entire name can appear on the Chart menu. Any characters or combinations of spaces and characters can be used.

---

5. Since **<RENAME>** is the active button, press **ENTER** and your chart will be renamed.
6. Select **Chart/Exit Chart** or press **F10** to return to the main spreadsheet screen.
7. Use **File/Save** to save the spreadsheet and the newly created chart.

Charting

When we say that the chart is saved, we don't actually mean that the picture that appears on the screen when you view the chart is saved. What's actually saved is the ranges of data that form the *X*- and *Y*-series, along with any titles, legends, or enhancements that you might have added. This is actually more useful than saving the chart because as data in your spreadsheet changes, the chart automatically will change as well. Let's see how this works.

8. Open the Chart menu.

    Notice that a new section consisting of the name of our new chart, *Expense Bar*, has been added to the *Chart* menu on this screen too. The name is preceded by a mark indicating that it is the current chart.

    The **Charts...** option is the same as the one we just used from the CHART screen, and can be used to rename, delete, or copy a chart. The other options are used to **View** the current chart, create a **New** chart or return to the CHART screen for the current chart (**Define**).

9. Select **View**.

    Take another look at the chart so that you can see how it changes when we change the data it includes.

10. Press any key.

    Let's suppose that you just received a late bill from one of your charge cards and need to update your budget.

11. Change the *Oct Actual* expenditure on *clothes* to: **125**

12. Use **Chart/View** or **SHIFT+F10** to view your chart again (Figure 6-36). The bar showing the *October Clothing* expenditure has been changed to reflect the changed spreadsheet entry.

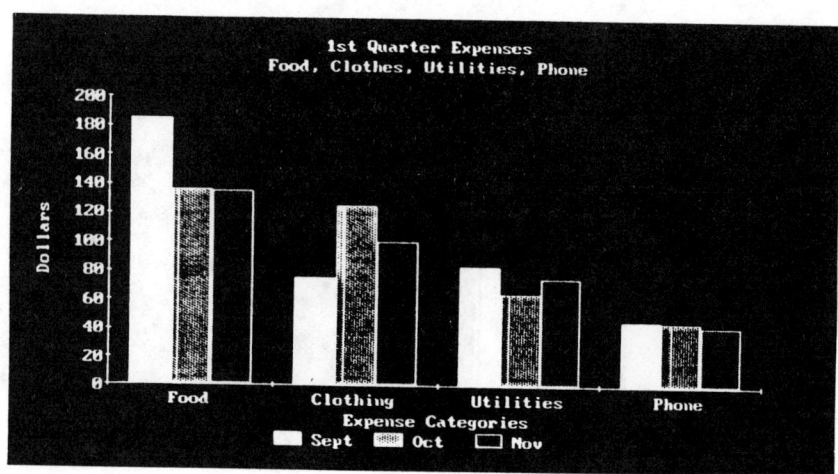

Figure 6-36

Printing a Chart Now let's try to print the graph. Since the educational version of *Works* has only one graphics printer setup, you may not be able to print your graph. You probably will be able to print it if you have an Epson or Epson-compatible printer (such as the IBM

Graphics Printer). You probably will not be able to print it on a Laser printer unless it has an Epson or IBM Graphics emulator. If you have printers not mentioned above, you may want to try to see if the graph will print. Assuming that your printer is capable of producing graphics, this problem would probably not occur with the retail version of *Works* because it has additional printer setups that would allow you to print the graph on a greater variety of printers. If you switch to the full version in the future you can retrieve spreadsheets created with the educational version and print any charts saved with the spreadsheet.

Caution: Do *NOT* attempt to print the graph unless you are using an Epson or Epson-compatible printer or have been told to do so by your instructor. As indicated at the beginning of this section, information used in printing graphics must be carefully tailored to the printer being used. If the Epson setup is not appropriate for your printer, your computer/printer may react by printing a string of characters, possibly using multiple sheets of paper, or your computer may lock. If this does happen to you and pressing the **ESC** key does not unlock the computer, try pressing **CTRL+BREAK**. It may be necessary to reboot the computer by pressing **CTRL+ALT+DEL** or by turning the computer off and on.

1. Select **Chart/Define** to return to the CHART screen for the current graph, *Expense Bar*.
2. Select **Print/Select Chart Printer**.

   The SELECT CHART PRINTER Dialog Box (Figure 6-37) is similar to the SELECT TEXT PRINTER Dialog Boxes that we used when printing documents, spreadsheets, and databases, except that the printer options are different. The **TTY** option that many of you selected for text printing does

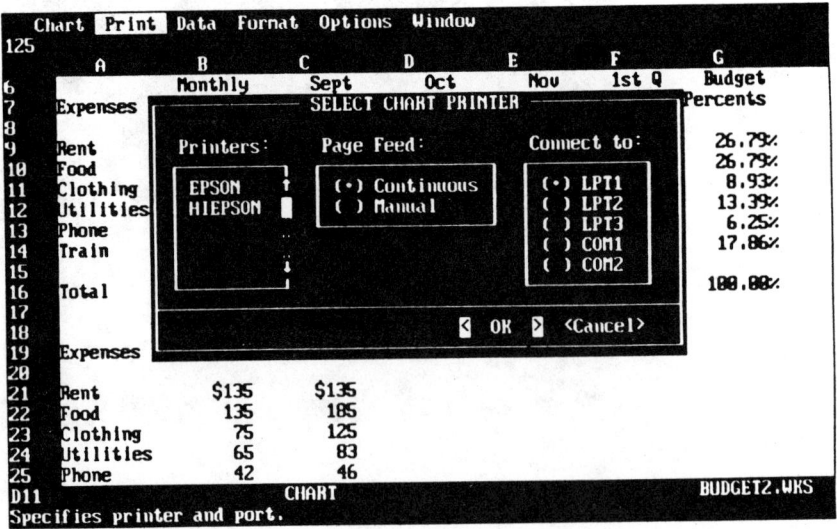

Figure 6-37

Charting

not appear because it does not have graphic capabilities. The two graphics options available in the educational version of *Works* are **EPSON** and **HIEPSON**. These both refer to Epson printers; **HIEPSON** produces a higher quality chart, but takes more time because the printer makes more than one pass at printing the chart. Choose either **EPSON** or **HIEPSON**.

See the section on selecting a text printer in Chapter 2 for information on the **Page Feed** List Box and **Connect to:** List Box settings. If you are using the same printer to print graphs as you used to print text, these settings should be the same as in the SELECT TEXT PRINTER Dialog Box.

3. Select **Print/Print**.

   Your chart will be printed horizontally on the paper as this is one of the default **Print Layout** settings.

Independent Extended Skills Project No. 4
Charting Changes in Budget Figures

In this project we are going to make slight modifications to **INDPROJ2.WKS**, the spreadsheet created in Independent Spreadsheet Project No. 2, and then use speed

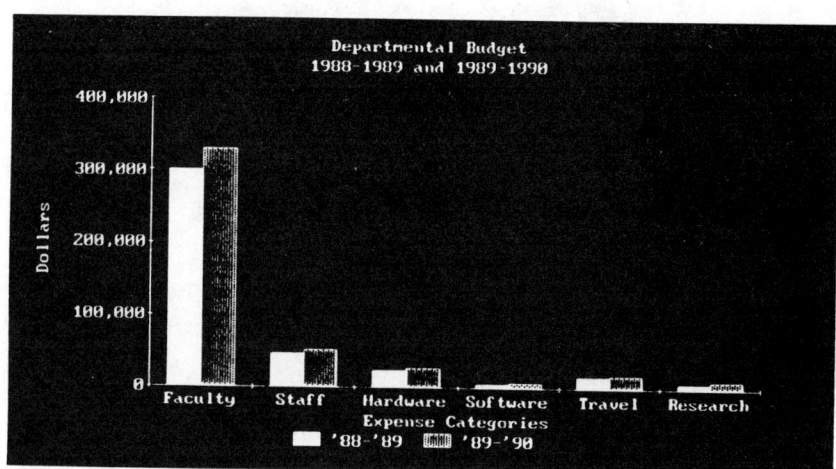

Figure 6-38

charting to graph the 1988/1989 and 1989/1990 budget data. Then we will add titles to enhance the chart. When finished, your chart should resemble Figure 6-38.

1. Open **INDPROJ2.WKS**. If you did not create this spreadsheet, follow steps 1 and 2 of the instructions in Independent Spreadsheet Project No. 2. It is not necessary to create the formulas because we will be graphing only the budget data and not the change or %change figures. Your spreadsheet should at least contain the information shown in Figure 6-39.

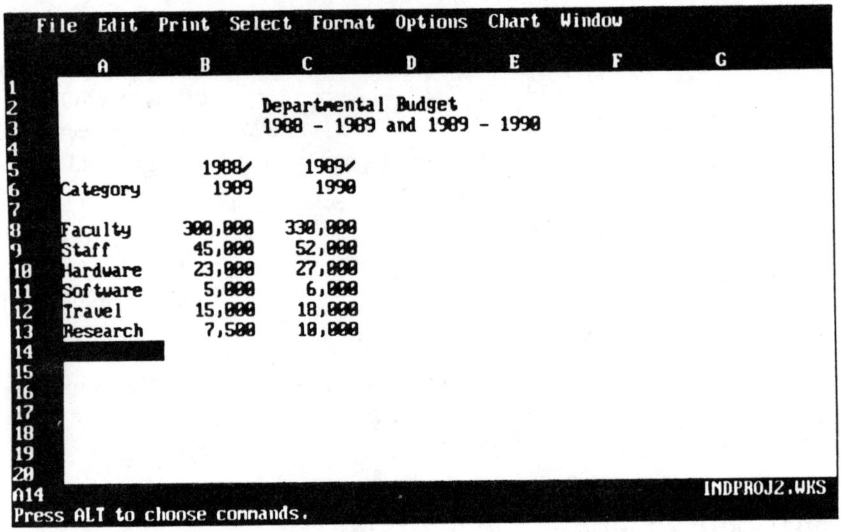

Figure 6-39

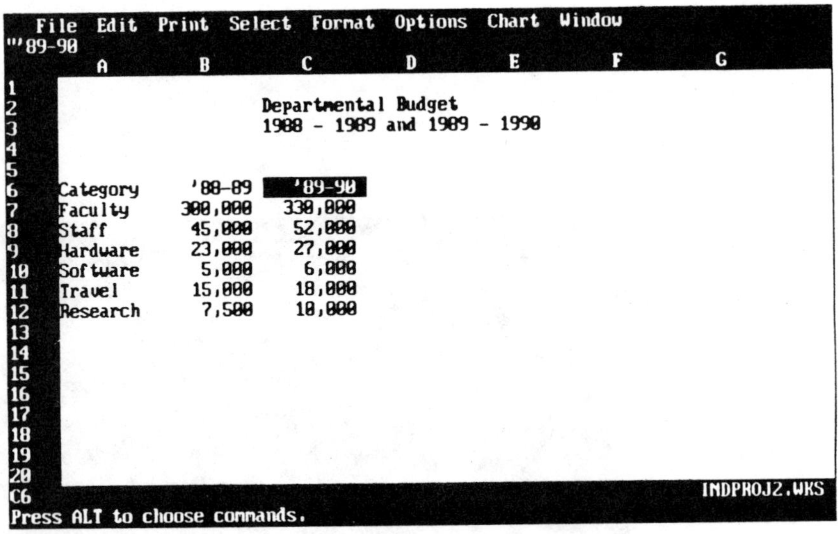

Figure 6-40

To see the full power of the *Works* speed charting, we will make two changes to the spreadsheet so that the information that we want to use for the *X*-axis labels and the legend are in the column/row immediately next to the data. When you have completed steps 2-5, your spreadsheet should resemble Figure 6-40.

2. To delete the blank row, row 7:
    a. Move the cursor anywhere in row 7 and choose **Select/Row**.
    b. Select **Edit/Delete**.
3. *Works* uses the information in only one cell for the *X*-axis labels or legends; therefore, we'll change our column titles so that they fit in one cell rather than two.

Database Queries 217

        a. Select cells *B5* and *C5*.

        b. Use **Edit/Clear** to delete the information in the cells.

4. Enter the following labels into cells *B6* and *C6*:

        B6: '88-89

        C6: '89-90

5. Create a new chart of the '88-89 and '89-90 budget figures as well as the adjacent row and column labels (i.e., cells *A6:C12*).
6. View the chart.
7. Add titles of your choice for the chart and the *X*- and *Y*-axes.
8. Rename your chart so that the name is more meaningful.
9. Save your spreadsheet.
10. Print the chart if it is possible to do so using your printer.

The Database Tool

In the database chapter we focused on the basic procedures for creating, saving, and printing databases. We expanded on these skills by learning to search for specific information, sort the database, and print only selected portions of the database. In our second look at databases you'll see how to add a field to an existing database and you'll expand your ability to use the database to answer questions about the data.

Database Queries

One of the most important aspects of a database is the ease with which you can locate records that meet specific criteria. We used several techniques in the database and integrated chapters to look for specific information. First, we used the **Select/Search** command. An advantage of this command is that the information searched for can be found regardless of the field in which it is contained. However, only the first record meeting the criteria is found. Additional key presses are required to find additional records. We used the **Query/Sort** command to order a database according to the information in one or more fields. Once the records are sorted, those containing specific information in the sort fields can be found, but this also requires additional steps.

Works contains other commands on the Query menu that are designed to rapidly locate and extract all of the records that contain specific information in one or more fields. You should remember from when we hid fields and then used the **Print/Print** command in Chapter 4 that database commands apply only to the records and/or fields that are currently on the screen. Therefore, although **Query** commands can be used simply to locate and read specific information, they are also frequently used prior to other database commands so that those commands will affect only some fields and records. For example, you could use a query followed by another command to print only selected records in the database, copy selected records to a word processing document, merge part of the database with a word processing document (a skill we'll cover later in this chapter), obtain a report on records meeting specific criteria, and so on.

It is possible to use queries to find records meeting very simple or very complex criteria. For example, assuming you had a personnel file containing the necessary information, you could create queries to find the records of everyone:

> Living in California,
>
> With a title of Manager in the Sales Department, or
>
> Earning between $30,000 and $50,000 a year, working in the Sales or Advertising departments, and hired after April 15, 1986.

In this project, however, we will limit ourselves to fairly simple queries that will introduce you to the basic skills you would need for more complex ones.

Extended Skills Project No. 6
Locating Records in Debbie's Database

In Chapter 4, Database Project No. 2, we created a database containing information on Debbie's painting clients. In this project we are going to add a field to that database and then create queries to find records meeting specific criteria.

The real power of the query command may not be apparent in the exercises that we are going to do. Since Debbie's database is small, you could quickly scan the data and find most of the information we will obtain. To get a better feel for the importance of the query commands imagine that Debbie's clientele—and database—has expanded to the thousands!

In this project you will learn:

- How to add a field to the end of the database.
- How to enter data in *List View*.
- What the **operators** used in query formulas are.
- How to create a simple query based on one field.
- How to create a query to find records that meet conditions in more than one field.

Adding a Field to the End of a Database Debbie has decided that it would be useful to record when she has a contract with a client to perform the work for which the estimate was given. Therefore, we must add a field to our database. Luckily, this is very easy to do.

1. Open the database, **PAINT2.WDB**, created in the second project in the database chapter. If you have not created this database, follow the instructions in Chapter 4, Database Project No. 2 until you are instructed to save the database using the name **PAINT2**.
2. Look at the Status Line to see if you are in *Form View* or *List View*. **PAINT2.WDB** will be opened to the view that you were using when you saved the database.
3. If you are in *List View*, press **F9** *or* select **Options/View Form** to switch to *Form View*.
4. Select **Options/Define Form**. The DESIGN screen should be displayed.

Database Queries 219

Note: **Define Form** is one of the choices on the Option menu when it is accessed from *Form View*. It is *not* one of the choices available from *List View*. Remember, menu options are not the same in each tool or on each screen within each tool. This can be most confusing in the database because it contains the most different screens. Appendix B contains a list of all of the *Works* commands; for the database tool, the specific screen(s) on which each command appears are listed.

5. Use the **DOWN ARROW** key to move the cursor two lines below the *Estimate:* field (Figure 6-41).

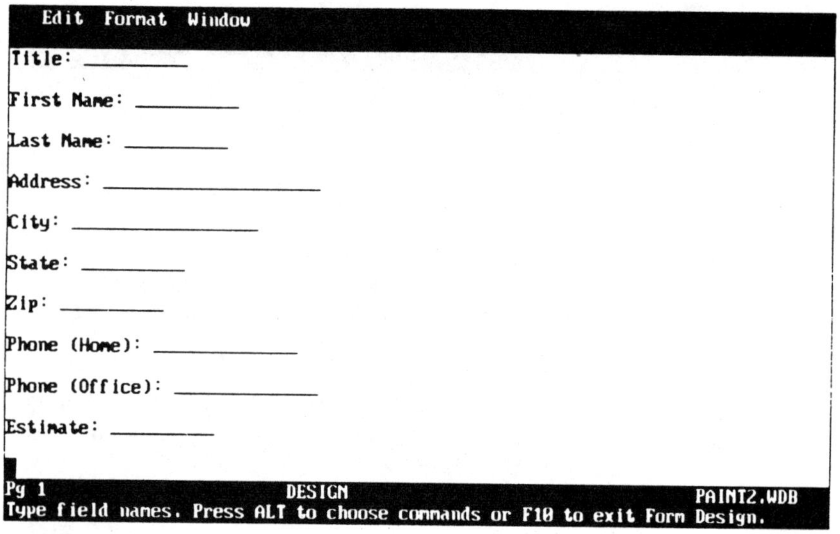

```
 Edit   Format   Window
Title: _____

First Name: _____

Last Name: _____

Address: _____

City: _____

State: _____

Zip: _____

Phone (Home): _____

Phone (Office): _____

Estimate: _____


Pg 1                    DESIGN                         PAINT2.WDB
Type field names. Press ALT to choose commands or F10 to exit Form Design.
```

Figure 6-41

6. You can create the *Contract* field using the same procedure used when you originally entered field names:

   a. Type: **Contract:**

Note: Remember you must type the colon at the end of a field name.

   b. Press the **ENTER** key (Figure 6-42).

Note: Fields also may be inserted in the middle of the database; just move the cursor to the desired position of the new field and follow the steps above. The **Edit/Insert** command may be used to enter blank lines to maintain the readability of the form. It inserts the blank line immediately above the line containing the cursor.

Extending Your Knowledge with Microsoft Works

```
  Edit  Format  Window
Contract:
Title: _____

First Name: _____

Last Name: _____

Address: _____

City: _____

State: _____

Zip: _____

Phone (Home): _____

Phone (Office): _____

Estimate: _____

Contract: _____
Pg 1                            DESIGN                          PAINT2.WDB
Type field names. Press ALT to choose commands or F10 to exit Form Design.
```

Figure 6-42

7. Press **F10** to leave the DESIGN screen.

We're now ready to enter data for the new field. We could enter the data in *Form View* as you have done before. However, it is also possible to enter data in *List View*. We'll do that now so that you can experiment with this method.

8. Press **F9** to switch to *List View*.

9. Move the cursor to the *Contract* field for Record 1 (Figure 6-43). Notice that the field name, *Contract*, appears on the screen, but the rest of the column is empty.

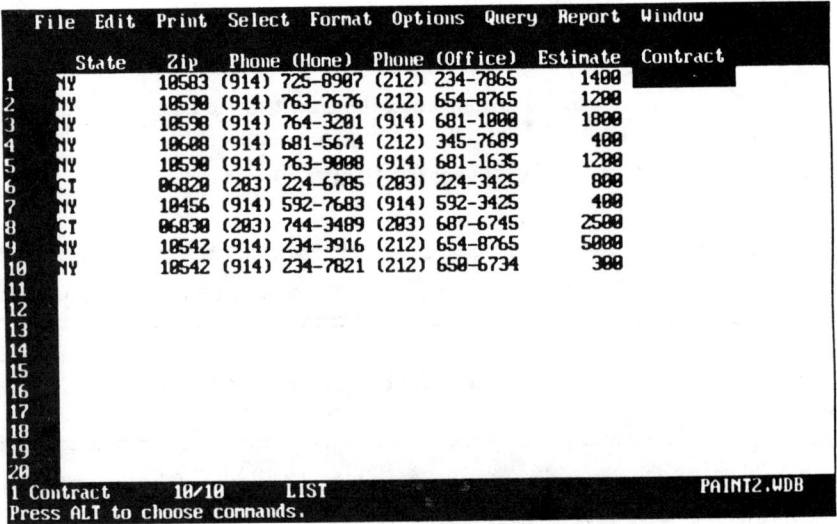

Figure 6-43

Database Queries 221

10. Add the data for the contract field. The contract entry for each record is listed below. Type each entry and then press the **DOWN ARROW** key.

Record No.	Contract
1	y
2	y
3	y
4	n
5	n
6	y
7	y
8	n
9	y
10	n

11. Save the database using the current name.

Querying the Database

Now we're ready to construct some queries of our database. First we must tell *Works* that we want to create a query:

1. Select **Query/Define**.

    The QUERY screen will appear (Figure 6-44). It contains each of the field names followed by a colon. The criteria on which a query is based are entered on the QUERY screen.

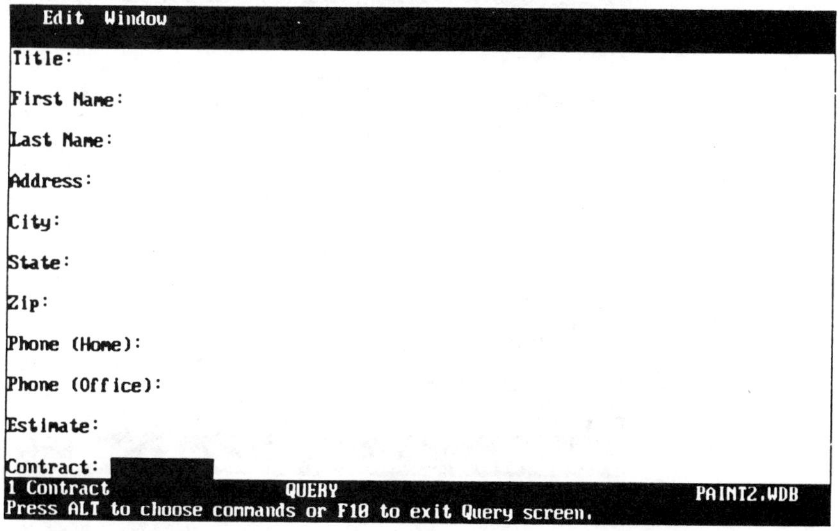

```
 Edit  Window
Title:
First Name:
Last Name:
Address:
City:
State:
Zip:
Phone (Home):
Phone (Office):
Estimate:
Contract:
1 Contract             QUERY                        PAINT2.WDB
Press ALT to choose commands or F10 to exit Query screen.
```

Figure 6-44

Each criterion is typed next to the field name to which it will be applied. The criterion contains an **operator** followed by the text or numbers to which the entries in each record are going to be compared. The operator defines the relationship between the records you want to find and the text or numbers you specify. For example, do you want records containing the exact *same* information? values that are *greater* or *less* than what is specified? only those records that do *not* contain certain information? Some of the operators used to define queries may be familiar to you. For example, to find those records in which the information is the same as or equal to the specified text or numbers, type = (equal sign). The basic *Works* operators are listed below:

Operator	Relationship
=	Equal to
<	Less than
>	Greater than
<=	Less than or equal to
>=	Greater than or equal to
<>	Not equal to

Let's try entering some criteria.

2. To find everyone whose estimate was equal to 1200:

   a. Move the cursor to the ESTIMATE field.

   b. Type: **=1200**

   c. Press **ENTER**. The query criterion now appears in the highlight box next to Estimate: (Figure 6-45).

Figure 6-45

3. Press **F10** to exit the QUERY screen and apply the query.

Database Queries

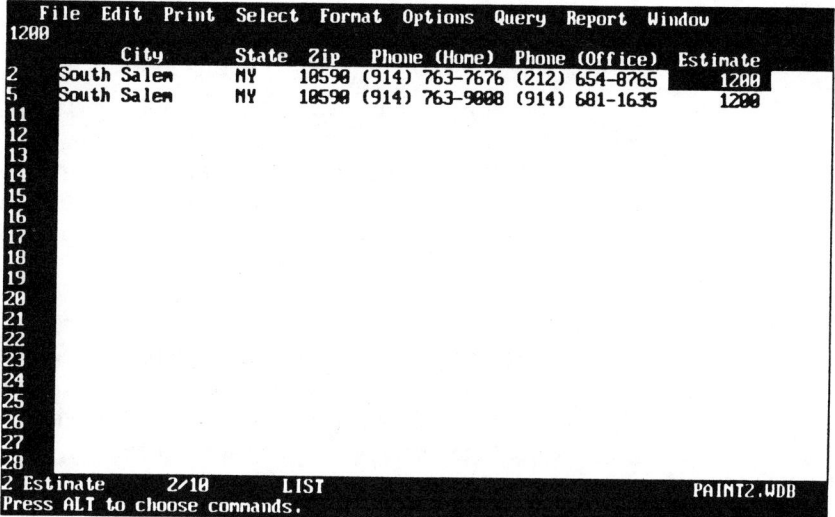

Figure 6-46

Since we entered the QUERY screen from *List View* all of the records for which the *Estimate* field equals **1200** have been extracted and appear on the screen (Figure 6-46). Notice that the original record numbers are retained; only records No. 2 and No. 5 appear because these are the only clients for whom the estimate equaled 1200.

Also note that the cursor remains in the position it was before you entered the QUERY screen, and only those fields previously visible are still visible. However, the entire record has been selected and other fields can be seen by moving the cursor to the left.

Now let's find everyone with estimates greater than 1200.

1. Select **Query/Define**.

   Notice that our previous query *Estimate: =1200* is still on the QUERY screen. We can edit this entry in order to change the query.

2. Move the cursor to the *Estimate* field.
3. Press **F2**, the same key you used to edit other entries in the database and spreadsheet tools.
4. Change the estimate entry to: **>1200**
5. Press **ENTER**.
6. Press **F10** to apply the query.

   The screen should show the four records with estimates greater than 1200.

This time we want to find everyone with an estimate greater than or equal to 1200. We'll enter this query by editing the existing query.

1. Select **Query/Define**.
2. Change the estimate entry to **>=1200**.
3. Apply the query.

The four records you obtained last time and the two found in our first query (*Estimate: =1200*) should now be on the screen, for a total of six records.

See how easy it is to extract records that meet specific criteria. We'll try some more queries, but the format of the command will be slightly different. The *Estimate* field contains numeric data. Our other fields all contain text. The same operators can be used with text fields, but the format of the query expression is slightly different. Let's try to find all of those clients who live in the state of New York.

1. Display the QUERY Screen.

    Since the previous query remains on the screen and we no longer want a query based on the *Estimate* field, we need to remove that entry completely. We will use the **Edit/Delete** command that erases all queries on the screen no matter where they are located.

2. Select **Edit/Delete**.
3. Move the cursor to the *State* field and type:

    ="ny"

Note: When the criterion contains text, the text should be enclosed in quotation marks.

Works' queries are not case specific—text can be entered in either upper- or lowercase letters or a mixture.

4. Press **ENTER** and then **F10**.

    Eight of the records have *NY* in the *State* field.

Caution: If some parts of the simple queries that we are now creating are omitted, the query still will work. However, if the same characters are omitted in slightly different or in more complex queries, *Works* either will look for different records than you intended or display an error message. It is therefore recommended that you habitually use the full, correct syntax, as presented in this book, for all queries.

Greater than and less than queries also can be applied to text. *Works* finds the entries that are alphabetically before or after the stated criterion.

1. Use the procedures above to find all of the records with a *Last Name* field **>"M"**.
2. When the query is applied and *List View* reappears on the screen, move the cursor so that the *Last Name* field is visible (Figure 6-47).

    Did the results surprise you? *Works* found all of the records with *Last Name* entries beginning with *M* or a letter occurring later in the alphabet. *Works* interprets the expression *>"M"* as any entry that would be alphabetized after the letter *M* followed by a blank space. Therefore, McDonald and Miller meet the criterion *>"M"*.

Database Queries

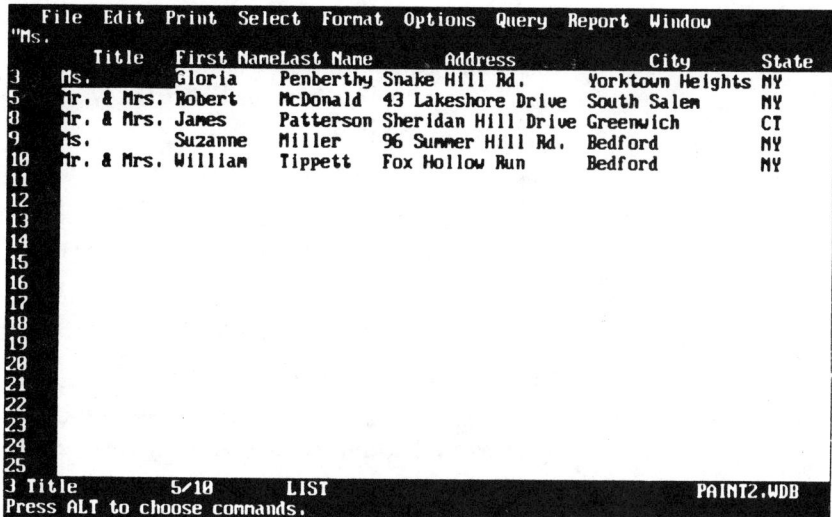

Figure 6-47

Now that we've practiced creating queries, let's use the information we've retrieved. Debbie wants each of her two assistants to take responsibility for approximately half of her clients. (Remember, we're pretending Debbie's company is growing rapidly!) To make it easier for client inquiries to be directed to the right person, the clients will be assigned alphabetically according to last name. Therefore, Debbie needs two separate printouts of client information—one of those whose names are in the first half of the alphabet and one of those in the second half. Obtaining a printout of those in the second half is fairly straightforward since those records currently are displayed on the screen. First we'll decrease the left and right print margins (as we did in the spreadsheet chapter) so that we can fit more information on a page, and then we'll print the selected part of the database.

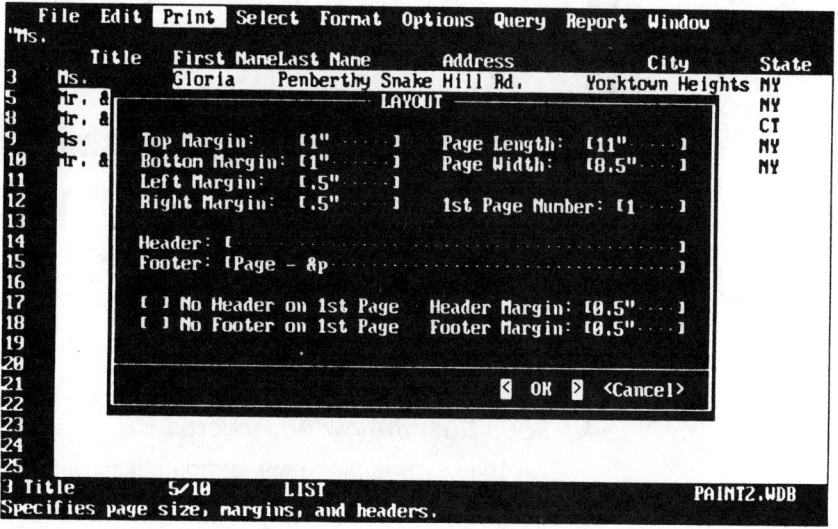

Figure 6-48

226 **Extending Your Knowledge with Microsoft Works**

1. Select **Print/Layout**.
2. Change the Left Margin and Right Margin Text Boxes to indicate margins of **.5"** (Figure 6-48). Press the **ENTER** key.
3. Select **Print/Print**.
4. Press the **ENTER** key.

   You will obtain a two-page printout. The first contains the first six fields of each record; the remaining fields are on page two.

We have obtained a printout of the second half of the alphabet. Now we can use another option on the Query menu to quickly display the remaining records.

1. Open the Query menu (Figure 6-49).

   The commands in the middle section: **Hide Record, Show All Records**, and **Switch Hidden Records** change the records that are visible on the screen.

2. Select **Switch Hidden Records** to hide the records currently visible and display the records that were hidden because they did not meet the last query criteria.

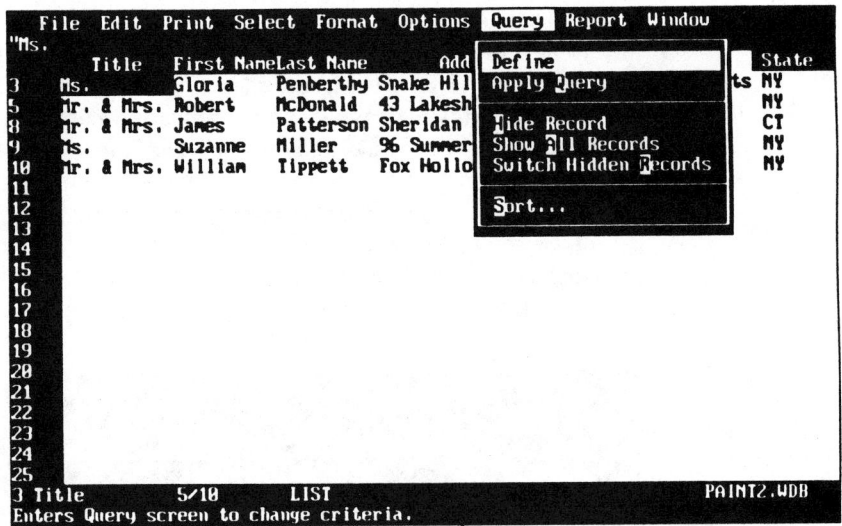

Figure 6-49

3. Use the **Print/Print** command to print the currently displayed records.

Now that we have finished using the results of our last query, let's redisplay all records.

4. Select **Query/Show All Records**.

   All 10 records in the database should reappear on the screen.

Suppose that after we had redisplayed all the records we remembered that we needed to do something else with the records extracted by the last query.

Database Queries 227

5. Select **Query/Apply Query**.

   The records meeting the criterion *Last Name: >"M"* are extracted once again.

   Since the QUERY screen retains our last created query until we delete it, that query can be repeated directly from the *List View* screen by using the **Apply Query** command. Also, if you save the database after defining a query, that query is saved and may be used the next time that you retrieve the file.

We've looked at the basic format for simple queries. The <, <=, and <> operators may be applied in the same way as the =, >, and >= operators that we used in the examples. There are many complex queries that can be constructed in *Works* that are beyond the scope of this book. However, before we finish our look at database queries, we will learn how to create queries that select records based on the data in more than one field.

Queries Using Criteria in More Than One Field   Debbie has decided that she wants her staff to make follow-up calls to all clients who have not yet signed contracts. Since she has two employees who are going to be making the calls, one in Connecticut and one in New York, she wants one list that shows those clients living in New York who have not signed a contract and one that shows clients in Connecticut who have not signed a contract.

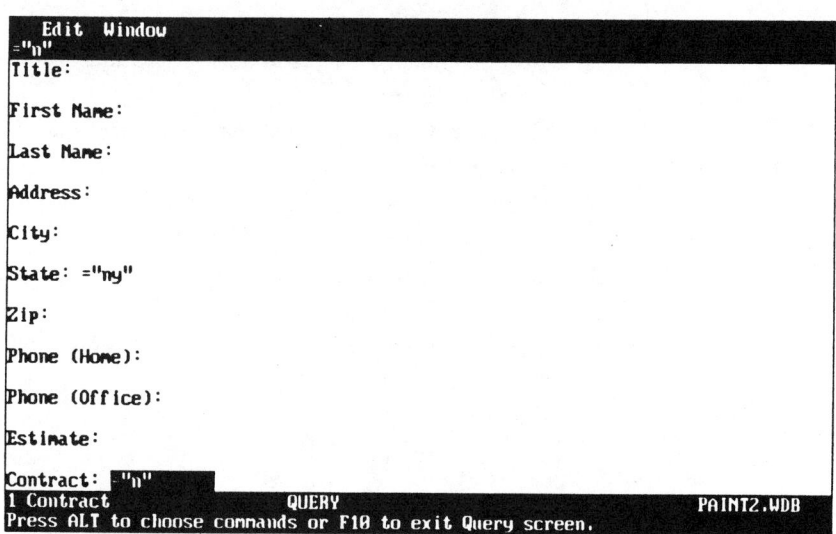

Figure 6-50

1. Select **Query/Define**.
2. Delete the criterion already on the QUERY screen.
3. Enter **="ny"** in the *State* field.

   Remember, the text used in queries may be typed in either upper- or lowercase letters.

4. Enter **="n"** in the *Contract* field (Figure 6-50).
5. Press **F10** to apply the query.

   The three records on clients living in New York who have not signed a contract are displayed.
6. Print the records.

Now we want to print the records of the clients living in Connecticut who have not signed a contract.

7. Edit the QUERY screen so that *State:* **="ct"**
8. Apply the query.

   The record of the one client in Connecticut who has not signed a contract is displayed.
9. Print the record.

Independent Extended Skills Project No. 5
Practicing Queries

Find and print the records in the **PAINT2.WDB** that meet the following criteria:

1. All of the clients who live the city of Bedford. (You should find two records.)
2. All of the clients whose estimate was less than or equal to 1400. (You should find seven records.)
3. All of the clients whose estimate was more than 1400. (You should find three records.)
4. All of the clients whose estimate was more than 1400 and who have signed a contract. (You should find two records.)
5. All of the clients for whom the city entry is Hartsdale. (What happens when you press **F10** to apply this query?)
6. All of the clients for whom the city entry is not equal to South Salem. (You should find eight records.)

Creating Reports from Your Database

We've just learned how to find records in the database that meet specific criteria. One of the other main uses of databases is to generate reports. It is possible to use *Works* to create customized reports containing not only your data, but summary statistics, explanatory text, calculations and formatting. A real strength of *Works'* reporting capabilities, however, is the ease with which you can let speed reporting create a report for you. What's more, once *Works* creates the report, you can edit it to make it better meet your needs. As many as eight report formats can be saved with your file and can be used repeatedly as data changes or to report on different parts of your database.

Creating Reports from Your Database 229

Extended Skills Project No. 7
Reporting on Debbie's Painting Clients

Debbie wants to use the data in **PAINT2.WDB** to see how her painting business is doing. A report listing the people to whom she has given estimates, their telephone numbers and the total estimates for those who have and have not signed contracts should give her an idea of the income range she can expect from potential jobs that she already knows about.

While completing this project you will learn:

- How to create a speed report.
- The types of information *Works* includes in a speed report.
- How to modify a speed report so that the information is grouped according to data in a different field.
- How to view and print the report.
- How to modify a speed report to delete some of the columns of data.
- How to name and save a report.

First we'll let *Works* create a report for us. Then we will do some simple editing to make the report better meet our needs.

To get ready:

1. If you have just finished Extended Skills Project No. 6, look to see that all 10 records are displayed. If they are not, select **Query/Show All Records**.

2. If you completed Extended Skills Project No. 6, but **PAINT2.WDB** is not open, open it and then display all 10 records if they are not already displayed.

3. If you have not completed Extended Skills Project No. 6, complete the section of Extended Skills Project No. 6 titled "Adding a Field to a Database."

4. If you are in *Form View*, change to *List View*.

Creating a Speed Report

Now you should be ready to create, view, and print a *Works* speed report.

1. Select **Report/New**.

   It will take a few seconds for *Works* to create the report. Then you will see the REPORT Screen (Figure 6-51).

The REPORT screen may seem incomprehensible at first glance. *Works* creates a tabular report. Each column on the REPORT screen relates to one field, or column, in your database. Each row contains explanatory text, data from your database, or summary statistics or formulas based on your data. The left-most column on the screen indicates the type of row. The rest of the screen shows the contents for each column in the row. The difficulty in reading the screen is compounded by the fact that many of the entries are too wide to fit in the columns, so one entry appears to run into the next. Before we discuss ways to make more sense of this information, let's print the report. The printed report may contain a few surprises, but it should help you see what the REPORT screen is doing.

230   **Extending Your Knowledge with Microsoft Works**

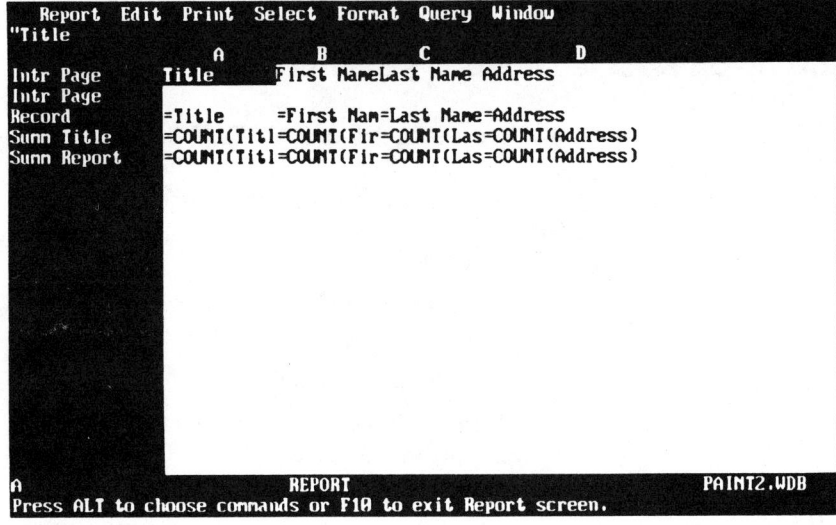

Figure 6-51

1. Use the **Print/Layout** command to change the left margin to **.15"** and the right margin to **.15"** so that we can fit more information on each page of our report.
2. Select **Print/Print** and press **ENTER** to print the report. Your report should look like the one shown below except that you will have more blank lines between the data and page numbers.

```
Title        First Name Last Name  Address              City             State  Zip
Dr.          Susan      Lippman    Whipporwill Drive    Darien           CT     06820
             1          1          1                    1                1   1  1
Dr. & Mrs.   Peter      Brody      456 Gilbert Street   South Salem      NY     10590
             1          1          1                    1                1   1  1
Mr. & Mrs.   Jerome     Adams      15 Martine Ave. #3M  White Plains     NY     10608
Mr. & Mrs.   Robert     McDonald   43 Lakeshore Drive   South Salem      NY     10590
Mr. & Mrs.   James      Patterson  Sheridan Hill Drive  Greenwich        CT     06830
Mr. & Mrs.   William    Tippett    Fox Hollow Run       Bedford          NY     10542
Mr. & Mrs.   Robert     Downey     52 Wilmot Circle     Scarsdale        NY     10583
Mr. & Mrs.   John       Fischer    P.O. Box 1118        Tarrytown        NY     10456
             6          6          6                    6                6   6  6
Ms.          Suzanne    Miller     96 Summer Hill Rd.   Bedford          NY     10542
Ms.          Gloria     Penberthy  Snake Hill Rd.       Yorktown Heights NY     10598
             2          2          2                    2                2   2  2
             10         10         10                   10               10 10  10

                                    Page - 1


         Phone (Home)    Phone (Office)   Estimate   Contract
         (203) 224-6785  (203) 224-3425      800     y
                  1               1          800            1
         (914) 763-7676  (212) 654-8765     1200     y
                  1               1         1200            1
         (914) 681-5674  (212) 345-7689      400     n
         (914) 763-9008  (914) 681-1635     1200     n
         (203) 744-3489  (203) 687-6745     2500     n
         (914) 234-7821  (212) 650-6734      300     n
         (914) 725-8907  (212) 234-7865     1400     y
         (914) 592-7683  (914) 592-3425     1000     y
                  6               6         6800            6
         (914) 234-3916  (212) 654-8765     5000     y
         (914) 764-3201  (914) 681-1000     1800     y
                  2               2         6800            2
                 10              10        15600           10

                                    Page - 2
```

Creating Reports from Your Database 231

The first line of the report lists the names of each field. Then there is a blank row and a listing of the data from each record in the database. However, you may notice that the records are no longer in the order that we entered them, and every so often the listing of data is broken and there are some numbers. How did this happen? When *Works* creates a report, it alphabetically sorts the database on the first field, and then inserts a break each time the information in the first field changes. The field used to order the report this way is called the **breakfield**. In our database *Title* is the first field, so it became the default breakfield.

In the speed report some kind of summary information, or summary statistic, is calculated for each field each time there is a break. For text fields like *Title*, *First Name*, *Zip*, etc., *Works* enters a count of the number of records. The 1's, 6's and 2's in your report are these counts. For fields with numeric data, such as the *Estimate* field, *Works* enters the sum of the values in the preceding subgroup of records. Thus, for the six people with the *Title* "Mr. & Mrs.", the number 6800 is entered since that is the sum of their estimates. Finally, the last line of the report provides a count or a sum of the data in each field for the entire report.

Now let's see if we can relate the information on the REPORT screen (Figure 6-51) to the printed copy of the report. The chart below shows the words in the leftmost column of the screen, which define the row type, and the information they produce in the speed report. Only the row types and information included in the speed report are included on the chart.

1. Make sure the REPORT screen is visible when you read the explanations below. If you are back in *List View*, select **Report/Define** to return to the REPORT screen.

Row Type	Information
Intr Page	Printed at the beginning of each page; speed reports contain one Intr Page with field names and a second blank one so that a blank line will follow the field name listing
Record	The REPORT screen lists the name of each field (e.g., =*Title*); the report lists the actual data for that field for each record
Summ breakfield[a]	Each column of the REPORT screen lists the function name followed by the fieldname[b]; the report lists summary information for each subgroup defined by the breakfield (counts are provided for text fields, sums for numeric fields)
Summ Report	Each column of the REPORT Screen lists the function name followed by the field name[b]; the report provides summary information (counts or sums) for all of the records in the report

Modifying a Speed Report The type of information included in the speed report is just the information Debbie could use—a listing of client information and figures on the total estimates. However, the organization and the subtotal figures do not make sense— *Title* is a meaningless field to use as a breakfield. Fortunately, the flexibility of *Works* report

---

a This entry is *Summ Title* on your REPORT screen because the breakfield is the field named *Title*.

b To see the entire entry for a column in a summary row, move the cursor to the entry and look at the Formula Bar.

Extending Your Knowledge with Microsoft Works

generator makes this difficulty very easy to overcome. Let's change our report so that *Contract* is the breakfield and the data within each contract subgrouping is listed alphabetically according to last name. We make this change by using a familiar command, **Query/Sort**.

1. Select **Query/Sort**.
2. Press the **ALT** key (Figure 6-52).

   The SORT Dialog Box is like the one we used to sort the database in the database chapter, except that Break and 1st Letter Check Boxes have been added. Therefore, when the **ALT** key is pressed, each of these options is followed by a bold letter. The bold letters *A*, *B*, *G*, and *H* apply to the characteristics of the *1st Field*; *C*, *D*, *I*, and *J* apply to the *2nd field*; and *E*, *F*, *K*, and *L* apply to the *3rd field*.

3. The *1st Field* Text Box should contain the name of the current breakfield, *Title*, and should be highlighted. If it is not, move the cursor to the *1st Field* Text Box.

4. Type: **Contract**

   Notice that the Break Check Box for the 1st field is marked. This means that *Works* will sort the database on the data in the *Contract* field and then insert a break each time the data changes. This is exactly what we want to happen.

5. Press **ALT+2** or **TAB** to the 2nd Field Text Box.
6. Type: **Last Name**

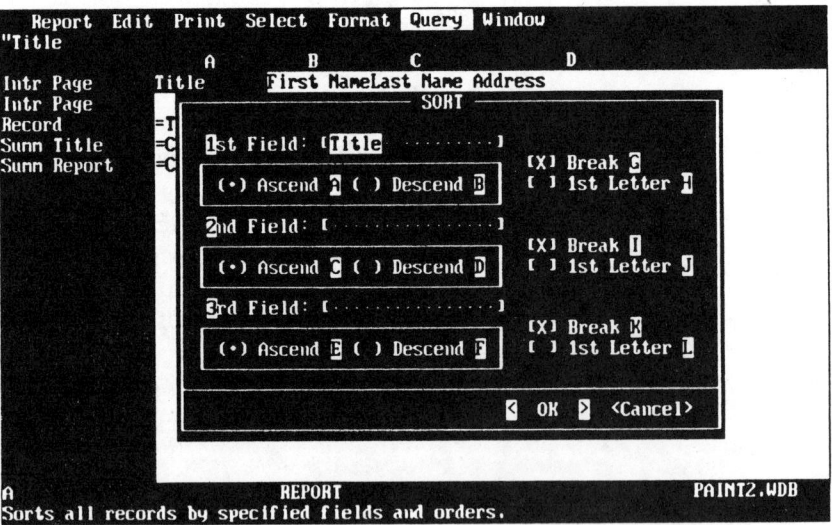

Figure 6-52

As you may remember from when you sorted the database in Chapter 2, the 2nd sort field is used only to order the records for which the data in the 1st field is the same. We do not want a break and summary statistics every time the last name changes. Therefore, we want to toggle off the Break Check Box for this field. (See

Creating Reports from Your Database   233

the end of Chapter 1 or Extended Skills Project No. 1 for more information on check boxes.)

7. **TAB** to the Break Check Box next to 2nd Field and press the **SPACE BAR** or press **ALT+I**.

8. If your SORT Dialog Box resembles Figure 6-53, press **ENTER**.

   Notice that *Summ Contract* has replaced *Sum Title* in the left-hand column of the screen, indicating that the summary information will be reported on the breaks in the *Contract* field.

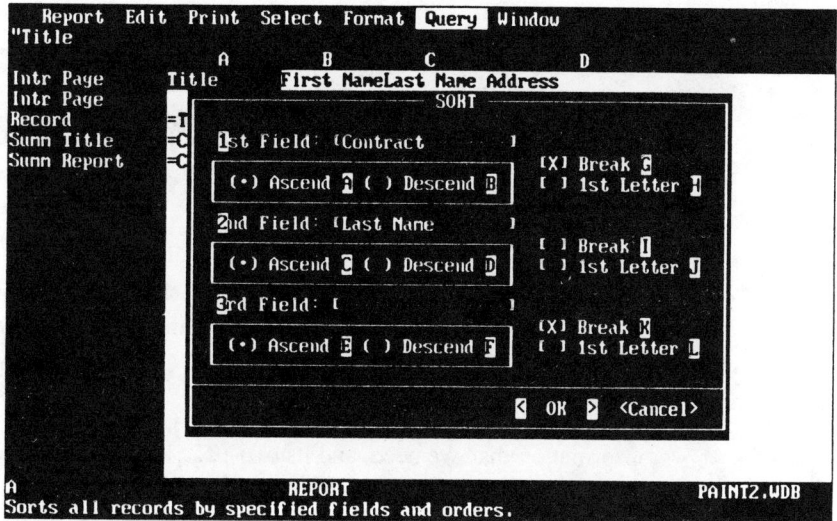

Figure 6-53

Note: We have not used the **1st Letter** Check Box. If this box is checked, breaks will be inserted when the first letter of the data in the field changes, rather than each time the data changes at all.

This time we'll view the report on the screen so that we don't need to print it until it looks as it should.

9. Select **Report/View**.

   A portion of the first page of your report will appear on the screen (Figure 6-54).

   The Message Line tells you to: *Press ENTER to continue or ESC To exit Report view.*

```
Title       First Name Last Name  Address              City             State

Mr. & Mrs.  Jerome     Adams      15 Martine Ave. #3M  White Plains     NY
Mr. & Mrs.  Robert     McDonald   43 Lakeshore Drive   South Salem      NY
Mr. & Mrs.  James      Patterson  Sheridan Hill Drive  Greenwich        CT
Mr. & Mrs.  William    Tippett    Fox Hollow Run       Bedford          NY
            4          4          4                    4                4         4
Dr. & Mrs.  Peter      Brody      456 Gilbert Street   South Salem      NY
Mr. & Mrs.  Robert     Downey     52 Wilmot Circle     Scarsdale        NY
Mr. & Mrs.  John       Fischer    P.O. Box 1118        Tarrytown        NY
Dr.         Susan      Lippman    Whipporwill Drive    Darien           CT
Ms.         Suzanne    Miller     96 Summer Hill Rd.   Bedford          NY
Ms.         Gloria     Penberthy  Snake Hill Rd.       Yorktown Heights NY
            6          6          6                    6                6         6
           10         10         10                   10               10        10

Page 1                                                              PAINT2.WDB
Press ENTER to continue or ESC to exit Report view.
```

Figure 6-54

10. Press **ENTER** until the top portion of page 2 appears on the screen (Figure 6-55).

This report is much closer to what we want. The four clients who do not have a contract are listed first and we know how much their estimates total. This information is followed by a listing of all those with contracts, the total of these estimates and, finally, the total of all of the estimates. However, this report contains more information than we need, and its two-page length hinders readability. Therefore, we'd like to eliminate the *Address*, *City*, *State* and *Zip* fields from our report.

1. Press **ESC** to return to the REPORT screen.
2. Move the cursor anywhere in the column headed *Address*.
3. Press **F8** and then use the right arrow key to **EXTEND** the highlight to the *Zip* column. *One* row in each column should be highlighted (Figure 6-56).

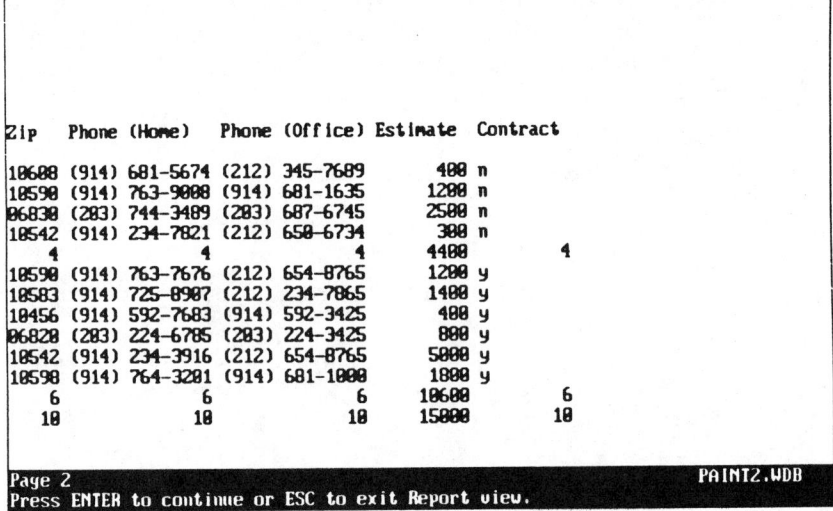

Figure 6-55

Creating Reports from Your Database

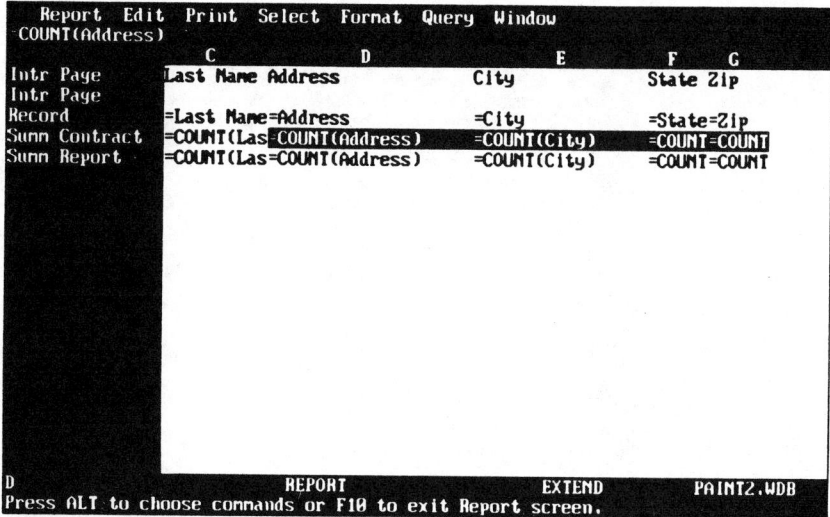

Figure 6-56

4. Choose **Select/Column** to select the *Address*, *City*, *State* and *Zip* columns.

5. Choose **Edit/Delete**.

   The fields containing address information have been deleted. The *Phone (Home)* field is now in column D.

6. Print the modified report.

Naming and Saving a Report

Now we have a printed report containing exactly the information that we want. However, if Debbie has to change any of the records in her **Paint2** database, or if she adds new clients, this printed report no longer will be valid. If you had to go through all the steps we just completed to generate this particular report format again each time the database changed, it would be very time consuming. Fortunately, *Works* will save a report format as part of the database file. If the database is updated, the report also automatically will be updated to reflect the new information. Let's look now at how to save a report as part of the database file.

1. Select **Report/Exit** to return to the *List View* screen. Notice that the records appear in the order in which they were sorted for our report.

2. Open the **Report** menu (Figure 6-57).
   Notice that a new section and the entry, *Report 1*, have been added at the bottom of the menu. This section of the menu is similar to the bottom section of the Chart menu in the spreadsheet tool. It lists all of the reports that are in the database. Report 1 is preceded by a mark indicating that it is the current report.

   The Report menu can be used to return to the REPORT screen for the current report (**Define**), to create a **New** speed report, to **View** the current report, or to rename, delete, or copy any listed report (**Reports**). Let's use this menu to give *Report1* a more meaningful name so that we can differentiate it from other reports that we might create.

Extending Your Knowledge with Microsoft Works

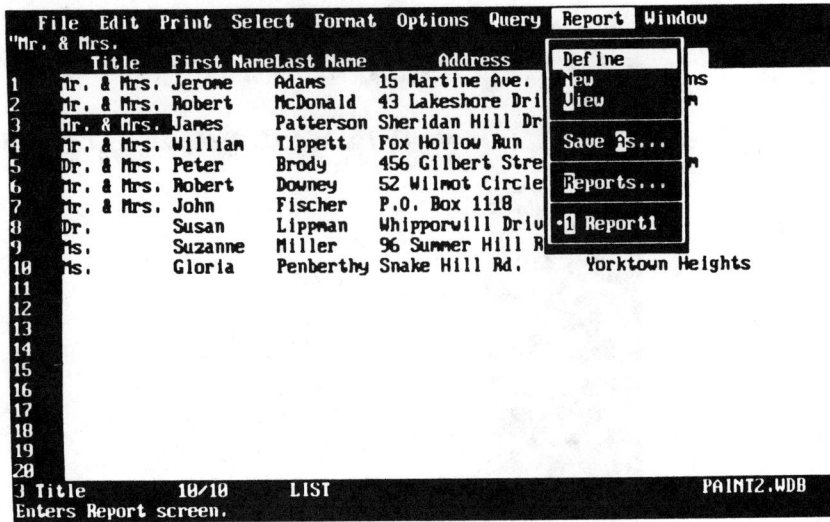

Figure 6-57

3. Select **Reports...**

   The REPORTS Dialog Box is very similar to the CHARTS Dialog Box used in Extended Project No. 5.

4. Make sure the current report is highlighted in the **Reports** List Box.

5. Use **ALT+N** or **TAB** to the Name Text Box.

6. Type a name for your report: **Contract Status** (Figure 6-58)

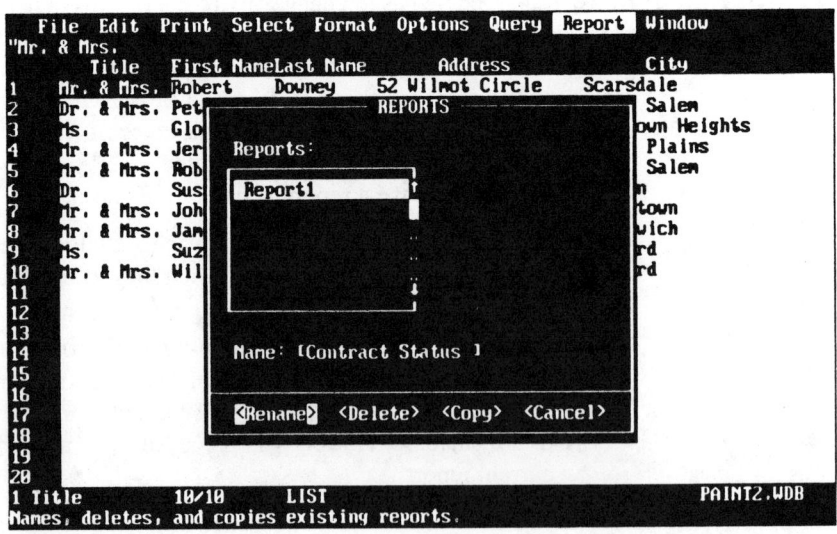

Figure 6-58

Creating Reports from Your Database 237

Note: The naming rules for reports are the same as for charts. Any characters or combinations of spaces and characters can be used. In order to have the entire name appear on the Report menu, use 15 characters or less.

---

7. Since **<RENAME>** is the active button, press **ENTER** and your report will be renamed.

Caution: The other option on the Report menu is somewhat confusing. The **Save As...** option will save the summary statistics from the report to a special file that then can be inserted in a *Works* word processing document. If you want to save the entire customized report, you must use the File menu commands, either **Save** or **Save As...**, to save the whole database file again.

---

8. Select **File/Save** to save the database and all reports using the current file name.

Note: You can generate up to eight different reports for each database, and when you save the database file, all eight automatically will be saved with it.

Independent Extended Skills Project No. 6
Creating a Second Report

We know that sometimes Debbie needs information on her clients separated by the state in which they live. A copy of a report that separates them this way is shown below.

```
Last Name  Address              City              State  Zip    Estimate  Contract

Lippman    Whipporwill Drive    Darien            CT     06820     800   y
Patterson  Sheridan Hill Drive  Greenwich         CT     06830    2500   n
              2                     2              2       2      3300          2
Adams      15 Martine Ave. #3M  White Plains      NY     10608     400   n
Brody      456 Gilbert Street   South Salem       NY     10590    1200   y
Downey     52 Wilmot Circle     Scarsdale         NY     10583    1400   y
Fischer    P.O. Box 1118        Tarrytown         NY     10456    1000   y
McDonald   43 Lakeshore Drive   South Salem       NY     10590    1200   n
Miller     96 Summer Hill Rd.   Bedford           NY     10542    5000   y
Penberthy  Snake Hill Rd.       Yorktown Heights  NY     10598    1800   y
Tippett    Fox Hollow Run       Bedford           NY     10542     300   n
              8                     8              8       8     12300          8
             10                    10             10      10     15600         10
```

1. Open **PAINT2.WDB** if it is not already open.
2. Create a **New** report.

3. Modify the report so that the records are sorted first by *State* and then by *Last Name*. We only want subtotals by state, so *State* should be a breakfield but *Last Name* should not.

4. Limit the report to include only the following fields:
   Last Name   Address   City   State   Zip   Estimate   Contract

5. Name the report: **CLIENTS/STATE**

Note: The **Report/Reports...** option is available from the REPORT screen so it is not necessary to return to the *List View* screen to name the report.

---

6. Print the report.

Hint: You may need to change the left and right margins on the print layout so that the report will print on one page.

---

7. Save the database again so that the new report format also will be saved.

Integrating Works

Now that we've taken another look at the Word Processor, Spreadsheet, and Database tools, we'll see another way that they can be integrated. In this exercise we'll use the database and word processor together to create personalized form letters.

Creating Form Letters

The Word Processor and Database files can be used together to create personalized letters or other documents. This **merging** of the data from database files with documents created in a word processor is the procedure used to generate the personalized mass mailings that we often receive and is thus often called a **mail merge**. It's also a technique that you can use whenever you want to create documents that are essentially the same but contain some variable information, and that **variable** information is available in a database file.

Extended Skills Project No. 8
Paul's Personalized Parent Letters

Paul wants to give each student a letter to take home to his/her parents. The general information is the same in each letter, but he wants to add a personal touch by including the student's name, parent's last name, and day of the lesson.

Creating Form Letters

Most of the steps involved in creating Paul's customized form letters involve skills you have already learned. However, while creating the letters, you will also learn how to:

- Insert a place holder in the word processor document for the variable information from the database.
- Print documents merging text from a word processor document and data from a database file.

The general steps used to create a letter that will include information from a database are:

- Open (or create) a database file containing the information that will be merged into each individualized document.
- Create the word processor document. Whenever variable information is to be included, use the **Edit/Insert Field** command to insert a place holder for the variable information.
- Select the records to be merged with the document.
- From the word processor document, use the **Print/Merge** command to print the documents with the variable information from the database file.

Let's implement these steps using the **PIANO2.WDB** database that you created in the database chapter of this book.

Creating a Word Processor Document Containing Variable Information from a Database

1. Close any open files.
2. Open **PIANO2.WDB**.
3. Select **File/New/Word Processor** to create a new word processor file.
4. Type today's date at the left hand margin.
5. Press the **ENTER** key six times.
6. Type: **Dear Mr./Ms.**
7. Press the **SPACE BAR** once.
8. To enter a field name:
   a. Select **Edit/Insert Field**.

   The names of all of the open databases will be shown in the Databases List Box (Figure 6-59).

   b. Use the **DOWN ARROW** key to highlight **PIANO2.WDB**.

   The fields in the selected database will be shown in the Fields List Box.

   c. Highlight: **Last Name** (See Figure 6-60)
   d. Press **ENTER**.

Extending Your Knowledge with Microsoft Works

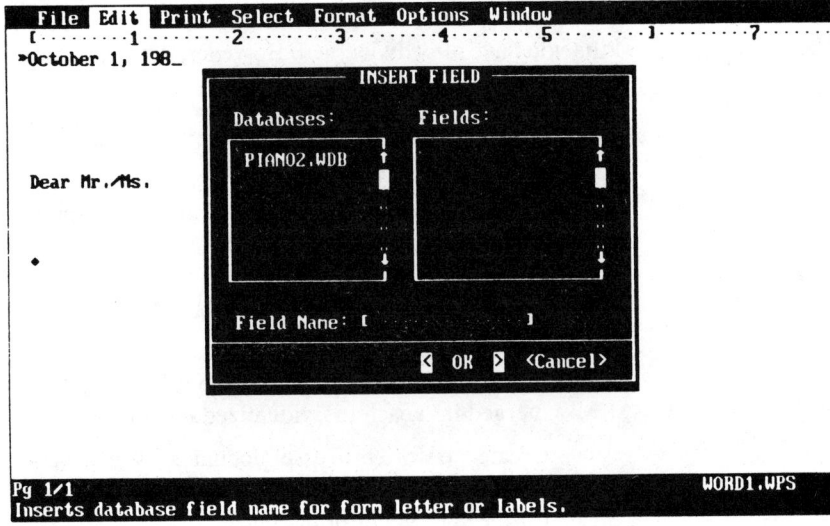

Figure 6-59

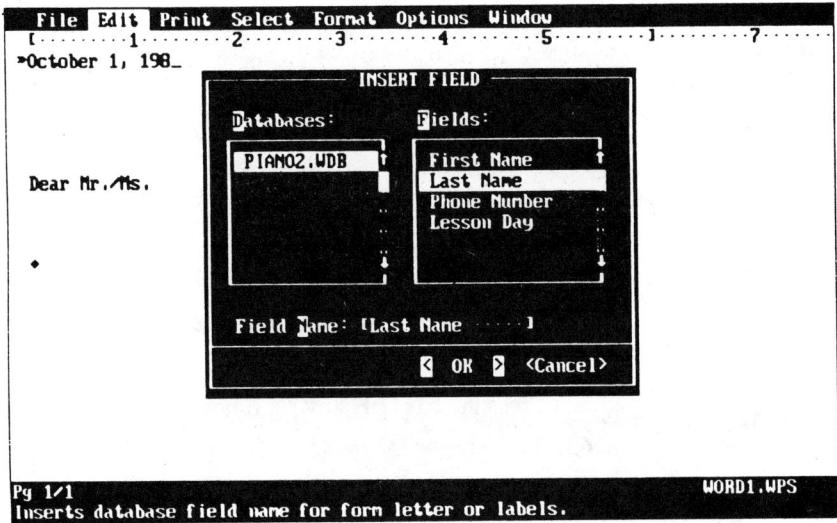

Figure 6-60

<<*Last Name*>>, the field name enclosed in double brackets, will be entered in the document.

9. Type: **:**
10. Enter the remainder of the letter as shown below.

Note: <<*Last Name*>>, <<*First Name*>>, and <<*Lesson Day*>> are included below to indicate where you should use **Edit/Insert Field** to place the field names.

Creating Form Letters

> Today's Date
>
>
> Dear Mr./Ms. <<*Last Name*>>:
>
> The students, some of the parents and I have been discussing the original schedule of recitals. Most students would prefer having small gatherings where they play for each other rather than the January 29th recital. A formal recital will still be held on June 13. <<*First Name*>> will participate in two small groups to be held at 7:30 p.m. on the first <<*Lesson Day*>> of November and February.
>
> Sincerely,
>
>
> Paul Harrison

Selecting Database Records to Merge If the **Print/Merge** command is used to print this letter, one letter will be printed for each record in the **PIANO2.WDB** file. Sometimes you want to print a letter for only some of the records in the database. There are several ways to do this. You may define a query to select only some records. Alternately, you may sort the database so that records are in order according to some criterion and then hide records, or you may hide individual or groups of records without first sorting the database.

Since this is a practice exercise, we do not want to print letters to all of Paul's clients. Let's use the **Query/Define** command to select records of those students whose last names begin with the letters A through G.

1. Select **Window/PIANO2.WDB**.
2. Change to *List View* if that is not currently on the screen.
3. Select **Query/Define**.
4. Move the cursor to the *Last Name* field and type: **<"H"**
5. Press **F10** to execute the query and return to *List View*. The records of those students shown in Figure 6-61 should be displayed.

Printing the Merged Document To print the document:

1. Return to the word processing document.
2. Select **Print/Merge....**
3. When the PRINT MERGE Dialog Box appears, select the name of the database that contains the information to be merged, **PIANO2.WDB**.

Extending Your Knowledge with Microsoft Works

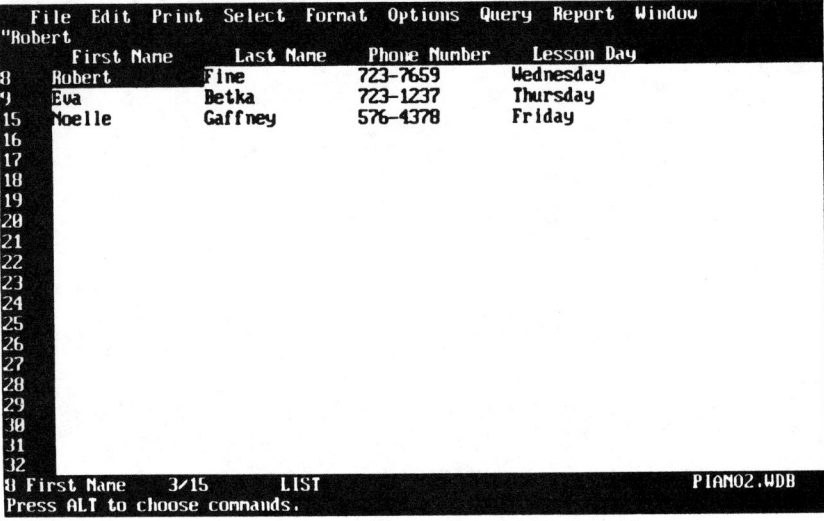

Figure 6-61

4. The PRINT Dialog Box should appear. Press the **ENTER** key to accept the default values.

   One copy of your letter will be printed for each one of the records that is currently displayed in the selected database. As the letters are being printed, the number of the current record whose data is being merged will appear on the middle of the Status Line.

   Works will word wrap the text correctly as the variable information is inserted.

Independent Extended Skills Project No. 7
Debbie's Customized Form Letters

Debbie wants to create a form letter that she can send to all clients to inform them of her estimate of the cost of painting their houses.

We will use fields from the database to enter the address, salutation, and estimate into the letter. Then we will print letters for all clients who do not have a contract. General instructions and a copy of the word processing document follow.

1. Open the database, **PAINT2.WDB** created in Database Project No. 2 and modified in Extended Skills Project No. 6. If you have not completed these projects, follow the instructions under the heading "Adding a Field to the End of a Database" in Extended Skills Project No. 6.

2. Use the **Query/Define** command to extract all the records for which the *Contract* field is equal to "**n**". This command should locate four records.

3. Create a new word processing document and type the text on the next page. *<<Last Name>>*, *<<First Name>>*, etc. are included to indicate where you should use **Edit/Insert Field** to place the field name.

4. From the word processing document, print the letter merged with the four selected database records.

Today's Date

<<Title>> <<First Name>> <<Last Name>>
<<Address>>
<<City>>, <<State>> <<Zip>>

Dear <<Title>> <<Last Name>>:

This is a written confirmation of the estimate we discussed during my visit to your home. The total fee for supplies and labor will be: $<<Estimate>>.

If this estimate is acceptable to you, please call me at 564-5464 to set up a work schedule. At that time I will send you a contract detailing the materials to be used, area to be painted, and work schedule.

Sincerely yours,

Debbie Starr

Conclusion

Our second look at *Works* has focused on some of the extras that make *Works* such a powerful, time-saving tool. In our return to the Word Processor tool we looked at ways to enhance and customize the appearance of our documents. Our second view of the Database and Spreadsheet tools began by making simple modifications to the structure of an existing database and spreadsheet. This was done to illustrate the ease with which they can be modified as your needs change. In the Database tool we also expanded our ability to organize, extract, and display specific information contained in a database. Our look at formulas in the Spreadsheet tool gave us a further feel for the flexibility, power, and ease of computing in Works. The spreadsheet charting capabilities provide another way to analyze and display data. The graphics ability of computers is widely used in business as a way of enhancing reports, presentations, and letters. Since charting is an integral part of the Spreadsheet tool, you can quickly turn the spreadsheet data into different graphs until you find the most effective presentation. Finally, we used the word processor and database together in one of the most widely used integration of these two types of programs—the creation of personalized form letters.

We have now looked at all of the main screens available in the Word Processor, Spreadsheet, and Database tools of *Works*. In addition to the specific skills learned,

Extending Your Knowledge with Microsoft Works

the additional experience with the menus should enable you to experiment with some of the commands not covered in this introductory book. Appendices containing a brief description of the commands and functions available in *Works* should further help your exploration.

Key Terms

The following important terms and commands have been introduced and explained in this chapter:

The Word Processor Tool:

Format/Paragraph	Format/Bold	Format/Underline
Format/Character	Format/Center	Format/Tabs
Format/Italic	SHIFT+ENTER	Format/Double

The Spreadsheet Tool:

Select/Column	Edit/Insert	F4 Reference key
Anchor the pointer	Chart	X-axis
Y-axis	Legend	Y-series
Speed Chart	Chart/New	Chart Screen
Chart/View	Data/X-series	SHIFT+F10
Data/Legends	Data/Titles	Chart/Charts
Chart/Exit Chart	Chart/Define	Select/Row
Edit/Delete	Print/Select Chart Printer	
Absolute cell address/reference		

The Database Tool:

Query/Define	Query Screen	Operator
Edit/Delete	Query/Apply Query	F10 (Apply Query)
Query/Show All Records	Query/Switch Hidden Records	
Report/New	Speed Report	Report Screen
Breakfield	Report/Define	Report/Exit
Report/Reports	F10 (Exit Report)	

Integrating Works:

Mail merge	Edit/Insert Field	Print/Merge

Chapter 7  A Brief Look at Communications

In this chapter you will learn:

- The hardware necessary for communications.
- Basic terminology used in communications.
- How to use *Works* to set up your computer to communicate with an on-line information service.

As you may have guessed by the limited nature of these objectives and the placement of this chapter at the end of the book, our treatment of the Communications tool is going to be different than that of the other *Works* components. That's because the Communications tool has some important differences from the three tools we have already examined. The word processor, database, and spreadsheet can all be used by themselves on a single computer to accomplish a task. The Communications tool is used to connect your computer with another computer. This requires separate hardware that many users of the educational version of *Works* do not have. In addition, each of you who do have the necessary hardware would wish to communicate with different computers or information-sharing systems. Therefore, instead of providing a project for you to complete, we will describe how to use the *Works* Communications tool to set up your computer to communicate with another. If you do not have the hardware necessary to use the Communications tool, this discussion should still give you an idea of some of the concepts involved. If you do have access to communications hardware as part of your course, your instructor can provide you with the specific information needed to use your communication source.

What is Communications Software?

The Communications tool is used to set up a connection between your computer and another computer so that they may exchange information. It most often uses a piece of hardware, known as a modem, and the telephone system to actually transmit information between the computers that are communicating. The process of communicating across large distances using telephones, teletypes, radios, or televisions is referred to as **telecommunications**.

A Brief Look at Communications

In order for two computers to communicate, they must have access to both specialized hardware and software. The types of information that you can access and the tasks that you can accomplish with a modem, a telephone, and a communications program such as the *Works* Communications tool is varied and growing daily. For example, you can leave or receive messages or exchange information or even non copywrited software (know as share-ware or free-ware) using one of the many Bulletin Board Systems sponsored by clubs, organizations, or groups of computer users. Dial-in computer information services (also called on-line information services) provide access to information such as stock quotes, airline schedules, book reviews, and the latest news or weather—generally for a fee. You may even initiate bank transactions, conduct bibliographic searches, shop, send mail or play games. Software, electronic mail, or data can also be exchanged with any other compatibly equipped computer. It is also possible to use your PC to receive and send data and commands to a larger computer at your school or office.

The Hardware—A Modem

If you want to use the telephone system to communicate with another computer, you must use a **modem**. Modems are necessary because computers and telephones represent information differently. Telephones use an **analog signal**, which is a continuous, smoothly varying signal well suited to the transmission of voices. Computers use a **digital signal**, which represents information by discrete on/off signals. The modem (short for MOdulator/DEModulator) sending the data converts the signal from digital to analog so that it can be transmitted via the telephone, and then the modem on the receiving end converts it back again. During communications each computer spends some time sending and some time receiving information so each modem spends some time converting from digital to analog and some time converting from analog to digital.

There are different types of modems. Acoustic modems use an acoustic coupler as a receptacle for an ordinary telephone handset. Once the handset is placed in the coupler, the coupler converts the computer signals so that they can be carried on the telephone system. Extraneous environmental sounds can interfere with data transmission when acoustic modems are used.

The newer modems, which you are much more likely to use, are either installed in your computer or alongside it and are actually plugged into standard telephone jacks. These modems tend to be more reliable and often have extra capabilities such as dialing for you, redialing busy numbers, and automatically receiving calls. *Works* can take advantage of these advanced features only if you are using a Hayes or Hayes-compatible modem. If you have an acoustic or non-Hayes-compatible modem you can still use it with *Works*, but without automatic dialing and some of the other time-saving features.

After purchasing a modem, you must install it in or next to your computer. If it is necessary for you to install a modem, consult the installation instructions provided with your modem in conjunction with Appendix E of this manual. Appendix E includes a table of modem settings that work best with *Works*.

It is also possible to directly wire two computers and use the *Works* Communications tool to enable the computers to communicate. This is a less frequently used application and will not be covered in this book.

The Hardware—A Modem 247

Communications Example
Communicating with an
On-Line Information Service

This example will illustrate the steps that you should use to access an on-line information service. The instructions will not enable you to actually carry out this activity because telephone numbers, account numbers, and similar information necessary to actually make the connection will not be supplied. If you have access to an on-line information service or bulletin board, you should be able to follow the general steps to establish communication.

The Communications Screen
The first step, just as when using any of the other tools, is to tell *Works* which tool you are using. If you have just loaded *Works*, select **Communications** from the NEW Dialog Box. If you are currently using *Works*, select **File/New/Communications**.

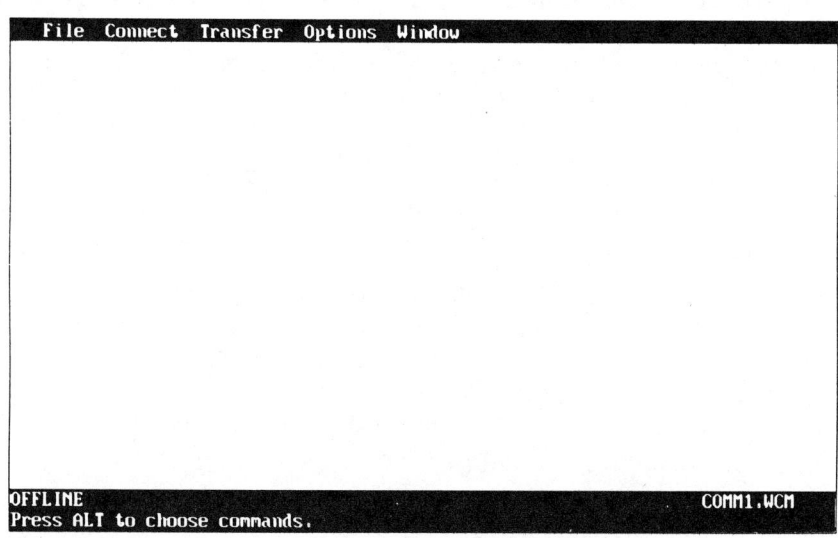

Figure 7-1

The general appearance of the communications screen (Figure 7-1) should be quite familiar. The Menu Bar contains the familiar **File** and **Window** menus as well as three new menus: **Connect, Transfer,** and **Options**. The **Options** menu is used to tell your computer how to communicate with a specific partner. The **Connect** menu is used to actually make the connection with the other computer. The **Transfer** menu is used only if you wish to save the information you receive to a file or send information from a file rather than by typing it in at the keyboard. We will not use the **Transfer** menu in this example.

The Work Area is currently blank and does not even contain the cursor. In the Communications tool the Work Area is used only to record the information being communicated between the two computers. Therefore, no information can be

A Brief Look at Communications

entered on it until your computer is connected to another computer. Prior to the connection, you may use the tool only to make menu selections that specify how the communications will take place.

The Status Line currently indicates that you are *OFFLINE*. This means that your computer is not currently communicating with another computer. Once you attempt to connect to another computer, the Status Line will indicate the time elapsed since you began the connection. The Status Line also indicates the current default file name: **COMM1.WCM**. Unlike the files that we created in the other tools, the communications file will not contain the information that is displayed in the Work Area. Instead, .WCM files contain the set up information used to establish contact with each information service or computer with which you communicate. This means that once you set up *Works* to communicate with a particular on-line information service, you can just open the existing .WCM file and skip the setup procedure described below.

Setting Up Works for Communication

Next, it is necessary to give *Works* information about the telephone number that you are calling and how you are making the call, about the way in which the information will be communicated between the two computers, and about the way the information will be displayed on your monitor. This information is entered using the three **Options** commands: **Terminal**, **Communication**, and **Phone**. We will discuss the settings available for each of these commands.

First lets fill in the **Phone** settings.

1. Select **Options/Phone**.

   The PHONE Dialog Box will appear (Figure 7-2).

2. Select **Phone Number**. Enter the telephone number of the information service. Type all of the numbers that you would need to dial if you were going to dial the number itself. The number can be entered as a string of digits or with parentheses and dashes as typically used when designating telephone numbers. Some examples of phone numbers are:

   (914)123-4567

   9141234567

   914-123-4567

   123-4567 (if you are calling a local number)

   9-123-4567 (if you are using a business phone that requires dialing 9 to access an outside line)

3. The **Modem Setup** Text Box can be used to send special commands to the modem that it will use when dialing. For example you can tell the modem to change volume or to allow a certain number of rings before assuming that a connection cannot be made. The specific commands available depend on your modem, so consult the modem's manual. It is not necessary to enter any information in this box.

4. If you have touch-tone service leave the Dial Type Option Box as it appears. If your phone only accepts pulse dialing, select **Pulse**.

Setting Up Works for Communication 249

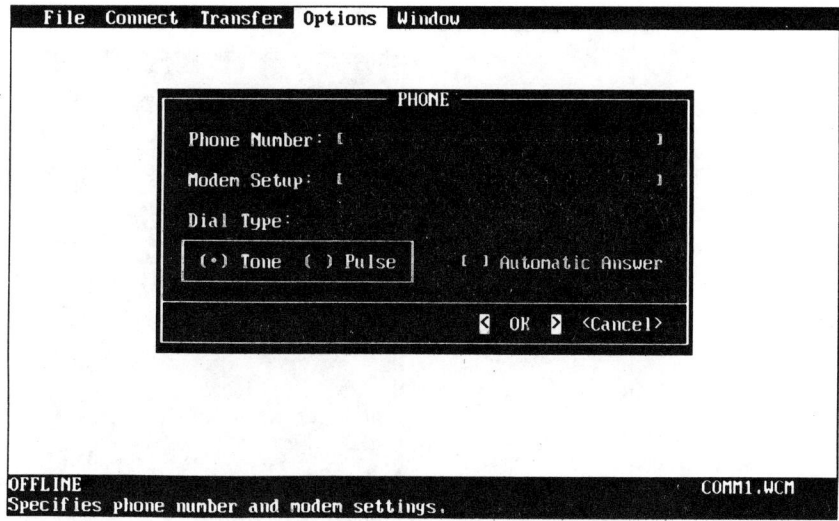

Figure 7-2

5. Since we are initiating a call, we are finished with this menu. Press **ENTER** to accept the current settings.

Note: The Automatic Answer Check Box is used only if you want to use your PC to accept a call from another computer.

We've finished setting up the computer so that it can dial the number of the information service. Remember, you can use the PHONE Dialog Box only to dial the information service number if you have a modem that uses Hayes commands.

Now, let's look at the settings that control how the information is actually transmitted. The speed and manner in which the data is transmitted is determined by a number of variables. The **Options/Communication** command is used to specify these variables for the current connection. Each of these settings will be briefly described. Don't worry if you don't understand what the settings really do. The important fact is that the settings you use *must correspond* to the settings being used by the receiving modem. When you subscribe to an information service they will tell you the settings that you need. In many cases these will be the same as the *Works* default settings. If they differ, all you have to do is use your knowledge of how to use *Works* Dialog Boxes to change the incorrect settings to those supplied by the information service.

The one piece of information that is related to your computer alone rather than to how the information will be exchanged between computers is the Port Option, so we will discuss that first.

1. Select **Options/Communication**.

    The COMMUNICATION Dialog Box will appear. (Figure 7-3 shows the dialog box as it appears if the **ALT** key is pressed after the box is displayed.)

A Brief Look at Communications

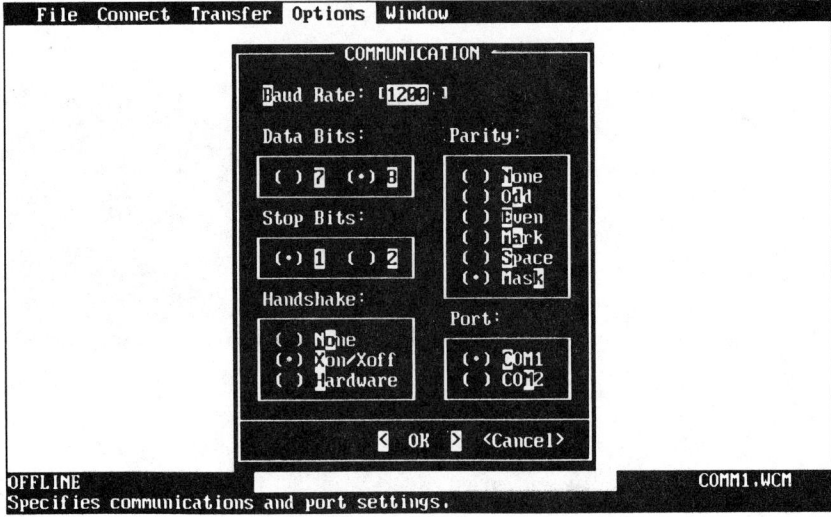

Figure 7-3

1. In Chapter 2 when we discussed how to setup your text printer, we mentioned that we had to tell *Works* the port, or slot, at the back of the computer to which the printer was connected. Similarly, we now need to tell *Works* the port to which the modem is connected. The modem can use only serial ports, which are named COM1 or COM2. Typically your modem will use COM1. If something else such as a serial printer is connected to COM1 and your modem is connected to COM2, type **ALT+M** to select COM2.

Note: If in doubt, leave the port as **COM1**. If this is the wrong choice, the message *Wrong COM port selected* will be displayed when you try to connect, and you can then select **Options/Communication** and change to COM2.

2. The **baud rate** refers to the speed at which data is being transmitted. The baud rate can be set anywhere between 50 and 9600. However, the baud rates for most communications using modems are 300, 1200, or 2400.

   Some information services give you a choice of baud rates, such as between 300 and 1200. You may need to experiment to see which is the more cost-effective option. Data is transmitted faster at 1200 baud than at 300 baud so the connect time (which is the time charged for) and the amount of time that you need to spend waiting for information to appear on your screen are shorter. However, many services charge less for a 300 baud connection than for one at 1200 baud.

   The faster response time afforded by a 1200 baud rate can be important when using an information service, since most of the communication involves the service's transmission of responses to your short queries for information. On the other hand, if you have a poor phone connection, a 300 baud rate should cause less loss of data. Also, if much of the time spent in

Setting Up Works for Communication 251

a particular situation involves your entering data at the keyboard, or if you want to read the information as it appears on the screen, a 300 baud rate might be more appropriate.

If you want to transmit at a rate other than 1200 baud, select **Baud Rate** and type the desired rate.

3. **Data bits** refers to the number of bits which make up a character. A bit is an electrical impulse which is the smallest unit of computer information. Works can transmit characters composed of 7 or 8 bits, although 8 bits is more typically used.

   If you need to send data as 7 bits, select **ALT+7**.

4. **Stop bits** are the number of bits used to indicate the end of each character. Most information services use one stop bit. If the service you are using requires two, select **ALT+2**.

5. **Parity** is a means of checking for errors. In *Works* if data bits is set at **8**, the parity setting must be **none**. If data bits is set at **7**, your service is probably using a parity check. Select the option in the Parity List Box that matches the parity type specified by your information service.

6. **Handshake** refers to the way in which the two computers know when the other is sending/receiving data and when it is involved in other tasks that might interfere with the transmission of data. The specific signals most often sent by on-line information services to indicate pauses and resumptions in data transmission conform to the rules of the **Xon/Xoff** convention. A **hardware** handshake involves computers attached via a cable rather than a modem, so it would not be used in this example.

   If you know that the other computer uses no handshaking, select **None** from the Handshake Option Box.

7. When you have selected the port to which your modem is connected, and set all of the other options so that they match the specifications provided by your information service, press **ENTER**.

The final group of settings refers to the way in which your monitor and keyboard will display and send information.

1. Select **Options/Terminal**.

   The TERMINAL Dialog Box will be displayed. (Figure 7-4 shows the Dialog Box as it appears if the **ALT** key is pressed after the box is displayed.)

Terminal is a term that originally referred to the video display and keyboard used to communicate with a large, multi-user computer before the development of personal computers. The TERMINAL Dialog Box is used to define the way your computer monitor displays and responds to information even if your computer is communicating with another personal computer. In addition, when a PC is used to communicate with a mainframe, the PC often needs to act like, or **emulate**, a specific type of terminal, and this Dialog Box is used to indicate the required terminal emulation.

2. **VT52** and **ANSI** refer to different terminal types.

A Brief Look at Communications

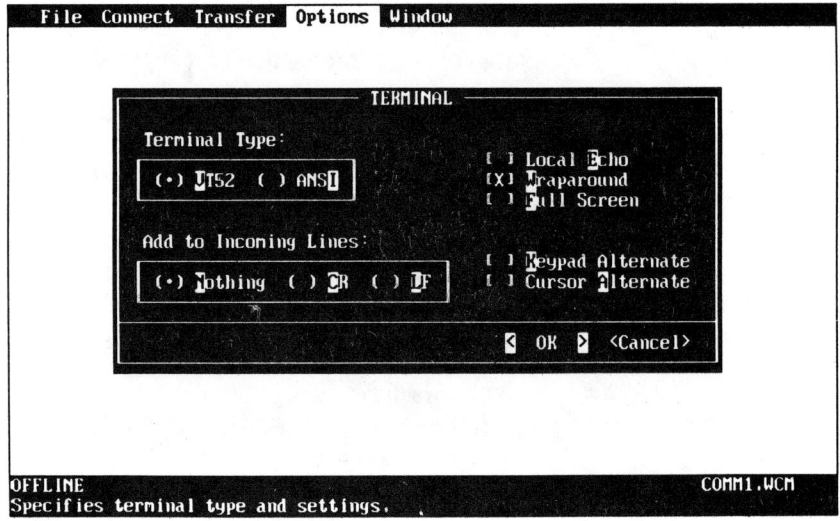

Figure 7-4

For most information services, VT52 is the correct setting even though, frequently, no terminal emulation is required.

Typically, the data transmitted by the information service will appear on your monitor in the same way that information that you type appears. If it doesn't, you will probably need to change the Add to Incoming Lines Option Box or the Local Echo, Wraparound, or Full Screen Check Boxes. The following explanation of these options is designed to give you an idea of how to correct potential problems. In most cases, however, the default settings will be fine for use with an information service.

3. Problems with line spacing can usually be resolved by changing the option selected in the Add to Incoming Lines Option Box. If the cursor seems to move to the right side of the screen and then get stuck or if the lines break in the middle of the screen, select **ALT+C** to add a carriage return.

   If the data keeps rewriting the same line on the screen, select **ALT+L** so that a line feed will be added and the cursor will move down one line. If incoming data is consistently double spaced, try selecting **ALT+C** or **ALT+N**.

4. The Wraparound Check Box will typically be checked so that incoming information that is too wide to fit on the screen will wrap to the next line. If Wraparound is not preceded by an X, select **ALT+W**.

5. The Local Echo Check Box does not usually need to be checked when using an information service. However, in some other applications, you may not be able to see what you are typing and transmitting to the other computer. If this is the case, select **ALT+E** to turn Local Echo on so that your transmission will be "echoed" back on your monitor. On the other hand, if you begin typing and notice that each letter is displayed twice (e.g., ttwwiiccee) and Local Echo is checked, select **ALT+E** to turn Local Echo off.

Making a Connection

6. Finally, if you want to see 25 lines at a time (instead of the 22 normally visible), select **ALT+F** to turn the Full Screen Check Box on. This will remove the Status, Menu and Message lines from the screen as soon as you try to connect to the other computer. If you press the **ALT** key, the Menu Bar will reappear, but it will disappear again as soon as you execute a command.

7. The *Keypad Alternate* and *Cursor Alternate* modes do not apply when using your PC to connect to an information system, so they should be left unchecked.

8. When the settings are selected, press the **ENTER** key.

The final step is to save the settings so that you will not need to reenter them the next time the same information service is used.

1. Select **File/Save**.
2. When the SAVE AS Dialog Box appears, give the file a name that will reflect the information service for which the settings are to be used. Remember to type only the one to eight character filename, allowing *Works* to add the **.WCM** extension.

Making a Connection

Once you have specified the settings, you are ready to begin communicating.

1. Select **Connect/Connect**.

   Several changes will occur on the screen (Figure 7-5). The left-hand side of the Status Line will change from *OFFLINE* to a digital indication of the hours, minutes, and seconds elapsed since **Connect** was selected.

Figure 7-5

The Work Area will display the modem setup command, if you entered one, and the modem's response to the command. (No modem setup command was used in the setup shown in Figure 7-5.) It then displays the command to the modem that tells it to dial the telephone number.

Next a message indicating the status of the attempt to connect with the information system will be displayed. The message *CONNECT*, sometimes followed by other information, will appear if the initial connection has been successful. If the telephone number is incorrect or the computer was unable to make contact for other reasons, the message *NO CARRIER* will appear.

2. When the *CONNECT* message appears, enter the commands required by your information system to **Sign-On** (begin communications). The sign-on procedure may involve use of key combinations and responses to prompts (which appear in the Work Area) sent by the information service. A user identification number and password issued by the information service is usually entered at this time.
3. Continue interacting with the information service until you are finished.
4. End the communication by typing the command used by your information service to indicate that you are done.
5. Select **Connect/Connect** again to discontinue the connection. The Status Line message should return to *OFFLINE*.

Conclusion

The Communications tool is fairly simple with far fewer commands than any of the other *Works* tools, but it adds an entirely different dimension to the use of a personal computer. With a modem and the Communications tool, your computer becomes the access line to a vast range of information and services. Most of this chapter described the preparations for communications. These steps need be carried out only once for each communications partner. Future connections can be made in seconds. Even if you do not currently have the hardware necessary to actually communicate with another computer, it is important to be aware of this aspect of computing. The use of computers linked by modems or connected in various types of networks is dramatically changing the information available in the work place and the way information is used by businesses.

Key Terms

The following important terms and commands have been introduced and explained in this chapter:

Telecommunications	Connect/Connect	Modem
Analog Signal	Digital Signal	Transfer Menu
Options/Phone	Options/Communication	
Options/Terminal	Baud rate	Data Bits
Bit	Stop bits	Parity
Handshake	Terminal	Emulate

Appendix A: System Requirements

The system requirements for running the educational version of *Microsoft Works* are listed below. Although some of the terminology will be familiar to you from explanations included throughout the seven chapters of this book, many of the terms are technical ones you may not be acquainted with. Your instructor will be able to provide you with explanations of these technical phrases, and inform you whether or not your system fulfills these requirements.

System Component	Requirement
Computer	An IBM Personal Computer or IBM Personal System/2 or Compatible
Memory	384 Kilobytes
Monitor	CGA, EGA, MCGA, VGA, or Hercules graphics adapter
Disk Drives	Two 360 kilobyte drives or one 720 kilobyte drive
Diskettes	5 1/4 or 3 1/2 inch disks (whichever is appropriate)
Disk Operating System	Version 2.0 or higher

Appendix  Microsoft Works Menu Commands

The following table lists the menu commands used in the Word Processor, Spreadsheet, Database, and Communications tools and describes the function of the specific commands. Most of the tools have File, Edit, Print, Select, Format, Options, and Window selections; however, some of the specific commands in each are different. There are additional menu commands in each tool depending on the specific capabilities of that tool. The menu commands listed in the following table are organized as they appear on the menu, integrating options from the various tools. *Note:* The Database uses five different screens and the Spreadsheet uses two different screens, which are listed in the explanation of abbreviatons.

Explanation of abbreviations

WP = Word Processor
SS = Spreadsheet
Ch = Spreadsheet Chart Screen
DB = Database
    D = Design screen
    F = Form screen
    L = List screen
    R = Report screen
    Q = Query screen
    C = Communications

File

Command	Tools	Function
New...	WP,SS,DB(F,L),C	Creates new *Works* file
Open...	WP,SS,DB(F,L),C	Opens existing *Works* file.
Save	WP,SS,DB(F,L),C	Saves active file on disk
Save As...	WP,SS,DB(F,L),C	Saves active file on disk with a new name
Save All	WP,SS,DB(F,L),C	Saves all open files on disk
Close	WP,SS,DB(F,L),C	Removes active file
DOS...	WP,SS,DB(F,L),C	Returns to DOS without exiting *Works*
Exit	WP,SS,DB(F,L),C	Exits *Works* and returns to DOS

Edit

Undo	WP	Reverses the last editing or formatting action
Exit Design	DB(D)	Exits Form Design screen
Exit Query	DB(Q)	Exits Query screen
Move	WP,SS,DB(D,F,L,R)	Moves selection to another location
Copy	WP,SS,DB(D,F,L,R)	Copies selection to another location
Copy Special...	WP,SS	Copies character or paragraph format to another location
Clear	SS,DB(F,L,R,Q)	Erases selection
Delete	WP,SS,DB(D,F,L,R,Q)	Deletes selected data
Insert	SS,DB(D,F,L,R)	Inserts rows, columns, lines before selected rows, columns, lines
Fill Right	SS,DB(L)	Copies first column of selection to rest of selection
Fill Down	SS,DB(L)	Copies first row of selection to rest of selection
Name...	SS,DB(L)	Names selection, deletes names, or lists names
Insert Special...	WP	Inserts special characters
Insert Field...	WP	Inserts database field name for form letter or labels
Insert Chart...	WP	Inserts spreadsheet chart
Field Name...	DB(R)	Enters name of specified field
Field Value...	DB(R)	Enters value of specified field
Field Summary...	DB(R)	Enters statistical summary of specified field

Print

Print...	WP,SS,Ch,DB,(F,L,R) DB(F,L,R)	Prints active file
Layout...	WP,SS,Ch, DB(F,L,R)	Specifies page size, margins, and headers
Set Print Area	SS	Specifies that print command print only the selected area
Insert Page Break	SS,DB(L,R)	Inserts page break before selected row or column
Delete Page Break	SS,DB(L,R)	Deletes page break before selected row or column
Font	SS,DB(F,L,R)	Specifies font for entire file
Title Font...	Ch	Specifies font for chart title
Other Font...	Ch	Specifies font for other titles and labels

Appendix B

Print Chart	SS	Prints active chart
Print Report	DB(F,L)	Prints active report
Print Merge...	WP	Prints one copy of file for each selected database record
Print Labels...	WP	Prints one mailing label for each selected database record
Select Text Printer	WP,SS,DB(F,L,R)	Specifies printer and port
Select Chart Printer...	Ch	Specifies printer and port

Select

Go To...	WP,SS,DB(F,L)	Moves the cursor to specified location
Search...	WP,SS,DB(F,L)	Selects next occurrence of specified text
Replace...	WP	Selects and replaces specified data
Row	SS,DB(R)	Extends selection to entire row
Column	SS,DB(R)	Extends selection to entire column
Record	DB(L)	Extends selection to entire row
Field	DB(L)	Extends selection to entire column

Format

Plain Text	WP	Removes all character formats from selection
Bold	WP	Applies bold character style to selection
Underline	WP	Applies this character style to selection
Italic	WP	Applies this character style to selection
Character...	WP	Controls character formats including style, position, and font
Normal Paragraph	WP	Removes all paragraph formats from selected paragraphs
Left	WP	Applies this alignment to selected paragraphs
Center	WP	Applies this alignment to selected paragraphs
Justified	WP	Applies this alignment to selected paragraphs

Microsoft Works Menu Commands

Single Space	WP	Applies this line spacing to selected paragraphs
Double Space	WP	Applies this line spacing to selected paragraphs
Paragraph...	WP	Controls paragraph formats including alignment, indents, and spacing
Tabs	WP	Sets and removes tab stops in selected paragraphs
General	SS,DB(D,F,L,R)	Applies this format to selection
Fixed...	SS,DB(D,F,L,R)	Applies this format to selection
Dollar...	SS,DB(D,F,L,R)	Applies this format to selection
Comma...	SS,DB(D,F,L,R)	Applies this format to selection
Percent...	SS,DB(D,F,L,R)	Applies this format to selection
Exponential...	SS,DB(D,F,L,R)	Applies this format to selection
Logical	SS,DB(D,F,L,R)	Applies this format to selection
Time/Date...	SS,DB(D,F,L,R)	Applies this format to selection
Style...	SS,DB(D,F,L,R)	Applies alignment, text style, and locks to selection
Width...	SS,DB(D,L,R)	Specifies width of columns in selection
Show Field Name	DB(D)	Displays field value either with or without field name
Bar	Ch	Applies this format to active chart
Stacked Bar	Ch	Applies this format to active chart
100% Bar	Ch	Applies this format to active chart
Line	Ch	Applies this format to active chart
Area Line	Ch	Applies this format to active chart
Hi-Lo-Close	Ch	Applies this format to active chart
Pie	Ch	Applies this format to active chart
X-Y	Ch	Applies this format to active chart
Data Format...	Ch	Specifies *Y*-series, color, pattern, and marker

Options

Split	WP,SS,DB(L)	Creates panes to view different part of file
Show Ruler	WP	Displays or hides ruler
Show All Characters	WP	Displays or hides special characters
Headers & Footers	WP	Displays or hides complex headers and footers
*Check Spelling	WP	Selects next misspelled word

*These menu commands do not apply to the educational version of Microsoft Works.

Appendix B 261

Manual Pagination	WP	Turns automatic pagination on or off
Paginate Now	WP	Paginates if manual pagination on
Freeze Titles	SS	Freezes rows and columns before selection
Unfreeze Titles	SS	Unfreezes rows and columns
Show Formulas	SS	Displays either formulas or values
Protect	SS,DB(F,L)	Protects the contents of a locked cell/field from being changed
Manual Calculation	SS	Turns automatic calculation on or off
Calculate Now	SS	Calculates spreadsheet if manual calculation is on
Define Form	DB(F)	Enters Form Design screen to change form
View List	DB(F)	Displays List screen
View Form	DB(L)	Displays Form screen
X-Axis...	Ch	Specifies axis scale and format
Y-Axis...	Ch	Specifies axis scale and format
Right Y-Axis...	Ch	Specifies axis scale and format
Two Y-Axes...	Ch	Assigns *Y*-series to left or right *Y*-axis
Mixed Line & Bar	Ch	Creates chart with both line and bar series
Format for B&W	Ch	Displays chart in either B&W or color
List Printer Formats	Ch	Lists either printer or screen formats in Data Format Dialog Box
Show Printer Fonts	Ch	Shows either printer or screen fonts in Chart View
Show Legends	Ch	Displays or hides legends
Show Border	Ch	Displays or hides border
Terminal...	C	Specifies terminal type and settings
Communication...	C	Specifies communications and port settings
Phone...	C	Specifies phone number and modem settings

Window

*Help Index	WP,SS,Ch,DB(All),C	Displays help index
*Tutorial Index	WP,SS,Ch,DB(All),C	Displays tutorial index
Settings...	WP,SS,Ch,DB(All),C	Changes color settings, units of measure, currency symbols, and date
Filenames (1-8)	WP,SS,Ch,DB(All),C	Activates selected open file

Chart

Define	SS	Enters Chart screen
Exit Chart	Ch	Exits Chart screen
New	SS,Ch	Creates new chart using selection
View	SS,Ch	Displays active chart in Chart View
Charts...	SS,Ch	Names, deletes, and copies existing charts
Chart Names (1-8)	SS,Ch	Activates selected chart

Data

1st Y-Series	Ch	Specifies selection as this series
2nd Y-Series	Ch	Specifies selection as this series
3rd Y-Series	Ch	Specifies selection as this series
4th Y-Series	Ch	Specifies selection as this series
5th Y-Series	Ch	Specifies selection as this series
6th Y-Series	Ch	Specifies selection as this series
X-Series	Ch	Specifies selection as this series
Series...	Ch	Selects and deletes existing series
Titles...	Ch	Specifies chart titles
Legends...	Ch	Specifies Y-series legends
Data Labels...	Ch	Specifies Y-series data point labels

Query

Define	DB(F,L,R)	Enters Query screen to change criteria
Apply Query	DB(F,L)	Applies current query to database records
Hide Record	DB(F,L)	Hides selected records
Show All Records	DB(F,L)	Displays all records
Switch Hidden Records	DB(F,L)	Displays hidden records and hides visible records
Sort...	DB(F,L,R)	Sorts all records by specified fields and orders

Appendix B

Report

Define	DB(F,L)	Enters Report screen
Exit Report	DB(R)	Exits Report screen
New	DB(F,L,R)	Creates new report
View	DB(F,L,R)	Displays active report in Report View
Save As...	DB(F,L,R)	Saves report in text form
Reports...	DB(F,L,R)	Names, deletes, and copies existing reports
Report Names (1-8)	DB(F,L,R)	Activates selected report

Connect

Connect	C	Connects to or disconnects from host
Dial Again	C	Redials if host busy or connection fails
Pause	C	Sends either pause or continue signals
Break	C	Sends break signal
Sign-On	C	Plays back recorded sign-on sequence
Record Sign-On	C	Starts and stops recording of sign-on sequence

Transfer

Capture Text...	C	Captures incoming text in specified file
End Capture Text	C	Stops capturing of text
Send Text...	C	Sends text file using no protocol
Receive Protocol	C	Receives file using XMODEM protocol
Send Protocol	C	Sends file using XMODEM protocol

Appendix C  Microsoft Works Function Keys

KEY	WORD PROCESSOR	SPREAD SHEET	DATA BASE	PURPOSE
F2		Edit	Edit	Changes data already entered
Shift + F3	Copy	Copy	Copy	Copies selected data to new location
F3	Move	Move	Move	Moves selected data to new location
F4		Reference		Makes cell reference absolute
F5	Go To	Go To	Go To	Moves cursor to specified location
Shift + F6	Previous Window	Previous Window	Previous Window	Moves cursor to previous split-screen windows
F6	Next Window	Next Window	Next Window	Moves cursor to next split-screen window
Shift + F7	Repeat Copy	Repeat Copy	Repeat Copy	Makes multiple copies of selected data or format
F7	Repeat Search	Repeat Search	Repeat Search	Finds and selects next instance of the search data
Ctrl + F8		Select Row	Select Row	Extends selection to entire row(s)/record(s)
Shift + F8	Shrink Selection			Cancels a selection made with F8
Shift + F8		Select Column	Select Column	Extends selection to entire columns/field
F8	Extend	Extend	Extend	Highlights data
F9	Paginate Now			Paginates file when manual pagination is turned on
F9		Calculate Now		Calculates all formulas

Microsoft Works Function Keys

F9		View List/Form	Switches between view and form screens
Shift + F10	View Chart	View Report	Displays chart or report
F10	Exit Chart	Exit	Exits report, chart, query or form design screen

*NOTE: The following keys are not used in the educational version:
    Shift+F1 (tutorial) and F1 (help).

Appendix D
Microsoft Works Functions

Most functions consist of the function name followed by a set of parentheses that include the values used to produce a new value. The values are called arguments: if there are multiple arguments, they are separated by commas. An argument may be a number, formula, function, cell address, or range address, as long as it represents a value. The following list describes the fuctions available in *Works*.

Date and Time Functions

Date(yy,mm,dd)	Displays the Equivalent Da*teNumber*, which then may be used in calculations
Day(DateNumber) or Day('dd/mm/yy')	Displays the day represented by the *DateNumber* as an integer
Month(DateNumber) Month('dd/mm/yy')	Displays the month as represented by the *DateNumber* as an integer
Year(DateNumber) Year('dd/mm/yy')	Displays the year as represented by the *DateNumber* as an integer
Time(Hour,Minute,Second) Time('hh,mm,ss')	Displays the equivalent *TimeNumber* which then may be used in calculations
Hour(TimeNumber) Hour('hh,mm,ss')	Displays the hour as represented by the *TimeNumber* as an integer
Minute(TimeNumber) Minute('hh,mm,ss')	Displays minutes as represented by the *TimeNumber* as an integer
Second(TimeNumber) Second('hh,mm,ss')	Displays seconds as represented by the *TimeNumber* as an integer
Now( )	Gives the D*ate* and *TimeNumber* for the current system date

Mathematical Functions

ABS(x)	Applies a positive value to x
ACOS(x)	Gives arccosine of x (measured in radians)
ASIN(x)	Gives arcsine of x (measured in radians)
ATAN(x)	Gives the arctangent of x (measured in radians)
ATAN2(x,y)	Gives the arctangent of an angle defined by x-and y-coordinates
COS(x)	Gives the cosine of x (measured in radians)
EXP(x)	Gives e (2.718...) to the power of x
LN(x)	The inverse of EXP. Gives the natural logarithm of x
INT(x)	Gives the integer or whole number part of x
LOG(x)	Gives the base 10 logarithm of x
MOD(Num,Den)	Gives the modulus (remainder) of Numerator/Denominator
PI( )	Gives the number 3.14159
RAND( )	Generates a random number
ROUND(x,Places)	Rounds x to a particular number of decimal places to the left or right of the decimal point
SIN(x)	Gives the sine of x (measured in radians)
SQRT(x)	Gives the square root of x
TAN(x)	Gives the tangent of x (measured in radians)

Appendix D

Logical Functions

FALSE( )	Gives the logical value 0
ISERR(x)	Used to test for errors. Gives the logical value 1 if x is the error value ERR. Else, gives logical value 0
ISNA(x)	If x is the value NA, ISNA gives the logical value 1. Otherwise, it gives the logical value 0
TRUE( )	Gives the logical value 1
IF(Condition,ValueIfTrue/ValueIfFalse)	Judges whether the condition is true or false and gives either the ValueIfTrue or ValueIfFalse

Financial Functions

CTERM(Rate,FutureVal,PresentVal)	Gives the amount of compounding periods
RATE(FutureVal,PresentVal,Term)	Gives the fixed interest rate per compounding period
PV(Payment,Rate,Term)	Calculates the present value of an ordinary annuity
FV(Payment,Rate,Term)	Calculates the future value of an ordinary annuity
TERM(Payment,Rate,FutureVal)	Gives the amount of compounding periods required for equal Payments earning a fixed Rate to accumulate a FutureValue
PMT(Principal,Rate,Term)	Gives the periodic payment for a loan or an investment
DDB(Cost,Salvage,Life,Period)	Gives depreciation using the double-declining method
SLN(Cost,Salvage,Life)	Gives depreciation using the straight-line method
SYD(Cost,Salvage,Life,Period)	Gives depreciation using the Sum-of-the-years-digits method
*IRR(Guess,RangeReference)	Gives the actual internal rate of return for a cash flow series
*NPV(Rate,RangeReference)	Gives the net present value of a series of cash flow payments

*RangeReference indicates a number, cell reference, range reference, or formula.

Statistical Functions

*AVG(RangeRef1,RangeRef2...)	Gives the average of the values in the specified cells
*COUNT(RangeRef1,RangeRef2...)	Gives the number of filled cells in a specified range
*MAX(RangeRef1,RangeRef2...)	Finds the greatest number in a set of references
*MIN(RangeRef1,RangeRef2...)	Finds the smallest number in a set of references
*STD(RangeRef1,RangeRef2...)	Gives the standard deviation of the values of the specified cells
SUM(RangeRef1,RangeRef2...)	Gives the total of all the values in the specified cells
VAR(RangeRef1,RangeRef2...)	Calculates the variance of the values in the specified cells

Special Functions

CHOOSE(Choice,Option0,Option1...)	Selects an option from a list based on the value of the choice formula
*COLS(RangeReference)	Counts the amount of columns in a range
ERR( )	Gives the error value ERR
*HLOOKUP(LookupValue,RangeRef, RowNumber)	Finds table entries based on rows
*VLOOKUP(LookupValue,RangeRef, ColumnNumber)	Finds table entries based on columns
*INDEX(RangeRef,Column,Row)	Gives the value of a cell in a range at the intersection of a column and a row
NA( )	Gives the numeric value NA meaning "not available"
*ROWS(RangeReference)	Counts the rows in a range

Appendix E
Modem Settings

In order to use a modem and the Communications tool to connect your computer with another, you must set up the modem so that it will interact properly with *Works*. Most modems contain a series of switches that control various settings. The exact switches and what they control vary, even for "Hayes-compatible" modems. The following information describes what the common settings should be so that your modem will function with *Works*. Use the documentation that came with your modem to determine how these settings are defined and set for your modem.

Modem Setting	Effect
Commands enabled	Permits the modem to respond to the commands *Works* sends
Result codes sent	Lets *Works* know the modem status
Word result codes	Displays descriptive messages on the *Works* screen describing what the modem is doing (e.g., *CONNECT*)
Respond to DTR	The modem hangs up when you end the connection
Characters echoed in the command state	Displays on the screen commands *Works* sends to the modem (e.g. *ATDT*)
Auto-Answer disabled	Disables auto-answer function so that *Works* can turn it on for you when you select the Auto-Answer option in the PHONE Dialog Box

271

Index

Absolute cell address/reference, 185–191, 198–201
Active cell, 71
Active file, 19
Addition, 74, 82
Alignment:
  changing, 98
  label, 72, 96
    months, 73
  value, 72, 96
ALT key, 3
  closing menus, 22
  description, 3
  in dialog boxes, 17, 25
  menu bar activation, 21, 109
Analog Signal, 246
Anchor the pointer, 194–197
Apply Query Command, 222–223
Arrow keys, 4. *See also* Cursor movement
  in dialog boxes, 17, 23, 26
  EXTENDING highlight, 87–88
  in menus, 20
  in spreadsheets, 71, 73, 77
  opening menus, 20, 22
Asterisk (*)
  multiplication, 74, 82
  wildcard character, 15

Backspace key:
  correcting errors, 38, 78, 112
  deleting tabs, 52
  description, 3
  text deletion, 41
Backup disks, 10–11
Baud Rate, 250–251
Beep, 39
Bit, 251
Boldface, 172–174
Bold letters:
  button selection, 18
  command selection, 20
  menu opening, 20
  option selection, 17
Boot system, 6
Breakfield, 231
Button, 17–18, 28, 30

Cancel button, 28
Canceling:
  commands, 28
  dialog boxes, 28
  EXTEND (highlight), 87–88
  printing, 62–63
CAPS LOCK key, 2, 38–39, 52
Cathode ray tube, 1
Cell:
  active, 71
  address (A1), 71, 81
  changing width, 95–96
  copying, 84–86
  description, 71
  editing, 78
  formatting, 87–89
  range, 87
Central Processing Unit (CPU), 1–2, 6
Changing drive command, 44–46

Charting, 201–217
  Creating, 206–213
  Modifying, 201, 215–217
  Printing, 213–215, 259
Chart menu commands:
  Charts, 201
  Define, 147, 201, 214, 262
  Exit Chart, 212, 262
  New, 206, 213, 262
  Save, 212–213
  View, 207–208, 213, 262
Chart screen, 203
Check box, 23, 30, 177, 233
Clear command, 102, 190, 258
CL message, 52
Close command, 50, 156–157
Closing:
  files, 50, 156–157
  menus, 22
Colon (:):
  anchoring cursor, 194–198
  field name designator, 110, 219
  in functions, 128
  range reference, 87, 100
Color settings, 21
Column
  hiding, 191
  select, 186
  spreadsheets, 71, 77, 84
  width, 95–96, 101
Column command, 186
Comma command, 98
Comma format, *see* Comma command
Command execution, 18
Commands:
  DOS:
    COPY, 13–14
    DEL, 14–15
    DIR, 11–13
    DISKCOPY, 10–11
    FORMAT, 8–9
  Works:
    Apply Query, 222–223, 227
    chart menu commands, *see* Chart menu commands
    choosing commands, 19–21, 22–29
    Close, 50, 156
    Clear, 102, 190, 217
    Column, 70, 259
    Comma, 98
    Communication, 17, 248–251
    Connect, 253, 263
    Copy, *see* Copy command
    data menu commands, *see* Data menu commands
    Define, 208, 213, 217, 221, 227, 231
    Define Form, 131, 219
    Delete, 216, 224
    Dollar, 88, 98
    edit menu commands, *see* Edit menu commands
    Exit, 32–33
    file menu commands, *see* File menu commands
    Fill Down, 101, 193
    Fill Right, 99, 101

Commands, Works (*Continued*)
    format menu commands, *see* Format menu commands
    Go To, 142
    Insert, 186, 219
    Layout, 62, 98, 125, 163–164
    Legends, 209–210
    Merge, 239
    Move, 25, 61
    New, 18, 23, 36, 108, 206, 213, 229
    Open, 18, 23–28
    options menu commands, *see* Options menu commands
    Phone, 247–248
    Print, 18, 48–49, 139
    print menu commands, *see* Print menu commands
    query menu commands, *see* Query menu commands
    report menu commands, *see* Report menu commands
    Save, 28–29, 44–46, 61–62, 91, 212, 237
    Save All, 166–167
    Save As, 23, 28–29, 46, 61–62, 91, 114, 120, 212, 237
    Search, 123–124
    Select Chart Printer, 213–215
    select menu commands, *see* Select menu commands
    Select Text Printer, 47–48, 125, 161
    Set Print Area, 92
    Settings, 21
    Show All Characters, 37, 42, 52
    Show All Records, 226
    Sort, 138–139
    Style, 87, 96
    Switch Hidden Records, 226
    Terminal, 251
    Titles, 211
    Undo, 174
    View, 207, 208, 213
    View List, 117
    Width, 95, 119, 130–136, 140
    X-series, 208
Communications:
    communication settings, 250–251
    connection, 253
    description, 245–246
    hardware requirements, 246–247
    modem, 246
    phone settings, 247–249
    saving, 248
    screen, 247
    setting up for, 258
    terminal settings, 248
    .WCM, 12, 248, 253
Connect menu commands, 247, 253–254
Copy command, 7, 13, 58–61
    Database to Word Processor, 148, 150–153, 156–158
    DOS, 13–14
    Spreadsheet:
        cell copying, 84–86
        to Word Processor, 162–166
    Word Processor:
        copying text, 58–61
        from Database, 148, 150–153, 156–158
        from Spreadsheet, 161–162
Copying, *see* Copy command
CPU, 1
CRT, 1, 4
CTRL key, 3
Currency, 87–89, 98
Current drive, 7–8, 25–26, 28

Cursor:
    description, 2, 17
    moving, *see* Cursor movement
    tool integration, 156–157
Cursor movement:
    CONTROL + END, 40, 81, 116, 118
    CONTROL + HOME, 40, 71, 116, 118, 123
    CONTROL + LEFT ARROW, 40
    CONTROL + PAGE DOWN, 72, 115, 118, 133, 136
    CONTROL + PAGE UP, 72, 117, 118, 136
    CONTROL + RIGHT ARROW, 40
    DOWN ARROW, 4, 18, 40, 70, 72, 76–77, 110, 115, 126, 133
    END, 4, 40, 119
    HOME, 4, 40, 80, 118
    LEFT ARROW, 4, 20, 40, 121
    PAGE DOWN, 4, 40, 72, 112, 118
    PAGE UP, 4, 40, 72, 112, 118
    RIGHT ARROW, 4, 20, 40, 71–73, 76, 196
    UP ARROW, 4, 18, 40, 128
Customized form letters, 238–241

Database:
    copying to Word Processor, 147, 150–153, 156–161
    creating, 107–108
    data entry, 112–114
        numeric data, 137–138
        numbers as text, 128–129
    description, 107
    designing, 126
    editing:
        in Form View, 112, 115–118, 121, 123, 130–136
        in List View, 117–119, 120–123, 136
    extension (filename), 12–13
    F8 (to select), 55
    field, 108, 118
    field, adding, 218
    field names, 110–111
    field width, 119, 130–137
    file, 109, 112
    hiding fields, 140–141
    moving within, 115–117, 119
    naming, 114
    printing, 124–125, 140
    querying, 112, 217–218, 221–227
    record, 109, 118
    redisplaying fields, 141–144
    reporting, 112, 228–237
    saving, 114–115, 130
    searching, 122–125
    selecting records, 123
    sorting records, 138–140
    viewing, 115–117, 136
Data bits, 25
Data menu commands (Charts):
    Legends, 209–210
    Titles, 211
    X-series, 208
Dates, *see also* Months
    entering as text, 74, 109
Decimals, 88–89
Default:
    button, 18
    drive, 7–8, 89
    file names, 37, 71
    settings, 37, 119
    in Word Processor, 37
Define Command:
    Chart, 260, 265
    Query, 274, 277, 282, 289
    Report, 287

Index

Define Form command, 219
DEL command (DOS), 7, 14–15
Delete command, 14–15
DELETE key:
  character deletion, 41
  Word Processor:
    deleting selected block, 56–57
    text deletion, 41, 56
Destination file, 148, 157, 160, 166
Dialog Box:
  canceling, 28
  execution, 18, 23, 28
  description, 17, 23–31
Digital Signal, 246
DIR command (DOS), 7, 11–13
Directory, works subdirectory, 15
Disk care and handling, 5–6
Disk drive, 1, 5, 35
  changing, 25–26
DISKCOPY command (DOS), 7, 10–11
Disk operating system, *see* DOS
Division, 82
Dollar command, 88, 98, 198
Dollar format, 88, 98
Dollar sign ($), 88
DOS, *see also specific commands*
  booting, 6–7, 205
  current drive, 7–8
  description, 6–7, 257
Double (spacing), 183

Edit menu commands:
  Database
    Delete, 224
    Insert, 220
  Spreadsheet:
    Clear, 101–102, 190, 217, 258
    Copy, 58, 61, 85–86, 99, 104, 258
    Delete, 216, 224, 235, 258
    Fill Down, 101, 104, 189, 193, 196, 258
    Fill Right, 99, 101, 258
    Insert, 186–187, 258
  Word Processor:
    Copy, 148
    Insert Field, 219, 239–240, 242, 258
    Move, 61, 258
    Undo, 56, 174, 258
EDIT message, 112, 153
Edit mode, 112, 153
Editing:
  Database:
    data, 120
    field names, 118
  Spreadsheet, 78, 101–102
  Word Processor, 41–44, 54–61, 153
Ellipsis (. . .), 23
Emulate, 251
END key, 4
Enhancing Text, 172–183
ENTER key, 3, 39, 181
Entering:
  Database:
    data, 112–114
    field names, 110–111
    numbers as text, 128–129
  Spreadsheet:
    formulas, 81–85
    labels, 72–74
    numbers, 79–81
    numbers as text, 74
    values, 72, 74–75
  Word Processor:
    blank lines, 39
    text, 38–40, 51, 54–61

Equal sign (=), formula designator, 82–83
Error messages, 31
ESC (Escape key):
  cancel command, 28, 36, 87
  cancel dialog box, 28
  cancel printing, 63
  de-activate menu, 22, 36
  description, 3, 36
  quit Extend, 87
Executing commands, 18
Exit command, 33
Exiting:
  Chart Screen, 212
  Form Design Screen, 109–110
  Microsoft Works, 32
  Query Screen, 258
  Report Screen, 235
EXTEND, 87, 96, 98, 101, 193, 196
EXTEND message, 58, 87
Extension, filename, 12

F2 key, 121, 223, 265
F4 key, 188, 265
F7 key, 123, 137–138, 154, 234, 265
F8 key, 102, 154, 186, 193, 265
F9 key, 121–122, 137–138, 218, 265–266
F10 key, 110–111, 127, 133–134, 212, 222, 266
Field:
  defining, 108–109
  description, 108
  naming, 117
  selecting, 140–142
  width, 119–121, 130–137
Field name, 110–114, 258
File:
  active, 19
  backup (DOS), 6–7, 13
  closing, 50, 157
  creating, 23, 108
  listing, 108
  naming, 29
  opening, 148–149
  printing, 47–49, 62
  saving, 28–29, 44, 114
  selecting, 26
  switching between, 148–149
File menu commands:
  Close, 50, 157, 161, 257
  description, 22
  Exit, 33, 72, 74, 257
  New, 18, 23, 36, 93, 126, 154, 257
  Open, 18, 24, 27, 122, 148, 157, 257
  Save, 27, 44, 53, 61, 89–91, 95, 109, 114, 237, 257
  Save All, 166, 257
  Save As, 28, 46, 61, 89–91, 137, 139, 237, 257
Filename:
  default, 37, 109
  extension, 12–15
    .WCM, 12, 248
    .WDB, 12, 115
    .WKS, 12, 90
    .WPS, 12
  rules, 12, 62
Fill Down command, 101
Fill Right command, 99, 101
Fixed Disk, 5–6, 7–8
Floppy Disk, 6
Footer, page layout, 49
Form Design Screen, 109–110
Form Entry Screen, 112
Form Letters, 238
Format command (DOS), 7–9

Format menu commands, 31
  Database:
    Width, 119, 132, 134, 140
  Spreadsheet:
    Comma, 98, 101
    Dollar, 88, 98
    Style, 96, 190
    Width, 95–96, 101, 136
  Word Processor:
    Bold, 172, 174, 260
    Center, 172, 174, 260
    Character, 172, 175–177, 260
    Double, 183, 260
    Italic, 172, 260
    Plain Text, 172, 260
    Format/Paragraph, 183
    Tabs, 179–183, 261
    Underline, 172, 174–175, 260
Formatting:
  alignment, 96, 98
  diskettes (DOS), 9–11
  tabs, 179–183
  values, 87–89
  width, 95–96
Formula:
  copying, 84–86
  description, 99–100
  designator (=), 100
  entering, 81
  pointing, 82–84
Formula bar:
  description, 70
  editing, 73, 112
Function:
  AVG, 199
  description, 99–100
  MAX, 194, 196, 199
  MIN, 194–196, 199
  pointing, 82–84, 99, 194–198
  SUM, 100, 194–197
Function keys, 3–4

Go To command, 142, 259
Graphics:
  monitor setup, 201–205
  printer setup, 201, 213–215

Handshake, 251
Hard drive, 5–6, 7–8
Hardware, 1, 251
Header, page layout, 125
Help Index, 31
Hiding columns, 191–192
Hiding fields, 140–144
Highlight
  EXTEND, 55
  in dialog boxes, 24–25
  in menus, 19–20
  selecting text, 55–56
  SHIFT + Arrow, 193
HOME key, 4

Indenting (TAB key), 39, 53
Insert command, 186
Inserting text, 42–43
Installing works, 15
Integrating tools, 144, 148, 161, 238
Interface, 16
Italics, 172

Justification, *see* Alignment

Keyboard, 1–4

Label, 72–74, 86–89, 94, 259

Layout command:
  footer, 62
  header, 125
  margins, 92, 163–164
Legend, 205
Line spacing, 183
List box, 26
Listing files:
  DOS, 11–12
  Works, 13, 37
List View:
  accessing, 117–119
  description, 117
  field width, 119–120
  hiding fields, 140–144
  moving around, 118
  redisplaying fields, 141–144
  searching, 122–125
  sorting, 139
Load a program, 6, 16

Mail merge, 238–239
Margin:
  changing, 92
  default, 37
Menu, *see also specific menu*
  activating, 19–20
  closing, 22
  opening, 19
Menu bar, 18–19, 36, 70, 112
Merge, 238, 241, 259
Message:
  CL, 39
  EDIT, 78
  ERROR, 31
  EXTEND, 87
  NL, 4
  POINT, 83
Message line, 19, 37, 71, 110, 112
Microsoft Works, 15
  starting, 16
  Educational version, 31–32
Mode:
  Design, 126–127
  Edit, 88, 120–121
  Extend, 88
  Insert, 43
  List View, 117
  Point, 194–198
Monitor, 1, 4
  graphics setup, 201–205
Months:
  in database, 114
  in spreadsheet, 73–74, 76–77
Move command, 61
Movement keys, *see* Cursor Movement
MS-Dos, *see* DOS
Multiplication, 74, 82

Naming:
  charts, 206–211
  fields, 110–111
  files, 12, 44, 53, 62–63
  reports, 235–237
New button, 18
New command, 18, 69, 108
  Charts, 206
  Files, 22, 69, 108
  Report, 229
NL message, 4
Numbers:
  entering, 73, 78, 98, 128
  formatting, 87–88, 96, 98
  as text, 128–129
  width of column/field, 191

Index

Numeric keypad, 4
NUM LOCK key, 4

OK button, 18
Open button, 18, 24
Open command, 18, 24
Operator, 221-222
Options, *see also specific commands*
   in dialog boxes, 17-18
Option box, 17-18, 26
Options menu commands
   Communications
      Communication, 248-250
      Phone, 248
      Terminal, 248, 251
   Database
      Define Form, 131, 134, 218-219
      View Form, 218
      View List, 117
   Word Processor, Show All Characters, 37, 42, 152-153, 162, 180, 183

Page layout, *see* Layout command
Parity, 251
PGDN, 4, 40, 72, 112
PGUP, 4, 40, 72, 112
Phone command, 247-249
POINT message, 82
Pointing, 82-84
Print area, 91
Print button, 18
Print command, 18, 258
Print menu commands:
   description, 47
   Layout, 49, 62, 92, 102, 125, 140, 161, 163, 230, 258
   Merge, 239, 241
   Print, 48-49, 91, 102, 125, 139-140, 217, 230
   Select Chart Printer, 214, 259
   Select Text Printer, 47-48, 125, 140, 161, 259
   Set Print Area, 91-92, 102, 258
Printer:
   description, 1, 4-5
   selecting, 47-48
Printing, *see also* Print menu commands
   cancelling, 63
   graphics, 213-215
   problems, 163, 177, 214

Query menu commands:
   Apply Query, 221, 262
   Define, 221, 223, 227, 241-242, 262
   Show All Records, 226, 229, 262
   Sort, 139, 217, 232, 262
   Switch Hidden Records, 226, 262
Query screen, 217, 228
Quotation mark, 72, 74, 77, 129, 133, 139, 224

RAM, 44
Range:
   description, 87
   selecting, 87
   separator, colon (:), 87
   Status Line message, 87
   in SUM function, 100
Record:
   copy to word processor, 148
   description, 109
   selecting, 115-117
Reference key, 187-188
Relative cell adjustment, 86, 185
Replacing text, 44
Reporting (database)
   Creating, 228-231
   Modifying, 231-235

Naming and saving, 235-237
Printing, 238, 259
Report menu commands:
   Define, 231, 235, 263
   Exit, 235, 263
   New, 229, 235, 263
   Reports, 238, 263
   Save, 237, 263
   View, 233, 263
Report screen, 229, 231
Row, 70, 259
Ruler, 37

Save All command, 166-167
Save As command:
   description, 28
   existing files, 44, 61, 89-90
   extension specification, 28-29
   new files, 46
   report menu, 235
Save command:
   charts, 212-213
   description, 28
   drive changing, 45
   existing files, 61, 89, 114-115, 166
   new files, 44, 89, 114-115
   reports, 235-237
Saving, *see also* Save command
   communications files, 248
   report summary statistics, 235
Screen:
   Database:
      Form Design, 109
      Form Entry, 112
      Form View, 115
      List View, 117, 231
      Query, 221, 223
      Report, 228, 231
   Scroll, 40
   Spreadsheet, 71, 80
      Chart, 201-217
   Word Processor, 18-19, 37, 40
Search command, 159, 259
Searching, Database, 122-125
Select menu commands:
   Database:
      Column, 235
      Go To, 142
      Record, 148, 150, 154
      Search, 123, 136, 150, 217
   Spreadsheet:
      Column, 186
      Row, 216
Select Chart Printer command, 214, 259
Select Text Printer command, 214, 259
Selecting:
   buttons, 18
   commands, 23-24
   Database:
      fields, 137, 140-141
      records, 115-117, 148
   disk drive, 6-8, 15-16
   extend key, 55-56, 88
   files, 33
   options, 26-28
   printer, 46-47
   Text, 55
   Spreadsheet
      columns, 99
      ranges, 86-87
   Word Processor text, 55-57
Set Print Area command, 92
Shift + Arrow key, 193
Shift key, 2-3
Shift + Enter, 181-182

Index

Shift + F10 keys, 208, 213
Shortcut keys, 175
Show All Characters command, 37, 42, 152–153, 162, 180, 183
Show All Records command, 226
Software, 1
Sort command, 139, 158, 217, 232
Sorting, *see also* Sort command
   by multiple fields, 138
Source file, 148, 157–158, 166
Space Bar, 2
Speed chart, 206–211
Speed report, 229–231
Spelling checker, 31
Spreadsheet:
   cell, 71, 185
      active, 71
      copying, 84–86, 185–187
      formatting, 185
   charting, 201–205
   copy to Word Processor, 162–166
   creating, 69
   description, 69
   editing, 78, 101
   F8 (to select), 162
   extension (.WKS), 71
   formatting, 87–89, 95–98
   formula:
      description, 81, 100, 185
      entering, 81
      pointing, 82–84, 99
      with functions, 100
   formula bar, 70, 78, 82
   functions, 100
   hiding columns, 191–192
   labels, 72–74, 76, 86–89, 94–96
   numbers, 70
   printing, 91–92
   printing charts, 213–215
   ranges, 87
   relative cell adjustment, 185
   row numbers, 70, 84
   saving, 89–91
   Screen, 71
   values, 72, 74, 79, 87–89, 94–97
Status line, 19, 37, 71, 206
Stop bits, 251
Storing, *see* Saving
Style command, 87, 96
Subtraction, 82
SUM (total) function, 100
Switch Hidden Records command, 226
Switching:
   between files, 148–149
   between Form and List Views, 115
System Unit, 1

TAB key, 2, 39, 52
Tabs, 25, 52, 179–183
Telecommunications, 245
Template, 61
Terminal command, 251

Text box, 28, 211
Titles command, 211
Toggle key, 2, 188, 232
Tools, 147–148, 161. *see also specific tool*
   integrating
Transfer menu, 247, 263
Tutorial, 31–32
Typing text, 38–40

Underlining, 172
Undo command, 49

Value, 72, 74, 79, 87–89, 94
View Command:
   Chart, 203
   Report, 233, 263
View Form command, 218
View List command, 117

.WCM, 12, 253
.WDB, 12, 115
Width command, 95, 118, 130–132, 138
Wildcard DOS, 15
Window Menu commands, 31, 150
   settings, 21–22
   switching between files, 147
   tutorial, 31–32
.WKS, 12, 90
Wordprocessor:
   blank lines, 59
   copying from database, 150–161
   copying from spreadsheet, 162–166
   copying from text, 58–61, 172
   default, 179
   description, 36–37, 147
   editing, 41–44, 153–155, 162–166
   extension (.WPS), 12
   form letters, 238
   formatting, 172, 175
   page layout changing, 62–63, 172
   printing, 46–49, 62
   reformatting, 153–154, 162–165
   saving, 44–46, 61–62, 166
   screen, 18–19, 37, 40
   selecting text, 55–61
   spacing, 183
   tabs, 153, 179–183
   tool, 172
Wordwrap, 39–42
Work area, 19, 37
Works
   See Microsoft Works
.WPS, 12

X-axis, 205
X-series command, 208, 262

Y-axis, 205
Y-series, 205, 262

Zip codes (entering), 128